Digitalization in Organizations

Digitalization in Organizations

Edited by

Mehmed Zahid Çögenli

Cambridge Scholars Publishing

Digitalization in Organizations

Edited by Mehmed Zahid Çögenli

This book first published 2021

Cambridge Scholars Publishing

Lady Stephenson Library, Newcastle upon Tyne, NE6 2PA, UK

British Library Cataloguing in Publication Data
A catalogue record for this book is available from the British Library

ISBN (10): 1-5275-7028-2
ISBN (13): 978-1-5275-7028-3

To my beautiful wife Elif

TABLE OF CONTENTS

Introduction x

Chapter One 1
Home Based Remote Work: Freedom or Slavery through Digitalization?
*Müge Klein (Assoc. Prof. Dr.) and *Sevgin Batuk (Assist. Prof. Dr.)

Chapter Two 24
The Catalyst Impact of the Covid-19 Pandemic on the Digital Transformation of Businesses
İbrahim Türkmen (Lecturer)

Chapter Three 44
Personalization is Possible with Digitalization
Emre Harorlı (PhD)

Chapter Four 61
Women Entrepreneurship in the Digital Age: Challenges and Opportunities
*Serap Sap (PhD) and *Erhan Aydın (Assoc. Prof. Dr.)

Chapter Five 75
Digital Aspect of Entrepreneurship: Crowdfunding
Alkan Alkaya (Assist. Prof. Dr.)

Chapter Six 94
Two Intersecting Clusters: The TQM Approach and ERP Systems
Mehmet Cıranoğlu (Assist. Prof. Dr.)

Chapter Seven 106
Toward a New Hybrid Model in Public Administration: Human and Artificial Intelligence
Şerafettin Erten (Assist. Prof. Dr.)

Chapter Eight 127
The Behavioral Dimension of Human Resources Management in the Age of Digitalization and Industry 4.0
Meryem Aybas (Assoc. Prof. Dr.)

Chapter Nine 145
The Impact of Covid-19 Pandemic on Human Resources Management and Digital Human Resources Management Practices
Selma Kılıç Kırılmaz (Assist. Prof. Dr.)

Chapter Ten 167
A Sectoral Analysis of the Reflections of Digital Transformation in Businesses to Human Resources (HR)
*Ebru Aykan (Assoc. Prof. Dr.) and *Yasemin Harmancı (Assist. Prof. Dr.)

Chapter Eleven 197
The Impact of Digitized Business Models on Employment in the Covid-19 Period: An Evaluation on Tourism Sector
Seda Karagöz Zeren (PhD)

Chapter Twelve 222
Digital Transformation and Education: Organizational, Cultural and Sociological Reflections
Gökhan Demirhan (Assist. Prof. Dr.)

Chapter Thirteen 236
Interaction between Digitalization and Financial Literacy: Impact of the Covid-19 Pandemic
*Ercan Özen (Assoc. Prof. Dr.) and *Maia Diakonidze (PhD)

Chapter Fourteen 256
Digital Change and Transformation of Occupational Health and Safety Practices in the Effect of Covid-19
*Mustafa Tatlıcan (Lecturer-OS Spec.-B) and *Yılmaz Karadaş (M.D.-Oc. Safety Spec.-B)

Chapter Fifteen 277
Reflections of Digitalization on Healthcare Services: E-Health Literacy and Cyberchondria
*Harun Kırılmaz (Assoc. Prof. Dr.) and *Kübra Öztürk (Master D.)

Chapter Sixteen 301
Digitalization and Data Security in Healthcare
Hüseyin Aslan (Assist. Prof. Dr.)

Chapter Seventeen 315
The City Hospitals and The Pandemi Science Committees in Turkey in the Context of Meta-Governance and Digitalization
*Yeliz Polat (Assist. Prof. Dr.) and *Meryem Kartal (PhD Candidate)

Chapter Eighteen 338
Digitalization in the Healthcare Sector
Emine Çetin Aslan (Assist. Prof. Dr.)

Chapter Nineteen 355
Psychosocial Problems of the Digitized Era: Psychological Violence and Harrasment in Organizations
*Mehmed Zahid Çögenli (Assist. Prof. Dr.) and *Fatih Ulukaya (Lecturer-OS Spec.-B)

INTRODUCTION

DIGITALIZATION IN ORGANIZATIONS

MEHMED ZAHID ÇÖGENLI (PHD), EDITOR

Technology; is an indispensable part of our lives. This concept is actually the lead actor in the world order that has changed and evolved quite rapidly over the last 30 years. Countries, nations, borders, economies, social structures, businesses and organizations. All systems are now almost divided into those who have and develop technology, or those who do not have and cannot develop it. The balance of power is on the side of those who invest and produce technology in every sense. The world is now shaped in the shadow of technology, led by international companies and organizations, not certain nation states. The new name for this transformation is the Digital Age. Digitization; that is, harmonization of each case with technology, is now a must. Imagine turning off your lights that you left on at home with a mobile phone app or turn on your combi half an hour before you get home and make it warm. What about showing your parents, who live 12,000 km away from you, the first steps of their grandchildren live? These are just a few simple examples of the social effects of digital transformation. In fact, if you were to say or write them 30 years ago, you would have been named a fictitious crazy or sci-fi writer by people. These examples are now the normals of us and the world we live in. So, can you imagine what would be normal in 30 years? Let me ask you a simpler question: What did you imagine about your new year in January 2020? More money, more power, more travel, more peace and happiness, or a virus? It's quite difficult to predict how technology will evolve and what will normalize after 30 years, but today we are going through a process called "The New Normal" in our social life, and causing this new normal is a Virus (Covid-19: "SARS-CoV-2"). An infectious disease resulting in the death of more than 1 million people as a result of Severe Acute Respiratory Syndrome (SARS) as of the end of 2020. As a result of the effects and rapid spread of the virus, which appeared in Wuhan, the capital of the Hubei region of China on December 1, 2019, a global outbreak was declared by the World Health Organization (WHO) on March 11, 2020 (Pandemic).

In light of all these, we basically need to talk about this. Digital transformation, which surrounds the earth and progresses quite rapidly under the influence of technology, has become a necessity with the Covid-19 Pandemic. With this process, which directly affects billions of people, it will not be quite difficult to observe that we need digitalization more and we are even being forced to digitise. Ten thousands of scientific publications have been published that deal with the process in medical terms. It would not be wrong to mention that the economic impact is hundreds of billions of dollars and that even estimating the damage it causes to the world economy will take years. It should also be noted that it collapsed our social life and created a new concept called "Social Distance" by eliminating the physical proximity of people with each other. However, it is not possible to ignore the contribution of digital transformation and, naturally, the effort of all humanity to adapt to this negative and frightening process while addressing the negative aspects of this process. This effort should be evaluated individually in each discipline.

With this study, we will attempt to carry out an evaluation of the digital transformation process, which has accelerated further with the influence of Covid-19, for organizations. We aim to provide an up-to-date perspective by addressing organizational aspects and activities of different social science disciplines. First of all, it is necessary to reveal that organizational studies were also carried out on the effects of digitalization before the pandemic process, but differences emerged with this process. Therefore, it is likely to say that the softer and slower developing digital transformation of organizations has become harder and faster in the name of sustainability.

With the contribution of 27 scientists, our book which has 19 chapters discusses the digital transformation of social and organizational studies related to disciplines such as Public Practices, Human Resource Management, Finance, Education, Occupational Health and Safety, Organizational Behavior, Health Management, Management Strategies, Entrepreneurship and Marketing. In this way, it will be possible to see and evaluate digitalization in many aspects in terms of organizations.

CHAPTER ONE

HOME BASED REMOTE WORK: FREEDOM OR SLAVERY THROUGH DIGITALIZATION?

MÜGE KLEIN AND SEVGIN BATUK

Introduction

Winning over highly qualified employees and retaining them on a permanent basis are crucial for the success of companies. Flexible working environments make a major contribution to increasing companies' attractiveness, because employees see greater flexibility in more easily combining work and private life (Hofmann and Nostdal, 2014; Kraus et al., 2020). Flexible work environments are diverse; flexibility can be seen in working times, in location, or even in the spread of risk (Hofmann and Nostdal, 2014; Kraus et al., 2020). Until recently, location-independent flexible working has been the ultimate dream of every white-collar employee. Also, companies that have realized the costs of keeping the workforce on-site, have changed their approach towards the importance of physical occurrence and have rather emphasized efficiency and productivity. This alternative view has opened up a new work arrangement, remote working, which has allowed employees to do their jobs outside traditional offices (Hardill and Green 2003).

Technological progress has always been important in terms of the design of the working environment. Digitalization, in the sense of Industry 4.0, can be seen as an essential driver for "Work 4.0", the conceptual framework of future work, which has been discussed over the last five years in Germany and the European Union (Federal Ministry of Labour and Social Affairs of Germany, 2017). The associated digital communication technologies open new possibilities for collaboration, which are independent of spatial and temporal constraints and lead to a tremendous ease of access to globally distributed knowledge, skills and resources. According to the possibility of working ubiquitously at any time thanks to digital information and communication technologies, companies tend to implement more flexible and adaptive work styles to retain high productivity (Kotera and Correa Vione, 2020). Even though digital technologies are sufficiently capable of technically supporting like never before the long desired remote work, based on the report of Owl Labs' Global State of Remote Work, at the beginning of 2020, 44% of companies globally still didn't allow remote work (Owl Labs, 2020). The reason that this is not as high as the potential acceptance of remote working may be the lack of an appropriate company and work culture in addition to the right technology, or psychological inhibitions (Engels, 2020).

The major role that digitalization plays in facilitating remote work became quite clear during the pandemic. The pandemic spread of the Covid-19 virus has resulted in a deep rift in the economy, society and the lives of almost everyone. The effects of the lockdown, which took place in numerous countries and has not yet ended, are forcing companies to offer their employees the option of working from home. Especially since the first months of 2020, the spread of the Covid-19 virus worldwide has caused companies to switch to "home-based" remote work, and the number of home-based remote workers has increased significantly in order to reduce the negative effects of the global epidemic. According to HR Drive (2020), 88% of the organizations worldwide, made it mandatory or encouraged their employees to work from home during the pandemic situation. Currently, the debate is on as to whether there will be a return to offices in the future even if the epidemic is over.

A study of home-based remote working could not have been fully attempted before, because remote-working was not prevalent enough in companies and it was in general time-restricted. The remote working scenario during the pandemic has thus created a great and novel opportunity to try out remote work, and it can be used to learn lessons from a large-scale remote home-working experiment.

The declaration of Karl Marx, "the worker is at home when he is not working, and when he is working he is not at home" calls attention to the importance of separation between work and private life (Marx, 1968). Unfortunately, due to home-based remote work the boundaries between work and private time are becoming increasingly blurred, and the ability to self-exploit through working at night or being permanently available is growing fast (Wimmer, 2019). Based on the fact that working remotely will be a part of company and employee life in the post-pandemic future, with this study we aim to achieve a better work-life balance and increase the efficiency of remote working. In this study, it is aimed to shed light on the employees' experiences of home-based remote working during the pandemic process, in order to support the future concepts of flexible working under the assumption that 80% of companies would like to continue offering home offices after the pandemic (HR Drive, 2020). In this respect, in-depth interviews will be conducted with white-collar employees working in multinational firms to understand how their well-being and work-life balance have been affected with remote working. The study will investigate if remote working has created advantages or disadvantages for employees and why their experiences are good or bad during this process. The objective is to find out if the employees are generally satisfied and happy with remote working and to evaluate the major reasons lying beneath their assessments.

Interrelationship between Remote Working, Digitalization, Work-Life Balance and Covid-19

It is crucial to attract and retain highly qualified employees for company success. On the one hand, flexible work environments increase the attractiveness of companies by enabling employees to integrate private and work life in a flexible way and on the other hand, they support a better utilization of the potential productivity and creativity of employees. The flexibility of work can be of different types as shown in Figure 1.1 (Degenhardt et al., 2012; Hofmann et al., 2015; Kraus et al., 2020):

- *Time flexibility*: This form of flexibility is about adapting working time, where employees can individually set their daily, weekly or annual working hours within a certain framework. For employers, the added value lies in the flexible adaptation to the workload. Typical appearances are shift work, overtime work, part-time working models and job sharing by the flexible assignment of individual content-related tasks to employees.
- *Location flexibility*: The focus here is on increasing the flexibility of the location from which the employees can carry out their work. Typical appearances are mobile working and home-based remote working.
- *Risk flexibility*: This form of flexibility is about relocating the company's risk of the permanent commitment of employees. The flexible disposition of the employees enables payments according to performance and thus costs can be reduced. Typical appearances are forms of temporary employment, agency work and outsourcing, where operational functions not belonging to the core business are carried out from other companies.

There is a mutual reinforcement between the different forms of flexibility which accelerates and intensifies the overall trend towards greater flexibility. An example of this mutual reinforcement could be the combination of time and location flexibility, for instance flexible part-time solutions for women with children, where they go to the office on two out of three working days ("time flexibility") and work from home on the third day ("location flexibility").

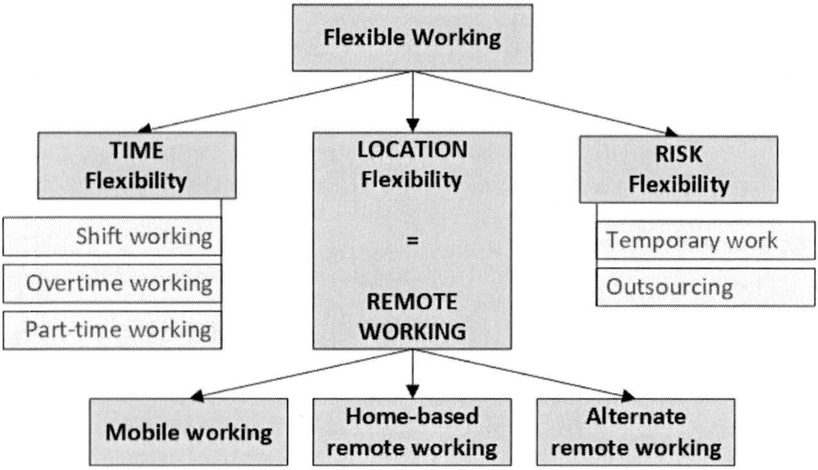

Figure 1.1: Flexible working types (Source: authors, based on Hoffmann et. al., 2015; Degenhardt et al., 2012)

The focus of this study is on location flexibility, where the employee can work remotely outside of the office. Depending on the place of work, a distinction is made between different forms of remote work (Degenhardt, et al., 2012): when remote work is performed from employees' homes, it is called home-based remote work. With mobile working, the workplace is completely variable and work is rarely done at the company's location. Mobile work takes place when the work activity is carried out at different locations (Breisig et al., 2017). Alternate remote working is the variant of remote work where people work alternately at home, in the company or somewhere else.

The reason why remote working is also called teleworking is that by remote working the connection to the company is maintained through various information and communication technologies (Perez Perez et al., 2003). According to Di Martino and Wirth (1990), telework is the work done away from head offices or production facilities, where the employee has no personal contact with employees in the head office or production facilities, but can communicate with them using new technologies.

By remote working the spatial distance to the company is balanced through a sort of information and communication technology. Feasibilities of information and communication technologies influence and define how remote work enviroments are structured and how working processes are run. Historical developments of digital technologies and digitalization of businesses, which can be summarized in four phases building on each other (Klein, 2019), influenced the development of remote work environments:

1. *Phase of the Personal Computer:* Digitalization began with the use of personal computers in the 1970s. At this time, electronic data processing in companies was possible and data banks were formed. Remote workers were able to connect to company mainframes and databases using personal computers and terminal emulation.
2. *Phase of the Internet:* The 1990s were the most important years of digitalization with the invention of the Internet, implicating the greatest changes on remote working. Remote working was then facilitated by so-called *groupware* tools, which aimed to enable information-system based communication, collaboration and cooperation between remote workers (Koch, 2008). The limited bandwidth of networks reduced the quality of the first videoconferencing attempts between remote workers and the company. As broadband Internet connections became more commonplace, remote workers had adequate bandwidth to link their homes to their corporate intranet and data sources.
3. *Phase of Mobile Technologies:* Since 2000 the hurdles of networking technologies have been overcome. Mobile phones and mobile network technologies such as 3G have made remote working more convenient.
4. *Phase of the Internet of Things:* Since 2010 the effects of the fourth industrial revolution, Industry 4.0 have been felt. Companies today are characterized by a high degree of digital communication and networking as well as large amounts of data that can be stored and accessed at any time (*cloud computing*). Work is becoming more and more mobile, decision-making is supported by IT-based mechanisms (e.g., *big data*), interactive forms of digital information exchange are practiced (e.g., *wikis, blogs, collaboration tools*) and other digital work practices are introduced (Thiemann and Kozica, 2019). Today, teleworkers carry smart devices enabling their steady and easy

access to company sources and communication among themselves using videoconferencing software (e.g., *Skype, Zoom*) that can be easily installed in seconds on every device.

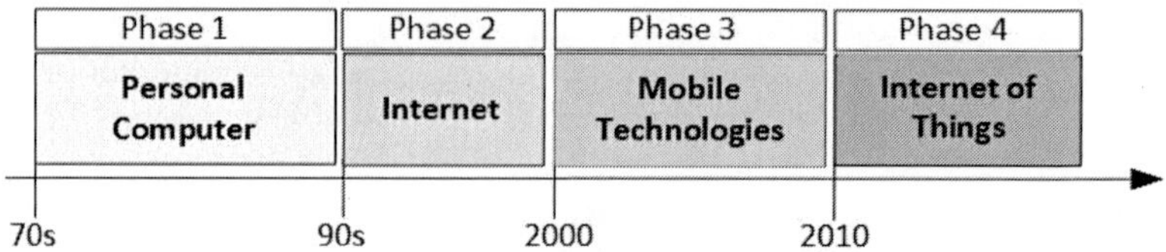

Figure 1.2: Digitalization Phases of Remote Working Environments (Source: Klein, 2019)

As already described in the above section, technological progress has always been important in terms of the design of the work environment and working life. Industry 4.0 influences the business models and business processes of companies, forces them towards digital transformation and also turns their organizational structures into a flexible and dispersed form (Klein, 2020). The Industry 4.0 derived concept, Work 4.0, is discussing the future scenarios of working environments as a response to developments in digital technologies (Vogler-Ludwig et al., 2016). Beneath globalization and demographic and cultural changes, digital transformation can also be seen as an essential driver for change processes around Work 4.0. The associated digital and mobile communication technologies offer new possibilities for collaboration, which are independent of spatial and temporal distribution, thus they lead to a tremendous ease of access to globally distributed knowledge, skills and resources: Work 4.0 is therefore more networked, more digital and more flexible (Rump and Eilers, 2017). Through Work 4.0, enabled modifications in companies' working environments can be mainly divided into three dimensions (see Figure 1.3): employment, skills and organizational structures (Federal Ministry of Labour and Social Affairs of Germany, 2017; von See and Kersten, 2017; Spath et al., 2012; Wimmer, 2019). The dimension of employment is about discussions of job losses and a definition of new jobs under the effects of digital transformation such as platform-oriented jobs. While some work will remain the same, complex and dynamic tasks can be added. The dimension skills deal with qualifications of leadership and employees in the new digital work life. The organizational structure dimension comprises flexible working arrangements including remote working supported by digital technologies, in order to build a more flexible, networked, mobile and agile organization.

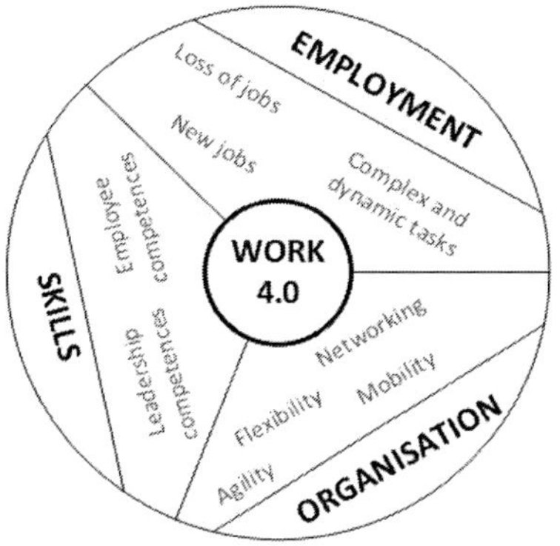

Figure 1.3: Dimensions of Work 4.0 (Source: authors)

Remote work is an elementary component of Work 4.0. Although remote work will be realized more efficiently than before thanks to digital technologies, the challenges may have remained the same, or be even greater. Lack of face-to-face social interaction can lead to loss of motivation, a decreased sense of belonging to the company and to troubles with the work-life balance of employees. The work-life balance is the state of equilibrium between the working life and personal life of an individual (Ratna & Kaur, 2016). The basic idea here is that work and life should be in such a relationship that one has the least negative impact on the other. The increasing flexibility of space and time due to digitalization may have a positive effect on work-life balance on the one hand, and negatively affect the private lives of employees on the other, with a compulsion for permanent availability and increased flexibility requirements (Rump and Eilers, 2017). Alongside the positive aspects, such as having more opportunities to spend time with family members and not to lose time on the way to work, it is also clear that working remotely from home implies the expectation that employees are reachable at all times and, as a result work longer, causing a blurring between people's work and personal lives (Cijan et al., 2019).

Owing to many possible reasons such as insufficient digital skills of employees, a perceived lack of value of the new technologies and insufficient development of an appropriate new company culture, remote-working scenarios have not been successfully integrated into existing work practices until today (Kaiser and Kozica, 2015). Furthermore, the corona crisis since the first months of 2020 has forced many changes in the economy and in the society. Since the global epidemic made staying at home mandatory, many companies around the world have had to migrate to "home-based remote working", which was not envisioned in any business plan. As shown in the next figure, Covid-19 has been beneath digitalization and a willingness to exploit the benefits of flexible working, a strong driver for home-based remote work and provides a very good and realistic opportunity to analyze the benefits and harms of remote working from home.

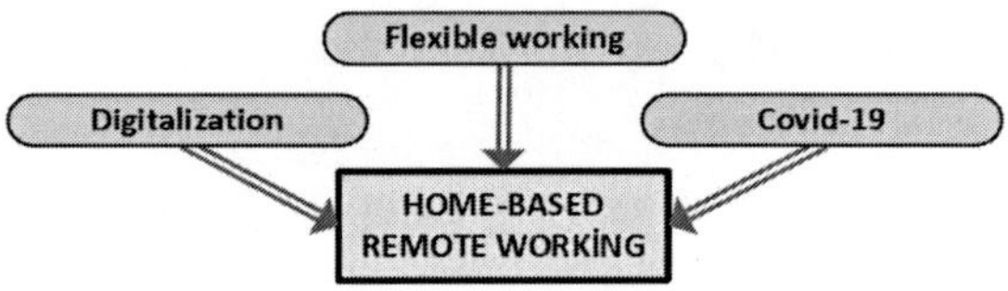

Figure 1.4: Drivers of Home-based Remote Working (Source: authors)

Previous Research

With the effect of Covid-19, research on remote work has grasped much more of the attention of scholars. Until today, research in this field has been limited. Papers have generally focused on the outcomes of remote work. In the conceptualization of these papers, remote working is seen as a flexible working opportunity offered by the company and it has mostly been considered as a positive concept. Today, with being obliged to work remotely at home, the employees' perceptions and evaluations may have differed. Therefore, understanding previously drawn conclusions can assist with making comparisons.

According to the literature, one of the major advantages of remote working from the employee side is considered to be the lower costs of transportation and clothing (Özkalp et al., 2013). The time lost in traffic jams is reduced (Toduk, 2014; Di Martino and Wirth, 1990; Karaca and Esen, 2019) and employees are able to spend more time at home and with family members (Özkalp et al., 2013). It is seen that remote work especially contributes positively to the work-life balance of working mothers (Karaca and Esen, 2019). It is also associated with higher autonomy and efficiency (Di Martino and Wirth, 1990; Johnson, 1997). Remote working is expected to lead to higher levels of autonomy; if the job role is appropriate, the workload is manageable and the supervisor trusts the employee (Karasek and Theorell, 1990). Notably remote workers who have greater autonomy are stated to require less supervision (Dimitrova, 2003). Especially home-based remote working is considered to contribute positively to self-management, work-life balance and job satisfaction (Wheatley, 2012;

Kurland and Bailey, 1999). It is also shown that for a positive work-life balance, the most important factor is managing the workload when it comes to remote working (Maruyama et al., 2009).

Remote working is also stated to offer advantages for organizations. Costs like real estate or electricity expenses can be reduced through the adoption of remote working arrangements (Toduk, 2014). Increased efficiency, increased life quality, decreasing costs and absenteeism are considered as major benefits of remote working (Alkan Meşhur, 2007; Di Martino and Wirth, 1990; Tozlu, 2011).

The other side of the coin focuses on the negative effects of remote working. One of the most debated outcomes of remote work is over the social isolation it may lead to (Kurland and Bailey, 1999; Harpaz, 2002). Remote workers are stated to experience higher levels of worry due to the isolation they face and the lack of communication with colleagues (Mann and Holdsworth, 2003). It has also been found that remote workers cannot separate their work and private lives, leading to diminished restorative effects of home (Hartig et al., 2007).

Study

Aim

The aim of this work is to investigate the extent to which the increase in digitalization in remote working changes the perceived work-life balance of the individual under the pandemic conditions.

Sampling and method of data collection

The sample of the study included employees working in one of the world's leading companies in the household appliance industry in Turkey. 19 semi-structured online interviews were conducted in 3 weeks, between 2 November 2020 and 21 November 2020. The interviews lasted 15 to 30 minutes and were recorded with the consent of the interviewees. The answers were transcribed verbatim and were content analyzed after decoding.

The questions included in the interview form aim to find out if remote working has created advantages or disadvantages for employees and to understand their experiences during this process in order to evaluate its effect on the work-life balance. The interview form basically consists of two types of questions. The first part includes items related to demographics such as age, tenure in work-life and in the company, marital status, etc. The second part is based on the perceptions, experiences and evaluations of participants regarding home-based remote working. In this respect, previous works on remote work, work-life balance and well-being were examined. Especially the tools and scales used for assessment were analyzed and common themes/patterns were determined.

Previous research shows that, in order to majorly assess the work-life balance, the effect of work on private life and the effect of private life on work were investigated (e.g., Netemeyer, Boles and McMurrian, 1996). In this respect, questions to evaluate the positive and negative effects of remote working on work life and private life were formulized and the participants were asked if they thought they were able to keep the balance between their work lives and private lives.

In order to assess the well-being level of employees, they were asked to define their experiences with adjectives as done in most of the well-being studies. Semantic scales that visualized two opposite sides via adjectives or items related to the emotions during work are majorly preferred to assess the well-being levels of participants (e.g., Warr, 1990; Van Katwyk et al., 2000). In this respect, respondents were asked to define the feelings and emotions they experienced during the remote-working process and to rate their overall happiness with home-based remote working.

Sample characteristics

The sample consists of 12 men and 7 women. The ages of the participants vary between 25 and 58. Most of the interviewees are between the ages of 31 and 50 (69%). Apart from one participant, all interviewees have more than 5 years of experience in work life (95%). 10 of the participants have subordinates under their span of control (53%). 18 of the respondents reside in Istanbul whereas 1 lives in İzmir. The demographics are indicated below in Table 1.1.

Table 1.1: Demographics

Characteristic	Category	Frequency	Percentage
Gender	Men	12	63%
	Women	7	37%
Age	≤30	2	23%
	31-40	9	23%
	41-50	4	46%
	≥51	4	8%
Educational level	Bachelor	11	58%
	Masters	8	42%
Marital status	Single	2	11%
	Married	17	89%
Family	Have children	11	58%
	Do not have children	8	42%
Tenure in work life	≤5 years	1	5%
	6-10 years	6	32%
	11-15 years	3	16%
	≥15 years	9	47%
Tenure in current organization	≤5 years	10	53%
	6-10 years	3	16%
	11-15 years	2	11%
	≥15 years	4	21%
Managerial role	Have subordinates	10	53%
	Do not have subordinates	9	47%

Findings

All the participants had the chance to work from home during the peak pandemic period between March 2020 and June 2020. In this respect, they were asked if they had the possibility to work remotely before the pandemic. All of the interviewees stated that they had this choice. The company allowed them to work remotely for a maximum of 4 days per month. Afterwards, the participants were asked if they had resorted to that option. 42% of them replied that they never or rarely used that option due to the requirements and structure of the work. 2 of the participants emphasized that they did not prefer to work remotely. The others mentioned that they usually used that option when it was offered.

Also, it was asked if they still continued to work remotely due to the pandemic or if they had returned to the usual practices. All of them mentioned they still have the option to work remotely since the pandemic situation still persists and they plan their working location according to the task requirements and the flow of work.

Afterwards, questions regarding the work-life balance were directed at the participants. First of all, they were asked to describe their work environment and working hours during the home-office. The participants replied that they tried to create an artificial office at their home, if possible, in a separate room. Most of the respondents especially emphasized that there was no established “work time” concept anymore. There were expected to be available most of the time. One of the respondents stated that he felt “neither at home nor at the office”.

Two of the fundamental questions were based on the positive and negative effects of remote working on the respondents’ work and private life. The frequency of the results is summarized below in Tables 1.2 and 1.3, where the positive and negative experiences of the interviewees were categorized under some headings according to their content.

As seen from Table 1.2 the negative effects of home-based remote working on work life (58%) are higher than the mentioned positive effects (42%). The most frequently mentioned effect of remote work was extended working hours and extended workload due to limitless availability. The second most voiced effect was also an issue of complaint, namely the lack of communication and socialization. In the third position of the mentioned effects on work life is a positive effect, that is to say the advantage of time savings due to not being obliged to spend time during transportation between home and work. Increased concentration, trust and self-management, flexibility, work efficiency, agility, and trust in technology achieved the next ranks as the most frequently repeated themes among the positive answers. In terms of negative effects on work life, too long meetings were especially mentioned as a loss of time and energy. Feelings of inefficient working, ergonomic discomfort at home, a blurring between private and working life, no lunch break, a lack of corporate culture and increased individualism were repeated negative themes among the answers.

Table 1.2: Effects of Remote Working on Work Life

Work-related effects		Frequency	Percentage
Positive effects	Time savings (no transportation)	8	8%
	Increased concentration	4	4%
	Increased perceived trust	4	4%
	Self-management/Time-management	4	4%
	Flexibility within comfort zone	3	3%
	Efficient work	3	3%
	Agility	3	3%
	Practicality/Innovativeness	3	3%
	Trust in technology	2	2%
	No distraction	2	2%
	Cost savings for company	2	2%
	Open data sharing	2	2%
	Time for self-development	2	2%
Sum of frequencies of positive effects		**42**	**42%**
Negative effects	Increased availability/extended work hours/increased workload	14	14%
	Loss of social interaction/loss of emotions	9	9%
	Too many and too long meetings	7	7%
	Inefficient work	7	7%
	Ergonomic discomfort	6	6%
	Blurriness between work and private life	6	6%
	No lunch break	4	4%
	Lack of corporate culture and belonging	4	4%
	Increased individualism/no feedbacks	1	1%
Sum of frequencies of negative effects		**58**	**58%**
Total sum		**100**	**100%**

The assessment of the effects on private life is exactly the opposite of those on work life: the ratio's positive feelings (63%) were higher than the negative ones (37%). The most mentioned effect of remote working on private life was a positive one: increased family time. The respondents were glad to spend more time with their families and they felt safe at home. Indeed, that feeling of safety was majorly associated with the pandemic rather than being a pure, direct effect of remote working. As the negative effects, the majorly mentioned factor was the loss of the "at home" feeling. This finding is, in a way, overlapping with the "blurriness between work and private life" factor given as a reply for the effects on work life. These two factors can be regarded as having a combined effect both on work life and private life.

Table 1.3: Effects of Remote Working on Private Life

Private life-related effects		Frequency	Percentage
Positive effects	Increased family time	8	30%
	Safety	6	22%
	Time flexibility	2	7%
	Increased physical well-being	1	4%
Sum of frequencies of positive effects		**17**	**63%**
Negative effects	Loss of "at home" feeling	5	19%
	Loss of family time	3	11%
	Loss of order	2	7%
Sum of frequencies of negative effects		**10**	**37%**
Total sum		**27**	**100%**

After that, the participants were asked to describe the emotions and feelings they experienced during the remote-working process with a few adjectives in order to gain insight about their overall well-being. The results are given below in Table 1.4. As seen from the table, negative adjectives were plural (68%). Mostly, the uttered adjectives were lonely and bored in addition to anxious. To objectively interpret these findings, the undeniable effect of the pandemic on causing loneliness shall not be ignored here. But in addition to that, participants mentioned that they felt bored during work processes and work time, because work relations had become something rather "robotic and non-human" as two of the respondents named it. Participants also felt anxious due to technology-related uncertainties, possible malfunctions, and, also due to personal inabilities regarding technological issues. Calm, joyful, efficient, enthusiastic and vigorous during home-based remote working were some of the positive emotions named by the participants.

Table 1.4: Emotions during Remote Work

Experienced emotions during remote work		**Frequency**	**Percentage**
Positive adjectives	Calm	4	8%
	Joyful	3	6%
	Efficient	3	6%
	Enthusiastic	2	4%
	Vigorous	2	4%
	Valued	1	2%
	Free	1	2%
Sum of frequencies of positive adjectives		**16**	**32%**
Negative adjectives	Lonely	9	18%
	Bored	8	16%
	Anxious/Stressful	5	10%
	Tired	4	8%
	Busy	3	6%
	Insufficient	3	6%
	Restricted	2	4%
Sum of frequencies of negative adjectives		**34**	**68%**
Total sum		**50**	**100%**

When the interviewees were asked if they believed they had achieved the establishment of a work-life balance during the remote-working process, they generally emphasized that work and private life had intertwined and therefore it had become hard to separate them. They generally thought they were not able to set the balance. At first, they felt overwhelmed but as time passed, they learned how to get along with the challenges better. It was mentioned that they always had work somewhere in their minds and therefore it was hard to rid themselves of that pressure to work further. Only 37% of the participants implied they were happy with the life they lived, whereas 63% of them asserted that they got used to it later but it was an exhausting process.

The participants were also asked if they evaluated remote work overall as positive or negative. 63% of the participants stated that they found remote work as a good opportunity, and therefore, their evaluations were on the positive side. As age increased, the participants' approach towards remote work changed. Elderly participants were not so eager to conduct work remotely, and mentioned that they would rather be at the office than at home whilst working. The difference observed between the deficient satisfaction with the work-life balance and the approach towards remote work could mainly stem from the positively perceived idea of being able to work remotely. The interviewees all mentioned that having this possibility at hand was always beneficial but full-time remote work would not be preferred by them.

The final question that was directed to the participants was about the future of work. They were asked if the ideal work model would be office-based, home-based or a hybrid model which incorporates both work arrangements to some extent. With no exception, all of the employees asserted that the future of work should be a hybrid model rather than just an on-site or remote-working style. They all stated that they would prefer a mixed, integrated model in which they could decide their work schedule in agreement with their supervisors or in accordance with their job requirements.

Discussion

The future is expected to be more digital day by day and new work arrangements will inevitably be based on technological advancements. Furthermore, the pandemic in 2020 has created an unexpected experimental environment in which the effects of remote working could be exercised and evaluated. From now on, it is impossible to think of work as the same old routine and expect classical ways of conducting tasks. Especially home-based remote work will be an inevitable part of work arrangements, therefore, understanding the dynamics of this process has become crucial. In this study, it is aimed to shed light on the employees' experiences of remote working during the pandemic process. In this respect, in-depth interviews were conducted with employees working in a multinational firm to understand how their well-being and work-life balance had been affected due to remote working. Since some of the participants had managerial roles within the company, their replies can also help to gain insights about the inclinations of the management perspective.

From the angle of the employees including the supervisors, the most mentioned advantage of home-based remote working was stated as "time savings". Most of the participants regarded this as a highly important benefit of working from home. As the majority of participants live in Istanbul, this result is not surprising. Employees especially living in metropolises waste so much time during travel to- and from work. Therefore, approximately 2 to 3 hours of the day have become utilizable for these employees.

The second most important contribution of remote work was considered to be "increased concentration". Employees generally stated that they had no distraction during working at home, therefore, they could focus on the work more easily, and as a consequence, felt that their efficiency was increased. Also, they indicated that they felt trusted by their supervisors and the company. No external control mechanisms were used during remote work to check the availability of the employees, they were able to self-manage their tasks and given the initiative. Therefore, this factor contributed positively to their sense of being valuable and trusted. They also stated that they were more innovative in finding solutions and they could also find some spare time for job-related self-development. They had the time and the opportunity to join online certificate programs or workshops to gain deeper knowledge in areas useful for their jobs.

From the management perspective, the agility of the organization was questioned during this process. The answers showed that being able to conduct jobs via home settings has provided proof that the company was agile, adaptive and able to cope with sudden change that could have, otherwise, led to a trauma. The trust in technology was stimulated and open data sharing was encouraged. One of the most important benefits for the organization had been the cost-reduction opportunity. Especially the participants who had managerial tasks supported remote working due to the advantage in terms of costs, and, therefore, evaluated it as beneficial for the organization in terms of financial concerns.

In terms of negative aspects, the most mentioned effects were "increased work hours and availability". These factors also led indirectly to blurriness between work and private life and the balance was lost. The frequent and unnecessarily long meetings were considered as having caused tiredness and inefficiency throughout the company. Another major complaint was "loss of social interaction". This has been claimed to have caused three major outcomes: first, things that could have been done during small talk required much more time to be completed; second, people felt lonely and helpless during working; and lastly, it hurt the corporate culture. People started losing their sense of belonging. This can also be regarded as an outcome that affects the organization. Managers had also stated that corporate culture was hard to build and sustain when working remotely. People should come together, transfer feelings and knowledge and share thoughts and experiences for the survival of a solid organizational culture. In addition to this, remote work was not appropriate for newcomers at the beginning of their career in the organization because it is hard to transfer the values and norms of the company to them. "Increased individualism" was also considered as a negative effect. It is a double-edged sword for both the employee and the company. Participants stated that they could not get proper feedback for their efforts, and due to being lonely, they were forced to continue alone and could not get proper help whenever needed. Besides providing advantages in terms of self-management and decision-making, this had also led to the loss of collective work and synergy. From the company perspective, teamwork was always encouraged and a shared culture was vital. Therefore, increased individualism posed a threat for both sides.

Most of the answers about remote-working experiences with regard to private life showed that the participants were happy to spend more time with the family. It was also a benefit derived from the time advantage brought about by staying at home. On the other hand, although time spent with the family increased, the quality of time did not. This means that most of the participants could not separate their private lives from work boundaries and therefore could not relax after work as they did before.

The participants were also asked to define their emotions during remote working with a few adjectives. The majority of the adjectives collected yielded negative emotions such as loneliness, boredom, anxiety and insufficiency. Keeping in mind that loneliness was doubled due to the pandemic and the lockdown situation, they majorly mentioned feeling alone in terms of doing the job. They were unable to find immediate support when needed, and due to the lack of communication, they also felt bored with no possibility for socialization. People generally consider work as a tool for socialization due to the fact that the majority of our daily time is spent with colleagues rather than with family. Therefore, colleagues are not solely professionals to work with, but they rather have a deeper meaning for most of us. Although the participants had prior remote-working experience, they doubted if this could be sufficient during this process. On the other hand, thanks to the isolation, the employees were able to set their own schedules most of the time and they felt calm and free. Also, this new experience facilitated a positive feeling of enthusiasm and joy towards this new way of doing things. Most importantly, they felt valuable to the organization in that the company let them stay at home and trusted them to do their job regardless of where they were.

The answers relating to achieving a work-life balance during the remote-working process showed that the participants generally thought they were not able to set the balance and they felt challenged by the expectations of both sides until they got used to it. This can be considered as an important explanation for the definition of the ideal work arrangement of the future made by the participants. None of them just favored office or remote work and all stated that, a hybrid or integrated/mixed model should be applied. According to the results mentioned before, the extent of location flexibility, in other words to which extent the work will be remote or on-site, should first be arranged between the employee and the supervisor, and second it should be compatible with the job characteristics and requirements.

Conclusion

Future work defined under the title of Work 4.0 envisages flexible remote-working environments independent of place and time thanks to digital technologies. Due to the high-power distance and hierarchical structures in countries like Turkey, where the general approach was based on micromanagement and close supervision, until today, remote work has not been preferred and utilized to a great extent. The pandemic has created a paradigm shift, so the meaning of remote work has become an exact meaning. Organizations worldwide were forced into a sudden change in which they had to adopt home-based remote work arrangements. Both companies and employees have altered their perspectives on remote work. It is seen that getting things done is much more important than where it is done. Supporting this, the employees who had remote-work experience prior to the pandemic, had confessed that they regarded remote work as time offered to them for their personal stuff. From now on, it will be considered as a true way of getting professional things done rather than spare time.

Based on the fact that there will be many more hybrid working environments in the future, this study was carried out to evaluate the perception of employees towards home-based remote working. In this context, the effects of remote working on work and private life and on the work-life balance of employees are analyzed on the basis of interviews. The results indicate that despite the greater negative impact on work life and the fact that most employees were challenged to maintain their work-life balance while working remotely at home, there was a positive perception about remote working. Employees feel obliged to be always available and do not know how to balance their work and private life. Therefore, due to the loneliness and boredom they have experienced, they do not favor full-time remote work so much. In this respect, a hybrid model which incorporates both work arrangements and offers location flexibility emerges as the most suitable option for now. It depends on the organization and the employee as to whether remote working will provide more benefits or more damages to both parties. It is seen that a combination of remote and on-site work will offer the most useful form of work for now.

This study shows that the digitalization of business that triggered and enabled remote work is neither freedom nor slavery. The organization and the employees should define the meaning of remote work together and decide whether it's beneficial or harmful, taking each other's needs and wants into account, in order to benefit from the advantages of location flexibility the most.

Keywords: *Remote working, well-being, work-life balance*

References

Alkan Meşhur, F. H. (2007). Geleceğin çalışma biçimi tele çalışmaya ilişkin yaklaşımlar. *Akademik Bilişim*, *7*(9), 265-272.

Breisig T, Grzech-Sukalo H, Vogl G (2017). Mobile rrbeit gesund gestalten – Trendergebnisse aus dem forschungsprojekt prentimo – präventionsorientierte gestaltung mobiler arbeit, prentimo, www.prentimo.de.

Cijan, A., Jenič, L., Lamovšek, A., & Stemberger, L. (2019). How digitalization changes the workplace. *Dynamic Relationships Management journal*, *8*(1), 3-12.

Degenhardt, B., Gisin, L., & Schulze, H. (2014). *Schweizerische umfrage „Home Office 2013" - Teil* 1. Olten: Hochschule für Angewandte Psychologie FHNW. http://www. fhnw. ch/aps/ifk/projekte/aktuelle-projekte/copy_of_home-office-2013/home-office-2013.

Di Martino, V., & Wirth, L. (1990). Telework: A new way of working and living. *International Labour Review*, *129*(5), 529-54

Dimitrova, D. (2003). Controlling teleworkers: supervision and flexibility revisited. *New Ttechnology, Work and Employment, 18*(3), 181-195.

Engels, B. (2020). *Corona: Stresstest für die digitalisierung in Deutschland* (No. 23/2020). IW-Kurzbericht Federal Ministry of Labour and Social Affairs of Germany (2017). Re-imagining work: Green paper work 4.0. Retrieved from https://www.bmas.de/SharedDocs/Downloads/DE/Publikationen/arbeiten-4-0-green-paper.pdf;jsessionid=02A1A6087AEADA4162C423E5F02F15C8.delivery1-replication?__blob=publicationFile&v=1

Hardill, I., & Green, A. (2003). Remote working - altering the spatial contours of work and home in the new economy. *New Technology, Work and Employment*, *18*(3), 212-222.

Harpaz, I. (2002). Advantages and disadvantages of telecommuting for the individual, organization and society. *Work Study*, *51*(2), 74-80.

Hartig, T., Kylin, C., & Johansson, G. (2007). The telework tradeoff: stress mitigation vs constrained restoration. *Applied Psychology: An International Review*, *56*(2), 231-253.

Hofmann, J., & Nostdal, R. (2014). Einsatz, bedeutung und rechtliche stellung von externen spezialisten in organisationen. Fraunhofer-Institut für Arbeitswirtschaft und Organisation, Stuttgart.

Hofmann, J., Bonnet, P., Schmidt, C., & Wienken, V. (2015). Die flexible führungskraft. Strategien in einer grenzenlosen arbeitswelt. Gütersloh: Bertelsmann Stiftung.

HR Drive (2020). Gartner: Over 80% of company leaders plan to permit remote work after pandemic. Retrieved from https://www.hrdive.com/news/gartner-over-80-of-company-leaders-plan-to-permit-remote-work-after-pande/581744/

Johnson, M. (1997). Teleworking in brief. 1. ed. UK: Butterworth-Heinemann.

Kaiser S, Kozica A (2015). Zukunftsfähige führung in fluiden organisationen und modernen arbeitswelten. In Widuckel W., de Molina K., Ringlstetter M. J., Frey D. (eds.) *Arbeitskultur 2020 (307-322)*. Berlin: Springer.

Karaca, S., & Esen, E. (2019). İş yeri inovasyonun bir örneği olarak uzaktan çalışmanın iş yaşam dengesine etkisi: Çalışan anneler üzerine bir araştırma, *International Social Innovation Congress,* İstanbul, Turkey, 16 - 17 October 2019, 22-0.

Karasek, R.A., & Theorell, T. (1990). Healthy work: Stress, productivity and the reconstruction of working life, Basic Books, New York, NY.

Klein, M. (2019). İşletme 4.0 kapsamında şirket 2.0. İşletme süreçlerinde sosyal yazılım kullanımı. Nobel Yayıncılık, İstanbul.

Klein, M. (2020). İşletmelerde dijital dönüşüm ve etmenleri. *Dijital Çağda İşletmecilik Dergisi*, *3*(1), 24-35.

Koch, M. (2008). CSCW and enterprise 2.0- towards an integrated perspective. *BLED 2008 Proceedings*, 15.

Kotera, Y., & Correa Vione, K. (2020). Psychological impacts of the new ways of working (NWW): a systematic review. *International Journal of Environmental Research and Public Health*, *17*(14), 5080.

Kraus, S., Grzech-Sukalo, H., & Rieder, K. (2020). Mobile arbeit–home-office, dienstreisen, außendienst–was ist wirklich belastend?. *Zeitschrift für Arbeitswissenschaft*, *74*(3), 167-177.

Kurland, N. B., & Bailey, D.E. (1999). Telework: The advantages and challenges of working here, there, anywhere, and anytime. *Organizational Dynamics*, *28*(2), 53-68.

Mann, S., & Holdsworth, L. (2003). The psychological impact of teleworking: stress, emotions and health. *New Technology, Work and Employment*, *18*(3), 196-211.

Maruyama, T., Hopkinson, P.G., & James, P.W. (2009). A multivariate analysis of work–life balance outcomes from a large-scale telework programme, *New Technology, Work and Employment*, *24*(1),. 76-88.

Marx, K. (1968). Ökonomisch-philosophische manuskripte,. In Marx-Engels-Werke, Bd. 40. Berlin (1844).

Netemeyer, R. G., Boles, J. S., & McMurrian, R. (1996). Development and validation of work–family conflict and family–work conflict scales. *Journal of Applied Psychology, 81*(4), 400-410.

OwlLabs (2020). Tha state of remote work report. Retrieved from *https://www.owllabs.com/state-of-remote-work#:~:text=44%25%20of%20global%20companies%20don,no%20option%20to%20work%20remotely*

Özkalp, E., Varoğlu, A., Varoğlu, D., Kırel, A. Ç., & Acar, P. (2013). Örgütsel davranış. 1. Ed. Eskişehir: Anadolu Üniversitesi.

Perez Perez, M., Martinez Sanchez, A., & Pilar de Luis Carnicer, M. (2003). The organizational implications of human resources managers' perception of teleworking, *Personnel Review*, *32*(6) 733-755.

Ratna, R., & Kaur, T. (2016). The impact of information technology on job related factors like health and safety, job satisfaction, performance, productivity and work life balance. *Journal of Business & Financial Affairs*, 5(171), 2167-0234.

Rump, J., & Eilers, S. (2017). Auf dem Weg zur Arbeit 4.0. Innovationen in HR. Berlin: Springer Verlag GmbH.

Spath, D., Bauer, W., Rief, Kelter, J., Haner, U. E., & Jurecic, M. (2012). Arbeitswelten 4.0. Wie wir morgen arbeiten und leben. Beiträge des Fraunhofer-Institut für Arbeitswirtschaft und Organisation, Stuttgart.

Thiemann, D., & Kozica, A. (2019). Digitalisierung der arbeitswelt: Eine empirische analyse relevanter handlungsfelder bei der digitalen transformation von geschäftsprozessen. *HMD Praxis der Wirtschaftsinformatik*, *56*(4), 721-734.

Toduk, Y. (2014). 2023 Lideri: Dijital çağın liderlik sırları. 1. Ed. İstanbul: Doğan Egmont Yayıncılık.

Tozlu, E.. (2011). Genel olarak esnek çalışma sistemleri ve tele çalışma ve sıkıştırılmış iş haftasının karşılaştırılması. *Süleyman Demirel Üniversitesi Vizyoner Dergisi*. 3(4), 99-116.

van Katwyk, Paul T., Fox, S., Spector P. E., & Kelloway K. (2000). Using the ob-related affective well-being scale (JAWS) to investigate affective responses to work stressors. *Journal of Occupational Health Psyhology*, *5*(2), 219-230.

Vogler-Ludwig, K., Düll, N., & Kriechel, B. (2016). Arbeitsmarkt 2030 - Wirtschaft und Arbeitsmarkt im digitalen Zeitalter. Prognose 2016. Munich: Economix Research & Consulting.

von See, B., & Kersten, W. (2017). Digitale transformation des arbeitsumfelds. In Norbert Gronau (ed.), Industrial Internet of Things in der Arbeits- und Betriebsorganisation, GITO Verlag.

Warr, P. (1990). Decision latitude, job demands, and employee well-being. *Work and Stress, 4*(4), 285-294.

Wheatley, D. (2012). Good to be home? Time use and satisfaction levels among home-based teleworkers. *New Technology, Work and Employment*, *27*(3), 224-241.

Wimmer, C. (2019). Industry 4.0 New challenges for the European world of work. Rosa-Luxemburg-Stiftung, Brussels Office. Retrieved from https://www.rosalux.eu/en/article/1363.industry-4-0.html

CHAPTER TWO

THE CATALYST IMPACT OF THE COVID-19 PANDEMIC ON THE DIGITAL TRANSFORMATION OF BUSINESSES

İBRAHIM TÜRKMEN

Introduction

Digitalization has become a strategic process for businesses along with the development in information and communication technologies. Digitalization is defined as the adoption and effective use of digital technologies to seize new value creation opportunities. As of the 2000s many leading businesses make investments in digitalization. However, digitalization has become a necessity for all public, private and non-governmental organizations during the Covid-19 pandemic process.

Covid-19 started in China and became a pandemic that has affected the whole world. The pandemic has caused an economic crisis as well as a health crisis for countries. Countries have taken lockdown decisions to stop the pandemic. Almost all sectors have been affected by the lockdown decisions. Countries have had to make flexible working and teleworking arrangements. This has promoted businesses to invest in digitalization. In the post-pandemic period, it is expected that the digitalization efforts of businesses will accelerate and become widespread.

The digitalization of businesses does not mean investing in or owning technology. Digitalization refers to a change and transformation. In order for the digitalization process to be successful in businesses, managers and employees need to change and develop their skills, competencies, thinking styles, communication and working styles. Also, the digitalization process in ever-changing and developing the work environment, forces businesses to change their business models. The business model is an effective means of focusing that businesses can utilize to get economic value from the digitalization process. Business models transformed in accordance with digitalization can increase the value created for internal and external partners and obtain competitive advantage by making the business different from its competitors.

This study focuses on the effect of the Covid-19 pandemic on the digitalization process in businesses. It is designed in three parts. The concepts of “digitization”, “digitalization” and “digital transformation”, the drivers of digitalization, the difficulties and obstacles experienced during the digitalization process of businesses, the factors affecting the success of digitalization and the effects of digitalization on business models are discussed in the first part. There is an attempt to explain the catalyst effect of the Covid-19 pandemic on the digitalization process of businesses in the second part. The recommendations for businesses are included in the third and concluding part.

Digital Transformation of Businesses

The Concept of Digitalization

The concepts "digitization" and "digitalization" are closely related, frequently used interchangeably, but different from each other. While “digitization” refers to the transformation of analog data into a digital form, “digitalization” refers to the adoption or the increase in the use of digital and computer technology (Brennen and Kreiss, 2016: 557). Digitization is a technical process that transforms the analog data developing with the use of computers into a digital form of binary numbers. The purpose of transforming data into a digital form is to make all digital data processable via the same technologies. The use of digital technologies for these purposes necessitates the development of new social, cognitive and technical models. This indicates that the concept of digitalization is different (Tilson et al., 2010).

Digitization is a simple process to digitize a document by scanning or do transactions without using paper and therefore it turns businesses into “paperless offices”. It contributes to the collection of documents that cannot be collected, reducing possible errors and increasing operational productivity by digitizing documents in public institutions, medical records in hospitals, student records in universities and data for the production process in businesses. However, digitization alone cannot change the usage of businesses and their value proposition and the implementation of new business models and basic business strategies. Digitalization is the foundation of information that can be used to create a change and act using the digitalized data. The digitalization process leads to digital transformation which means complete reconstruction of the business around the new opportunities and new demands offered by digital technology (Gobble, 2018a; Gobble, 2018b).

Digitalization refers to "the increasing penetration of digital technologies in society with the associated changes in the connection of individuals and their behaviors" (Gimpel and Röglinger, 2015: 5). Digitalization is defined as "the use of digital technologies to change a business model and provide new income and value creation opportunities and a transition process to a digital business" (Gartner Glossary, accessed 29.10.2020). Digitization is a larger concept than digitizing existing processes or making business processes technologic (Parviainen et al., 2017). As a conclusion, digitization is a technical process focusing on digital technologies. Digitalization is a socio-technical process focusing on the individual, organizational and social adoption and use of digital technologies (Legner, et al., 2017).

Drivers of Digitalization

Four factors stand out as the drivers of digitalization. They are: (1) the development of digital technologies, (2) changes in the demands and expectations of people, (3) falling barriers for the entry to the sector, and (4) support for entrepreneurs (Schreckling and Steiger, 2017).

Digitalization is based on technology. There are four main technologies affecting the digitalization process of businesses. The first of these is analytical technologies which help managers and employees to analyze big data, obtain innovative information and take decisions. Mobile technologies are the second. Mobile applications and devices enable the establishment of new business affairs with all partners. Cloud technologies are the third. These provide flexible, reliable, low cost and shareable digital skills for businesses. The fourth and final one is social media technologies. Social media and the web empower customers by raising awareness and reducing information asymmetry. Therefore, they make businesses customer-oriented (Gimpel and Röglinger, 2015; Wade and Marchand, 2014).

Of course, the effect and contribution of technology in the digitalization process of businesses cannot be denied. However, it is not enough for businesses to have and invest in technology alone for digital transformation (Papagiannidis et al., 2020). In other words, technology alone does not promote the change, transformation and cooperation (Bonnet and Nandan, 2011). With technology, visionary and transformational leadership applications and employees have to be open to change and development (Attaran, 2004). Employee and customer behaviors changing with the development of digital technologies offer businesses many opportunities for the business model and value proposition. However, there are some difficulties in seizing these opportunities and turning them into a competitive advantage. The first of these difficulties is the individualization of the demands of the customers with the awareness of the customers. Changing employee behaviors and thought patterns are the second. Third is the increase in competition as a result of new competitors' easy entry to markets due to the increase in transportation possibilities and low entry barriers (Gimpel and Röglinger, 2015).

Digital Transformation

Digital transformation consists of three stages: "digitization, digitalization and digital transformation" (Verhoef et al., 2021: 889). Digitization, the first stage, is a technical process related to digitizing analog signals. Digitalization is a socio-technical process about creating a change by using digitized data. The digitalization process leads to change and digital transformation in businesses (Gobble, 2018a).

Businesses tend to see their investments in digital technologies as digital transformation. However, this causes great mistakes and failure. Digital transformation is not solely the use of digital technologies in business processes. Although this is considered as a digital change that creates some benefits, it does not include a transformation. For instance, businesses can accelerate their business processes, reduce their costs and increase their productivity and sales by investing in digital technologies. However, all of these are not actually transformational (Soto-Acosta, 2020).

Digital transformation refers to the "managed adaptation of companies in light of progressing digitalization in order to assure sustainable value creation" (Gimpel and Röglinger, 2015: 5). Put simply, digital transformation is "the increasing adoption of digital tools and technologies by an organization to fundamentally change both internal and external processes and functions" (Bonnet and Nandan, 2011: 4). There are also some definitions regarding digital transformation as a process. For instance, Vial (2019: 118) defines digital transformation as "a process that aims to improve an entity by triggering significant changes to its properties through combinations of information, computing, communication, and connectivity technologies". Morakanyane et al. (2017: 437) define it as "an evolutionary process that leverages digital capabilities and technologies to enable business models, operational processes and customer experiences to create value".

Based on the definitions in the literature, digital transformation is regarded as the changes in working conditions, employee roles and business processes resulting from the adoption of digital technologies in a business. Digital transformation refers to changes at various levels (Parviainen et al., 2017: 64):

- *Process level: digitalization necessitates the adoption of new digital tools and the simplification of processes by reducing manual steps.*
- *Organization level: digitalization forces the organizational structure and culture to change.*
- *Business domain level: digitalization changes the way of business and business models.*
- *Society level: digitalization changes the needs and demands of the society.*

Businesses digitize their business, business processes, products and business models in the digitalization process (Schreckling and Steiger, 2017). Digital technologies transform operations, products and services in large, small, public, private and non-governmental organizations. Digital transformation is seen as a solution for both productivity and efficiency difficulties (Heavin and Power, 2018; Bonnet and Nandan, 2011). In addition, digitalization and the use of information technologies were found to be an effective factor in increasing financial performance (Eller et al., 2020).

The Obstacles and Challenges of Digital Transformation

Digital transformation offers many opportunities and benefits for businesses, but it is a challenging process. Many businesses fail due to the obstacles and challenges they encounter in the digitalization process. The fact that businesses see digital transformation as just investing in technology or owning it and consider it as a sufficient condition causes the process to fail. Resistance is possible since the change and transformation are often perceived as a threat by employees (Tabrizi et al., 2019). In this context, businesses and managers should determine the obstacles and challenges of digital transformation and take the necessary measures.

The obstacle and challenges of businesses in digital transformation can be divided into four categories: data, technology, human beings and management. The first is related with the failure to collect sufficient and standard data, the lack of data integration and sharing and the inability to analyze and transform the data into new and usable information. Second, the basic condition for digitalization is to have a suitable technological infrastructure. The technological and software shortcomings of businesses will challenge the success of digitalization. Third, employees' bias towards digitalization, and knowledge, skill and competency shortcomings will create obstacles. The last category is about the management of digitalization. Digitalization is not only the task of one department, but all units. It is the management that will assure this task (Fernandez and Gallardo-Gallardo, 2020).

In the study by Parviainen et al. (2017), it was determined that the biggest challenge and obstacle to digital transformation are either that businesses do not change their mindsets and processes or they cannot build a culture that can promote change. Gjellebaek et al. (2020) stated that managers', especially mid-level managers, and employees' lack of sufficient competence in digital transformation, lack of knowledge about how to manage the transformation, and inability to ensure cooperation within the business were obstacles and difficulties.

Current organizational culture can be one of the obstacles to digital transformation. The obstacle to digital transformation is the human, not the technology. Too many businesses invest in technologies without getting their culture and employees ready for the digital transformation. Thus, businesses neglect the social aspect of digital transformation while focusing on the technical aspect. Failure is not a surprise for businesses that cannot realize that digital transformation is a socio-technical process (Forgo et al., 2020; Bonnet and Nandan, 2011). In this case, managers should make the necessary effort to increase the competencies of the employees and to evolve the organizational culture towards technology-based innovation (Azoeva et al., 2020; Ancarani and Di Mauro, 2018).

Although today's technological developments create opportunities for businesses such as flexibility, speed, productivity and product individualization, they also create various challenges such as adaptation to change, increasing uncertainty, changing customer preferences and legal requirements. In spite of all of these challenges, it is not possible for businesses to ignore digitalization, change and transformation (Rachinger et al., 2019; Gimpel and Röglinger, 2015).

Factors Important to the Success of the Digital Transformation

Businesses make important investments in digital transformation. It is estimated that the economic value of digital transformation reached $ 20 trillion, more than 20% of global GDP. It is expected that investments will continue and the amount expected to be spent on digital transformation by 2023 will reach $ 2.3 trillion (International Data Corporation, 2019). In spite of large-scale investments, 70% of the digital transformation enterprises fail (Tabrizi et al., 2019). Although there is variance according to the sector, the businesses desiring to be successful in digitalization need to specialize in the following six domains (Table 2.1): "customer, value proposition, operations, data, organization, [and] transformation management" (Gimpel and Röglinger, 2015).

Table 2.1: Six Domains to Specialize for Success in Digitalization

Customer	**Data**
➢ *Customer Experience Management* ➢ *Customer Insights* ➢ *Multi/Omni Channel Management* ➢ *Hybrid Customer Interaction*	➢ *Data Integration* ➢ *Data Analytics* ➢ *Data Ownership & privacy* ➢ *Data Security*
Value Proposition	**Organization**
➢ *Smart Products* ➢ *Smart Services* ➢ *Individualization* ➢ *Digital Ecosystems*	➢ *Organizational Agility* ➢ *Workplace of the Future* ➢ *Digital Skill Set* ➢ *Digital Mindset*
Operations	**Transformation Management**
➢ *Integrated IT* ➢ *Flexible Operations* ➢ *Digital Supply Network* ➢ *Digital Manufacturing*	➢ *Digital Strategy* ➢ *Transformation Leadership* ➢ *Change Management* ➢ *Digital Value Assurance*

Source: Gimpel and Röglinger (2015: 9)

Businesses not only provide their customers with appropriate goods and services, but also customer experience (Kudyba, 2020). Customer experience is not only limited to customer interaction in businesses; it occurs at all of the stages that customers interact with businesses and includes the customer's personal cognitive, emotional and behavioral responses to the business during the search, purchasing, consumption and after-sales stages (Grewal et al., 2009; Verhoef, et al., 2009).

Although digitizing the interaction with customers delivers solution for many customers, it will not always offer a perfect customer experience (Markovitch and Willmott, 2014). The only and best way to know where and how to make changes and improvements to customer experience is to get comprehensive and in-depth information from customers (Tabrizi et al., 2019). In this context, insights regarding the real needs of customers should be obtained by analyzing data about the customers. In addition, businesses should integrate their customers into the main business processes at the strategy, system and process levels and establish strong and loyal relationships. Therefore, businesses should try to offer a holistic, smooth, satisfactory and personalized customer experience by consolidating many different channels (Gimpel and Röglinger, 2015).

Understanding what increases customer value as a result of customer experiences is a prerequisite for designing a value proposition. The basic dimensions of customer value guide customer behaviors (Rintamaki and Kirves, 2017). Businesses can integrate their customers into the product designing process through digital technologies, design smart products and services and therefore, expand their value propositions (Gimpel and Röglinger, 2015).

Businesses can digitize their knowledge-intensive processes, accelerate recycling times and reduce process costs by up to 90% (Markovitch and Willmott, 2014). Mobile digital technologies such as IoT, cloud, big data, artificial intelligence, robotics, and automation help to increase productivity, efficiency, flexibility and diversity in businesses. In addition, they change business models, production processes and ways of working and cooperation (Foerster-Metz et al., 2018). Digitization also enables structured and unstructured data from different sources to be obtained, integrated and analyzed (Parviainen et al., 2017). At this point, specialization in data analysis, assuring data privacy and safety should be one of the most important targets for businesses (Papagiannidis et al., 2020).

Technological changes trigger and affect organizational change. Leaders must have the courage and strength to make the necessary arrangements for their organizations to benefit from this technology-driven transformation. For this reason, digital transformation is about leadership as much as technology (Pratt, 2019; Bonnet and Nandan, 2011). Using information technologies triggers a transformation from vertical bureaucracy to horizontal companies as well as the reorganization of tasks and positions (Castells, 2009). For the success of digital transformation, businesses should transform from hierarchically managed line organizations to more creative and participatory organizations that are self-managed, project-oriented, and agile by expanding the range of control (Gjellebaek et al., 2020; Kudyba, 2020; Foerster-Metz et al., 2018; Schwer and Hitz, 2018; Zuboff, 1995).

The success of investments in digitalization depends on the development of intrabusiness skills and employees' different abilities (Markovitch and Willmott, 2014). Cognitive skills are replaced for action-based skills with the use of information technologies (Zuboff, 1995). Besides cognitive skills, a number of soft skills such as emotional intelligence, openness to development and change, sacrifice and cooperation became important (Nokelainen et al., 2018). This promotes businesses to invest in human and social capital (Kudyba, 2020). Since human capital and social capital are mostly business specific, they make all businesses unique (Schneider, 2018).

To tell the truth, digitalization changes the working ways of people. For this reason, it is necessary to develop the technical and human skills of employees and also their digital competencies to increase productivity (Soto-Acosta, 2020). Employees should have continuous learning and interdisciplinary skills. The management should create a digital mindset and transformative vision in the whole organization (Gimpel and Röglinger, 2015). If the leaders lack the right mindset to change people and are not appropriate for the cultural transformation, the failure of the digital transformation is inevitable. In this context, businesses should determine their strategies to manage the transformation and the leaders should make their businesses, organizational culture and employees volunteer and appropriate for change through transformational and visionary leadership practices (Tabrizi et al., 2019).

The Effect of Digitalization on Business Models

It is regarded that today's economy has become more digital and is described as the "digital economy" (Soto-Acosta, 2020). Digitalization transforms businesses from new cooperation with customers and interaction models to newly designed products and services (Gimpel and Röglinger, 2015). Digital transformation also fundamentally changes consumer expectations and behaviors (Verhoef et al., 2021). For these reasons, digital transformation disables traditional business models (Bonnet and Nandan, 2011).

Digitalization changes the settled ways of business and transforms business models. Companies such as Uber, Facebook, Alibaba and Airbnb indicate how new business models have changed in the digital economy. Uber is the largest taxi company providing an urban transportation service although it does not own a single car. Facebook has become the world's most popular media owner with no content. Alibaba is the world's most valuable retailer although it does not have any inventory. Airbnb is the world's largest accommodation company although it has no real estate. As seen in the examples, new business models develop in today's digital economy and settled business models should be evaluated again (Gimpel and Röglinger, 2015: 5). Basically, the business model is "ways of business in which a company can sustain itself, that is, generate income" (Rappa, 2010: 1). The business model is to mediate for creating economic value using technology (Chesbrough and Rosenbloom, 2002).

Business model and strategy are different concepts (Zott et al., 2011; Chesbrough and Rosenbloom, 2002). Clarifying the difference between the strategy and business model will be important for readers. Strategy is often defined as a conditional action plan designed to reach a particular target. Strategy refers to the selection of a business model that will be used by the business. In other words, the business model is "considered as a reflection of the strategy" (Casadesus-Masanell and Ricart, 2010: 205).

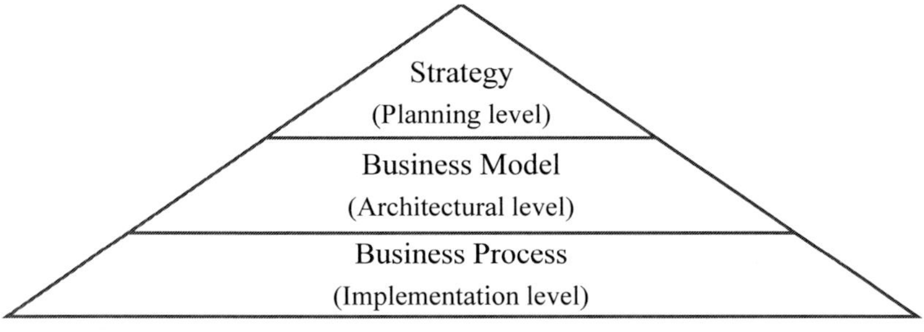

Figure 2.1: Business Logic Triangle (Osterwalder and Pigneur, 2002: 2)

Osterwalder and Pigneur (2002: 2) state that the business model is "the conceptual and architectural implementation of a business strategy and the fundamental of business processes". Since the business model defines how the strategy will be operated and represents the main logic of the business and strategic choices, it is at the operational level. The business model defines "the way the business presents its strategy and value proposition to customers" (Onetti et al, 2012: 362). Even if businesses produce similar products to meet customers' needs and even use the same strategies, they can do this with different business models. The business model and strategy are not substitutes, but complementary to each other (Zott and Amit, 2008). A business model has six main functions (Chesbrough and Rosenbloom, 2002: 533):

- A business model refers to value proposition.
- A business model determines a market segment and the mechanism of income generation.
- A business model defines the value chain in the company for creating and distributing value proposition.

- A business model enables an estimation of the cost structure and profit potential of the generating value proposition by considering the selected value proposition and the value chain structure.
- A business model determines the position of the business in the value network connecting the opponents, suppliers and customers.
- A business model helps the business to formulate its strategy that will provide sustainable competitive advantage.

Businesses commercialize by converting their new ideas and technologies into economic value through business models. For this reason, businesses need to improve their business model innovation skill (Chesbrough, 2010). Many businesses often use digital technologies to develop business models rather than transform them (Li, 2020). This fully technology-centered approach usually fails because digital transformation is initially an organizational business transformation (Bonnet and Nandan, 2011).

Covid-19 as a Catalyst

Covid-19 is a disease caused by a novel coronavirus called Sars-CoV-2. Covid-19 was first seen in December 2019 in Wuhan Province, People's Republic of China. Coronavirus infection spreads from person to person especially during close contact with an infected person. Due to this feature of the coronavirus, it spread all over the world in a short time. This spread was accepted as a global epidemic and the World Health Organization announced it as a pandemic on March 11, 2020. As of 5 December 2020, there were more than 65 million confirmed cases and 1.5 million deaths worldwide due to coronavirus (WHO, 2020).

The Covid-19 pandemic is becoming the biggest economic crisis since the Great Depression, as well as being a health crisis (Soto-Acosta, 2020). Due to the economic crisis caused by the pandemic, a decrease of 4.5% of GDP worldwide is expected in 2020 and a decrease of 7.9% in Europe (OECD, 2020a). Unemployment in OECD countries is expected to reach about 10% at the end of 2020, from 5.3% at the end of 2019, and rise to 12% if a second pandemic wave hits (OECD, 2020b).

The Covid-19 pandemic has seriously affected all countries and people economically, socially and psychologically. Many governments fighting the pandemic have had to make decisions to restrict the actions of their citizens and the activities of businesses. These restrictions include transportation restrictions, curfews, and the temporary closure of “non-essential” businesses. Under these conditions, people have had to work at home (Pan et al., 2020). While there are remarkable differences between businesses, those that work mainly as office-based have turned towards flexible and home working. However, many businesses that need personnel to work physically and deal directly with customers have had to close down during the lockdown (Papagiannidis et al., 2020). This has required businesses to apply innovative tactics to survive (Kudyba, 2020).

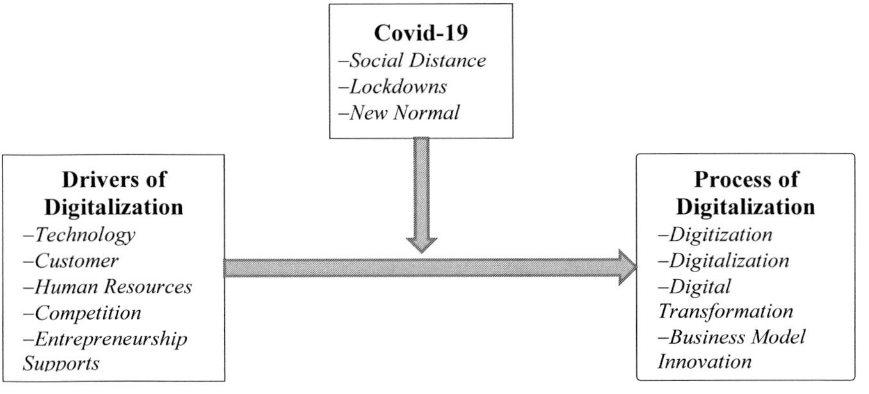

Figure 2.2: Catalytic effect of Covid-19

The most important consequences of the Covid-19 pandemic are social distance, lockdown and the new normal. The pandemic forces much work to be performed remotely. The pandemic accelerated the adoption and implementation of digital technologies although people have already had the opportunity to reach out to the technologies that enable remote working. In this context, businesses had to accelerate digital transformation as the only solution to prevent economic collapse. As a conclusion, many projects on digital transformation were launched by businesses that want to make remote working easy (Soto-Acosta, 2020). Digitalization was encouraged before the pandemic, but became a necessity during the pandemic. This emphasis is now evident in almost every private sector, public sector and non-governmental organization. The destructive effect of Covid-19 necessitated the rapid transformation in business processes and operational practices (Kamal, 2020).

The Covid-19 outbreak caused lockdowns in countries across the world; as a result, all industries and service sectors including healthcare, education, travel, tourism, and manufacturing were affected by the Covid-19 process. During the Covid-19 pandemic, the dependence on technology and online platforms increased exponentially in many aspects of society.

This sudden change forced businesses and employees to adapt to new working conditions (Herath and Herath, 2020; Richter, 2020). On the one hand, businesses needed to employ new information technology systems during the course of the pandemic, and on the other hand, other businesses needed to entirely rethink their business models, transition to online services and products and create new business channels for those lost or eliminated by the epidemic (Papagiannidis et al., 2020).

Covid-19, of course, caused organizational changes. It forced the business strategies of private and public businesses to be redefined and acted as an accelerator for digital transformation (Agostino et al., 2020; Carroll and Conboy, 2020; Gabryelczyk, 2020). For example, distance education technologies existed before the pandemic, but lockdown due to the pandemic required the use of these technologies in mainstream education. Therefore, educational activities continue as distance education in many countries in the world (Soto-Acosta, 2020). To tell the truth, the pandemic is not a short-term process and these new and technology-based practices will be part of the "new normal" (Carroll and Conboy, 2020). Just transitioning to the use of remote working systems and video conferencing and the increase in network capacity does not mean a digital transformation has taken place (Gabryelczyk, 2020).

The Covid-19 crisis offers an opportunity to further disrupt the status quo and bring about radical change. However, businesses need to have the potential to turn this opportunity into an advantage. There is no guarantee that the transformation will actually happen and lead to better events. Moreover, excessively hasty reactions are more likely to lead to new crises. Businesses try to reproduce their physical activities online rather than achieve digital transformation. Putting face-to-face meetings online and collecting data digitally through technologies are not a transformation. We need to transform the way we do things. If we want to be transformed, technology has a great transformative potential. Digitizing core activities is a start but this alone is not enough (Davison, 2020).

Businesses need to permanently normalize new applications to benefit from a digital transformation and the use of technology to achieve goals through these applications (Carroll and Conboy, 2020). Thus, it is necessary for businesses to significantly improve the digital competencies of managers, employees and customers. In this context, employees should become more skilled in using digital working tools that bring new routines and habits to their lives. Managers should ensure that the business will continue even when employees are physically away from the workplace. As customers learn that their needs continue to be met by different digital ways of working, organizations should explore a broader way to interact with customers (Richter, 2020).

Conclusion

There are challenges with digital transformation not only in emergencies such as Covid-19, but also in the normal period. These challenges pertain to social and organizational factors as well as technology as a facilitator for digital transformation. They can be new roles and competencies, flexibility, remote working, performance, security, etc. (Agostino et al., 2020; Papagiannidis et al., 2020). Businesses can benefit from employee competencies that are difficult to replicate when transforming digitally. These competencies are empathy, intuition, interpersonal sensitivity, emotional intelligence, reasoning, problem solving, creativity, i.e., some special interpersonal human competencies that machines currently do not have. Therefore, businesses should focus on how technology can be used to enable employees to do their jobs more effectively, rather than on whether or not their labor force will be replaced by machines; because creating value from technology is not only a matter of managing technical uncertainty (Kudyba, 2020; Levit, 2018; Chesbrough and Rosenbloom, 2002). Another important issue is that digital transformation requires significant changes to current business models or the creation of new business models (Soto-Acosta, 2020; Chesbrough and Rosenbloom, 2002).

Many jobs have begun to be done remotely and the employees' homes have turned into offices with the Covid-19 pandemic. Where knowledge is the raw material of work, it has never been necessary for all people to be in the same place at the same time. As this event spreads, the situation that Charles Handy expressed as "business is what you do, not where you go" will have come true (Handy, 1995). Whether this trend will go on or not after the pandemic can be questioned. However, it can be said that the tangible and intangible benefits and the digitalization trend of businesses that appeared as a result of the successful management of the digital transformation accelerating with the pandemic will continue or should continue after the pandemic (Soto-Acosta, 2020).

In addition, the world experienced the 2003 SARS pandemic and the 2012 MERS pandemic and now experiences the 2019 Covid-19 pandemic. People have been exposed to three fatal pandemics in the last 17 years. These pandemics will not be the last and similar fatal pandemics are likely to occur in the future (Haselltine, 2020). For this reason, businesses should not consider the digitalization process to be specific to the epidemic period, but should be prepared for such situations in the future. It does not seem possible for businesses that are caught unprepared or cannot provide the necessary transformation to survive. During the coronavirus period, businesses, employees and customers in all sectors have understood the importance of digitalization and have adopted digital technologies. Businesses should consider "pre-Covid-19", "during Covid-19" and "post-Covid-19" environments as an opportunity to develop their practices (Herath and Herath, 2020: 280).

Keywords: *Digitization, digitalization, digital transformation, business model, Covid-19*

References

Agostino, D., Arnaboldi, M., & Lema, M. D. (2020). New Development: COVID-19 as an Accelerator of Digital Transformation in Public Service Delivery. *Public Money & Management*, 1-4. doi: https://doi.org/10.1080/09540962.2020.1764206.

Ancarani, A., & Di Mauro, C. (2018). Successful Digital Transformations Need a Focus on the Individual. In F. Schupp, & H. Wöhler, *Digitalisierung im Einkauf*, (pp. 11-26). Wiesbaden: Springer Gabler.

Attaran, M. (2004). Exploring the Relationship between Information Technology and Business Process Reengineering. *Information & Management, 41(5)*, 585-596. doi: https://doi.org/10.1016/S0378-7206(03)00098-3.

Azoeva, O. V., Mikhalevich, L. Y., Ostapenko, V. A., & Shim, G. A. (2020). The Labor Nature Changes and its Regulation Challenge Caused by Global Digitalization of Business. *International Journal of Organizational Leadership, 9(4)*, 170-183.

Bonnet, D., & Nandan, P. (2011). *Transform to the Power of Digital: Digital Transformation as a Driver of Corporate Performance.* Capgemini Consulting. Available at: https://www.capgemini.com/wp-content/uploads/2017/07/Transform_to_the_Power_of_Digital.pdf. Accessed 21 November 2020.

Brennen, J. S., & Kreiss, D. (2016). Digitalization. In Jensen, K.B., Rothenbuhler, E.W., Pooley, J.D. and Craig, R.T. (Eds), *The International Encyclopedia of Communication Theory and Philosophy*, (pp. 556-566). Wiley-Blackwell, Chichester.

Carroll, N., & Conboy, K. (2020). Normalising the "New Normal": Changing Tech-driven Work Practices under Pandemic Time Pressure. *International Journal of Information Management, 55*, 102186. doi: https://doi.org/10.1016/j.ijinfomgt.2020.102186.

Casadesus-Masanell, R., & Ricart, J. E. (2010). From Strategy to Business Models and onto Tactics. *Long Range Planning, 43* , 195-215. doi: https://doi.org/10.1016/j.lrp.2010.01.004.

Castells, M. (2009). *The Rise of the Network Society.* Malden: Wiley-Blackwell.

Chesbrough, H. (2010). Business Model Innovation: Opportunities and Barriers. *Long Range Planning, 43*, 354-363. doi: https://doi.org/10.1016/j.lrp.2009.07.010

Chesbrough, H., & Rosenbloom, R. S. (2002). The Role of the Business Model in Capturing Value from Innovation: Evidence from Xerox Corporation's Technology Spin-off Companies. *Industrial and Corporate Change, 11(3)*, 529-555. doi: https://doi.org/10.1093/icc/11.3.529

Davison, R. M. (2020). The Transformative Potential of Disruptions: A Viewpoint. *International Journal of Information Management, 55*, 102149. doi: https://doi.org/10.1016/j.ijinfomgt.2020.102149.

Eller, R., Alford, P., Kallmünzer, A., & Peters, M. (2020). Antecedents, Consequences, and Challenges of Small and Medium-sized Enterprise Digitalization. *Journal of Business Research, 112 (May)*, 119-127. doi: https://doi.org/10.1016/j.jbusres.2020.03.004.

Fernandez, V., & Gallardo-Gallardo, E. (2020). Tackling the HR Digitalization Challenge: Key Factors and Barriers to HR Analytics Adoption. *Competitiveness Review*, 1059-5422. doi: http://dx.doi.org/10.1108/CR-12-2019-0163.

Foerster-Metz, U. S., Marquardt, K., Golowko, N., Kompalla, A., & Hell, C. (2018). Digital Transformation and its Implications on Organizational Behavior. *Journal of EU Research in Business, 2018(2018)*, 1-14. doi: https://doi.org/10.5171/2018.340873

Forgo, Z., Tolvaly-Roşça, F., & Farmos, R. (2020). Digitalization of Production - A Challenge for the Industry and Education. *Műszaki Tudományos Közlemények, 12*, 38-41. doi: https://doi.org/10.33894/mtk-2020.12.05.

Gabryelczyk, R. (2020). Has COVID-19 Accelerated Digital Transformation? Initial Lessons Learned for Public Administrations. *Information Systems Management, 37(4)*, 303-309. doi: https://doi.org/10.1080/10580530.2020.1820633.

Gartner Glossary. (2020). *Information Technology.* Available at: https://www.gartner.com/en/information-technology/glossary/digitalization. Accessed 29 October 2020.

Gimpel, H., & Röglinger, M. (2015). *Digital Transformation: Changes and Chances—Insights Based on an Empirical Study.* Augsburg/Bayreuth:

Project Group Business and Information Systems Engineering BISE) of the Fraunhofer Institute for Applied Information Technology FIT.

Gjellebaek, C., Svensson, A., Bjorkquist, C., & Grunden, K. (2020). Management Challenges for Future Digitalization of Healthcare Services. *Futures, 124*, 1-10. doi: https://doi.org/10.1016/j.futures.2020.102636.

Gobble, M. M. (2018a). Digitalization, Digitization, and Innovation. *Research-Technology Management, 61(4)*, 56-59. doi: https://doi.org/10.1080/08956308.2018.1471280.

Gobble, M. M. (2018b). Digital Strategy and Digital Transformation. *Research-Technology Management, 61(5)*, 66-71. doi: https://doi.org/10.1080/08956308.2018.1495969.

Grewal, D., Levy, M., & Kumar, V. (2009). Customer Experience Management in Retailing: An Organizing Framework. *Journal of Retailing, 85(1)*, 1-14. doi: https://doi.org/10.1016/j.jretai.2009.01.001.

Handy, C. (1995). Trust and the Virtual Organization. *Harvard Business Review, 73(3)*, 40-50.

Haselltine, W. A. (2020, 02 29). *Want to Prevent another Coronavirus Epidemic?* Scientific American. Available at: https://blogs.scientificamerican.com/observations/want-to-prevent-another-coronavirus-epidemic/. Accessed 12 November 2020.

Heavin, C., & Power, D. J. (2018). Challenges for Digital Transformation – Towards a Conceptual Decision Support Guide for Managers. *Journal of Decision Systems, 27(1)*, 38-45. doi: https://doi.org/10.1080/12460125.2018.1468697.

Herath, T., & Herath, H. S. (2020). Coping with the New Normal Imposed by the COVID-19 Pandemic: Lessons for Technology Management and Governance. *Information Systems Management, 37(4)*, 277-283. doi: https://doi.org/10.1080/10580530.2020.1818902.

International Data Corporation. (2019). *Worldwide Digital Transformation Strategies.* IDC Analyze the Future. Available at: https://www.idc.com/getdoc.jsp?containerId=IDC_P32570. Accessed 20 November 2020.

Kamal, M. M. (2020). The Triple-edged Sword of COVID-19: Understanding the Use of Digital Technologies and the Impact of Productive, Disruptive, and Destructive Nature of the Pandemic. *Information Systems Management, 37(4)*, 310-317. doi: https://doi.org/10.1080/10580530.2020.1820634.

Kudyba, S. (2020). COVID-19 and the Acceleration of Digital Transformation and the Future of Work. *Information Systems Management, 37(4)*, 284-287. doi:

https://doi.org/10.1080/10580530.2020.1818903.

Legner, C., Eymann, T., Hess, T., Matt, C., Böhmann, T., Drews, P., . . . Ahlemann, F. (2017). Digitalization: Opportunity and Challenge for the Business and Information Systems Engineering Community. *Business & Information Systems Engineering, 59*, 301-308. doi: https://doi.org/10.1007/s12599-017-0484-2.

Levit, A. (2018). *Humanity Works: Merging Technologies and People for the Workforce of the Future.* London: Kogan Page Publishers.

Li, F. (2020). The Digital Transformation of Business Models in the Creative Industries: A Holistic Framework and Emerging Trends. *Technovation, 92-93*, 102012. doi: https://doi.org/10.1016/j.technovation.2017.12.004.

Markovitch, S., & Willmott, P. (2014). *Accelerating the Digitization of Business Process.* McKinsey&Company. Available at: https://www.mckinsey.com/business-functions/mckinsey-digital/our-insights/accelerating-the-digitization-of-business-processes#. Accessed 20 November 2020.

Morakanyane, R., Grace, A., & O'Reilly, P. (2017). Conceptualizing Digital Transformation in Business Organizations: A Systematic Review of Literature. *30th Bled Econference: Digital Transformation – From Connecting Things to Transforming Our Lives*, (pp. 427-444). Bled, Slovenia.

Nokelainen, P., Nevalainen, T., & Niemi, K. (2018). Mind or Machine? Opportunities and Limits of Automation. In C. Harteis , *The Impact of Digitalization in the Workplace: An Educational View,* (pp. 13-24). Cham, Switzerland: Springer International Publishing.

OECD. (2020a). *Economic Outlook*. Available at: https://www.oecd.org/economic-outlook/. Accessed 22 November 2020.

OECD. (2020b). *Employment Outlook*. Available at: http://www.oecd.org/employment-outlook/2020/#report. Accessed 22 November 2020.

Onetti, A., Zucchella, A., Jones, M. V., & McDougall-Covin, P. P. (2012). Internationalization, Innovation and Entrepreneurship: Business Models for New Technology-based Firms. *Journal of Management & Governance, 16*, 337–368. doi: https://doi.org/10.1007/s10997-010-9154-1.

Osterwalder, A., & Pigneur, Y. (2002). An e-Business Model Ontology for Modeling e-Business. *15th Bled Electronic Commerce Conference e-Reality: Constructing the e-Economy*, (pp. 1-12). Bled, Slovenia.

Pan, S. L., Cui, M., & Qian, J. (2020). Information Resource Orchestration during the COVID-19 Pandemic: A Study of Community Lockdowns in China. *International Journal of Information Management, 54*, 102143. doi: https://doi.org/10.1016/j.ijinfomgt.2020.102143

Papagiannidis, S., Harris, J., & Morton, D. (2020). Who Led the Digital Transformation of Your Company? A Reflection of IT Related Challenges during the Pandemic. *International Journal of Information Management, 55*, 102166. doi: https://doi.org/10.1016/j.ijinfomgt.2020.102166.

Parviainen, P., Tihinen, M., Kaariainen, J., & Teppola, S. (2017). Tackling the Digitalization Challenge: How to Benefit from Digitalization in Practice. *International Journal of Information Systems and Project Management, 5(1)*, 63-77. doi: https://doi.org/10.12821/ijispm050104.

Pratt, L. (2019). *Organisational Change in Times of Digital Transformation*. HRD Connect. Available at: https://www.hrdconnect.com/2019/06/12/organisational-change-in-times-of-digital-transformation/. Accessed 30 November 2020.

Rachinger, M., Rauter, R., Müller, C., Vorraber, W., & Schirgi, E. (2019). Digitalization and its Influence on Business Model Innovation. *Journal of Manufacturing Technology Management, 30(8)*, 1143-1160. doi: https://doi.org/10.1108/JMTM-01-2018-0020.

Rappa, M. (2010). *Business Models on the Web.* digitalenterprise.org. Available at: http://digitalenterprise.org/models/models.html. Accessed 31 November 2020.

Richter, A. (2020). Locked-down Digital Work. *International Journal of Information Management, 55*, 102157. doi: https://doi.org/10.1016/j.ijinfomgt.2020.102157

Rintamaki, T., & Kirves, K. (2017). From Perceptions to Propositions: Profiling Customer Value Across Retail Contexts. *Journal of Retailing and Consumer Services, 37*, 159-167. doi: https://doi.org/10.1016/j.jretconser.2016.07.016.

Schneider, M. (2018). Digitalization of Production, Human Capital, and Organizational Capital. In C. Harteis, *The Impact of Digitalization in the Workplace: An Educational View* (pp. 39-52). Cham, Switzerland: Springer International Publishing.

Schreckling, E., & Steiger, C. (2017). Digitalize or Drown. In G. Oswald, & M. Kleinemeier, *Shaping the Digital Enterprise: Trends and Use Cases in Digital Innovation and Transformation* (pp. 3-27). Walldorf: Springer.

Schwer, K., & Hitz, C. (2018). Designing Organizational Structure in the Age of Digitization. *Journal of Eastern European and Central Asian Research 5(1)*, 1-11. doi: https://doi.org/10.15549/jeecar.v5i1.213.

Soto-Acosta, P. (2020). Covid-19 Pandemic: Shifting Digital Transformation to a High-Speed Gear. *Information Systems Management, 37(4)*, 260-266. doi: https://doi.org/10.1080/10580530.2020.1814461.

Tabrizi, B., Lam, E., Girard, K., & Irvin, V. (2019). Digital Transformation in not about Technology. *Harvard Business Review, March*.

Tilson, D., Lyytinen, K., & Sorensen, C. (2010). Digital Infrastructures: The Missing IS Research Agenda. *Information Systems Research, 21(4)*, 748-759. doi: http://dx.doi.org/10.1287/isre.1100.0318.

Verhoef, P. C., Broerhuizen, T., Bart, Y., Bhattacharya, A., Qi Dong, J., Fabian, N., & Haenlein, M. (2021). Digital Transformation: A Multidisciplinary Reflection and Research Agenda. *Journal of Business Research, 112(C)*, 889-901. doi: https://doi.org/10.1016/j.jbusres.2019.09.022.

Verhoef, P. C., Lemon, K. N., Parasuraman, A., Roggeveen, A., Tsiros, M., & Schlesinger, L. A. (2009). Customer Experience Creation: Determinants, Dynamics and Management Strategies. *Journal of Retailing, 85(1)*, 31-41. doi: https://doi.org/10.1016/j.jretai.2008.11.001.

Vial, G. (2019). Understanding Digital Transformation: A Review and a Research. *Journal of Strategic Information Systems, 28*, 118–144. doi: https://doi.org/10.1016/j.jsis.2019.01.003.

Wade, M., & Marchand, D. (2014). *Are You Prepared for Your Digital Transformation? Understanding the Power of Technology AMPS in Organizational Change.* Lausanne, Switzerland: IMD Tomorrow's Challenges.

WHO. (2020). *Coronavirus disease (COVID-19) pandemic*. World Health Organization, Available at: https://covid19.who.int/. Accessed 06 December 2020.

Zott, C., & Amit, R. H. (2008). The Fit Between Product Market Strategy and Business Model: Implications for Firm Performance. *Strategic Management Journal, 29 (1)*, 1-26. doi: http://dx.doi.org/10.1002/smj.642.

Zott, C., Amit, R., & Massa, L. (2011). The Business Model: Recent Developments and Future Research. *Journal of Management, 37(4)*, 1019-1042. doi: https://doi.org/10.1177/0149206311406265.

Zuboff, S. (1995). *In the Age of the Smart Machine : The Future of Work and Power.* New York : Basic Books.

CHAPTER THREE

PERSONALIZATION IS POSSIBLE WITH DIGITALIZATION

EMRE HARORLI

Introduction

Developing technology and internet accessibility have led to widespread digitalization, which has excellent effects on life. Digitalization has also caused significant changes in the marketing strategies of businesses.

Due to the rapid developments in technology and digitalization, businesses and consumers have met digital marketing, where efficient marketing management uses digital channels. Besides, with the development of databases and increased ease of use, it has been possible to effectively use personal messages by following consumer attitudes and behaviors at the individual level. It has become possible to have interactive communication where consumers can quickly evaluate personalized messages and respond to these messages instantly with the development of technology.

In an increasingly competitive environment, businesses are trying to reach their customers with some strategies. One of these strategies is personalization. Consumers want to feel more special and unique. For this, businesses are trying to address their customers with personalized messages and personalized goods/services. However, this becomes a big challenge for businesses with thousands of customers. Digital marketing can mitigate or even eliminate these challenge effects.

This chapter is designed as follows, respectively. First, a piece of general information about digital marketing and its relation with personalization will be presented, and then the marketing contributions of digitalization to businesses will be discussed. Finally, the future impacts of digitalization will be evaluated from a business perspective.

Digitalization and Digital Marketing

Today, technological innovations and developments cause changes to the forms and functions of communication tools and lead to new communication platforms. Digitalization and the Internet play a leading role in these technological changes. The Internet, which provides information dissemination to the world through computers and smart devices, remote cooperation and mutual interaction, worldwide broadcasting, and similar opportunities, has become an indispensable part of daily life by contributing to many critical socio-economic changes. Also, with digitalization, traditional approaches give up their place to technology-based new approaches. Similarly, as a result of digitalization, consumers have turned to new product searches (Demirci Aksoy, 2014). Parallel to these, the Organization for Economic Cooperation and Development (OECD) states that changes and developments in the digital world can also support countries' sustainable development. The effects of technological advances in the mobile Internet, the Internet of things, information automation, 3-D printers, cloud systems, and robotics on the economy in recent years have only just been seen (Kotler et al., 2017).

The number of Internet users continues to increase on a global scale. As of October 2020, active Internet users consist of approximately 4.66 billion people. This number makes up about 59% of the global population. Smart mobile device users account for 91% of total internet users (Clement, 2020). Considering that active Internet users commonly use the digital world for shopping, the Internet becomes an essential tool for businesses that want to benefit from such a large target audience (Peter & Dalla Vecchia, 2020).

New approaches and trends that steer modern marketing undergo specific and critical changes every day with the rapid advance of communication and information technologies. By taking this into consideration, marketing managers need to accommodate these transformations while using digital marketing techniques. It will be useful to understand the meaning of the concept of digitization, which is increasingly developing and contributing to socio-economic life. As a technical term, digital is "the language of machines made of ones and zeros" (Schneider, 2019). Digitalization started with the transition from mechanical and analog technology to digital technology in the 1980s and continues today with personal computers and smart devices (Musnaini et al., 2020); it enables information to be spread easily, cheaply, securely, and quickly. Besides, digitalization has enabled information to be easily accessible anytime and anywhere without any time or space limit.

The development of technology causes the differentiation of customer needs and demands. Similarly, businesses that want to keep up with these developments better understand that customers' in-store purchases, that is, traditional purchasing behavior, evolve into online purchasing behavior, and therefore strive to take their place in the digital world (Peter & Dalla Vecchia, 2020).

Digitalization is not a new phenomenon for consumers. Consumers have especially used personal computers and smart devices for years. However, today technology is used in almost every field and more than in every previous year. For example, with home automation and the digitalization of things, refrigerators can digitally interact with retailers or easily create a shopping list (Hagberg et al., 2016).

As a result of digitalization, consumers' daily lives, routines, and purchasing behavior are continually changing. Businesses that want to know their changing customers better and introduce their products to a broader audience try to use information and communication technologies more and benefit from some of the opportunities that they offer to businesses (Durmaz & Efendioglu, 2016).

Due to these changes in technology and society and increasing competitive conditions, it has become a necessity for businesses to continually keep themselves up to date. There are also updates on marketing from past to present. With the industrial revolution, a product- and market-oriented marketing strategy, namely Marketing 1.0, dominated businesses. Subsequently, companies that wanted to prove themselves to their customers in an increasingly competitive environment started to adopt a customer-oriented marketing strategy, Marketing 2.0. With Marketing 3.0, businesses have adopted a value-oriented marketing strategy by considering the society and environment in which the consumers live. During this period, companies aimed to attract consumers by striving to make the world more livable with social responsibility projects. Today, that technology and digitalization are effective, Marketing 4.0 is mentioned. In other words, a very active marketing system has emerged, in which the activities of businesses and customers can be followed instantly from the digital world (Büyükkalaycı & Karaca, 2019; Durukal, 2019; Kotler et al., 2017).

Until Marketing 1.0 became Marketing 4.0, businesses did not wholly abandon the previous marketing approach. On the contrary, companies have tried to create and maintain a combination of each marketing approach. In other words, a business that adopts a Marketing 4.0 approach; should be product-, customer-, and community-oriented, and in addition to these, it should try to maintain its marketing strategies in parallel with digitalization.

A New Market: The Digital World

Today, people socialize more through social media, and they can continue their professional business life more comfortably and efficiently with computers, smart devices, and some communication and presentation applications (Keenan, 2015). In parallel with the developments in digital platforms, consumer behavior is also changing (Gani & Faroque, 2020). Consumers can now quickly examine and control the businesses' promises and easily evaluate brand positioning in the digital world. Above all, transparency is very high due to the rapid flow of information on social media. Therefore, businesses avoid making unverifiable or even false promises. With these developments, the brand images of the business gain importance rather than brand identities (Kotler et al., 2017). In other words, with digitalization, the dominant side of the market is rapidly evolving from the suppliers to those who demand (Hagberg et al., 2016). With this increased transparency, the widespread use of better products throughout the market, and worthless products being vanquished from the market, the competition becomes fair (Järvinen, 2011).

In the last decades, e-commerce has become an essential part of global trade. Especially in today's life, as the digital world takes up more space, consumers have benefited more from some of the advantages of online transactions. In 2019, the estimated number of consumers purchasing goods and services through digital platforms reached 1.92 billion. In the same year, online sales worldwide exceeded $ 3.5 trillion (Statista Research Department, 2020).

With digitalization, customers' actions, requests, and related areas can be quickly followed and recorded. Thus, by creating a database about existing and potential customers, personalized products can be easily created and presented (Güven, 2020). Besides, promotional videos are prepared for the products in the virtual environment, and real consumer comments affect the customers' decision-making processes and help them to make more manageable and more accurate decisions (Durmaz & Efendioglu, 2016). In this context, it is clear that digitalization increases decision support processes. New products, product development, market communication, purchase-sale decisions, brand management, customer relationship management, etc., and significant progress have been welded with digitalization (Gedik, 2020).

In a highly competitive and globalized market environment, it is difficult for businesses to retain existing customers and acquire new customers. In addition to these difficulties, the consumers' shopping habits in the digital world, and the businesses' traditional marketing strategies gradually become invalid. In this context, it is evident that digitalization has become a cornerstone of companies.

Digital Marketing

As a result of the digitalization in the business world, digital marketing has emerged with the adaptation of marketing and sales departments, which are an essential part of the businesses, to this change. With digital marketing, the aim is to react quickly and flexibly to changes in the market and consumer needs through digital channels and tools (Peter & Dalla Vecchia, 2020). Digitalization has significant effects on consumption and marketing issues such as the consumer concept, consumption, consumer applications, retailer-consumer interfaces, channel integration, market communication, and business models (Hagberg & Kjellberg, 2020). Digital marketing has become pivotal in overcoming the marketing challenges that businesses face, managing their relationships with consumers worldwide, and communicating with them more easily. In other words, digital marketing has become a marketing approach that allows businesses to adapt to the digital world.

The term digital marketing first appeared in the 1990s. With the increasing use of personal computers in daily life, it has become an important part of marketing technology, especially in customer relationship management applications. Kotler and Armstrong define digital marketing as "a direct marketing form that enables sellers and consumers to communicate interactively with each other in an electronic environment by using digital technologies such as e-mail, online blogs, forums and newsgroups, social media, interactive television, display advertising, search engines via smart devices" (Kotler & Armstrong, 2018). In other words, digital marketing is "the comprehensive and practical use of the internet, digital media platforms, and marketing tools to achieve success in an intensely competitive environment" (Gani & Faroque, 2020).

In particular, the integration of the production industry with the Internet and developing technology has led to the emergence of Industry 4.0, and with the inclusion of the marketing process in parallel with this integration, Marketing 4.0 has emerged (Güven, 2020).

Digital marketing is definitely not an alternative to traditional marketing, but rather a complementary strategy. In establishing communication between businesses and customers, traditional marketing plays a vital role in creating awareness and interest, and digital marketing comes to the fore in meeting the unique demands of customers as a result of the close relations that the business establishes with them. A marketing mix is a classic tool that helps companies to determine what and how it should be presenting to the target audience, briefly referred to as 4P (product, price, place, and promotion). However, due to the increasing competitive conditions and widespread digitalization, adopting a customer-oriented and customer-focused strategy has been revised as 4P, 4C (co-creation, currency, communal activation, and conversation) (Kotler et al., 2017).

Customers take an active role in many stages of digitalization, from creating a new product idea to product design (Narayanan & Kartheeswaran, 2019). With co-creation, businesses that allow customers to customize their products can offer excellent value suggestions (Kotler et al., 2017).

Opportunities such as personalized discounts and dynamic pricing for different customers in online and in-store sales are possible with digitalization (Hagberg et al., 2016). Today, the pricing of products sold through digital channels is evolving from a standardized price to a dynamic price. Dynamic pricing is not new to most situations and industries (transport and accommodation, etc.). However, with digitalization, dynamic pricing has now become suitable for many product/service categories. Many businesses can sell their products on their websites and instantly apply dynamic prices to different consumer groups on the products that consumers browse and transact while looking at the website and offer e-coupons of distinct values (Kannan & Kopalle, 2001).

The innovations brought by digitalization also affected the place mix. Many sectors, from banking to car rental, from the accommodation sector to the food and beverage industry, were directly or indirectly affected by the innovations and opportunities provided by digitalization (Kotler et al., 2017). Consumers have the opportunity to make money transfers and evaluate their investments more quickly through the crypto money markets, book accommodation at affordable prices for short-term travel, rent a car with a driver, and order food whenever they want, through various mobile applications.

The concept of promotion has also changed depending on the innovations brought about by digitalization. In traditional marketing, businesses were always able to establish a one-sided relationship. However, especially with the widespread use of social media, mutual interaction with customers can be easily achieved, and it is also possible for customers to consult among themselves (Kotler et al., 2017).

The digital world, which provides a real-time interactive environment between buyers and sellers, facilitates new relationships between these two communities. Businesses that process the data they obtain with digital tools can offer their customers some personal privileges by transforming mass marketing into personalized marketing with the help of flexible production technology that has developed over time (Dewan et al., 1999; Yüksel, 1999).

Digital Marketing and Personalization

Customers demand unique goods and services to be designed for them. Businesses that want to keep their customers by meeting this demand can produce products designed by their customers for a small additional fee, even if they have mass production systems.

The efficient execution of CRM activities especially depends on technology. Implementing customer-oriented CRM applications, which require intense customer information, can be possible with the correct recognition and clear understanding of the customers. Digital marketing facilitates personalization as it has an advanced internet marketing concept and can meet customer expectations with offline customer interactions and online technologies (Gedik, 2020).

Personalized marketing provides an enhanced customer experience by processing consistent data obtained, increasing the return on investment (ROI) by identifying the right channel for each customer and establishing efficient interactions, creating both high brand loyalty and competitive advantage by providing unique experiences with data obtained from customers, and finally, cross-channel consistency. It provides several advantages to businesses such as enabling creation (Murray, 2017).

Businesses today frequently utilize personal marketing to differentiate themselves from their competitors, to express and fully reach their target audiences, and get the income they desire (Bullock, 2018). At this point, digitalization enables businesses to fulfill these desires. Businesses can easily monitor and analyze the behavior of the target audience at an individual level with digitalization. Thus, businesses that have the information needed for personalized marketing can deliver personalized messages to their target audiences and prepare and present goods and services in line with customers' demands. For example, regularly tracking the customer's products and offering similar products or providing easy access to these products' consumables are only a small part of the digitalization benefits. With digitalization, businesses are more likely to quickly follow consumers' interests on social media platforms, make suggestions that are compatible with these interests, and communicate with personalized messages. In particular, the widespread development of smart mobile devices has a positive contribution to the spread of digitalization in marketing; for example, businesses that used to operate in fixed retail stores had the opportunity to move their stores to the digital environment and continue their activities with the development and widespread use of the Internet and smart mobile devices (Hagberg et al., 2016).

Many e-retail sites make suggestions to their users with visual remarks such as "Frequently purchased with this product" or "Users who viewed this product also viewed the following products." 44% of the users carefully check out such suggestions and buy from the recommended products. These visual remarks are supported by digital marketing with very comprehensive data. Similarly, streaming platforms strive to provide personalized services with data obtained from users' viewing history. They highlight new movie and series suggestions that are compatible with the users' viewing history and also automatically design the movies' and series' covers using the actors' and actresses' visuals that the user likes to watch (Bullock, 2018). Thus, users can easily choose for themselves the most suitable movie or series from the thousands of movies and TV series; that is, they can easily access the service offered.

According to the current information provided by the International Data Corporation (IDC), more than 59 zettabytes (ZB 1ZB = 10^{21} byte) of data will be created and consumed worldwide at the end of 2020. Due to the Covid-19 pandemic, there was a greater need for information and communication technologies for activities such as working from home, distance education, video conferencing, and streaming (International Data Corporation (IDC), 2020). Such estimates can differ significantly between different professional market analysts. However, it can be easily predicted that an enormous amount of data is produced each year compared to the previous years, and this will continue to increase. It is also clear that such vast amounts of data can create unprecedented opportunities. However, in such a large "data ocean," it is crucial for businesses to reach their desired destination without drowning. In this context, customer analytics, which is a technology- and model-supported approach to utilize customer and market data to improve the marketing decision-making process, increases businesses' productivity (Germann et al., 2021). Customer analytics guides businesses as to who their customers are, what they do, what they want, and how, where, and when to reach them. Thus, businesses can easily offer a personalized customer experience to gain loyal customers.

Customers show a more positive attitude towards businesses that clearly understand them and fulfill their special requests. Besides, businesses try to convey individual messages to their customers through channels such as television, billboards, and social media tools to attract their target audience's attention. However, today, many messages are directed to the target audience and it is thus getting more and more challenging to attract their attention. At this point, personalization lends a helping hand to businesses as they use it to create campaigns, product content, and experiences to attract the target audience's attention by collecting and analyzing data about the target audience's demographic characteristics, purchasing behavior, and interests.

A personalized marketing strategy consists of four main processes. The first process is identify, which is collected data such as gender, age, and location. Then comes the differentiate process, in which the collected data are analyzed, and the target audience is segmented into niches. The third process is interact, which is communicating with prospective or existing customers through the correct identified channels. In the last stage, personalization is carried out successfully (Galetto, 2017). Businesses that apply a proper personalization strategy can increase customer satisfaction by enriching their customers' experiences, thus obtaining more revenue and long-term customer loyalty.

Digitized Marketing's Contributions to Business

Market data gain importance in determining which products customers are most interested in. The amount of data that businesses need for their personalization strategies both increases and becomes more accessible. This opportunity is significant for marketing managers.

Digital marketing supports businesses in increasing their market shares by providing the opportunity to reach millions of target audiences worldwide and also offers personalized products to this target audience. Also, businesses provide these target audiences with the opportunity to advertise much more quickly and at affordable costs, manage their campaigns more efficiently, and easily measure their interactions with customers.

There is much literature showing that small businesses' competitiveness, capacity, and performance increase faster with digitalization. Besides, in similar studies, it has been determined that digitalized businesses' lack of information has decreased, and international network capabilities have improved (Gedik, 2020).

With digitalization, businesses can offer consistent offers to their target audiences, increase the customer lifetime value with personalized up-selling and cross-selling offers, and communicate with their customers interactively with the right message at the right place at the right time. Besides, with digitalization, businesses reduce the risk of losing their customers by detecting their customers' trends with a high accuracy rate through their databases. With personalized marketing, businesses increase their sales and support them to have a satisfied customer portfolio. Communication between customers and businesses is getting stronger, mainly due to the communication established through personalized messages.

Also, customers can communicate the problems they encounter during their shopping through social media. Businesses that adopt a customer-centric approach can quickly act in light of the existing data at hand to eliminate such problems. Today, customers turn the increasingly competitive environment in their favor and continuously seek smooth and even perfect purchasing experiences. With the help of digitalization, businesses fulfill these wishes of consumers by offering personalized content and products and strengthening their relationships with their customers.

In digital marketing, activities can be carried out with more affordable costs compared to traditional marketing. Also, businesses can easily access large amounts of data with the use of digital marketing. Businesses can have opportunities such as spreading complete and in-depth information about their products, determining the target audience very clearly, delivering the most appropriate personalized messages to the target audience, and having a high sales potential with digital marketing (Musnaini et al., 2020). However, despite the need to seize the opportunities offered by digital technology through adaptation to digital market environments and the development of relevant operations, most businesses are not yet taking a step towards digitalization, despite the need (Negricea & Purcarea, 2017).

Quarantine and Digitalization

As in previous years, every business completed its 2020 plans, determined its strategies, and dreamed of implementing its activities according to these plans and strategies. Unfortunately, with the sudden rise of Covid-19, many businesses had to make very definite changes in their projects. The curfew and restriction decisions within the scope of the fight against Covid-19 had negative operational consequences on businesses of all sizes. As a result of these decisions taken by countries within the scope of combating the pandemic, there was naturally a significant decrease in consumer demand and a noticeable decrease in businesses' profitability. As a precaution, businesses also made mandatory restrictions in their expenditures, apart from their necessary operational expenses, and had to suspend their intensive business activities (International Telecommunication Union (ITU), 2020). During this period, significant disruptions were experienced in supply chains. The World Trade Organization stated that the global trade volume could drop by 32% due to the pandemic (Gujrati & Uygun, 2020). Due to these negativities, countries had to revise their economic growth forecasts. It is thought that the pandemic may have a more devastating effect than the economic depression in 1929 (Rostomyan, 2020).

However, every crisis brings some opportunities with it. There was a significant increase in demand during the pandemic, especially in the information and communication technologies industry. Digital technologies have played a supportive role in the continuity of daily life. In this process, commercial activities worldwide continued through digital platforms, and many businesses achieved their sustainability through digitalization. Although it is difficult to reach consumers who cannot go out due to restrictions, the challenges posed by this problem have been easier to overcome for many businesses with a digital infrastructure already in place. While their competitors were preparing to make a new digitalization investment, they continued their communication with their customers without significant disruptions and interruptions. In other words, businesses that have the opportunity to sell online have a significant competitive advantage in this process. With such a crisis, there was a noticeable increase in the digitalization efforts of businesses. According to a survey completed in May 2020 with 3,032 executives in the UK, USA, Australia, France, Germany, and Scandinavian countries, it was determined that 52% of businesses plan to increase their investments in digitalization (IFS, 2020). According to another research study, a record was reached with 22 billion visits to online shopping sites globally in June 2020 (Statista Research Department, 2020).

Similarly, the financial sector, which has mostly completed its digitalization, has been profitable because consumers, who cannot/do not want to go out during the pandemic, prefer home delivery options and make payments with credit cards because of hygiene concerns (Global Entrepreneurship Research Association (GERA), 2020).

The pandemic affects not only the operations of the businesses but also the behavior of the customers. This change in consumers' behavior can only be valid during the pandemic, and it is likely to continue after the pandemic (Junusi, 2020). Consumer behavior has rapidly changed because of the pandemic. Many businesses have had to close their doors or turn to take away services. On the other hand, consumers have turned to e-commerce and delivery to their home to buy many of their needs, such as food, electronics, and clothing, without leaving their homes. There are two situations to be considered here. While consumers are motivated to have the product and engage in social interactions when shopping at a store, there are easy access and affordable shopping motivations in online shopping (Kim, 2020).

Significantly, many businesses that want to get out of the economic recession with the least damage caused by the Covid-19 pandemic and similar global crises have better understood the importance of digitalization and accelerated their investments in this direction. It will not be complicated to predict that businesses' investments in the digital industry will be larger in the periods after the economic crisis.

The Future Potential of Digitalization

Digital marketing is not a temporary trend, but rather a marketing strategy that gradually strengthens. Due to the increase in digitalization, the number of social media networks and digital platforms, and the global spread, digital marketing's importance will increase even more (Ferié, 2020). This is why understanding the future potential of digital marketing is essential.

Today, shopping on the Internet reaches significant dimensions. In the future, consumers will order almost all of the products they need over the Internet, and businesses will turn to more digitalization (Güven, 2020). According to retail sector research, e-commerce development will occur at 20.2% in Turkey between 2020 and 2024 and will rank first between chosen countries (Coppola, 2020). The technological advances and digitalization efforts of businesses are gradually taking place. However, even these gradual transitions continue at an extraordinary pace. In this context, businesses must keep up with this pace. Businesses should explore the digital world more and adapt their marketing activities to this world to provide a successful customer experience.

Communication with customers is essential for customer-oriented businesses; especially as Internet access has become more comfortable and easier worldwide, online communities' influence increases more, and customers can communicate their product experiences to a broader audience. As a result of these developments, customers' access to information becomes both easier and deeper. Accordingly, businesses should better understand the importance of the digital world and digital marketing, the negative effect of ineffective customer communication, and have more focus on digitalization investments.

Besides, it can be easily predicted that 3-D printers will play an essential role in the future. Consumers will obtain the product they want in their homes or offices quickly through various software. Such a future could pose both a great opportunity and a significant threat to businesses.

Conclusion

Digital marketing, a practical approach in executing strategies based on measurable marketing communication, which is sensitive to new technologies and obtained through digital tools, enables extensive data to be easily obtained through digital platforms and analyzed and interpreted with a high rate of hits. Thus, businesses can make decisions based on reliable quantitative information in their specific campaigns compared to traditional marketing campaigns. Besides, businesses gain a competitive advantage by accurately analyzing and interpreting the data they obtain through digital marketing and communicating their differences with their competitors to their customers more clearly. Businesses can also accurately evaluate their customers' requests and offer personalized messages and goods and services with digital marketing.

Businesses should make digital marketing the most fundamental part of their business culture and provide the skills and financial resources needed to achieve this, re-motivate their existing personnel with a digital marketing approach, and recruit new personnel accordingly, to implement successful digital marketing practices.

In today's world, where competition is experienced in such an intense and brutal way, businesses have to be customer-focused to fulfill their customers' requests. Businesses should not only be customer-focused but also should make their customers feel valuable and memorable. In order to achieve this, the existence of personalized messages and goods and services, is of critical importance. Customers are intensely exposed to a massive number of messages during the day, which is a severe challenge for businesses. In such a situation, businesses should prepare personalized messages specially designed to stand out from those of their competitors and reach their target audience. It is also important to design and deliver personalized goods and services to customers with customers' data. However, it is impossible to design personalized messages and goods and services for businesses whose target audience reaches millions with traditional marketing strategies and practices.

Some problems that traditional marketing cannot deal with can be alleviated or eliminated with digital marketing; for example, a business with a customer-oriented approach can personalize its products more effectively with digital marketing. Besides, with the development of online protection methods, these businesses, which offer digital payment options to their customers with peace of mind, can also provide their customers with a personalized shopping experience with dynamic price alternatives. In the world, which has become a small village in parallel with the developments in information and communication technologies, even a small business can appeal to comprehensive geography by using digital marketing opportunities, to gain customers and competitive power. While doing all this, businesses can realize their communication with their customers more efficiently, in a much shorter time, and with a mutual interaction compared to traditional marketing.

Businesses should never be afraid of digitalization and digital marketing applications. Contrary to one-sided communication, customers' mutual communication with the business, and even customers' communication among themselves, is critical today. Interactive communication is a great opportunity, especially for businesses with a customer-oriented strategy. Thanks to digital marketing applications, many factors that businesses overlook but negatively affect the quality of goods and services can be easily detected by customers. In other words, businesses can easily obtain information that can quickly respond to their customers' requests and warnings thanks to interactive communication supported by digital marketing.

Customer analytics is essential for customer relationship management. With customer analytics, businesses can know their customers more efficiently and effectively. The performance of marketing activities and other business activities, in general, can be increased thanks to customer analytics from big data obtained by digital marketing.

The development of information communication technologies causes consumers to have more detailed information about goods and services. As a result of sharing consumer experiences with everyone through digital platforms, they have more details on competing goods and services. As a result, customers can more loudly convey their personalized goods and service requests to businesses. With digitalization, businesses can offer their customers the experience of owning personalized goods and services by allowing them to choose from a wide variety of options and successfully stand out from their competitors.

Keywords: *Digitalization, digital marketing, personalization*

References

Bullock, L. (2018). *5 Brands Taking Personalized Marketing to the Next Level.* https://www.forbes.com/sites/lilachbullock/2018/12/28/5-brands-taking-personalized-marketing-to-the-next-level/?sh=2c7eac03c8ff

Büyükkalaycı, G., & Karaca, H. M. (2019). Pazarlama 4.0:Nesnelerin

İnterneti. *Üçüncü Sektör Sosyal Ekonomi Dergisi*, *54*(1), 463–477. https://doi.org/10.15659/3.sektor-sosyal-ekonomi.19.03.1105

Clement, J. (2020). *Global digital population as of October 2020*. Statista. https://www.statista.com/statistics/617136/digital-population-worldwide/

Coppola, D. (2020). *Retail E-commerce Sales CAGR Forecast in Selected Countries from 2020 to 2024*. Statista. https://www.statista.com/statistics/220177/b2c-e-commerce-sales-cagr-forecast-for-selected-countries/

Demirci Aksoy, A. (2014). Tüketimin Dijitalleşmesi. In *Tüketici Yazıları* (Issue IV, pp. 46–64). TÜPADEM.

Dewan, R., Jing, B., & Seidmann, A. (1999). One to One Marketing on the Internet. *Proceedings of the 20th International Conference on Information Systems*.

Durmaz, Y., & Efendioglu, I. H. (2016). Travel from Traditional Marketing to Digital Marketing. *Global Journal of Management and Business Research: E-Marketing*, *16*(2), 33–40.

Durukal, E. (2019). Pazarlama 1.0'dan Pazarlama 4.0'a Doğru Değişim. *İnsan ve Toplum Bilimleri Araştırmaları Dergisi*, *8*(3), 1613–1633. https://doi.org/10.15869/itobiad.549402

Ferié, F. (2020). Digital Marketing. In *The Palgrave Encyclopedia of Interest Groups, Lobbying and Public Affairs* (Issue 2019, pp. 1–5). Springer International Publishing. https://doi.org/10.1007/978-3-030-13895-0_6-1

Galetto, M. (2017). *What Is Personalized Marketing? A Look at How Personalized Marketing Works, Benefits, Best Practices, and More*. https://www.ngdata.com/what-is-personalized-marketing/

Gani, M. O., & Faroque, A. R. (2020). Digital Marketing. In *Cross-Border E-Commerce Marketing and Management* (Issue October, pp. 172–202). https://doi.org/10.4018/978-1-7998-5823-2.ch008

Gedik, Y. (2020). a New Window in Marketing: Digital Marketing. *Journal of Business in The Digital Age*, *3*(1), 63–75. https://doi.org/10.46238/jobda.726408

Germann, F., Lilien, G. L., Moorman, C., Fiedler, L., & Groβmaβ, T. (2021). Driving Customer Analytics From the Top. *Customer Needs and Solutions*, *7*(3–4), 43–61. https://doi.org/10.1007/s40547-020-00109-2

Global Entrepreneurship Research Association (GERA). (2020). *Diagnosing COVID-19 Impacts on Entrepreneurship Exploring policy remedies for recovery* (Issue September).

Gujrati, R., & Uygun, H. (2020). Covid-19: impact on global economics. *Amity Journal of Computational Sciences*, *4*(1), 24–29.

https://www.researchgate.net/publication/342962154

Güven, H. (2020). Industry 4.0 and Marketing 4.0: In Perspective of Digitalization and E-Commerce. In B. Akkaya (Ed.), *Agile Business Leadership Methods for Industry 4.0* (pp. 25–46). https://doi.org/10.1108/978-1-80043-380-920201003

Hagberg, J., & Kjellberg, H. (2020). Digitalized markets. *Consumption Markets & Culture*, *23*(2), 97–109. https://doi.org/10.1080/10253866.2020.1694209

Hagberg, J., Sundström, M., & Egels-Zandén, N. (2016). The Digitalization of Retailing: an Exploratory Framework. *International Journal of Retail & Distribution Management*, *44*(7), 694–712.

IFS. (2020). *Press Release*. https://www.ifs.com/us/news-and-events/newsroom/2020/06/30/70-percent-of-businesses-increase-or-maintain-digital-transformation-spend-amid-pandemic-ifs-study-s/

International Data Corporation (IDC). (2020). *IDC's Global DataSphere Forecast Shows Continued Steady Growth in the Creation and Consumption of Data*. https://www.idc.com/getdoc.jsp?containerId=prUS46286020

International Telecommunication Union (ITU). (2020). Economic Impact of COVID-19 on Digital Infrastructure Report of economic experts roundtable organized by ITU. In *International Telecommunication Union* (Issue July).

Järvinen, J. (Thesis). (2011). *The Impact of Digitalization on Marketing Communications Measurement Process. Case of Global B2B Industrial Companies* (Issue October). UNIVERSITY OF JYVÄSKYLÄ.

Junusi, R. El. (2020). Digital Marketing During the Pandemic Period ; A Study of Islamic Perspective. *Journal of Digital Marketing and Halal Industry*, *2*(1), 15–28.

Kannan, P. K., & Kopalle, P. K. (2001). Dynamic pricing on the Internet: Importance and implications for consumer behavior. *International Journal of Electronic Commerce*, *5*(3), 63–83. https://doi.org/10.1080/10864415.2001.11044211

Keenan, D. (2015). *Teaching in a Digital World*. https://donnakeenan.wordpress.com/2015/03/24/the-digital-world-what-does-it-mean/

Kim, R. Y. (2020). The Impact of COVID-19 on Consumers: Preparing for Digital Sales. *IEEE Engineering Management Review*, *48*(3), 212–218. https://doi.org/10.1109/EMR.2020.2990115

Kotler, P., & Armstrong, G. (2018). *Principles of Marketing - Pazarlama İlkeleri* (A. E. Gegez (ed.)). Beta Basım Yayım.

Kotler, P., Kartajaya, H., & Setiawan, I. (2017). *Marketing 4.0 Moving from Traditional to Digital*. John Wiley & Sons, Inc.

Murray, J. (2017). *What Is Personalized Marketing?* https://emarsys.com/learn/blog/what-is-personalized-marketing/

Musnaini, M., Suherman, Wijoyo, H., & Indrawan, I. (2020). *Digital Marketing* (Issue August). Pena Persada.

Narayanan, R. L., & Kartheeswaran, K. (2019). Future of Digital Marketing in 2020. *Digital Marketing: Scope and Opportunities*, *November 2019*, 10. https://www.researchgate.net/publication/337304612_FUTURE_OF_DIGITAL_MARKETING_IN_2020

Negricea, C. I., & Purcarea, I. M. (2017). Building a Path toward Digital Marketing Maturity. The impact of digital marketing in healthcare. *Holistic Marketing Management Journal*, *7*(3), 07–21. http://holisticmarketingmanagement.ro/RePEc/hmm/v7i3/2.pdf

Peter, M. K., & Dalla Vecchia, M. (2020). The Digital Marketing Toolkit: A Literature Review for the Identification of Digital Marketing Channels and Platforms. In *Studies in Systems, Decision and Control* (Vol. 294). Springer International Publishing. https://doi.org/10.1007/978-3-030-48332-6_17

Rostomyan, A. (2020). *The Impact of Coronavirus on Digitalization Do you use digital social platforms in your teaching ?* 1–6.

Statista Research Department. (2020). *E-commerce Worldwide - Statistics & Facts*. Statista.

Yüksel, B. (1999). İşletme-Müşteri İlişkilerini Kişisel Boyuta İndirgemede Kitlesel Kişiselleştirme (Mass Customization) Stratejisinin Rolü. *Sosyal Bilimler Dergisi*, *3*, 207–224.

CHAPTER FOUR

WOMEN ENTREPRENEURSHIP IN THE DIGITAL AGE: CHALLENGES AND OPPORTUNITIES

SERAP SAP AND ERHAN AYDIN

Introduction

Digital technologies have been widely adopted by organizations into their routine activities and they have simultaneously changed the organizations in many ways. Digitalization causes many disruptive changes in organizations (Matzler, Bailom, Eichen & Anschober, 2016). Various and continuously growing research studies show that digitalization is reshaping businesses environments. According to Kikovska-Georgievska (2013), improvement in technology provides opportunities to organizations such as access to markets, meeting customer expectations and survival in the market. In the same vein, Ahmad and Murray (2019) examined the effect and effectiveness of digitalization on company performance. The results of their investigation demonstrate a positive relationship between a company's digitalization investment and sales. Since digitization is a very wide field in research, it is fragmented from different angles. The main studies are mostly gathered around digital innovations, organizational structures, learning and agility (Kuusisto, 2017).

During an organization's digitalization process, managers/executives/ entrepreneurs play an important role in implementing the strategies and encouraging and motivating the employee adaptation process (Wipulanusat, Panuwatwanich, & Stewart, 2017). Although there are many important factors affecting the digitalization of organizations, studies mainly concentrate on the skills of entrepreneurs and the digitalization of organizations. It is suggested that organizations can digitalize in two ways; being born into digitalization or gradually digitalizing over time (Basly & Hammouda, 2020). In both ways, entrepreneurs hold a pivotal role to attain the organization's technology adoption aim. Scholars have pointed out that organizations' technology adoption operations are gender-blind (Henry, Orser, Coleman, Foss & Welter, 2017), others contend that managers or entrepreneurs' gender affect the organization's technology adoption process (Kahraman & Ndubisi, 2005). In addition to this, Zgheib (2018) emphasizes that women entrepreneurs are faced with various barriers in the business socio-cultural environment, the corporate cultures and organizational policies and practices. With the gap in the sex or gender-based analysis in the digitalization process of organizations, this research aims at exploring the role of digitalization in the success of women entrepreneurship through considering patriarchal institutions.

The study is structured as follows: a discussion of the existing literature is followed by an introduction of research methods and findings and then a conclusion with theoretical and practical implications as well as the limitation of the research.

Digitalization in Organizations

Digitization is a very broad and inclusive term that depends on the context in which it is used. Digitalization is a driving force in the business world because it allows the usage of new technologies that create an impact on all of society (Unruh & Kiron, 2017). Digitalization refers to the process of converting analog and complex information into digital data (Brennen & Kreiss, 2016) that aim to improve performance. Digitalization allows organizations to enhance performance and expand the business scope (Westerman, Calméjane, Bonnet, Ferraris & McAfee, 2011). Digitalization in an organization provides it with a competitive advantage in terms of direct and indirect benefits (Ahmad & Murray, 2019). By using digital technologies in their operations companies can gain various advantages in terms of the utilization of resources, the decreasing of certain costs, the increasing of efficiency and the productivity of organizations, thus enhancing customer satisfaction and loyalty (Kagermann et al., 2015; Loebbecke & Picot, 2015; Rachinger, Rauter, Müller, Vorraber & Schirgi, 2019). In their study, Gregori and Holzmann (2020) aim to gain a deeper insight into how sustainable entrepreneurs use digital technologies in the organization's business model to create social and environmental value. In their study, they collected and analyzed qualitative data from 28 entrepreneurs. Their findings show that usage of appropriate digital technologies to create value increases the convenience and efficiency in the organization while decreasing the costs. In the current digitalized era, advanced improvements in information and communication technologies affect organizations extensively. Organizations are currently facing major changes in the way they do business operations and in leadership due to the latest technological advances (Colbert, Yee, & George, 2016).

Digitalization and Entrepreneurship

Digitalization in organizations is related to adopting or increasing the volume of digital tools, such as artificial intelligence, 3D printing, etc. (Brennen & Kreiss, 2016). The usage of digital tools enhances the digital capabilities of the organization in terms of new possibilities for action that can be used by actors such as entrepreneurs (Autio, Nambisan, Thomas & Wright, 2018; Nambisan, Lyytinen, Majchrzak, & Song, 2017). Recent studies show that the usage of digital technologies provides new opportunities to entrepreneurs and the development of new business models (Hinings, Gegenhuber & Greenwood, 2018; Täuscher & Laudien, 2018; Nambisan et al., 2017). As a top manager, the management and handling of the digitalization process is the responsibility of the entrepreneur (Gratton, 2016). Therefore, developing appropriate business models and implementing them, and managing employee adaptation are the responsibility of entrepreneurs (El Sawy, Kræmmergaard, Amsinck, & Vinther, 2016; (Wipulanusat, Panuwatwanich & Stewart, 2017). While managing the digitalization process in their organizations, entrepreneurs need to be role models for their employees to help their adaptation process (Day, Fleenor, Atwater, Sturm, & McKee, 2014). Digitalization affects organizations, the work environment and processes, and also, creates new challenges for entrepreneurs to deal with.

During the digitalization process, entrepreneurs should reconcile with different employees' technological ability (Dimitrov, 2018). Entrepreneurs need to focus on employees' adoption of new technology. The inspiration and motivation of employees are also challenges for entrepreneurs (Horner-Long and Schoenberg, 2002); for instance, working with virtual teams causes worker alienation as a result of less social bonding, collaboration and accountability (Roman et al., 2018). This distance communication method negatively affects the trust between the entrepreneur and their employees (Savolainen, 2014). Therefore, it is the entrepreneur's responsibility to motivate and promote employees, help them to feel less isolated by increasing interactions, and support them to complete tasks (Schwarzmüller et al., 2018).

Another challenge of digitalization for entrepreneurs is its damage to the work-life balance. Being reachable all the time increases the volume of information transition between the two parties and causes an increase in the range of topics or issues that need attention (Barley, Meyerson, & Grodal, 2011; Schwarzmüller et al., 2018). The increase in workload causes an increase in the stress level of entrepreneurs (Gordon & Martin, 2019; Kane et al., 2019). At the same time, fast-track digital tools require entrepreneurs to make decisions faster than usual (Pulley & Sessa, 2001). Although digital tools allow two-way communication and more data for decision-making (Cortellazzo, Bruni & Zampieri, 2019), they also increase the stress level of entrepreneurs. The need to be informed and to understand novel digital technologies forces entrepreneurs to regularly update their technical knowledge and be a lifelong learner to follow the trends in the digital world (Sousa & Rocha, 2019; Schwarzmüller et al., 2018).

While some scholars claim that organizations' technology adoption process is independent of the entrepreneurs' gender (Henry, Orser, Coleman, Foss & Welter, 2017), other studies highlight the opposite (Kahraman & Ndubisi, 2005). Orser, Riding and Li (2019) conducted empirical research to explore gender-related barriers during the adoption of technology. They collected qualitative data from 21 semi-structured interviews with women entrepreneurs who are expert in digital technology. Their findings highlight the gender influence on the digital economy, showing that organizations with women entrepreneurs are perceived as having a lack of technical capacity. Therefore, as a response strategy to deal with this perception, they suggest enhancing confidence for women entrepreneurs.

The research by McKinsey Global Institution (Madgavkar et al., 2019) suggests that technological advancement will be part of both women's and men' jobs in the next decades. However, the research results highlight that women are more affected in terms of the transition process in catching opportunities because of gender-related barriers. Although, technology offers various opportunities for women to increase their participation in the business world and to decrease the barriers to becoming an entrepreneur. Women entrepreneurs still suffer when reaching out to technology, to improve skills and to find technology-dominated jobs. Therefore, these barriers exclude women from the potential benefits of digitalization. For this reason, this research addresses the challenges and opportunities faced by women entrepreneurs as part of the digitalization of organizations and working in a new way.

Research Method

This research aims to demonstrate the challenges and opportunities of women entrepreneurship in the digital age which introduces many digital business and talent platforms. The reason behind the digitalization of business processes is that it provides advantages in decreasing the operational costs of organizations which is why it is preferred by entrepreneurs. As existing studies related to the digitalization of organizations have a gender-blind approach, this research focuses on women entrepreneurs and the barriers and opportunities that they face. To explore the challenges and benefits of the digitalization processes for both companies and entrepreneurs, we conducted 16 semi-structured, qualitative and in-depth interviews with the graduates of business administration departments at public universities in Turkey. The main reason for adopting qualitative research is to gain a deeper understanding and to explore the experiences of women individuals who want to start an online business (Flick, 2009). Table 4.1 shows the participants of this research. To protect participants' privacy, and for other confidentiality and anonymity issues, we gave them nicknames as presented in Table 4.1.

Table 4.1: Participants' Demographic Information

	Participant Name	**Gender**	**Age**
1.	Dona	Woman	22
2.	Fatma	Woman	21
3.	Zeynep	Woman	23
4.	Dilara	Woman	22
5.	Melek	Woman	23
6.	Medine	Woman	21
7.	Ahu	Woman	23
8.	Ajda	Woman	24
9.	Adile	Woman	23
10.	Alara	Woman	21
11.	Arife	Woman	23
12.	Asya	Woman	22
13.	Aynur	Woman	23
14.	Beste	Woman	25
15.	Burcu	Woman	23
16.	Buse	Woman	22

In this research, we adopt snowball sampling to ensure access to participants. The snowballing sampling method is preferred by researchers when the individual networks are vital to the society's culture in which the data have been collected (Coleman, 1958). First, we reached out to three graduates based on personal networks. Then, each participant let us find another participant with similar characteristics or experiences that matched our research aim. Data collection was ended after the completion of sixteen qualitative interviews as data reached the saturation level that refers to stopping the interviews when researchers have no new information (Francis et. al., 2009). The interview protocol included three stages: an introduction, responses to interview questions and the end of the interview. In the introduction stage, we informed every participant of the aims and objectives of the present research. Moreover, they confirmed that they were volunteering to attend the interviews and gave us permission for voice records. We confirmed confidentiality to participants that the records would not be shared with any other individuals and institutions. Every interview took about 30-40 minutes. To eliminate the negative effect of the Covid-19 pandemic, we used an online platform and completed face-to-face interviews via Google Meet. NVIVO 12 analytics software was used to transcribe and analyze the interview data. This software helped researchers to categorize data and find themes.

Findings

In view of the limited literature on women entrepreneurs in the digital age 16 semi-structured interviews were conducted. In consideration of the limited literature, this research aims to explore the role of digitalization in the success of women entrepreneurship through considering patriarchal institutions. According to the findings of the semi-structured interviews, four main themes were identified within the scope of this research. Two of them are related to the challenges of digitalization for women entrepreneurship: a "lack of access to the target market" and "adopting technological advancement". The remaining themes are related to the benefits of digitalization that are "providing [a] work-life balance" and "access to [a] talented labor force". Table 4.2 presents the findings.

Table 4.2: Identified Themes

Barriers Faced by Women Entrepreneurs	Opportunities of Digitalization
• Lack of access to the target market • Adopting technological advancement	• Work-life balance • Access to a talented labor force

Lack of Access to the Target Market

In the scope of this research, all participants demonstrate an intention to run a business on digital platforms that include websites and social media accounts. The reason behind working on digital platforms is the cost advantage. Young women entrepreneurs have a budget barrier as they graduated a few years before. This is why it is hard for them to save money for a bricks-and-mortar business. In addition to this, young entrepreneurs do not have an expanded network in the market because of a lack of experience. Therefore, finding an investor for their business idea might be difficult in their early career. Therefore, they mostly focus on starting their business via online platforms. However, even though digital platforms provide a cost-saving opportunity for women entrepreneurs, the platforms bring critical challenges for them. For instance, Melek mentions this situation, as follows:

> I bought a website and also, I created an Instagram profile for my business. However, since it is a new account, my followers are mostly my friends and relatives. I need more than them. I need to be followed by my potential consumers. (Melek, 23)

As the participant states, the main challenge for women entrepreneurs in the early stage is to reach potential consumers. Even though the entrepreneurs have digital platforms, they need to do promotional activities such as advertisements in order to gain access to the consumers in their target market. For this reason, they use social media accounts, and Google Ads that provides online advertisement in both search engines and digital platforms such as YouTube and Facebook. However, this brings additional costs for the early career women entrepreneurs. For instance, Buse raises the issue of online advertisement as follows:

> Digital platforms are definitely very useful since we do not give any rent. However, I need to reach more people who do not know me because I need to sell my service to someone that I do not know. For this reason, I have a budget to place an advertisement on Instagram. I am in the early stage and I need to spend more money to reach more people in my target market. (Buse, 22)

The findings demonstrate that women entrepreneurs in their early career face the challenges of accessing the target market and they overcome this issue through promoting advertisements on digital platforms. Even though they spend money for access to the target markets, they are aware of some problems that stem from the algorithms of the digital advertisement platforms. For instance, Dona discusses this situation as follows:

> I have problems about accessing the consumers in my field. I pay lots of money to the digital platform for advertisements. However, it is too weak and I don't reach that much consumers. I think the algorithms of the platforms are designed to get more money. It creates a challenge for me because I do not have that much money to spend for advertisements. (Dona, 22)

As discussed above, the algorithms of the advertisements on the digital platforms are subject to various changes and these may have an impact on the efficiency of online advertisements. For this reason, three main issues result in a lack of access to the target market. These issues are the lack of followers who can be potential consumers, the online advertisement costs and the algorithms of the digital platforms that make online advertisement costly.

Adopting Technological Advancements

Digital platforms that women entrepreneurs use to promote their businesses consistently and regularly update their software and interface. For this reason, to successfully manage promotional activities or understand the needs of potential customers, entrepreneurs need to follow and understand the technological advancements. Entrepreneurs need to improve their knowledge of technology in regard to the changing software and algorithm structure of the digital platforms to stay connected. Otherwise, as the technology changes so fast, entrepreneurs can lag behind in the trends and the market. For instance, Beste raises this issue as follows:

> I mostly use Facebook and Instagram. Maybe, I use Instagram more than Facebook. They always update their system in terms of how they look. For instance, Instagram recently changed the buttons on the program. Also, it has a more professional perspective to creating advertisements since it introduces Reels and Shops on the digital platform. There are a lot of technological developments in software based platforms. For this reason, it is difficult to catch the trend. I think this creates a critical challenge for women entrepreneurs. (Beste, 25)

As Beste states, adopting technological advancements is a challenge for women entrepreneurs. Also, some entrepreneurs compare women entrepreneurs' technological skills with those of men entrepreneurs. For instance, Zeynep introduces this comparison as follows:

> Men have skills for adopting technological changes. However, women do not have that many skills. This has an impact on adopting technological advancements for women. For example, I am really terrible at using the technological tools and even digital platforms. I always ask for help from my brother. (Zeynep, 23)

The findings of this research demonstrate that some women entrepreneurs face challenges to provide the adoption of technological changes in terms of the digital platforms' usage. For this reason, the theme of "adopting technological advancements" has been considered as a challenge for women entrepreneurs.

Providing a Work-Life Balance

Work-life balance refers to feeling "comfortable with both work and family commitments" (Johari et al., 2018). Women entrepreneurs face difficulties in managing both their life and their business. The main reason for this situation comes from the need for hard work at the beginning of a business. However, digitalization brings possibilities to manage both private life and business. For instance, Dilara discusses this situation as follows:

> I graduated from business administration and my expertise is in the accounting field. Since it can be given as a service in the digital platforms, I do not need to go to any workplace. I can manage all my work at home. Thus, it creates an opportunity to have more time for my private life. Also, I may marry someone in the future, and I may have a child. Therefore, it is good to work at home and I think this is the main benefit of digitalization for women entrepreneurs. (Dilara, 22)

The findings demonstrate that women entrepreneurs mostly focus on the advantage of being at home or of having more time for their private life. Digitalization of work and businesses provides a critical advantage for women entrepreneurs since they also consider their roles as a mother, sister and child. These social roles shape their understanding of how they can manage their lives and businesses.

Access to a Talented Labor Force

A talented labor force is a critical input and cost of operating a business. SMEs usually have financial restrictions around employing highly-skilled staff. It is difficult for them to pay high salaries and keep talented and skilled individuals for the long-term. For this reason, one of the advantages of digitalization is to reach talented individuals through digital platforms. For instance, Fullet et al. (2020) suggests emerging digital platforms for a talented workforce such as Freelancer and Catalant. Thus, such platforms help women entrepreneurs to find talented individuals who do project-based work instead of permanent work.

Alara discusses this situation as follows:

> A labor force is critical for my work since I provide websites for small-medium sized companies. I need a team that also know about software management. For this reason, I use Freelancer as a talented individuals pool and I work for someone there on a project basis. This is a great opportunity for me because if I do not reach that pool, it will be difficult to have full-time employees. Of course, employing part-time employees is also challenging for me. (Alara, 21)

The findings of this research demonstrate that access to a talented or highly-skilled labor force provides a critical benefit for women entrepreneurs. By using digital platforms like Freelancer and People Per Hour, entrepreneurs can find the most appropriate staff from anywhere in the world with a short-term agreement. This enables new-born companies to decrease their labor cost while increasing the quality of their product, services and operations.

Conclusion

The main contribution of this study is to extend the knowledge of women entrepreneurship through adopting the role of digital tools and networks for their success. Also, in terms of the practical contribution, the present research creates suggestions to encourage women entrepreneurship in society through digitalization and governmental institutions because the current literature consists of traditional entrepreneurship that does not cover the impact of digitalization. This research adopts a qualitative approach to gain new insights into the women entrepreneur phenomenon. Therefore, 16 semi-structured interviews were conducted with snowball sampling. The qualitative data were analyzed with NVIVO 12 software to create main themes. According to the findings, four interesting themes have emerged.

In terms of the barriers that women entrepreneurs face in their online business, these are classified under two main issues; lack of access to the target market and difficulties in adopting technological advancement. Although using digital platforms requires fewer financial resources for businesses, women entrepreneurs highlight that they still need a certain budget level. To promote their product or services or to reach the target market, digital entrepreneurs still have expenditure on promotional activities. Besides, our findings show that a lack of technical skill is an important barrier for women entrepreneurs. Based on our findings, the usage of digital platforms requires technical skill, and also, following improvements to online channels, requires continuous improvement of their technical skills. In the same vein, Sousa and Rocha (2019) state that digital entrepreneurs need to regularly update their technical knowledge in order to follow the trends, otherwise they might become out-of-date. In addition to this, our findings support the existing literature that women entrepreneurs are perceived as having a lack of technical knowledge; therefore, there is a bias against women entrepreneurs (Orser, Riding & Li, 2019). Thus, women entrepreneurs need to have confidence in their situation to realize the problem and develop solutions.

However, young women entrepreneurs highlight two important opportunities that they discovered while working online: a work-life balance and easy access to a talented labor force. According to our findings, women entrepreneurs found that working online provides them with the freedom to work anywhere or anytime. An entrepreneur who has children can stay at home while taking care of children and work online. This finding is very surprising because according to the literature, being reachable all of the time increases the workload and stress of entrepreneurs (Gordon & Martin, 2019; Kane et al., 2019). However, women entrepreneurs perceive it as an opportunity as they also have to think about their family life and children. The other surprising opportunity is easy access to highly-skilled employees from anywhere in the world. Although young entrepreneurs highlight their financial restrictions, they are willing to pay money to skilled employees to increase their product, service and operational quality. Although, spending money on outsourcing creates a cost in the short-term, they believe that increasing the quality provides benefits in the long-term.

Keywords: *Digitalization, women entrepreneurship, entrepreneurship*

References

Ahmad, M. U., & Murray, J. (2019). Understanding the connect between digitalization, sustainability and performance of an organisation. *International Journal of Business Excellence*, *17*(1), 83-96.

Autio, E., Nambisan, S., Thomas, L. D., & Wright, M. (2018). Digital affordances, spatial affordances, and the genesis of entrepreneurial ecosystems. *Strategic Entrepreneurship Journal*, *12*(1), 72-95.

Barley, S. R., Meyerson, D. E., & Grodal, S. (2011). E-mail as a source and symbol of stress. *Organization Science*, *22*(4), 887-906.

Basly, S., & Hammouda, A. (2020). Family businesses and digital entrepreneurship adoption: A conceptual model. *The Journal of Entrepreneurship*, *29*(2), 326-364.

Brennen, J. S., & Kreiss, D. (2016). Digitalization. *The international encyclopedia of communication theory and philosophy*, 1-11.

Colbert, Amy; Yee, Nick; And George, Gerard. (2016). The digital workforce and the workplace of the future. *Academy of Management Journal*. 59, (3), 731-739.

Cortellazzo, L., Bruni, E., & Zampieri, R. (2019). The role of leadership in a digitalized world: a review. *Frontiers in psychology*, *10*, 1938.

Day, D. V., Fleenor, J. W., Atwater, L. E., Sturm, R. E., & McKee, R. A. (2014). Advances in leader and leadership development: A review of 25 years of research and theory. *The leadership quarterly*, *25*(1), 63-82.

Dimitrov, A. (2018). The digital age leadership: a transhumanistic perspective. *Journal of Leadership Studies*, *12*(3), 79-81.

El Sawy, O. A., Kræmmergaard, P., Amsinck, H., & Vinther, A. L. (2016). How LEGO built the foundations and enterprise capabilities for digital leadership. *MIS Quarterly Executive*, *15*(2).

Flick U. (2009). *An Introduction to Qualitative Research* (6th. Edition). London: Sage publication.

Francis, J. J., Johnston, M., Robertson, C., Glidewell, L., Entwistle, V., Eccles, M. P., & Grimshaw, J. M. (2010). What is an adequate sample size? Operationalising data saturation for theory-based interview studies. *Psychology and health*, *25*(10), 1229-1245.

Fuller, Joseph B., Manjari Raman, Allison Bailey, and Nithya Vaduganathan (2020). "*Rethinking the On-Demand Workforce.*" Harvard Business Review 98(6), 96–103.

Gordon, V., & Martin, D. (2019). The 21st-century CEO: Intrinsic attributes, worldview, and communication capabilities. *Journal of Leadership & Organizational Studies*, *26*(2), 141-149.

Henry, C., Orser, B., Coleman, S., Foss, L., & Welter, F. (2017). Women's entrepreneurship policy: A 13-nation cross-country comparison. In *Entrepreneurial Ecosystems and Growth of Women's Entrepreneurship*. Edward Elgar Publishing.

Hinings, B., Gegenhuber, T., & Greenwood, R. (2018). Digital innovation and transformation: An institutional perspective. *Information and Organization*, *28*(1), 52-61.

Horner-Long, P., & Schoenberg, R. (2002). Does e-business require different leadership characteristics?: An empirical investigation. *European Management Journal*, *20*(6), 611-619.

Johari, J., Tan, F. Y., & Zulkarnain, Z. I. T. (2018). Autonomy, workload, work-life balance and job performance among teachers. International Journal of Educational Management. 32(1), 107-120.

Kagermann, H., Riemensperger, F., Hoke, D., Helbig, J., & Stocksmeier, D. (2015). Smart Service Welt-Recommendations for the Strategic Initiative Web-based Services for Businesses. acatech–National Academy of Science and Engineering. *Germany, Berlin.*

Kahraman, C., & Ndubisi, N. O. (2005). Malaysian Women Entrepreneurs: Understanding the ICT Usage Behaviors and Drivers. *Journal of Enterprise Information Management*, *18*(6), 23-35.

Kikovska-Georgievska, S. (2013) 'Ecommerce challenge for sustainable development of companies', *Journal of Sustainable Development*, 4,(7),71–83.

Kuusisto, M. (2017). Organizational effects of digitalization: a literature review. *International Journal Of Organization Theory and Behavior*, *20*(03), 341-362.

Loebbecke, C., & Picot, A. (2015). Reflections on societal and business model transformation arising from digitization and big data analytics: A research agenda. The Journal of Strategic Information Systems, 24(3), 149-157.

Madgavkar, A., Manyika, J., Krishnan, M., Ellingrud, K., Yee, L., Woetzel, J., ... & Balakrishnan, S. (2019). The future of women at work: transitions in the age of automation. New York: McKinsey Global Institute. Retrieved March 18, 2020, from https://www.mckinsey.com/featured-insights/gender-equality/the-future-of-women-at-work-transitions-in-the-age-of-automation.

Matzler, K., Bailom, F., von den Eichen, S.F. and Anschober, M. (2016), *Digital Disruption. Wie Sie Ihr Unternehmen auf das digitale Zeitalter vorbereiten*, Vahlen, München.

Nambisan, S., Lyytinen, K., Majchrzak, A., & Song, M. (2017). Digital Innovation Management: Reinventing innovation management research in a digital world. *Mis Quarterly*, *41*(1).

Pulley, M. L., & Sessa, V. I. (2001). E-leadership: tackling complex challenges. *Industrial and commercial Training*.

Rachinger, M., Rauter, R., Müller, C., Vorraber, W., & Schirgi, E. (2019). Digitalization and its influence on business model innovation. *Journal of Manufacturing Technology Management*, 30(8), 1143-1160.

Roman, A. V., Van Wart, M., Wang, X., Liu, C., Kim, S., & McCarthy, A. (2019). Defining e-leadership as competence in ICT-mediated communications: an exploratory assessment. *Public Administration Review*, *79*(6), 853-866.

Savolainen, T. (2014). Trust-building in e-leadership: A case study of leaders' challenges and skills in technology-mediated interaction. *Journal of Global Business Issues*, *8*(2).

Schwarzmüller, T., Brosi, P., Duman, D., & Welpe, I. M. (2018). How does the digital transformation affect organizations? Key themes of change in work design and leadership. *mrev management revue*, *29*(2), 114-138.

Schwarzmüller, T., Brosi, P., Duman, D., & Welpe, I. M. (2018). How does the digital transformation affect organizations? Key themes of change in work design and leadership. *mrev management revue*, *29*(2), 114-138.

Sousa, M. J., & Rocha, Á. (2019). Skills for disruptive digital business. *Journal of Business Research*, *94*, 257-263.

Täuscher, K., & Laudien, S. M. (2018). Understanding platform business models: A mixed methods study of marketplaces. *European Management Journal*, *36*(3), 319-329.

Unruh, G., & Kiron, D. (2017). Digital transformation on purpose. *MIT Sloan management review*, *6*.

Westerman, G., Calméjane, C., Bonnet, D., Ferraris, P., & McAfee, A. (2011). Digital Transformation: A roadmap for billion-dollar organizations. *MIT Center for Digital Business and Capgemini Consulting*, *1*, 1-68.

Wipulanusat, W., Panuwatwanich, K., & Stewart, R. A. (2017). Exploring leadership styles for innovation: an exploratory factor analysis. *Engineering Management in Production and Services*, *9*(1), 7-17.

Zgheib, P. (2018), "Multi-level framework of push-pull entrepreneurship: comparing American and Lebanese women", International Journal of Entrepreneurial Behavior and Research, 24(3), 768-786.

CHAPTER FIVE

A DIGITAL ASPECT OF ENTREPRENEURSHIP: CROWDFUNDING

ALKAN ALKAYA

Introduction

With the emergence of Web 2.0 technology, internet users have turned into an asset that not only consumes content but also produces content. Internet users are now seen as a resource. James Surowiecki (2004) revealed in his article "Wisdom of the Crowd" that the masses can do some jobs more effectively than experts, and businesses are starting to take advantage of this. He called this concept crowdsourcing. Wikipedia can be seen as one of the most important examples of a crowd source (Niederer & Van Dijck, 2010). Entrepreneurs also see the masses on the internet as a resource for finding funds. Entrepreneurs have been forced to use different methods to find financial resources due to the changes occurring on a global scale. This financing method is called crowdfunding. This concept, first introduced by Michael Sullivan in 2006, is defined as an innovative method of fundraising for entrepreneurs who have become increasingly popular in the internet age (Gobble, 2012). The crowdfunding method draws attention as an alternative financing method that has been put into practice in recent years to overcome the problems encountered in the financing of entrepreneurship. Entrepreneurs have now begun to benefit from the masses on the internet due to the difficulties and disadvantages they face in taking advantage of traditional funding sources. Thanks to this method which takes advantage of the power and wisdom of the crowd, it is possible for individuals or businesses with innovative ideas to access the financing they need regardless of geographic boundaries.

Crowdfunding started as an online extension of conventional funding by family and friends. In the spread of crowdfunding, artists and entrepreneurs, who had difficulty in finding support for their projects due to the economic crisis in 2008, have a significant share in alternative methods. During this crisis period, the willingness of the banking sector to lend decreased and the trust in banks deteriorated (Kuti & Madarász, 2014). In a short time, crowdfunding gained interest in many developed economies, including the UK, Australia, Italy, the United States and the Netherlands. This prominent phenomenon is now gaining great attention in the developing world (Best et al., 2013).

Crowdfunding Concept

One of the most important obstacles to initiatives is the lack of necessary funding. Entrepreneurs' ability to realize their thoughts and be successful in their activities depends on their ability to easily find funds from the necessary knowledge, managerial support, money and capital markets. At this stage, entrepreneurs may encounter many alternative financing methods and the problems that these methods bring with them.

Newly-established businesses can find the funding sources they need in two ways, formal and informal. Formal sources of funds are those obtained through borrowing from third parties such as credit institutions, venture capital, banks and the government (Karasioğlu & Duman, 2006). Non-formal funding sources can be classified as equity, family, friends, relatives, angel investors and crowdfunding platforms (Er et al., 2015).

Entrepreneurs are dependent on their relatives and friends as a source of capital other than their own resources in the first stage of growth. Family and friends can provide small amounts of seed capital (Aldrich, 2014). However, the self-financing option limits asset diversity, and family, friends, and relatives are often poor financial intermediaries. In addition, relatives and friends may want to control or interfere with the entrepreneur's independence in entrepreneurship. For these reasons, entrepreneur companies seek official and professional sources of financing such as commercial banks or venture capital (Brophy & Shulman, 1992). Asset-backed lenders such as banks and commercial loan companies are not interested in beginner entrepreneurs who have partially insufficient assets in order to secure possible loans. Angel investors are another alternative. However, crowdfunding may lead to missed opportunities due to the methods of evaluating new venture proposals and the long evaluation period (Aldrich, 2014).

Crowdfunding is an internet-enabled way for businesses or other organizations to raise money from multiple individuals in the form of donations or investments. This new form of capital formation originated in large part due to the difficulties that artisans, entrepreneurs and early-stage businesses faced in finding funds in the 2008 financial crisis. Due to the fact that banks are less willing to lend, entrepreneurs began to seek capital elsewhere (Best et al., 2013).

Crowdfunding, defined as a financial contribution to products, projects, or business ideas by a number of investors, has recently been seen as an alternative for individuals to find resources (Agrawal et al., 2013; Kleeman et al., 2008; Unterberg, 2010; Wenzlaff, 2012). The concept of finding financing in small amounts dates back to old times (Fiedler & Horsch, 2014; Harrisson, 2013; Zademach & Baumeister, 2013). Unlike conventional financial investments, crowdfunding is basically open to everyone (Blohm et al., 2013; Wenzlaff, 2012). Crowdfunding first became popular with the funding of artists or creative projects and then spread to more industries (Bradford 2012; Meinshausen et al., 2012). Crowdfunding is closely linked to micro borrowing (Vitale, 2013). Micro borrowing refers to the idea of financing individuals who do not have access to traditional finance from credit institutions (Armendariz & Morduch, 2010).

Crowdfunding represents one dimension of crowdsourcing, as well as crowd-creation and crowd-voting (Leimeister, 2012; Leimeister & Zogaj, 2013; Richter et al., 2014). The term crowdsourcing consists of "crowd" and "outsourcing", referring to the meaning of outsourcing certain functions to a group of external people (Kleeman et al., 2008). This concept comes from the idea of "the wisdom of the crowd" (Surowiecki, 2004). Howe (2006) was the first to describe crowdsourcing in his online article in 2006. To date, his definition is the most important scientific one, which we have therefore followed (Brabham, 2009; Starbird, 2012).

There are many definitions of crowdfunding, none of which are generally scientifically accepted (Tomczak & Brem, 2013). The currently considerable definitions are thus presented in the Table 5.1 below:

Table 5.1: Definitions of Crowdfunding

Authors	Definition
Howe, 2006: 1	The act of taking a job traditionally performed by a designated agent (usually an employee) and outsourcing it to an undefined, generally large number of people in the form of an open call.
Belleflamme et al., 2010: 5	Crowdfunding mainly involves an open call to provide financial resources over the internet, in the form of donations, or in exchange for some form of reward or voting right.
Fiedler & Horsch, 2014: 92	Crowdfunding includes types of capital supply where capital-seeking companies present themselves publicly on certain internet-based platforms to a large group of potential capital providers based on innovative business ideas and offer this group the opportunity to engage in fund allocation.
Hemer et al., 2011: 5	Crowdfunding is a form of project and innovation funding with micropayments.
Lambert & Schwienbacher, 2010: 4	An open call, mainly on the internet, to provide financial resources either in the form of donations or in exchange for some form of award or voting right to support initiatives for specific purposes.
Tomczak & Brem, 2013: 338	The act of outsourcing, usually to a large group of people, not defined as obtaining a loan/funding and an open search, traditionally performed by a particular representative.
Voorbraak, 2011: 1	The process of one party requesting and receiving money and other resources from many people to fund a project in exchange for a monetary or non-monetary return on investment.
Wenzlaff, 2012: 1	Crowdfunding is a form of fundraising for creative projects as well as companies. The most important thing is that crowdfunding is open, uses Web 2.0 methods for communication, and often has some kind of material or immaterial reward.
Ordanini, Miceli, Pizetti & Parasuraman, 2011: 444	Crowdfunding is a fundraising initiative by collecting small to medium-sized investment amounts from many people (masses) for new projects submitted by individuals.
Joenssen, Michaelis & Müllerleile, 2014: 1	Crowdfunding is the initiation of commercial or non-commercial projects by individuals or organizations in a public call to raise funds, value market potential and build relationships with customers.

Originally, crowdfunding was carried out using websites and/or online social networks. As an example, in 1997, the British music group Marillion collected the $60,000 it needed for a tour to the United States (USA) from its supporters through an online donation campaign (Bradley III & Luong, 2014).

The development of Web 2.0 technologies and the success of crowdsourcing have led to the emergence of special crowdfunding platforms that bring together entrepreneurs and potential funders, providing an information flow and facilitating transactions. Crowdfunding platforms bring project owners and potential funders together through a web-based application (Zvilichovsky et al., 2015). Most crowdfunding happens on platforms that provide payment facilities and project management tools. These platforms direct funds from donors, lenders or investors to the project owner (Röthler & Wenzlaff, 2011).

A website called "ArtistShare", the first website to use crowdfunding in the USA in 2003, mediated for many artists to realize their projects with the money they collected from their supporters (Sakızlı, 2018). Maria Schneider's jazz album was ArtistShare's first crowdfunding project. She collected approximately $130,000 from her fans with her ArtistShare campaign and received a 2005 Grammy award for her album. This success of ArtistShare has led to the emergence of numerous crowdfunding platforms, primarily Indiegogo in 2008 and Kickstarter in 2009. Financing campaigns for arts (fine arts, dance, comics, design, film and video, music, fashion, photography, theater and creative writing) and social issues (animals, community, education, environment, health, politics and religion) have been started on these platforms (Freedman & Nutting, 2015).

Although the crowdfunding method usually collects small amounts of money, it is possible to achieve very large amounts of financial resources. One of the most successful projects within the scope of crowdfunding is the cooler project named "The Coolest Cooler". A total revenue of $13,285,226 was generated with this campaign, in which 62,642 people participated (Kickstarter, 2020a). Another successful project is the "Pebble Watch" smart watch project. Within the scope of this project, a total of $10,266,845 of income was obtained from 68,929 people (Kickstarter, 2020b). These projects are important in terms of demonstrating the power of crowdfunding as an alternative financing method. Crowdfunding not only generates large financial resources for high-tech products; for the "An Hour of Code for Every Student" project, which was initiated within the scope of teaching children computer programming, approximately $5 million was earned from 2,895 people (Indiegogo, 2020). It is seen that the crowdfunding application is also used in the field of politics. Barack Obama earned $631 million with the donation-based crowdfunding campaign he started for the presidential elections in 2012 (Kappel, 2008).

Crowdfunding Ecosystem

To understand how the crowdfunding ecosystem works, it is important to identify the stakeholders and their impact on the process (Beaulieu et al., 2015). In general, stakeholder means "any group or individual that can affect or be affected by the organization's achievement of its goals" (Freeman, 2010: 53). Stakeholders are not isolated groups, but dynamic groups that interact with each other (Laplume et al., 2008). There are three types of main stakeholders or players in the crowdfunding system; fund seekers, and funder and crowdfunding platforms (Ordanini et al., 2011).

Fund seekers are people who make an open call to large masses through crowdfunding platforms to raise the funds they need to implement their projects or business ideas (Atsan & Erdoğan, 2015). Instead of the concept of fund seekers, concepts such as "entrepreneur", "creator", "firm", "borrower", "founder", "start-up", "owner", are also used. However, most of these concepts are narrow and do not always express all participants. For example, a crowdfunding person may not have the goal of starting a business and may instead attempt to raise funds for different purposes. Therefore, the concept of "fund seekers" refers to individuals, groups, charities, businesses, etc., seeking funds for different commercial or non-commercial purposes (Beaulieu et al., 2015).

Funders are the supporters of crowdfunded projects, and equally important to the crowdfunding ecosystem. In the literature, funder is also expressed in terms such as "supporter", "backer", "consumer", "lender", "investor", and "contributor" (Beaulieu et al., 2015). Funders contribute to the realization of projects by examining projects offered by entrepreneurs on crowdfunding platforms and investing money in the projects they want to support. In return for their contribution, they can expect a specific financial reward or return, or they may not expect any material or financial reward. Founders benefit from the crowdfunding model with intrinsic motivations such as being a community member and philanthropy, as well as external motivations such as financial gain and reward (Gerber et al., 2012).

In essence, crowdfunding is provided through technology; thus, website providers have a very important role in the crowdfunding concept. Crowdfunding platforms are internet-based websites that bring together fund seekers and funders (Karaaslan & Altuntaş, 2015). Entrepreneurs put their project photos and videos or the first prototype of their product on their funding platform and get the funds they need from their donors or investors (Akyüz, 2016). Crowdfunding platforms are commercial sites which charge a certain percentage of the total funding amount determined by the platforms (Agrawal et al., 2013). They may act as orchestrators, intermediaries, distribution channels and rule enforcers, and in addition to these, they are also used for the testing of projects, marketing, promoting, and obtaining information about consumer preferences (Atsan & Erdoğan, 2015; Ordanini et al., 2011).

Types of Crowdfunding

There are four main types of crowdfunding: donation, reward, debt and share (equity) based crowdfunding (Nesta, 2012; Chervyakov & Rocholl, 2019). Key characteristics of the crowdfunding types are outlined in Table 5.2 (Cicchiello, 2019):

Table 5.2: Key Features of Crowdfunding Models

Model	Purpose of Financing	Expected Return	Main Sector
Donation-based	Funding of non-profit charitable projects	No expectation of returns	Charities, foundations
Reward-based	Funding for creative projects	Non-monetary rewards or products	Art, music and design
Debt-based	Providing loans to individuals and companies requesting debts	Repayment of capital and interest	Education and research
Equity-based	Equity investment mostly in start-ups	Profit sharing	Technology and innovation

Source: Cicchiello, 2019: 3

Donation-based crowdfunding is the financing of social or charitable projects by collecting money from the masses (Röthler & Wenzlaff, 2011; Nesta, 2012). This funding model is for non-profit charitable projects. The reason it is called "donation-based" is that the charity or project owner running the campaign does not offer any financial or intangible rewards to supporters in return for the funds they provide. For funders, the motivation provided by the model is intrinsic, and this is often an important motivation for a long-term donor relationship (De Buysere et al., 2012).

Large charities can collect donations through their websites or organize various donation campaigns. However, with the emergence of donation-based crowdfunding platforms, small charities and individuals have also gained the opportunity to raise funds from large masses for charity. For example, GoFundMe, established in 2010 as a donation-based crowdfunding platform, mediated the collection of over $9 billion in donations from more than 120 million participants from its establishment until 2020 (www.gofundme.com). Donation-based crowdfunding is a crowdfunding method mostly used in social responsibility projects. In this method, the money collected from the participants is used in projects such as providing aid and medical supplies to victims. GiveForward, FirstGiving and GoFundMe are major donation-based internet platforms.

In the reward-based crowdfunding type, fund seekers do not provide any financial return such as interest or shares to those who contribute to their projects (funders), but if their initiative is successful, they give various tangible or intangible awards according to the amount of their contribution (Nesta, 2012; Gulati, 2014). These awards are of symbolic value but will please the funder, such as mentioning their name on the project, sending a letter of appreciation, or giving small gifts (De Buysere et al., 2012). This funding is a type of crowdfunding that is widely used in the financing of social, cultural and creative projects and business ideas. Reward-based crowdfunding is a method used by small businesses, non-profit organizations, and people from different branches of the arts. Through this funding, it is possible to finance projects in many categories such as fine arts, creative writing, education, dance, environment, design, health, video, music, theater, food, fashion, sports, plays, publishing, and technology (Freedman & Nutting 2015; Sakızlı, 2018). ArtistShare and Indiegogo are examples of reward-based crowdfunding. Kickstarter is the world's largest reward-based crowdfunding platform in terms of visitor traffic. One of the most successful examples of reward-based crowdfunding, Pebble Watch, generated pre-sales revenue of $10 million for the first run and $20 million for the second run through Kickstarter (Bellavitis et al., 2017).

Debt-based crowdfunding, which takes the biggest share from the crowdfunding market in terms of transaction volume, is the matching of parties who want to borrow (loan) and parties who want to lend through a crowdfunding platform (Kirby & Worner, 2014). In the debt-based crowdfunding model, fund seekers collect funds from the fund providers, not from the banks, by borrowing on the internet platform, on the condition of repayment on the agreed date (Atsan & Erdoğan, 2015). In this model, while fund seekers have the opportunity to finance by paying interest, those who provide funds without the mediation of banks also earn interest income (Beaulieu et al., 2015). This funding model is currently the largest crowdfunding method with the largest trading volume in the crowdfunding market at approximately 99.6% (Schmidt, 2020). The reason why debt-based crowdfunding has such a large share is that the platforms in China collect huge funds with this method. Regionally, debt-based crowdfunding is 99.7% in China, 93.3% in the USA, 89.8% in the UK, 83.5% in the Asia-Pacific region excluding China and 79.1% in Europe, compared with other crowdfunding methods (Garvey et al., 2017).

People often take advantage of debt-based crowdfunding for home renovation, credit card reloading, car or home purchase, and many other personal reasons. Crowd2fund, Zopa and Funding Circle, Lending Club, Prosper, and Peerform are examples of KF platforms operating in the debt-based model (Monica, 2020).

Another type of crowdfunding application is equity-based crowdfunding, which allows equity investment and profit sharing to businesses or projects. This type of crowdfunding is less developed than other types due to its complexity and regulatory constraints, so it has the lowest transaction volume in the crowdfunding market (Nesta, 2012; Kirby & Worner, 2014; Atsan & Erdoğan, 2015). In equity-based crowdfunding, entrepreneurs present their business ideas to investors through the platform, and those investors who think the project has a promising future become partners by purchasing shares in the business. Entrepreneurs, instead of reaching only one investor or a limited number of investors, meet their financing needs faster and by maintaining the management of their business with the funds they collect from a large number of investors in small amounts. The aim of the investors who become partners in the project or the business by purchasing shares may be to get a share of the profit, to obtain voting rights or to gain value increase (Röthler & Wenzlaff, 2011). Although it is possible to generate more income with this method, the fact that the participants are entitled to the shares they obtain complicates the management of the company (Demiray & Burnaz, 2019). Examples of platforms operating in this model are Ourcrowd, Crowd Cube, Seedrs and Syndicate Room, AngelList, Wefunder and Start Engine. A comparison of crowdfunding financing models is shown in Table 5.3 (Monica, 2020; Best et al., 2013):

Table 5.3: Key Features of Crowdfunding Models

Model	Business Model	Pros	Cons
Donation	Donation-based donors Money is used to support a charitable project or sponsor an individual	No risk	Donors do not acquire security interest. Entrepreneurs have difficulty raising substantial capital.
Donation	Reward-based supporters Investors receive some kind of reward in return for the investment. The reward may be tangible or intangible	Low risk (primarily fulfillment and fraud risk). No real potential for financial return	Potential return is small. No security is acquired, and there is no accountability mechanism. Most entrepreneurs may have difficulty raising substantial capital without a product with mass appeal to sell.
Reward	Equity-based investors Investors receive equity in the firm in return for the investment provided by them	Potential to share in the profitability of the venture. Unlimited potential for financial gain. May attract relatively large numbers of investors.	Potential loss of investment. Equity holders are subordinate to creditors in the event of bankruptcy. Securities laws related to crowdfund investing may be complex.
Reward	Lending-based investors Investors receive interest in return for the funding	Pre-determined rate of return agreed upon between the lender and borrower. Debt holders are senior to equity holders in the	May be subordinate to senior creditors. Start-ups' high-failure rate presents similar risk of loss as an equity investment, but with capped

	provided by them	case of bankruptcy. Secured status may make it easier for entrepreneurs to raise capital.	potential returns. Requires a business already generating cash flow. Existing/established, cash flow positive businesses may consider this option because they can offer a more structured exit opportunity than typical equity offerings.

Source: Best et al., 2013:20; Monica, 2020: https://medium.com/@mahzeb/top-10-crowdfunding-platforms-of-2020-b837efcf25c2

The most common and preferred crowdfunding platforms in the world are Kickstarter, Indiegogo, Crowdfunder, AngelList, GoFundMe, Patreon, Funding Circle, Seeders, CrowdRise, and Give (Monica, 2020). In practice, two types of platforms have emerged: "All-Or-Nothing" (AON), and “Keep-It-All” (KIA) (Cumming et al., 2014; Freedman & Nutting, 2015). In the AON model, if the amount collected from the funders within the specified period is below the fund amount determined by the project owner, the project is considered to be unsuccessful and the money that the funders committed is not withdrawn from their credit cards. In the case that the project fails, the project owner has not been able to receive any funding. The success of this model is only possible if the specified amount of money is collected within the target period. Platforms such as Circle Up and Kickstarter are built on the AON model. In the KIA model, the amount collected during the campaign period is transferred to the entrepreneur regardless of the recovery of the targeted amount. In the KIA model, the commission rates received by the platforms may be higher. Projects using the AON model have higher targeted funds and a higher probability of success than projects using the KIA model. According to a study based on IndieGoGo data, while the chances of success of big projects increase in the KIA model, it has been determined that the AON model, where the entrepreneur takes on all the risks, is more suitable for small projects (Cumming et al., 2014).

Types of Crowdfunding

The intermediary role of traditional financial institutions between fund seekers and funders is generally also present in the crowdfunding system. But crowdfunding has some important differences and advantages over traditional funding. These can be expressed as follows (Anbar, 2000):

- Opportunities to reach more people
- Eliminating time and geographical border barriers
- Democratization of capital and transparency
- Specificity and value change
- Simplicity and convenience
- Using it as a market research and marketing tool
- Lower capital cost and higher return opportunity
- Distribution of risk.

The advantages of crowdfunding can be listed as follows (Kirby & Worner, 2014; Zengin et al., 2017);

- Combining entrepreneurship financing and social networking opportunities
- Changing the funding cycle, expanding the geographical range of angel investment
- Product validation, supporting networks and providing collaboration
- Providing access to support networks
- Allowing for the market and cooperation
- Helping economic growth by increasing credit flows to SMEs and other users in the real economy
- Filling the gap left by banks
- Presenting a new product for portfolio diversification
- Effective cost
- Increasing competition.

Just as every financing method has advantages and disadvantages, crowdfunding has some drawbacks and risks. One of these risks in terms of fund seekers is that the project is not accepted by the crowdfunding platform or, even if it is accepted, the targeted fund amount cannot be reached within the specified period (Holtland & Van Heck, 2019). Some young and inexperienced entrepreneurs may fail to manage and therefore fail in the fundraising process in terms of project preparation, presentation, and communication with potential funders (Fettahoğlu & Khusayan, 2017). There are also some risks for funders. For example, in reward-based crowdfunding, fund seekers may not deliver on time or not deliver their promised rewards in exchange for the raised funds. Fund seekers may not be able to fulfill their obligations such as interest and principal repayments. In share-based crowdfunding, investors may experience difficulties in liquidity by selling their shares due to the underdeveloped secondary markets. Fund seekers may not reveal all the information about their projects or provide information about potential risks. This situation may cause asymmetric information and transparency problems in terms of fund providers. Apart from these, failure, organizational closure, and cyber-attack are also risks that can occur in crowdfunding (Kirby & Worner, 2014; Polena & Regner 2016).

Conclusion

The economic crisis experienced in 2008 clearly revealed the fragility of entrepreneurs in accessing traditional financial resources. The damage caused by the Covid-19 epidemic, which started to spread around the world in early 2020, significantly restricts the access of entrepreneurs who want to start a new enterprise to the necessary financial resources and makes the crowdfunding method more attractive. Crowdfunding was initially a method mostly used by charities and artists, but later became an alternative financing method for startups and innovative entrepreneurial ideas (Schwienbacher & Larralde, 2010).

Crowdfunding, which was first introduced in the UK in 2007, was implemented in China in 2013, a date that can be considered a little later than in other countries. With the help of its performance in the field of technology and its increase in production capacity in recent years, China has become the biggest player in crowdfunding, leaving the USA behind in 2018. In 2019, China had a 37% share in the global crowdfunding market, while the USA had a share of 32% and Europe 18% (QYR_Research 2020).

Crowdfunding uses crowd-based decision-making and innovation to implement the financing of products, businesses and projects. Individuals and companies using social media and web-based communications have raised billions of dollars in donations, debt, and equity for their projects over the past five years. For example, Kickstarter, the market leader in donation-based crowdfunding, has raised over $815 million from 4.9 million supporters worldwide (29% invested in multiple projects) since 2009. According to the estimates of the World Bank, crowdfunding is expected to reach a transaction volume of $96 billion in 2025. China stands out in the crowdfunding market with a resource expectation of $50 billion (Best et al., 2013).

Due to the fact that the internet is a "borderless" entity, legal regulations must come to the countries where these websites operate. “Crowdfunding” is a formation that emerged with the supply-demand dynamics and innovation of markets, and legitimizing this formation with a regulation framework that will exclude the possibilities of “abuse” and limit the risks exposed will contribute to the diversity of the financial system.

Keywords: *Crowdfunding, crowdsourcing, entrepreneurship*

References

Agrawal, A., Catalini, C. and Goldfarb, A. (2013) The Simple Economics of Crowdfunding, Innovatio n Policy and the Economy. Chicago: University Press.

Akyüz, A. (2016). *Yeni Medya Araştırmaları 2. M.G. Genel (Der.), Sosyal medyada kitlelerin gücü: Kitlesel fonlama:79-94*. Bursa: Ekin Yayınevi.

Aldrich, H. E. (2014). The Democratization of Entrepreneurship? Hackers, Makespaces, and Crowdfunding. *Academy of Management Annual Meeting,* 2014 (1).

Armendáriz, B., & Morduch, J. (2010). *The economics of microfinance*. MIT press.

Atsan, N. & Erdoğan, E. O. (2015). Girişimciler için alternatif bir finansman yöntemi: Kitlesel fonlama. *Eskişehir Osmangazi Üniversitesi İİBF Dergisi, 10*(1): 297- 320.

Beaulieu, T., Sarker, S., & Sarker, S. (2015). A conceptual framework for understanding crowdfunding. *Communications of the Association for Information Systems, 37*(1), 1.

Belleflamme, P., Lambert, T., & Schwienbacher, A. (2010, June). Crowdfunding: An industrial organization perspective. *In Prepared for the workshop Digital Business Models: Understanding Strategies', held in Paris on June* (pp. 25-26).

Bellavitis, C., Filatotchev, I., Kamuriwo, D. S., ve Vanacker, T. (2017). Entrepreneurial finance: New frontiers of research and practice. *Venture Capital, 19*(1-2), 1-16.

Best, J., Neiss, S., Swart, R., Lambkin, A. & Raymond, S. (2013) *Crowdfunding's potential for the developing world.*

http://documents.worldbank.org/curated/en/409841468327411701/Crowdfundings-potential-for-the-developing-world (Accessed: 20/09/2020).

Blohm, I., Leimeister, J. M., Wenzlaff, K., & Gebert, M. (2013). Crowdfunding-Studie 2013/14. *Analysen, Perspektiven und Erfolgsfaktoren innovativer Unternehmens-und Projektfinanzierungen*. epubli.

Brabham, D. C. (2009). Crowdsourcing the public participation process for planning projects. *Planning Theory, 8*(3), 242-262.

Bradford, C. S. (2012). Crowdfunding and the federal securities laws. *Columbia Business Law Review*, *1*, 1-150.

Bradley III, D. B., & Luong, C. (2014). Crowdfunding: A new opportunity for small business and entrepreneurship. *The Entrepreneurial Executive, 19*, 95.

Bretschneider, U., Knaub, K., & Wieck, E. (2014). Motivations for crowdfunding: What drives the crowd to invest in start-ups? *ECIS 2014 Proceedings - 22nd European Conference on Information Systems, Tel Aviv.*

Brophy, D. J., & Shulman, J. M. (1992). A finance perspective on entrepreneurship research. *Entrepreneurship Theory and Practice, 16*(3), 61-72.

Chervyakov, D., & Rocholl, J. (2019). *How to make crowdfunding work in Europe* (No. 2019/6). Bruegel Policy Contribution.

Cicchiello, A. F. (2019). Harmonizing the crowdfunding regulation in Europe: need, challenges, and risks. *Journal of Small Business & Entrepreneurship,* 1-22.

Cumming, D., Leboeuf, G., & Schwienbacher, A. (2014). Crowdfunding Models: Keep-it-All vs. All-or-Nothing. *SSRN Electronic Journal.* doi:10.2139/ssrn.2447567.

De Buysere, K., Gajda, O., Kleverlaan, R., Marom, D., & Klaes, M. (2012). A framework for European crowdfunding, https://www.fundraisingschool.it/wp-content/uploads/2013/02/European-Crowdfunding-Framework-Oct-2012.pdf (Accessed: 20/09/2020).

Demiray, M., & Burnaz, S. (2019). Positioning of crowdfunding platforms: Turkey as an emerging market case. *Journal of Management Marketing and Logistics, 6*(2), 84-94.

Er, B., Şahin, E., & Mutlu, M. (2015). Girişimciler için alternatif finansman kaynakları: Mevcut durum ve öneriler. *Uluslararası Ekonomi ve Yenilik Dergisi, 1*(1), 31-54.

Fettahoğlu, S. & Khusayan, S. (2017). Yeni finansman olanağı: Kitle fonlama. *Uşak Üniversitesi Sosyal Bilimler Dergisi, 10*(4), 497-521.

Fiedler, S., & Horsch, A. (2014). Crowdinvesting als finanzierungsalternative. *ZfKE–Zeitschrift für KMU und Entrepreneurship, 62*(1), 91-98.

Freedman, D. M., & Nutting, M. R. (2015). *Equity crowdfunding for investors: A guide to risks, returns, regulations, funding portals, due diligence, and deal terms*. John Wiley & Sons.

Freeman, R. E. (2010). Strategic management: A stakeholder approach. Cambridge University Press.

Garvey, K., Ziegler, T., Zhang, B. Z., Wardrop, R., Rau, P. R., Gray, M., & Ridler, S. (2017). Crowdfunding in East Africa: Regulation and policy for market development. *Available at SSRN 3621303.*

Gerber, E. M., Hui, J. S., & Kuo, P. Y. (2012, February). Crowdfunding: Why people are motivated to post and fund projects on crowdfunding platforms. In *Proceedings of the international workshop on design, influence, and social technologies: techniques, impacts and ethics, 2*(11),10. Northwestern University Evanston, IL.

Gobble, M. M. (Ed.). (2012). Everyone is a venture capitalist: The new age of crowdfunding. *Research technology management, 55*(4), 4-7.

Gulati, S. 2014. Crowdfunding: A Kick Starter for Startups Special Report, *TD Economics,* 29 January: 1-19.

Harrisson, R. (2013). Crowdfunding and the revitalization of the early-stage risk capital market: catalyst or chimera? *Venture Capital: An International Journal of Entrepreneurial Finance, 15(*4,) 283-287.

Hemer, J., Schneider, U., Dornbusch, F., & Frey, S. (2011). *Crowdfunding und Andere Formen Informeller Mikrofinanzierung in der Projekt-und Innovationsfinanzierung*, Final Report. Karlsruhe: Fraunhofer ISI.

Holtland, H. & Vicky, V. H. (2019). *Institutional Investors & Crowdfunding: The Right Match*. Whitepaper, VBDO.

Howe, J. (2006). The Rise of Crowdsourcing. *Wired Magazine, 14*(6), 1-5.

Howe, J. (2008). *Crowdsourcing: How the power of the crowd is driving the future of business.* Random House.

Indiegogo (2020). An Hour of Code for Every Student. https://www.indiegogo.com/projects/an-hour-of-code-for-every-student (Accesed: 20/09/2020).

İşler, S. T. (2014). Modern finansmanda yeni bir dönem: Kitlesel fonlama-crowdfunding. *Gösterge*, Sonbahar, 51-65.

Joenssen, D., Michaelis, A., & Müllerleile, T. (2014). A link to new product preannouncement: Success factors in crowdfunding. *Available at SSRN 2476841.*

Kappel, T. (2008). Ex ante crowdfunding and the recording industry: A model for the US. *Loy. LA Ent. L. Rev., 29*, 375.

Karaarslan, M. H., & Altuntaş, B. (2015). Sosyal pazarlamanın yeni aracı: Kitle fonlaması. 20. *Ulusal Pazarlama Kongresi Bildiri Kitabı, Anadolu Üniversitesi-Eskişehir*, 487-497.

Karasioğlu, F., Duman, H. (2006). Gelişmekte olan ülkelerde girişimcilik kültürü ve risk sermayesi üzerine bir inceleme", *Kırgızistan-Türkiye Manas Üniversitesi Uluslararası Girişimcilik Kongresi, 25- 27 Mayıs 2006*, 145- 158.

Kickstarter (2020a). *Coolest cooler: 21st century cooler that's actually cooler.* https://www.kickstarter.com/projects/ryangrepper/coolest-cooler-21st-century-cooler-thats-actually (Accessed: 20/09/2020).

Kickstarter (2020b). *Pebble time- awesome smartwatch, no compromises.* https://www.kickstarter.com/projects/getpebble/pebble-time-awesome-smartwatch-no-compromises (Accessed: 20/09/2020).

Kirby, E., & Worner, S. (2014). Crowd-funding: An infant industry growing fast. *IOSCO Research Department*. https://www.finextra.com/finextra-downloads/newsdocs/crowd-funding-an-infant-industry-growing-fast.pdf (Accessed: 20/09/2020).

Kleemann, F., Voß, G. G., & Rieder, K. (2008). Un (der) paid innovators: The commercial utilization of consumer work through crowdsourcing. *Science, technology & innovation studies, 4*(1), 5-26.

Kuti, M., & Madarász, G. (2014). Crowdfunding. *Public Finance Quarterly, 59*(3), 355.

Lambert, T., & Schwienbacher, A. (2010). An empirical analysis of crowdfunding. *Social Science Research Network, 1578175*, 1-23.

Laplume, A. O., Sonpar, K., & Litz, R. A. (2008). Stakeholder theory: Reviewing a theory that moves us. *Journal of Management*, *34*(6), 1152-1189.

Leimeister, J.M. (2012). Crowdsourcing: crowdfunding, crowdvoting, crowdcreation, *Zeitschrift für Controlling und Management, 2012*(56) 388-392.

Leimeister, J.M. & Zogaj, S. (2013). Neue Arbeitsorganisation durch Crowdsourcing, *Hans-Böckler-Stiftung Arbeitspapier Arbeit und Soziales*, *2013*(287).

Meinshausen, S., Schiereck, D., & Stimeier, S. (2012). Crowdfunding als finanzierungsalternative. *WiSt-Wirtschaftswissenschaftliches Studium, 41*(11), 583-588.

Monica, M. (2020). *Top 10 Crowdfunding Platforms of 2020.* https://medium.com/@mahzeb/top-10-crowdfunding-platforms-of-2020-b837efcf25c2 (Accessed: 20/09/2020).

Nesta (2012). An Introduction to Crowdfunding. https://www.em-a.eu/fileadmin/content/REALISE_IT_2/REALISE_IT_3/IntroToCrowdfunding.pdf (Accesed: 20/09/2020).

Niederer, S., & Van Dijck, J. (2010). Wisdom of the crowd or technicity of content? Wikipedia as a sociotechnical system. *New Media & Society, 12*(8), 1368-1387.

Ordanini, A., Miceli, L., Pizzetti, M., & Parasuraman, A. (2011). Crowdfunding: Transforming customers into investors through innovative service platforms. *Journal of Service Management, 22*(4), 443-470.

Pierrakis, Y. (2019). Peer-to-peer lending to businesses: Investors' characteristics, investment criteria and motivation. *The International Journal of Entrepreneurship and Innovation, 20*(4), 239-251.

Polena, M. & Regner, T. (2016). Determinants of Borrowers Default in P2P Lending Under Consideration of The Loan Risk Class. *Jena Economic Research Papers, No. 2016-023*, Friedrich Schiller University Jena

QYR Research (2020). *Global Crowdfunding Market Report, History and Forecast 2015-2026.* https://www.qyresearch.com/index/detail/1638305/global-crowdfunding-market (Accessed: 20/09/2020).

Richter, C., Seidler-de Alwis, R., & Jötten, M. (2014). Crowdsourcing als chance für mittelständische unternehmen. *ZfKE–Zeitschrift für KMU und Entrepreneurship, 62*(1), 1-29.

Röthler, D., & Wenzlaff, K. (2011). Crowdfunding schemes in Europe. *EENC Report, 9*, 2011.

Sakızlı, E. (2018). *Alternatif bir finansman yöntemi: Kitlesel fonlama.* İstanbul: İktisadi Kalkınma Vakfı.

Schmidt, J. (2020). Crowdfunding Statistics Worldwide: Market Development, Country Volumes, and Industry Trends. https://p2pmarketdata.com/crowdfunding-statistics-worldwide/ (Accessed: 20/09/2020).

Schwienbacher, A., & Larralde, B. (2010). *Crowdfunding of small entrepreneurial ventures. Handbook of entrepreneurial finance*, Oxford University Press, Forthcoming.

Starbird, K. (2012). What" Crowdsourcing" Obscures: Exposing the Dynamics of Connected crowd work during disaster. *arXiv preprint arXiv:1204.3342.*

Statista, (2020a). *Worldwide digital population as of October 2020.* https://www.statista.com/statistics/617136/digital-population-worldwide/ (Accessed: 20/09/2020).

Statista, (2020b). Smartphone users worldwide 2016-2021. https://www.statista.com/statistics/330695/number-of-smartphone-users-worldwide/ (Accessed: 20/09/2020).

Surowiecki, J. (2004). *The wisdom of crowds: Why the many are smarter than the few and how collective wisdom shapes business, economies, societies, and nations*, New York: Doubleday.

Tomczak, A., & Brem, A. (2013). A conceptualized investment model of crowdfunding. *Venture Capital, 15*(4), 335-359.

Unterberg, U. (2010) *Crowdsourcing*, In Michelis, D. and Schildhauer, T. (eds.), *Social Media Handbuch: Theorien, Methoden, Modelle*. Baden-Baden: Nomos Verlag, 121-135.

Vitale, M. (2013). Crowdfunding: Recent international developments and analysis of its compatibility with Australia's existing regulatory framework. *Available at SSRN 2324573.*

Voorbraak, K. J. P. M., Tanrisever, F., & Mahieu, R. J. (2011). *Crowdfunding for financing new ventures: Consequences of the financial model on operational decisions*. Technische Universiteit Eindhoven.

Wenzlaff, K., (2012). Definition von crowdfunding. http://www.ikosom.de/2012/06/11/definition-von-crowdfunding-beta/ (Accesed: 20/09/2020).

Zademach, H. M., & Baumeister, C. (2014). Wagniskapital und entrepreneurship: grundlagen, empirische befunde, entwicklungstrends. In *Wertschöpfungskompetenz und Unternehmertum* (121-144). Springer Gabler, Wiesbaden.

Zengin, S., Yüksel, S., & Kartal, M. T. (2017). Kitle fonlaması sisteminin Türkiye'ye faydaları (Benefits of crowdfunding system to Turkey). *Banka ve Sermaye Piyasası Araştırmaları Dergisi, BSPAD, 1*(2).

Zvilichovsky, D., Inbar, Y., & Barzilay, O. (2015). Playing both sides of the market: Success and reciprocity on crowdfunding platforms. *Available at SSRN 2304101.*

CHAPTER SIX

TWO INTERSECTING CLUSTERS: THE TQM APPROACH AND ERP SYSTEMS

MEHMET CIRANOĞLU

Introduction

While studies in the field of business often focus on productivity, efficiency and costs, these concepts are attempted to be filled. What is meant by filling these concepts is the search for an answer to the question of what approaches and practices will provide these results for businesses. At the beginning of the 1900s, efforts to develop scientific approaches to management began (by Taylor, 1911) and various approaches have been put forward since then.

Among these approaches, the total quality management (TQM) approach, whose validity has been proven especially in Japan, has been the most widely studied and one of the most common approaches in practice (Flynn et al., 1994: 342).

One of the most important goals of any business is to satisfy its customers. For this reason, tracking customer needs and any development based on these needs will contribute to the total quality of the product. Efforts to improve all kinds of processes and the integration of the business with customers, employees, suppliers, and ultimately with each other, are included in the development (Gitlow et al., 1989: 23).

Being in continuous development in a competitive environment is only possible if the quality approach covers all activities of the enterprise (Madu et al., 1996: 57). TQM, which is constantly developing with various applications and models, is an approach with this inclusive perspective. While this approach requires a collective change in organizational culture, it obliges all employees, processes, production tools and products to be handled in an integrated manner (EFQM, 2011: 28).

The main purpose of TQM is to fully meet customer expectations on time and every time. In this respect, ensuring customer satisfaction requires the participation of all departments and all employees in the organization (Cravens and Shipp, 1991: 55).

One of the factors that support efficiency in a business is IT applications. However, IT applications, which were initially seen as a support element, have become one of the main sources of efficiency for businesses with rapid developments in this field. Management information systems and software have been important factors in ensuring efficiency (Bessen, 2002: 461; Willcocks and Lester, 1997: 1084).

As an example, an enterprise resource planning (ERP) system is software that combines key business processes (Nah et al., 2001). These systems facilitate the flow of information within the organization, ensuring the integration, optimization and control of all production processes and other processes required to increase efficiency and maintain a competitive position (Basu and Biswas, 2013: 39).

So, in order to stand out against the competition, TQM's comprehensive management approach is needed, and in order for this understanding to be effective within the organization, the integrated data/information flow provided by ERP systems is needed. From this point of view, it can be said that the intersection set of TQM and ERP systems is "integration".

In this study, it will be revealed that intersection points to the TQM approach, which envisages an inclusive (integrated) management approach as a philosophy, and the ERP software that envisages an interdependent (integrated) system on the data/information plane in practice.

The TQM Approach and ERP Systems

TQM is a management system based on customer satisfaction for all its activities, originating in America and developed in Japan. Although there is no consensus on the definition and scope of TQM, which is used by businesses in many countries to gain competitive advantage, it can be defined as an approach that increases the competitiveness, efficiency and flexibility of an organization as a whole (Oakland, 1993: 3). TQM is a management philosophy and set of rules that are based on continuous improvement and progress in the organizational structure (Dale and Cooper, 1994: 20). TQM is a management style that prioritizes the development of all processes, products and services through full participation, maintains internal and external customer expectations above all, and creates the quality defined by the customer within the product and service during the execution of all activities (Konstadt, 1990: 83). The

TQM philosophy is a whole with its principles and techniques, and as understood by the word total, it starts from the idea that every decision taken in the organization, every activity and process carried out, has an impressive role in product and service quality.

Elements of TQM can be summarized as customer focus, "human first" understanding, full participation, continuous improvement and group work (Garvin, 1991: 84; Oakland, 1993: 12). TQM is based on continuous improvement, the aim of which is not to reach a certain standard, but to improve the level continuously and at a fast pace (Flynn et al., 1994: 341).

The main benefits of TQM can be stated as the development of the market power of the products, the increase of the company image, the reduction of waste, the development of resource use, the reduction of costs, the possibility of quality assurance activities, the reduction of audit costs, the motivation of distribution channels and employees, and the development of competitive power as a result (Morden, 1993: 183).

By ERP systems, we mean the whole technology, applications and services that serve to collect, store, process, access and distribute information (Ang et al., 2000). The ERP system is a formal information system that collects, processes, stores and reports the data required for management to make decisions from different sources. Formal information systems can be computer-aided or manual. However, today when it comes to ERP systems, computer-aided information systems come to mind. Computer-aided information systems rely on computer software and hardware technology to process and write information (Laudon & Laudon, 1996: 9). Like every system, ERP systems consist of certain parts that are related to each other. The six parts of these systems are the inputs that form the center of any information system, processes, data files and outputs, as well as the hardware and people that use and control them (Hicks, 1993: 3).

In the early 1980s, information systems were generally classified as data processing systems or management information systems. There are six types of information systems, although the boundaries between them are not very clear today. These are business transaction systems, office automation systems, senior management information systems, expert systems, decision support systems and management information systems (Hicks, 1993: 157).

ERP systems, which are included in management information systems and can be designed module by module, developed rapidly in the second half of the 1990s (Forslund, 2010: 353). These systems, which contribute to a management's effective and rapid decision-making, have become professional over time and gained a specificity to focus on each process separately (Gupta and Kohli, 2006: 691). The success of an ERP system in any business is possible with the presence of people who know the processes within the business, and can correctly construct and discover the inter-process relations. The presence of these people is as important as the software skills of those who designed the ERP system. In a business, people who take this holistic view of processes are usually quality managers concerned with the effectiveness of processes (Laframboise and Reyes, 2005: 51).

The purpose of this study is to explain the intersection points of ERP systems, which include integrating processes from the outside, and TQM concepts which include integrating internally (Themistocleous et al., 2001: 197).

The Intersection Points of the TQM Approach and ERP Systems

The main purpose of TQM is to fully meet customer expectations on time and every time, and this goal requires the participation of all departments and employees in the organization (Cravens & Shipp, 1991: 55).

The "customer satisfaction chain" indicates that business activities should be handled as a process. It starts with the determination of customer needs and requests and ends with meeting them. Another important point is that the customer satisfaction process is continuous, with products being modified and new products being developed in parallel with the changes in requirements and demand. Ensuring customer satisfaction requires the inclusion in the quality management process of all employees and departments within the business, and all suppliers and customers outside the business. This relies on the establishment of interdepartmental cooperation based on group work within the enterprise, and the development of cooperation with suppliers and customers outside the enterprise. This necessary cooperation for the successful implementation of TQM, requires the establishment of a communication system that will organize internal and external relations and allow the maximum benefit of information.

In the light of the explanations made so far, it is understood that knowledge is a fundamental factor in the successful application of TQM. As a matter of fact, Juran and Deming emphasize the importance of data collection and analysis in quality improvement. This reveals the importance of ERP systems as an effective tool in collecting, processing and distributing information (Jurison, 1994: 6). The place and importance of ERP systems in the TQM approach can be discussed in terms of their contribution to the applications used in the TQM approach.

At this point, the mentioned contribution – or, if we express it within the scope of our study: the intersection points – can be listed as follows (Dale et al., 1994: 7; Saraph et al., 1989: 814; Ahire et al., 1996: 27): *process flow management, customer involvement, involvement of employees in the quality process, cooperation with suppliers, benchmarking* and lastly *quality data and reporting.*

Process Flow Management

Perhaps the most evident issue in the function of ERP systems within the organization is the linking of processes. Inter-departmental data flow is provided by these links established online. This flow contributes to maximizing efficiency while trying to integrate with the least number of errors (Gong et al., 1997: 1022). The fact that data can be seen as both fluid and holistic is a situation that makes the job of decision-makers quite easy. Managers who can see the relationship and permeability between processes as a whole can make decisions faster (Gupta and Kohli, 2006: 689). In addition, each datum can be evaluated comparatively at any time, providing important power to prevent possible problems. Seeing a process flow from supply to after-sales services in a holistic manner is a valuable resource for businesses in every sense (Furslund, 2010: 354).

On the other hand, if the subject is handled separately for processes, the three-dimensional contribution of ERP systems can be seen. It is important to be able to categorize the data of each process which shed light on the processes before and after, and to be able to compile instant data simultaneously (Laframboise and Reyes, 2005: 50). This contribution, which means that decision-makers who manage processes can detect errors that are not caused by them, is one of the desired results in most quality proposals when evaluated together with the support of senior management (Themistocleous et al., 2001: 199).

Customer Involvement

The essence of TQM is to ensure continuous customer satisfaction by producing in accordance with the needs and wishes of the customer. In order to achieve this, information about the expectations of the customer and the performance of the product must be collected continuously. Getting customers' expectations and opinions about the product will increase the quality of the product. For this, a database related to customers should be created. Recently, new techniques such as "quality function development" (Quality House) have been developed in order to include customer demands in the new product development process. The main purpose of quality function development is to involve the customer in the design process to determine what the customer really wants (Chase & Aquilano, 1998: 178-179). At this point, ERP systems play an important role in ensuring customer participation because the ERP system can help to determine the alternatives that will best meet the customer needs by comparing the product features with the customer needs. It also provides the opportunity to arrange the products in a suitable way for the customers; for example, a travel company can easily and quickly determine a holiday option that suits the customer's specific needs through ERP systems. Another example can be given from the cosmetics industry. Companies like Elizabeth Arden and Shiseido use information technology to increase their sales. The system allows the cosmetologist to automatically try different makeup combinations on the computer and even determine the most suitable product for the skin structure of the customer (Alter, 1996: 309). Information technologies are also used to achieve "mass customization", which is the essence of TQM, in providing customer satisfaction. This approach is widely used, for example, in the construction of prefabricated houses in Japan. The sellers design the house in accordance with the wishes of the person by bringing together thousands of parts that have been produced on the computer, depending on the customer's request. The designed house is delivered to its owner within 30 to 60 working days (Alter, 1996: 310).

Involvement of Employees in the Quality Process

Ensuring the participation of employees in the quality process is critical in quality improvement. Therefore, almost every TQM application constitutes quality improvement groups. In order for these groups to work effectively, they must be equipped with sufficient information in terms of quantity and variety (Rivers & Bae, 1999: 283). This is because the contribution of employees to quality improvement activities depends on whether they have the knowledge necessary to make a decision. Therefore, employees should be adequately informed about the product, production processes, organizational performance, and competing products and services (Matta & Chen, 1998: 448). ERP systems have an important place in ensuring the full participation of employees. By using ERP systems, it will be possible to establish an effective bi-directional communication system between employees within the organization. In this way, an effective communication opportunity will be provided both between managers and employees, and employees and employees (Bradley, 1993: 216). One of the main ways to realize the implementation of quality groups under the TQM umbrella with the support of information technology is to create discussion groups on the intranet (Cravens & Shipp, 1991: 57).

Cooperation with Suppliers

The successful implementation of TQM necessitates some changes in the nature of the relationship with suppliers.

In order to produce quality products and services, all inputs used in the production process must be of high quality. Porter (1985: 33) approaches this issue in terms of the "value chain" and defines the activities between interdependent value chains as value systems. In the value system, the output of any unit is the input of the other, and the mismatch between the output of one unit and the expectation of the customer, due to the incoordination between activities, leads to disruptions and ultimately large amounts of corrective actions. Lindberg and Trygg (1991: 59) divide value activities into two groups, intra and inter activities, in order to emphasize the importance of activities between value chains based on Porter's model. Intra activities include activities within a value chain, while inter activities include activities between value chains that are part of a value system.

Based on this determination of Lindberg and Trygg, it can be said that the successful implementation of TQM requires the support of suppliers to a large extent. As Porter states, whether the buyers can benefit positively from this interdependence between value chains depends on increasing cooperation with suppliers. Establishing a full cooperation model with suppliers requires a bi-directional and transparent flow of information between the buyer and the supplier. ERP systems allow businesses to integrate with suppliers and exchange data very quickly and effectively.

Today, ERP systems are widely used to increase cooperation with suppliers. Long-term relationships are established with a limited number of suppliers, rather than competitive relationships with many suppliers. For example, Ford contracts with its suppliers for at least five years or the life of a particular model. However, in order for any business to be selected as a supplier, it must establish an electronic data exchange connection with Ford and use a computer-aided design (CAD)/computer-aided manufacturing (CAM) system determined by Ford. Similarly, Xerox has reorganized its relationships with its suppliers through its "leadership through quality" program. It is also stated that Benetton regulates its relations with its suppliers through ERP systems and CAD/CAM technologies (Bradley, 1993: 129).

Benchmarking

Benchmarking is an easy concept to define; it is a comparison of the current performance of organizational activities with the performance of an organization outside the organization (usually the best in that sector). The purpose of benchmarking is to determine the organizations and their applications that show superior performance in the relevant process, whether in the sector or not, and to achieve a long-term competitive advantage in the market by adapting these applications to the business (Bradley, 1993: 236). Many businesses have been successful in quality improvement by setting a standard for products, services, and other activities and then measuring performance against that standard.

ERP systems contribute to benchmarking activities in many ways; for example, thanks to the transparent data shared in the market, many companies use ERP software to follow successful applications in product development and analyze them for themselves. Generally, these researches are in an impressive position to realize the Kaizen plan or to develop alternative solutions to problems (Cravens and Shipp, 1991: 54).

Quality Data and Reporting

One of the basic principles foreseen in the TQM approach is the operation of the control mechanism, which is also expressed as "you will write what you do, you will do what you write". The basis of this audit activity, which is designed to increase the efficiency of enterprises with the aim of having the quality and means to follow up every process and function, lies in the collection and reporting of data (Zadrozny & Ferrazzi, 1992: 17). ERP systems play an active role here as well as in collecting and reporting all kinds of data within the organization.

The quality management modules of ERP systems, whose most basic function is to compile, classify and report data (comparatively when necessary), usually collect information that is included in different processes but will be useful for quality management, and reports the information in a holistic perspective within the quality approach. It provides important advantages regarding the steps to be taken (Laframboise and Reyes, 2005: 61).

Conclusion

Today, as a result of economic and technological developments, the globalization of markets has changed the international competition in shape and dimension. While globalization creates an opportunity for businesses due to the increase in production and sales opportunities, it also becomes a threat due to the increase of competitors in national and international markets. The success of businesses in the global competitive environment depends on increasing their ability to meet consumers' increasing expectations in matters such as product quality and reliability, product variety, customer service, etc. This requires the enterprises to make adjustments in their current production systems in a way that allows them to produce quality and flexible production at an appropriate cost level.

As a result of the increase in global competition, consumers are able to choose from products produced in any country in the world, so their expectations about quality increase (Laudon & Laudon, 1996: 477). For this reason, an enterprise operating in the domestic market should take into account the quality level of external competitors as well as internal competitors while determining the quality level of the products and services it produces. The increasing importance given to quality with the changing market structure has made TQM a modern management model by laying the groundwork for the implementation of quality as a management philosophy in enterprises.

In the case that TQM is implemented in order to gain competitive advantage by ensuring customer satisfaction, business managers should take into account that TQM is a knowledge-intensive management system. In other words, for the successful implementation of TQM, they should ensure that more information is obtained and processed in terms of quantity and variety, as well as the establishment of a system that will enable the timely transfer of the obtained information to relevant units inside and outside the enterprise. Otherwise, it will be very difficult to obtain the benefits expected from TQM application. In this context, in this study, the intersection points of ERP systems with TQM are analyzed from two angles. Firstly, due to the effectiveness of an ERP system in collecting, processing and distributing information, its contribution to process flow management, customer participation, the involvement of employees in the quality process, cooperation with suppliers, benchmarking and quality data and reporting approaches, which have a very important place in TQM implementation, has been explained with examples in terms of concretization. Secondly, ERP systems also contribute to the establishment of interdepartmental cooperation based on group work, which is one of the basic elements of TQM implementation.

As a result, considering the contribution that ERP systems can make to the successful implementation of TQM, it can be suggested to business managers that, with the TQM application, businesses should invest in ERP systems suitable for their own structures and needs.

On the other hand, although different quality management systems have been developed in different parts of the world in different periods, it is stated that the successful implementation of any of these quality management systems will help others to increase their effectiveness. For this reason, it is recommended that organizations adopt any of these quality management systems with a clear purpose and consistently follow the principles and methodologies stipulated by the quality system in question until they reach their goals (Kumar et al., 2017: 1057).

ERP and TQM implementation levels are positively correlated, indicating that there are similar factors that make businesses choose ERP and TQM (Laframboise & Reyes, 2005: 53). One of these factors can be attributed to skilled human resource elements, namely workforce management and employees' attitudes and behaviors (Martinez-Lorente et al., 2004: 88), as today's business environment requires managers to use more advanced technologies and management systems. More qualified employees have the skills to use ERP and get the most out of TQM. Another factor is that both elements (ERP systems and the TQM approach) have the ability to develop a holistic view for the organization. Therefore, it is inevitable that these two elements, which integrate all processes and managers within the enterprises in a flow, will be the source of advanced competitive advantage if integration is achieved between them (Themistocleous et al., 2001: 197).

Keywords: *Digitalization, ERP and TQM*

References

Ahire, S.L., Golhar, D.Y. and Waller, M.A. (1996). Development and validation of TQM implementation constructs, *Decision Sciences*, 27(1): 23-56.

Alter, S., (1996). *Information Management: A Management Perspective*, The Benjamin Cummings Publishing Co., California.

Ang C., M. Davies and Paul, N.F. (2000). Measures to assess the impact of information technology on quality management, *International Journal of Quality & Reliability Management*, 17: 42-66.

Basu, R. and Biswas, D. (2013). An Approach to Identify Failure Factors of Enterprise Application Implementation in Indian Micro Enterprises. *International Journal of Managing Value Supply Chains*, 4(1): 37–47.

Bessen, J. (2002). Technology adoption costs and productivity growth: The transition to information technology. *Review of Economic Dynamics*, 5(2): 443–469.

Bradley, S.P. (1993). The Role of IT Networking in Sustaining Competitive Advantage, S.P. Bradely, J.E. Hausman ve R.L. Nolan (Ed.), *Globalization, Technology and Competition*, Harvard Business School Press, Boston.

Chase, R.B. and Aquilano, N.J. (1995). *Production and Operations Management*, 7th. Ed., Irwin, London.

Cravens, D.W. and Shipp, S.H. (1991). Market Driven Strategies for Competitive Advantage, *Business Horizons*, 34 (1): 53-61.

Dale, B.G., Boaden, R.J. and Lascelles, D.M. (1994). `Total quality management: an overview', in Dale, B.G. (Ed.) *Managing Quality*, Prentice Hall International, Hemel Hempstead, pp. 3-40.

EFQM Publishing, (2011). *Introducing to EFQM Excellence Model*, EFQM Pub., Brussels.

Flynn, B.B., Schroeder, R.G. and Sakakibara, S. (1994). A framework for quality management research and an associated measurement instrument, *Journal of Operations Management*,11 (4): 339-366.

Forslund, H. (2010). ERP systems' capabilities for supply chain performance management, *Industrial Management & Data Systems*, 110(3): 351-367.

Garvin, D.A. (1991). How the Baldrige Award really works, *Harvard Business Review*, 69(6): 80-95.

Gitlow, H., Gitlow, S., Oppenheim, A. and Oppenheim, R. (1989). *Tools and Methods for the Improvement of Quality*. IRWIN Pub., Boston.

Gong, L., Jwo, W. and Tang, K. (1997). Using on-line sensors in statistical process control, *Management Science*, 43(7), 1017-1028.

Gupta, M. and Kohli, A. (2006). Enterprise resource planning systems and its implications for operations function, *Technovation*, 26(5), 687-696.

Hicks, J.O. (1993). *Management Information Systems*, 3rd Ed., West Publishing Company, USA.

Jurison, J. (1994). The Role of Information Systems in Total Quality Management, *Knowledge and Policy*, 7(2), 3-16.

Konstadt, P. (1990). The unending quest for quality, *CIO*, 3(11): 83-5.

Kumar, V., Verma, P., Sharma, R.R.K. and Khan, A.F. (2017). Conquering in emerging markets: critical success factors to enhance supply chain performance, *Benchmarking: An International Journal*, 24(3): 570-593.

Laframboise, K. and Reyes, F. (2005). Gaining competitive advantage from integrating enterprise resource planning and total quality management, *Journal of Supply Chain Management*, 41(3): 49-64.

Laudon, K.C. and Laudon, J.P. (1996). *Management Information Systems*, 4th Ed., Prentice-Hall, New Jersey.

Lindberg, P. and Trygg, L. (1991). Manufacturing Strategy in the Value System, *International Journal of Operations and Production Management*, 11(3): 52-62.

Madu, C.N., Ajeto, J., Kuei, C.H. and Winokur, D. (1996). Adoption of Strategic Total Quality Management Philosophies: Multi-Criteria Decision Analysis Model, *International Journal of Quality & Reliability Management*, 13(3): 57-72

Martinez-Lorente, A.R., Dewhurst, F., and Dale, B.G. (1998). Total quality management: Origins and evolution of the term, *The TQM Magazine,* 10(5): 378–386.

Matta, K. and Chen, H-G. (1998). The Information Requirements of Total Quality Management, *Total Quality Management*, 9(6), 445-461.

Morden, T. (1993). *Business Strategy and Planning: Text and Case*, McGraw-Hill, London.

Nah, F.F., Lau, J.L. and Kuang, J. (2001). Critical Factors for Successful Implementation of Enterprise Systems, *Business Process Management Journal*, 7(3): 285-296.

Oakland, J.S. (1993). *Total Quality Management: The Route to Improving Performance,* 2nd ed., Butterworth Heinemann, London.

Porter, M.E. (1985). *Competitive Advantage*, The Free Press.

Rivers, P.A. and Bae, S. (1999). Aligning Information Systems for Effective Total Quality Management Implementation in Health Care Organizations, *Total Quality Management*, 10 (2): 281-289.

Saraph, J.V., Benson, P.G. and Schroede, R.G. (1989). An instrument for measuring the critical factors of quality management, *Decision Sciences*, 20(4): 810-829.

Taylor, W. F. (1911). *The Principles of Scientific Management*. Harper and Brothers Publishiers. New York/London.

Themistocleous, M., Irani, Z. and O'Keefe, R.M. (2001). ERP and application integration, *Business Process Management Journal*, 7(3): 195-204.

Willcocks, L.P. and Lester, S. (1997). In search of information technology productivity: Assessment issues. *Journal of the Operational Research Society*, 48(11): 1082–1094.

Zadrozny, M.A and Ferrazzi, K.E. (1992). Building a technology base for TQM, *Chief Information Officer Journal*, 5(2): 16-21.

CHAPTER SEVEN

TOWARD A NEW HYBRID MODEL IN PUBLIC ADMINISTRATION: HUMAN AND ARTIFICIAL INTELLIGENCE

ŞERAFETTIN ERTEN

Introduction

Debates and transformation in the field of public administration have recently focused on two main axes. The first includes transferring business understanding to public administration and the problems in the implementation of public transformation and recommendations for solutions to these problems. The second pertains to the effects of new technologies on public administrations developing both within and independently from the first axis.

Since the last quarter of the twentieth century, public administrations have been exposed to criticisms of clumsiness, unproductivity and inefficiency. They found the answer just next to them. The idea of transferring private sector structures, practices and techniques to the public sector, which can be regarded as a kind of isomorphism, has been put into practice under the new public management (NPM) theory. Different practices such as privatization, sharing administrative responsibility, restructuring, total quality management and strategic management have emerged within the framework of the NPM approach (Brown et al., 2003; Dunleavy et al., 2006). However, factors such as the increasingly strengthening globalization wave, technological developments, transformation in the workforce and changing competition conditions have put great pressure on traditional patterns in the production of goods and services. As a result, collaborative structures related to production and management have emerged among sectors (Miller et al., 2008).

In terms of public administrations, this situation has resulted in hybrid structuring consisting of a combination of the private sector and public sector which are regarded as opposite poles. Hybrids as adaptations from two different types of organizations have been designed as structures acting as customer-oriented and productive companies on the one hand, and performing essentially public tasks on the other. Hybrids have had a wide organizational diversity such as public sector, private sector and third sector partnerships, social enterprises, forums, buyer-supplier models and contracts, and administrative networks (Kickert, 2001; Laihonen and Kokko, 2020; Williamson, 1991).

The second important discussion axis in terms of public administrations is the effect of technology. The period in which we live is the process where a major technological transformation occurs on a global scale called the fourth industrial revolution (FIR). The FIR, both qualitatively and quantitatively, includes different technologies that can be transformative for almost all structures such as social, economic, political, etc. (Bruckner et al., 2017). Corvalán (2019) suggests that there are two important features that distinguish the FIR from other technological revolutions. The first is the change in the structure and meaning of time and space concepts due to the intensive use of technology; and the second is the emergence of new ways of data and information processing for many human-specific activities.

The new structure created by the FIR naturally brings with it many risks, difficulties and opportunities for public administrations. Artificial intelligence (AI) is one of the leading technological developments expected to fundamentally change society, including the public sector and public officials. AI systems have been known and used for many years. However, early AI systems were essentially utilized for the automation, support and improvement of daily operational tasks. These systems operated in certain tasks within the framework of defined rules and in a limited way. It is the powerful or super AI that is discussed today and constitutes the subject of this study. These are the systems which try to imitate and go beyond human beings in all areas of intelligence, can simulate the logical-rational and linguistic elements of human intelligence and can improve themselves by their cognitive skills (Etscheid, 2019; Loukis et al., 2019).

It is anticipated that new forms of AI will also lead to great changes in production, employment, labor relations and ways of working as well as in all fields of life (Batra et al., 2017). An increase in the virtual labor force called smart automations both in the public and private sectors, increasing the current labor force skills, labor and capital increase, cost efficiency and savings is considered to be among the essential changes and benefits of AI (Wirtz et al., 2019).

Purdy and Daugherty (2016) consider AI to be a capital-labor force hybrid because AI can perform labor activities much more rapidly and on a much larger scale. It may also take the form of physical capital. As Miller et al. (2008) stated, hybrids are not organizational forms only consisting of the combination of the market and hierarchy. Hybrids are new phenomena produced from two or more elements that are normally separate. Hybridization itself is a process which takes different forms. Hence, they can also be seen as organizational arrangements, practices or forms of expertise that do not correspond to traditional hybrid models. The main assumption of this study is that public administrations whose main capital is human beings (public personnel) will create a new and different hybrid form at least in the short and medium term with the use of artificial intelligence.

Public Administration and Artificial Intelligence

Revolutions in industry and technology have had great and important effects on societies and individuals throughout history (Makridakis, 2017). However, today's technological revolution occurs on a scale and structure unlike the previous ones. Technological innovations such as the internet of things, big data, machine learning and artificial intelligence have begun to deeply shape our lives (Agarwal, 2018). These new technologies update the transformation of muscle power by machines in the past to cognitive power which is now considered as an indispensable human ability (Bruckner et al., 2017). It is now accepted that we are in a new era of automation in which technologies such as robots, artificial intelligence and cognitive information systems seize human performance in many activities including those that require cognitive abilities and even perform them better from time to time (Manyika et al., 2017).

It is considered as inevitable that technological developments will transform traditional administrative structures and processes in the near future (Agarwal, 2018). Therefore, public institutions at all administrative levels from small units to large central administrations try to use these technologies today in order to overcome the problems and provide better services (Mehr, 2017). In this context, the relationship between public administrations and artificial intelligence is discussed as a significant title. However, before starting to analyze this relationship, it should be revealed exactly what we need to understand from the concept of artificial intelligence.

Artificial Intelligence

Intelligence is "the quality that enables a living creature to function accurately, properly and by predicting what is happening in its environment". It is thus a quality found in many living creatures. However, it ranges between the levels of various animals and simple machines at the bottom to human beings at the top. What makes people different from these others is their distinctive features such as reasoning, perception of languages, perception and interpretation of visual and emotional inputs, an ability to synthesize information and the creation of works of art. In this context, AI is “all of the activities to bring intelligence to machines” (Nilsson, 2009).

The early modern studies on AI began with Alan Turing’s paper published in 1950. To replicate intelligence at a human level in a machine was the objective. Different types of AI have emerged in a long line of development. Recent developments in the field have increased the interest in AI. Early AI systems are already in use and their effects are observed. However, it is thought that types of AI that are expected to emerge in the future will make the real change. AI is a technology which includes a heterogeneous set of tools, techniques and algorithms. It includes numerous applications and techniques such as machine learning, perception, reasoning, natural language processing, pattern recognition, deep learning and genetic algorithms. AI is also seen as part of digital systems and cognitive information systems that automate and replicate intelligent behavior (AI Now, 2016; Boyd and Wilson, 2017; Brooks, 1991; Desouza, 2018; Jarrahi, 2018; Nilsson, 2009).

This heterogeneous structure has led to different definitions of AI. Mehr (2017) approached AI as "programming computers to do tasks that normally require human intelligence". This includes the ability to understand and follow visual, spatial and auditory information, reasoning and making predictions, interacting with people and machines and continuous learning and improvement. According to Tinholt et al. (2017) AI is “a technology which allows digital systems to monitor, analyze, move, interact, remember, estimate, sense, moralize and create”. Wirtz and Weyerer (2019) defines AI as "human-like intelligent behavior and problem-solving ability of a computer system through certain basic competencies which include perception, understanding, action and learning".

In terms of defining artificial intelligence, the evolution or classifications in the process are also important, as early or simpler AI practices are already in use as previously mentioned. In general, it is possible to divide the classifications in the literature into three as artificial narrow intelligence (weak), artificial general intelligence (strong) and artificial super intelligence (Etscheid, 2019; Wirtz et al., 2019; Boyd and Wilson, 2017):

- Artificial narrow intelligence: This is the system that is usually able to solve a certain problem only in a certain field and is not able to transfer its abilities to different fields (Rosa and Feyereisl, 2016). In this first level AI is able to perform automated tasks by monitoring, analyzing and acting on the basis of rule-based programming (Tinholt et al., 2017). AI is rather used in this level as a support system in decision-making (Barth and Arnold 1999).
- Artificial general intelligence: This aims to have a human-level skill and problem-solving ability (Rosa and Feyereisl, 2016). In addition to the previous level, it also gains interaction, memory and anticipation abilities. It is able to adapt to new conditions, learn from the previous experiences and make more accurate analyses based on anticipation (Tinholt et al., 2017). In this level, also called expert systems, AI can apply complex logic and establish connections independently. However, it still has a limited mobility depending on the data source it is fed (Barth and Arnold, 1999). The best-known example of this type is DeepBlue developed by IBM. The system consists of a combination of hardware and software with a special use. It became a current issue after beating the world chess champion Garry Kasparov in a chess match in 1997 (Nilsson, 2009).
- Artificial super intelligence: This represents a much more advanced form of software than the human mind. It occurs when a system multiplies a person's intelligence level by several orders of magnitude (Pohl, 2015). In this final level of AI evolution three consciousness levels get involved in addition to other levels. In the third level, AI is able to sense, make morally guided decisions and create new things independently. Unlike its predecessors, artificial super intelligence transforms into an artificial existence that is independent from repetitive and contextualized systems (Tinholt et al., 2017). This final level of AI is incomparably different from the other two levels. Artificial super intelligence is the systems with values and motives which can go beyond the initial programming and acquire judgment abilities thanks to their autonomous and independent learning abilities (Barth and Arnold, 1999). The robot called STAIR made by Andrew Ng, one of the Stanford University professors, can be indicated as an example of these systems. STAIR is a robot which is designed to assist home and office work and can use many methods including machine learning, vision, manual manipulation, planning, reasoning and natural language processing (Nilsson, 2009).

It is the third level of AI which is the subject of discussion and research today, and artificial super intelligence is also considered and discussed in this study. It can interact with people through natural language processing as a cognitive information system. It is context sensitive and remembers the past, i.e., it has a memory and can personalize consequences. It can make reliable recommendations that can be performed by people. It can adapt itself to conditions according to new data and information and can improve itself. It is cyclic and can start over again and again to solve the problems. Most importantly, it constantly collects data and can learn from both data and human interactions repetitively by creating new information and models based on the data it obtains (Desouza, 2018; Desouza et al., 2020; Jarrahi, 2018; Susar and Aquaro, 2019).

As Tinholt et al. (2017) state, AI has "digital eyes, ears, noses, tongues and skins". It collects information through sensors and saves important data. This function gives it cognition. An AI can learn through one of two ways: supervised or unsupervised. In supervised learning each record in data sets is labeled according to the class it belongs to, therefore the system learns what makes a record more or less possible in all data sets. In unsupervised learning the system itself discovers previously unknown patterns or sets in the data (Desouza et al., 2020). In both ways, it processes the information with what it learns, identifies the patterns, perceives the trends, fulfills the tasks and initiates certain processes (Tinholt et al., 2017).

The literature on AI is quite extensive and constantly growing around the discussions. AI is not an issue that can only be discussed technically. It has many dimensions such as social, economic, political, cultural, moral, legal, etc., within the possibilities and practices. Therefore, attitudes and approaches towards AI also change. Makridakis (2017) discusses current attitudes and approaches within the framework of four general trends. The first trend consists of optimists who dream of a utopic future where AI will prevent diseases, create limitless wealth and perform all the activities of human beings, and people will live in prosperity and happiness. The second trend consists of pessimists who rather draw attention to potential dangers. According to pessimists, human beings will only be second-class living creatures or slaves in a world where AIs make all the decisions and do all the work. Another trend consists of beneficiaries. According to the beneficiaries, human beings should definitely use the power of AI and make use of it. However, AI has harms and threats as well as its benefits. Therefore, they argue that we need to be one step ahead in order to prevent possible destructive consequences. The final trend consists of skeptics who believe that artificial intelligence will not be possible and will not be a threat for humanity. Skeptics suggest that no machine will replicate the human brain, so there will be no machine beyond human beings.

Why Artificial Intelligence in Public Administration?

The use of AI in public administration is not a new phenomenon. However, it has been observed that it was used in artificial narrow intelligence and artificial general intelligence levels until recently (Tinholt et al., 2017). The use of computers instead of typewriters and calculators, the widespread use of the internet and information technologies since the 1990s and the use of e-Government 1.0 and the later e-Government 2.0 applications are the most common examples (Charalabidis et al., 2019; Ojo et al., 2019).

Digital technologies and the internet have changed many things for public administrations. The digital government/administration has been very effective, especially in the search for solutions to the problems of the business management approach. In terms of public administrations, the 1990s are considered as the beginning of the post-bureaucratic or post-new public management era. It is noteworthy in this new paradigm that technology is used more intensively as a part of strategic management (Dunleavy et al., 2006; Ojo et al., 2019).

As a result of this trend and due to the developments in AI, the use of AI in various and different public service areas has recently increased in the public sector (Mikhail et al., 2018; Sun and Medaglia, 2019). This great interest also diversifies the AI applications used and to be used in public administrations. According to Wirtz et al. (2019: 3-4) "AI-based information management software, AI process automation systems, virtual units, predictive solutions and data visualization, identity analyses, cognitive robotic and autonomous systems, suggestion systems, smart digital assistants, speech analyses and threat intelligence" are among the leading applications.

As the artificial intelligence applications begin to be more included in public administrations, discussions also increase in parallel. Some of the ideas suggested about positive or negative aspects of AI systems are based on current applications, and some are based on anticipations. However, it is an inevitable process to integrate new technologies into public administrations. Technological developments must be considered as an important part of strategic management in public administrations. Therefore, in the context of current applications and views (Corvalán, 2019; Desouza, 2018; Eggers et al., 2017; Kouziokas, 2017; Mikhail et al., 2018; Ojo et al., 2019; Shrum and Gordon, 2019; Susar and Aquaro, 2019; Tinholt, et al., 2017; Wirtz et al., 2019) a SWOT analysis for artificial intelligence applications in public administrations will be useful in explaining the process.

Table 7.1: Public Administration SWOT Analysis for AI

Strengths	Weaknesses
- Public force privilege - Being able to participate in international governance mechanisms - Current experience about the use of technology - Access to more and larger resources - Hybridization experience - Using executive power	- Resource constraints - Qualified personnel shortage - Bureaucratic processes - Excessive legal rules and regulations - Limitation of movements, stiffness - Being closed to innovation/ Doubt about innovation - Strong resistance to preserving the status quo - Inadequate technological infrastructure in the AI level - Lack of legal framework for AI - Political preferences
Opportunities	**Threats**
- Increase in workforce capabilities - Diversification of public services - Increase in public service quality - Increase in efficiency and productivity - Ability to process large amounts of data - Decrease in workload and shifting human labor to high value services - Efficient use of resources and cost savings - Decrease in stationery and shortening in work times - Real-time monitoring of relevant information - Clearer complex analysis about policies, plans, programs and decisions - Forecasting and managing the crises - The emergence of new jobs and tasks - Creating clearer solutions for public problems - Clearer monitoring of public service consequences - Increase in access to the public - Increase in public value	- Replacement of AI for public personnel - Failure to provide cyber security - Invasion of privacy - Creating ethics and values and conflicts with human ethics and values - Adoption of AI, but distrust for AI by citizens - Disconnection in human-machine and machine-machine interaction - Responsibility of decisions by AI - Control of AI - Violation of the field of rights and freedoms by AI

This analysis has two important deductions for this study. First, despite the current weaknesses and threats, artificial intelligence applications are indispensable for public administrations. Second, public administrations need a series of innovations, including the paradigm and model search, in order to obtain the maximum benefit from artificial intelligence applications.

Hybridization in Public Administration

According to Miller et al. (2008), "impurity is the rule, hybrids are the norms despite the relaxing limits of the areas in which concepts such as economy, society, technology and politics are effective." It is possible to evaluate all actors, creatures, objects, institutions, applications, processes and expertise areas with impurities in the hybrid category. Therefore, as in many fields, in terms of public administration, hybridity is a concept that has a long history, is frequently used and is still discussed (Billis, 2013; Denis et al., 2015; Skelcher, 2012).

Many reasons have been presented for the emergence of hybridization in public administrations. The leading factors that accelerate hybridization are paradigm changes, public reforms, changes in management and governance, blurring of the boundaries between public-private-third-sector organizations, the fact that the environment in which public institutions operate consists of numerous, diverse and sometimes conflicting demands, ideas and needs, and technological developments (Billis, 2013; Christensen and Lægreid, 2011; Denis et al., 2015; Skelcher and Smith, 2015; Polzer et al., 2016).

The fundamentals of today's public administration hybrids are based on new public management and neoliberal economy approaches (Hyyryläinen and Viinamäki, 2011). Especially after the 1980s, with the effect of neoliberal policies, pure public sector forms have regressed and a new public management field with pervious borders has emerged with multiple actors and sectors. With the influence of the business management approach, discussions on public service delivery have been carried out through long-standing dilemmas such as public/private, market/hierarchy and consumer/citizen. Citizens as common producers and non-profit organizations delivering public services, i.e., the "third sector" have also been included in today's discussions (Denis et al., 2015; Dickinson, 2016). Hybridization movements, based on two classical neoliberal principles such as efficiency and productivity in the field of public service in the early periods, resulted in a structure where legitimacy was preferred to productivity at the end of the process (van der Heijden, 2015).

The fact that hybridity is a very meaningful and controversial concept prevented a specific definition of hybrid in the public administration literature. Hybridity in the literature is mostly associated with organizational structure, administration and governance expressions (Christensen and Lægreid, 2011; Denis et al., 2015; Quélin et al., 2017; Skelcher, 2012). However, in public administrations hybridity is evaluated and applied in a wide range from inter-sectoral cooperation and alliances to initiatives combining social, economic and cultural activities (Quélin et al., 2017).

Hybridity can be considered as participation in various, opposite and socially structured applications, routines and beliefs followed by actors with different values and goals (Quélin et al., 2017). It expresses the coexisting features of different structural and cultural dimensions with another approach. It is also used for characterizing cultural factors in different departments of government or public institutions. Hybrids are also considered as multi-functional things combining different tasks, values, ideas and organizational forms (Christensen and Lægreid, 2011). In this context, according to Skelcher and Smith (2015: 433), in the field of public administration, it is possible to see a variety of hybrid examples such as "public-private partnerships, contracted service delivery structures, semi-autonomous institutions and user-managed public facilities, various types of collaborative forums, social enterprises and network governance systems."

There is no general theory or model agreed on in the literature regarding how hybridization emerged and developed, its dimensions and hybrid types. It is seen that current approaches are discussed under four titles: governance, organizational structure, organizational culture and conducted activities.

Denis et al. (2015) discussed the hybridization in public administrations in four dimensions as structure (organization design), agency (activities), organizational context (environment, culture) and identities (labor force) within the perspective of governance theory, organizational theory, actor-network theory and identity. According to these four theoretical perspectives, hybridization may occur as mixed governance structures, changes in archetypes and institutional logic, a combination of information, values and processes and hybrid roles and identities of individuals and groups.

Similar to Denis et al. (2015), Grohs (2014) determined three hybridity levels as field hybridity, governance hybridity and organizational hybridity. Field hybridity refers to the organization of three main sectors: state, market and community. Governance hybridity pertains to whether the administration tool of organizational fields is state-centric or market-oriented or community-oriented. Organizational hybridity refers to the main structural characteristics with which organizations manage their internal instructions, resource allocation and personnel policies.

Karré (2011) explains the hybridization with three groups and ten sub-dimensions. The first group is structures and activities. This group includes legal format, ownership, activities, financing and market atmosphere. These dimensions present the fundamentals and activities of the hybrid. The second group is strategy and culture. This group includes strategic orientation and value orientation dimensions. These dimensions express the general strategic orientation of the hybrid and its values system. The final group is governance and policy. This group includes the relation with political authority, administrative autonomy and executive autonomy. The dimensions summarized here indicate the relation of organizations with public principles and whether organizations have autonomy in both administrative and executive terms. An ideal hybrid organization is one that shows half the public and half private sector characteristics in each of these three groups and ten dimensions.

In the study by Skelcher and Smith (2015), when the hybridization of public and non-profit organizations was analyzed, five types of hybrids were revealed by using organizational logic theory. The first is segmented hybridity. In this type, functions for different organizational logics are divided into departments in organizations. Functions for different institutional logics in the segregated hybrid are divided into departments as separate but associated organizations. Basic organizational logic in the assimilated hybrid adopts some applications and symbols of a new organizational logic. In blended hybridity, elements of current organizational logic are synergistically included in a new and contextually specific organizational logic. In blocked hybridity, organizational dysfunctions occur due to the failure to eliminate the tensions among competing organizational logics.

Polzer et al. (2016) used the concepts of blending and layering as the analysis levels of hybrid organizations. These two levels represent two different mixing methods of the original components. Blending refers to hybridity as "a combination with the original components that are no longer distinguishable". The components are mixed to form a new combination. In layering, various elements of different administrative paradigms are added to or next to each other, but the paradigms here are still individually distinguishable.

Hybridity is generally regarded as a combination of the public and private sectors and recently the third sector (De Waele et al., 2015; Kickert, 2001). This combination reveals benefits for public administrations such as finding new financial resources and markets, specialization, increased organizational and individual productivity, openness to change and innovation, enrichment of culture, and the creation of governance mechanisms representing different interests. However, the combination of components with different structures, values, principles, norms and cultures does not always result in compliance. Hybrids have challenges and threats as well as benefits. Uncertainty in values and strategies, failure to clarify targets, difficulties in providing motivation and most importantly, problems in creating new identities are the leading challenges of hybrids (Hyyryläinen and Viinamäki, 2011).

Combination of Human and Artificial Intelligence

Studies on hybridization in the literature focus around administrative paradigms such as organizational design and governance. However, there has recently been an increase in different and new perspectives. The approaches addressing hybridity more comprehensively from a sociological perspective or examining how hybridity affects and changes the structure of the state and public administrations can be indicated as examples (Polzer et al., 2016; Quélin et al., 2017). Hybridization is not a one-dimensional phenomenon and has a great driving force. Scientific and technological innovations are the leading driving forces. The new opportunities that scientific and technological innovations offer to shape and manage institutions, activities and relationships are the main factors that cause them to force hybridization (Denis et al., 2015).

It is seen that artificial intelligence is rapidly adopted in all sectors. AI offers governments and public administrations unprecedented opportunities because of the many benefits such as increasing speed and quality simultaneously, reducing costs and providing options for how to do things better. Therefore, AI is also anticipated to increase inter-sectoral hybridization on the one hand and intra-organizational hybridization on the other (Eggers et al., 2017; Shrum and Gordon, 2019).

The biggest concern expressed in a great majority of research on the use of artificial intelligence is its negative effects on production and employment. It is assumed that artificial intelligence will completely eliminate human labor and replace human beings in the labor force. Although there is some merit in these concerns, studies indicate that people are not completely excluded from production and employment (Corvalán, 2019; Susar and Aquaro, 2019). Even with the most pessimistic estimation the human factor will continue to play a large part in employment in the short and medium term. Considering the current technologies today, it is anticipated that only a small part of the professions such as 5% can be completely automated. Also, only half of the various activities in the current professions can be automated (Manyika et al., 2017). It is also known that new technologies usually replace certain tasks rather than eliminate professions and often create new products, new markets and new professions by increasing employee productivity (Bruckner et al., 2017).

The main question that should be asked at this point in terms of governments, organizations and individuals is how to achieve the balance between human and artificial intelligence in employment (World Economic Forum, 2020). In this respect, ensuring a human-artificial intelligence combination is a priority for public administrations, regarded as the largest employer in most countries, whose main capital is human (Tinholt et al., 2017). In this context, it is evident that public administrations will have a hybrid form consisting of human and artificial intelligence which are different actors as the main logic of hybridization is to combine the strengths of parties with different structures in order to increase efficiency and productivity in public services and provide public interest (Mikhaylov et al., 2017).

It is possible to realize human and artificial intelligence hybridity in public administrations in various forms and sizes. In this study which is based on a human-AI combination, hybridization is discussed under the titles of organizational structure and governance. Division of labor and employee abilities are under the title of organizational structure, and decision-making and administrative discretion are under the title of governance.

One of the main ways to analyze the effect of new technologies in workplaces is to distinguish between professions/jobs and tasks/activities. Each profession contains various tasks that require different cognitive abilities and levels. In parallel, it is possible to classify the tasks in two dimensions as manual-cognitive and routine-non-routine. Routine tasks are ones that are based on well understood procedures and can be defined by clear rules and algorithms. On the contrary, non-routine tasks require flexibility, creativity, complex problem-solving and human interaction. In the short and medium term, it seems possible for artificial intelligence to perform manual or cognitive routine tasks and support experts in non-routine tasks. In addition, it will allow for the personnel who especially perform routine duties and activities in public organizations to improve themselves and take up tasks that require creativity and innovation as well as social and interpersonal skills. Such a hybridization in terms of the division of labor will enable the optimization of the labor force and more efficient use of resources by directing public personnel to more value-added jobs (Bruckner et al., 2017; Corvalán, 2019; Eggers et al., 2017; Makridakis, 2017; Manyika et al., 2017; Young et al., 2019).

A different approach is addressed through the distinction between intuitive decision-making and analytical decision-making. Jarrahi (2018) approached the human-AI relationship through uncertainty, complexity and doubleness which are the main problems of decision-making activities. In this context, decision-making is separated into analytical and intuitive. While analytical approaches for decision-making are based on deep knowledge, intuitive approaches rather focus on scope by addressing the problem with a holistic and discrete perspective. While the problem-solving ability of AI is analytical, that of humans is intuitive. These two types do not externalize each other; in contrast, they can be used as parallel decision-making systems to think through various possibilities more effectively. One way to embody the synergistic relationship between AI and human beings is to combine the speed of AI with the superior intuitive judgment and insight of human beings in collecting and analyzing information. AI can help people overcome complexity with its analytical skills, but people's intuition is required against the ambiguity and doubleness of decision-making. Jarrahi (2018) conceptualized the combination of human-AI as symbiosis, which is called hybridization in this study.

The human-AI hybridity is possible in the use of administrative discretionary power as a special type of decision-making in public administrations. AI can be considered as a governance tool in the field of administrative discretion. AI can be used to make rational decisions regarding uncertain tasks in the context of criteria such as efficiency, productivity, equity, accountability, manageability and political feasibility. This administrative discretionary power called artificial discretion may be included as a governance component which increases, supports or changes human appreciation in administrative tasks with too little or too much information, results that may cause various possibilities or more than one reasonable solution depending on competitive values (Barth and Arnold, 1999; Young et al., 2019).

It is possible to evaluate the presented human-AI combination within the framework of the hybridization approaches (Denis et al., 2015; Grohs, 2014; Karré, 2011; Polzer et al., 2016; Skelcher and Smith, 2015) discussed in this study. First, human-AI hybridity should be considered as layering. The abilities, skills and capabilities of humans and AI should be combined; however, they should continue to exist as separate and different structures. Human-AI hybridity is an organizational hybridization because no other actors outside organizations participate. In this context, it is necessary to make radical changes in organizational logic. In the short and medium term, separated or divided hybridization, and in the long-term blended hybridization are likely to occur. In addition, there should be a change in the structure, operation and personnel policies of organizations in the organizational context. Cooperation in areas such as making decisions, creating policies and the use of administrative discretion makes this combination a governance hybrid.

There are several points that public administrations should take into consideration to ensure the human-AI combination. Above all, the process of making public administrations "smart" should be considered within the framework of a "social technology" or "humanizing automation" approach. This means that artificial intelligence is not regarded as a replacement for humans in their current activities. In this context, technology should be designed to carry out routines, fulfill the backlogs and shift employees to more value-added tasks in order to reduce the burden of public administrations and personnel. By dividing the current works the tasks should be redefined, the jobs that the artificial intelligence can do alone should be determined and public personnel should be assigned to others. The capabilities of human and artificial intelligence should be combined and the way to create value should be chosen by supporting human labor with technology. Institutions should take care to choose the most appropriate artificial intelligence application depending on their current duties and structures. Financial savings as a result of the use of artificial intelligence should be directed towards the training of employees so they can improve themselves and obtain more benefits and productivity (Corvalán, 2019; Eggers et al., 2017; Tinholt et al., 2017).

When the historical process is examined, it is seen that technological revolutions do not reduce the general demand for human labor in the long run, instead they reinforce it. Technology does not eliminate professions, but it does change how things are done and the number of people required to do them. However, due to the nature of technological revolutions, short-term troubles and problems definitely occur in industries, sectors and organizations. Today’s digital revolution is expected to lead to more automation in production and services. Therefore, similar troubles and problems will appear for today's industries, sectors, organizations and employees (Bruckner et al., 2017).

Conclusion

Toffler (1980) suggested the idea that industrialization ended and a new civilization began in the third wave, in which everything was radically changed. The concept of civilization pointed out by Toffler today appears with different names such as knowledge era, information age, digital era and fourth industrial revolution. Knowledge is now considered in classical production factors. Technological innovations rapidly change the means of production. A great transformation is observed in all conceivable social structures such as the economy, culture, politics, administration, language, religion, etc.

Schwab (2016) stated that the technological developments in the new period have great effects on organizations in all sectors. Organizations are now turning to new forms of collaboration and new digital models are replacing traditional operational models. This works similarly for public organizations because governments and public administrations are the organizations most affected by the process. On the one hand, governments and public administrations have to manage the great transformation, and on the other hand, they have to keep up with the transformation.

AI is one of the most discussed and popular technologies today. It is anticipated that it will perform many activities in the future, such as learning, perceiving, interpreting, judging and applying cognitive systems. For public administrations this means new searches for ensuring the human-AI combination. Hybridization appears to be a method in which both elements are and operate in harmony. The hybridization experience of public administrations is quite old. Early AI systems have also been used by public administrations for a long time. Therefore, it will be easier to establish such a structure in public administrations.

The major concern with AI, including public administrations, is that it replaces the human workforce. However, it is impossible for AIs to fulfill all administrative tasks in spite of their potential value. The convenience of an AI for a particular administrative role depends on several factors. Numerous factors such as task complexity, quality and availability of data, technical requirements, limitations of AI systems, task-related risks and uncertainties and political returns are determinants for the use of AI in public institutions (Young et al., 2019).

As a conclusion, it is not possible to prevent technological developments and avoid using them. Public administrations, on the contrary, have to be a big part or partner of this event. Therefore, the simplest and most reasonable solution to relieve AI's pressure on public administrations and public personnel would be to establish a hybrid structure based on a partnership between AI and human beings which will provide the best results in all cases.

Keywords: *Public administration, artificial intelligence, hybridity, strategic management*

References

Agarwal, P. K. (2018). Public administration challenges in the world of AI and bots. *Public Administration Review, 78(6)*, 917-921. doi: https://doi.org/10.1111/puar.12979.

AI Now. (2016). *The AI now report: The social and economic implications of artificial intelligence technologies in the near-term*. Retrieved from https://ainowinstitute.org/AI_Now_2016_Report.pdf.

Barth, T. J., & Arnold, E. (1999). Artifical intelligence and administrative discretion: Implications for public administration. *American Review of Public Administraton, 29(4),* 332-351. doi: https://doi.org/10.1177/02750749922064463.

Batra, G., Queirolo, A., & Santhanam, N. (2017). *Artificial intelligence: The time to act is now*. McKinsey & Company. Retrieved November 03, 2020, from https://www.mckinsey.com/industries/advanced-electronics /our-insights/artificial-intelligence-the-time-to-act-is-now#.

Billis, D. (2013). *The symbiotic relationship between social enterprise and hybridity*. EMES-SOCENT Conference Selected Papers, no. LG13-30. Liege.

Boyd, M., & Wilson, N. (2017). Rapid developments in artificial intelligence: How might the New Zealand government respond? *Policy Quarterly, 13(4),* 36-43. doi: https://doi.org/10.26686/pq.v13i4.4619.

Brooks, R. A. (1991). Intelligence without representation. *Artificial Intelligence, 47*, 139-159. doi: https://doi.org/10.1016/0004-3702(91)90053-M.

Brown, K., Waterhouse, J., & Flynn, C. (2003). Change management practices: Is a hybrid model a better alternative for public sector. *International Journal of Public Sector Management, 16(3),* 230-241. doi: https://doi.org/10.1108/09513550310472311.

Bruckner, M., LaFleur, M., & Pitterle, I. (2017). *Frontier issues: The impact of the technological revolution on labour markets and income distribution*. UN Department of Economic & Social Affairs.

Charalabidis, Y., Loukis, E., Alexopoulos, C., & Lachana, Z. (2019). The three generations of electronic government: From service provision to open data and to policy analytics. In I. Lindgren et al. (Ed.), *18th IFIP WG 8.5 International Conference, EGOV 2019,* (pp. 3-17). San Benedetto Del Tronto: Springer.

Christensen, T., & Lægreid, P. (2011). Complexity and hybrid public administration-Theoretical and empirical challenges. *Public Organization Review, 11*, 407-423. doi: https://doi.org/10.1007/s11115-010-0141-4.

Corvalán, J. G. (2019). PROMETEA: Artificial Intelligence to Transform Public Organizations. *International Journal of Digital and Data Law, 5*.

De Waele, L., Berghman, L., & Matthyssens, P. (2015). Defining hybridity and hybrid contingencies in public organizations: An alternative conceptual model. *Contingency, Behavioural and Evolutionary Perspectives on Public and Nonprofit Governance (Studies in Public and Non-Profit Governance, Vol. 4)* (pp. 113-154). Emerald Group Publishing Limited.

Denis, J.-L., Ferlie, E., & Van Gestel, N. (2015). Understanding hybridity in public organizations. *Public Administration, 93(2),* 273-289. doi: https://doi.org/10.1111/padm.12175.

Desouza, K. C. (2018). *Delivering artificial intelligence in government: Challenges and opportunities*. Washington, DC: IBM Center for The Business of Government.

Desouza, K. C., Dawson, G. S., & Chenok, D. (2020). Designing, developing, and deploying artificial intelligence systems: Lessons from and for the public sector. *Business Horizons, 63*, 205-213. doi: https://doi.org/10.1016/j.bushor.2019.11.004.

Dickinson, H. (2016). From new public management to new public governance: The implications for a 'new public service'. In J. R. Butcher, & D. J. Gilchrist (Ed.), *The Tree Sector Solution* (pp. 41-60). Australia: ANU Press.

Dunleavy, P., Margetts, H., Bastow, S., & Tinkler, J. (2006). New public management is dead—Long live digital-era governance. *Journal of Public Administration Research and Theory, 16(3),* 467-494. doi: https://doi.org/10.1093/jopart/mui057.

Eggers, W. D., Schatsky, D., & Viechnicki, P. (2017). *AI-augmented government: Using cognitive technologies to redesign public sector work*. Deloitte University Press.

Etscheid, J. (2019). Artificial intelligence in public administration: possible framework for partial and full automation. In I. Lindgren et al. (Ed.), *18th IFIP WG 8.5 International Conference* (pp. 248-261). San Benedetto Del Tronto: Springer.

Grohs, S. (2014). Hybrid organizations in social service delivery in quasimarkets: The case of Germany. *American Behavioral Scientist*, 58, 1425-1445. doi: https://doi.org/10.1177/0002764214534671.

Hyyryläinen, E., & Viinamäki, O.P. (2011). Benefits of hybridity in organizations: Views from public, private and the third sector. *The International Journal of Management Science and Information Technology*, *2*, 16-54.

Jarrahi, M. H. (2018). Artificial intelligence and the future of work: Human-AI symbiosis in organizational decision making. *Business Horizons, 61(4),* 577-586. doi: https://doi.org/10.1016/j.bushor.2018.03.007.

Karré, P. M. (2011). *Heads and tails: both sides of the coin: An analysis of hybrid organizations in the Dutchwaste management sector*. The Hague: Eleven International Publishing.

Kickert, W. J. (2001). Public management of hybrid organizations: Governance of quasi-autonomous executive agencies. *International Public Management Journal, 4,* 135-150.

Kouziokas, G. N. (2017). The application of artificial intelligence in public administration for forecasting high crime risk transportation areas in urban environment. *Transportation Research Procedia, 24*, 467-473. doi: https://doi.org/10.1016/j.trpro.2017.05.083.

Laihonen, H., & Kokko, P. (2020). Knowledge management and hybridity of institutional logics in public sector. *Knowledge Management Research & Practice*. doi: https://doi.org/10.1080/14778238.2020.1788429.

Loukis, E., Maragoudakis, M., & Kyriakou, N. (2019). Economic crisis policy analytics based on artificial ıntelligence. In I. Lindgren et al. (Ed.), *18th IFIP WG 8.5 International Conference* (pp. 262-275). San Benedetto Del Tronto: Springer.

Makridakis, S. (2017). The forthcoming artificial intelligence (AI) revolution: Its impact on society and firms. *Futures, 90,* 46-60. doi: https://doi.org/10.1016/j.futures.2017.03.006.

Manyika, J., Chui, M., Miremadi, M., Bughin, J., George, K., Willmott, P., & Dewhurst, M. (2017). *A future that works: Automation, employment, and productivity*. McKinsey Global Institute.

Mehr, H. (2017). *Artificial intelligence for citizen services and government*. Cambridge: Ash Center for Democratic Governance and Innovation.

Mikhail, B., Aleksei, M., & Ekaterina, S. (2018). On the way to legal framework for AI in public sector. *In Proceedings of the 11th International Conference on Theory and Practice of Electronic Governance*. Galway, Ireland: April 2018 (ICEGOV'18). doi: https://doi.org/10.1145/3209415.3209448.

Mikhaylov, S. J., Esteve, M., & Campion, A. (2017). Artificial intelligence for the public sector: Opportunities and challenges of cross-sector collaboration. *Phil. Trans. R. Soc. A, 376(20170357)*, 1-21. doi: https://doi.org/10.1098/rsta.2017.0357.

Miller, P., Kurunmaki, L., & O'Leary, T. (2008). Accounting, hybrids and the management of risk. Accounting, *Organizations and Society, 33*, 942-967. doi: https://doi.org/10.1016/j.aos.2007.02.005.

Nilsson, N. J. (2009). *The quest for artificial intelligence: A history of ideas and achievements*. Cambridge University Press.

Ojo, A., Zeleti, F. A., & Mellouli, S. (2019). A realist perspective on AI-era public management: An analysis of mechanisms, outcomes and challenges of AI solutions in the public sector. *In Proceedings of dg.o 2019: 20th Annual International Conference on Digital Government Research* (pp. 159-170). June 18, 2019: Dubai, United Arab Emirates. doi: https://doi.org/10.1145/3325112.3325261.

Pohl, J. (2015). *Artificial Superintelligence: Extinction or Nirvana?* InterSymp-2015. Baden: International Institute for Advanced Studies.

Polzer, T., Meyer, R. E., Höllerer, M. A., & Seiwald, J. (2016). Institutional Hybridity in Public Sector Reform: Replacement, Blending, or Layering of Administrative Paradigms. *In How Institutions Matter! (Research in the Sociology of Organizations 48B*) (pp. 69-99). Emerald Group Publishing Limited.

Purdy, M., & Daugherty, P. (2016). *Why artificial intelligence is the future of growth*. Accenture. Retrieved from, https://www.accenture.com/t20170524t055435__w__/ca-en/_acnmedia/pdf-52/accenture-why-ai-is-the-future-of-growth.pdf.

Quélin, B. V., Kivleniece, I., & Lazzarini, S. (2017). Public-private collaboration, hybridity and social value: Towards new theoretical perspectives. *Journal of Management Studies, 54(6)*, 763-792. doi: https://doi.org/10.1111/joms.12274.

Rosa, M., & Feyereisl, J. (2016). A Framework for Searching for General Artificial Intelligence. arXiv:1611.00685 [cs.AI]. Retrieved November 05, 2020, from https://arxiv.org/abs/1611.00685.

Schwab, K. (2017). Fourth industrial revolution. England: Portfolio Penguin.

Shrum, K., & Gordon, L. (2019). Artificial intelligence and the future of work. In A. R. Shark (Ed.), *Artifical Intelligence and Its Impact on Public Administration* (pp. 9-15). Washington D.C.: National Academy of Public Administration.

Skelcher, C. (2012). *What do we mean when we talk about 'hybrids' and 'hybridity' in public management and governance?* Working Paper, Institute of Local Government Studies. Birmingham: University of Birmingham. Retrieved from http://epapers.bham.ac.uk/1601/1/Hybrids_working_paper_%2D_march_2011.pdf.

Skelcher, C., & Smith, S. R. (2015). Theorizing hybridity: Institutional logics, complex organizations, and actor ıdentities: The case of nonprofits. *Public Administration, 93(2)*, 433-448. doi:

https://doi.org/10.1111/padm.12105.

Sun, T. Q., & Medaglia, R. (2019). Mapping the challenges of artificial intelligence in the public sector: Evidence from public healthcare. *Government Information Quarterly, 36,* 368-383. doi: https://doi.org/10.1016/j.giq.2018.09.008.

Susar, D., & Aquaro, V. (2019). Artificial intelligence: Opportunities and challenges for the public sector. In S. Ben Dhaou, L. Carter, & M. Gregory (Ed.), *Proceedings of the 12th International Conference on Theory and Practice of Electronic Governance* (pp. 418-426). Melbourne: ACM.

Tinholt, D., Enzerink, S., Sträter, W., Hautvast, P., & Carrara, W. (2017). *Unleashing the potential of artificial intelligence in the public sector.* Capgemini Consulting. Retrieved from https://www.capgemini.com/consulting/wp-content/uploads/sites/30/2017/10/ai-in-public-sector.pdf.

Toffler, A. (1980). *The Third Wave*. New York: William Morrow.

van der Heijden, J. (2015). Interacting state and non-state actors in hybrid settings of public service delivery. *Administration & Society, 47(2),* 99-121. doi: https://doi.org/10.1177/0095399713481349.

Williamson, O. E. (1991). Comparative economic organization: The analysis of discrete structural alternatives. *Administrative Science Quarterly, 36(2)*, 269-296. doi: https://doi.org/10.2307/2393356.

Wirtz, B. W., & Weyerer, J. C. (2019). Artificial intelligence in the public sector. In A. Farazmand (Ed.), *Global Encyclopedia of Public Administration, Public Policy, and Governance*. Springer, Cham. doi: https://doi.org/10.1007/978-3-319-31816-5_3701-1.

Wirtz, B. W., Weyerer, J. C., & Geyer, C. (2019). Artificial intelligence and the public sector-Applications and challenges. *International Journal of Public Administration, 42(7)*, 596-615. doi: https://doi.org/10.1080/01900692.2018.1498103.

World Economic Forum. (2020). *The future of jobs report 2020*. Geneva: The World Economic Forum.

Young, M. M., Bullock, J. B., & Lecy, J. D. (2019). Artificial discretion as a tool of governance: A framework for understanding the impact of artificial intelligence on public administration. *Perspectives on Public Management and Governance, 22*, 301-313. doi: https://doi.org/10.1093/ppmgov/gvz014.

CHAPTER EIGHT

THE BEHAVIORAL DIMENSIONS OF HUMAN RESOURCES MANAGEMENT IN THE AGE OF DIGITALIZATION AND INDUSTRY 4.0

MERYEM AYBAS

Introduction

Due to the dazzling effect of Industry 4.0, which is the technological transformation used in production, and digital technologies, the work itself, employee qualifications and expectations, and employee management have largely changed. In the business environment that has changed with Industry 4.0, the behavior and attitudes of individuals in the organization have also changed and will continue to do so. In this framework, the organizational context and the individual, which were the subject of organizational behavior researches in the past, now differ from the past. The management of the behaviors of individuals in the digitalized business environment with the new context will require different strategies. Within the scope of this chapter, after examining the behavioral dimension of human resources management (HRM), there will be an attempt to express what kinds of changes are expected in the context of Industry 4.0 and digitalization, and what will be the research areas. Additionally, within the scope of this chapter, there will be a discussion of how HRM can lead human behavior towards the strategic goals of the firm.

Behavioral Issues in HRM

HRM represents the dimension of the business functions related to the labor process within the production factors. Behavioral theories and approaches, which have gained importance with the human relations movement in management theory, played an important role in the development of HRM (Evans, 1999, Mahoney and Deckop, 1986, Bruce and Nyland, 2011).

Ensuring employee commitment, which is one of the main objectives of HRM, is based on the assumption that employees will be more satisfied, more productive and, more adaptable. For an organization, commitment means more loyalty and better performance, as well as results such as an individual's self-worth, dignity, psychological involvement, and identification (Guest, 1987). In the researches, it is stated that there are many hidden reasons behind the apparent reasons for employees to leave their jobs (Hartley, 2005, Chang et al., 2013). These include the workplace that does not meet expectations, mismatches between the business and the person, too little coaching and feedback, too few growth and development opportunities, feeling unworthy and unrecognized, overwork and stress from a work-life imbalance, and loss of faith and trust in senior leaders. Most of these reasons are behaviorally manageable (Torrington et al., 2014).

The models of HRM based on human behavior involve a psychological exchange that involves full dedication to work based on a psychological contract, beyond a definite formal contract that includes the individual's labor in return for a measurable wage. With this psychological contract, now the employees have a strong acceptance and belief in the goals and values of an organization, a willingness to work on behalf of the organization, and a strong desire to maintain organization membership (Guest, 1987; Bruce and Nyland, 2011). In this sense, organizational behavior researches have facilitated HRM to manipulate the behaviors of the individual in line with firm purposes. Organizational behavior aims to have information about the different characteristics and attitudes of employees to implement HRM practices that look towards organizational effectiveness (Yıldız, 2013). Many HRM models also target outcomes such as job satisfaction, retention, and attraction (Heneman et al., 1989). Employee interviews during recruitment and performance interviews, interviews with managers, focus group studies, employee engagement, motivation, job satisfaction, organizational culture, attitude and equality of opportunity towards minority groups, commitment to the organization and its reasons, clarification of business objectives, and goal-oriented behaviors provide useful information to the firm on organizational issues and problems, areas to be improved and strengths (Torrington et al., 2014).

According to the skill, motivation and opportunity model that can be shown as a model in which behavioral research affects HRM strategies; it is assumed that employees have the necessary knowledge and skills, are motivated with appropriate incentives, and will reach high performance when the necessary support and tools are provided in their work environment. In some studies, the "ability, motivation, and opportunity" model has been synthesized with Lawler's high involvement performance model and high involvement work programs have been used to explain; accordingly, ability; "education" in the Lawler model, motivation; "pay" includes the opportunity, "communication" and "empowerment". This expressed model explains the relationship between HRM and performance, which is described as the "black box" (Marin-Garcia, 2013, Juarez Tarraga et al., 2019).

The researches in the field of organizational behavior are important regarding how human resources can be developed. An example of this is why some employees are more engaged than others, and the reasons for organizational citizenship behavior are analyzed. How senior managers helped subordinates and how they indirectly transferred their experiences over the years through implicit knowledge can be examined (Barney et al., 2001). The studies in the field of HRM, which constitute the application-level form of organizational behavior, can form a bridge in this sense. According to Boxall and Purcell (2000), strategies based on a resource-based approach; instead of focusing on a limited set of tired structures in work psychology in the HR context, a broad understanding of HR strategy that includes all the effects of work and employment systems is needed because it includes topics such as learning, agility, adaptation, and innovation. HR strategy should be linked to other key aspects of management and understood dynamically. In a study by Kehoe and Collins (2017), to clarify the targeted potential value of the human resources (HR) system, in the context of knowledge-intensive work, the rare effects of a relationship-oriented HR system, and a high-commitment HR system on unit performance have been investigated. In this study, the authors found that the high-commitment HR system has a positive effect on firm performance. According to this, the increase in collective employee commitment increases general and firm-specific human capital as it facilitates the exchange of knowledge in a social context. They also argued that the relationship-oriented HR system contributes to unit performance through its positive effects on employees' collective access to information, by encouraging employees to continuously access and exchange information flows within and outside their units and the wider organization. Also, in the context of the information-resource-based approach, it is seen that the studies aimed at obtaining a sustainable competitive advantage for companies have changed direction from examining the characteristics of the resources of the companies as a source of competitive advantage, to understanding the managerial actions that structure, organize, transform and direct companies' resources (Huy and Zott, 2019). On this subject, we see that the studies are detailed in the context of defining the dynamic capabilities of the manager, manager cognition, emotional intelligence, human capital, and the power to transform social capital. Collins (2020) developed the resource-based vision model of strategic HR and CEO dynamic management capabilities. In this model, the author sought to develop an understanding of how and when a high-commitment HR system can achieve competitive advantage and higher firm performance due to employee-based resources through the CEO's dynamic management capabilities. Challenging the current basic assumption of the resource-based approach in this model is the strategic HR research that creating potentially valuable, employee-based resources should always provide a competitive advantage and higher firm performance; instead, the author argued that dynamic management capabilities of the CEO were necessary to unlock employee-based resource potential (Collins, 2020). Collins (2020) claims that the CEO's management cognition, social capital, and human capital potentially lead to larger firm-level employee-based resources while pursuing a high-commitment-based HR strategy, and when firms can effectively manage the CEO's management cognition, this suggests its use for competitive advantage. While the adoption of a firm-level high-commitment HR strategy is easily imitable, it is more complex to repeat the effective implementation of the policies underlying an HR strategy. The reason for this is, due to the abilities and motivations of frontline leaders to implement policies that are different, that there is a large variability even in the degree of implementation of high-commitment HR policies in different departments within a company (Collins, 2020). One of the approaches that combine the resource-based view with strategic management is Huy and Zott's (2019) study, approaching the subject in terms of psychological processes at the individual level, focusing on certain emotion regulation actions as the emotional basis of dynamic management abilities. According to this; emotion regulation refers to the manipulation and changing of one's own and other people's emotions for a specific purpose, and shows how differences in managers' interest in emotion regulation affect the extent to which they can mobilize resources to pursue market opportunities. By regulating the emotions of others, facilitating judgments of legitimacy helps to mobilize social capital, while helping them to mobilize human capital resources by creating psychic benefits through emotional regulation for themselves. The study of Huy and Zott (2019) explains that managers' emotion regulation capacity constitutes an important basis of their dynamic management abilities and how the structure is linked to other basic conceptual foundations, namely managerial human and social capital.

There are previous studies that address various aspects of management cognition, such as mental models and knowledge structures or mental processes and cognitive abilities (Helfat and Martin, 2015, Huy and Zott, 2019). However, considering the transformative nature of digital processes in organizational life, it can be said that how dynamic managerial capabilities can be combined through artificial intelligence will increase its importance among the research topics of the coming period. The following section discusses the possible effects of digitalization on HRM in the context of managing human behavior.

Digitalization, HRM and Human Behavior

A socio-technical system perspective is needed to understand how Industry 4.0 and digitalization affect the behavioral dimension of HRM (Stone et al., 2015). Socio-technical systems claim that there is an interaction between the social system and the technological system and that each affects the other. Accordingly, none of the social and technological elements of the system alone are determinative. Job satisfaction, motivation, job design, monotony, absenteeism, learning, teamwork, etc., and many other issues are considered in the context of socio-technical systems (Trist, 1981). Industry 4.0 is a socio-technical system. Therefore, determining the effects of the new technological system created by new technologies on working life will depend on understanding the technology-human interaction. Industry 4.0 is technology that has never been used in production, i.e., unmanned factories, autonomous robots, the internet of things, smart products, artificial intelligence, smart processors (operators), smart machines, etc. Therefore, there is a need to rethink the human-technology interaction. For the integration of people, processes, cultures, and goals that are parts of the system, organizational goals should be aligned with HR strategy, technology, culture, and procedures or processes within the organization (Sony and Naik, 2020).

With Industry 4.0, as business activities become increasingly digital, autonomous and "smart", they are transforming the roles and responsibilities of employees in the workplace and their skills and competency needs. Digitalization disrupts traditional career paths in all sectors of employment. This change in employees' roles, responsibilities, and skill needs requires the adoption of a new approach in all practices of HRM, including the recruitment, development, and relocation of employees (Munsamy and Telukdarie, 2019). Digital technologies have transformed the current way that HR processes are managed, particularly in terms of how they collect, store, use, and disseminate information about job applicants and current employees. Additionally, they have changed the nature of jobs, business relationships, and control (Stone et al., 2015, Stone and Deadrick, 2015). Parallel to the development of digital technologies, with applications such as web-based applications, virtual teams, and remote work, it has been possible for employees to work from home or interact with team members across geographic boundaries. This situation has also reduced the effect of distance between organizations. Moreover, it has enabled organizations to recruit individuals with special skills (e.g., software developers) in remote parts of the world (Stone et al., 2015). According to Connelly et al. (2020), because digital technologies have developed, organizational processes and the nature and meaning of work continue to evolve; thus, work has evolved into a more modular, granular, networked, and decontextualized form that is more flexible, *ad hoc* and part-time (Spreitzer et al., 2017, Connelly et al., 2020).

The impact of technology on the work environment and workflows is a determinant of human behavior in organizations because changes in technology can affect both the organizational structure of the firm and the individual characteristics of the workforce. Technology-structure researches are a very important part of the approach described as the condition dependency or contingency approach in management (Fry, 1982). As a result of technological developments in the place where work is done and where production and exchange of goods and services take place, the concept of "factory" has lost its privileged channel and is questioned. Accordingly, new working models have been observed for a while, instead of the traditional Fordist working models based on command and control under the supervision of a supervisor in a factory. Employees in new working models are now required to work autonomously and on a project basis. Therefore, what matters is not how, when, and where they work but the results of their work (Seghezzi and Tiraboschi, 2018). Traditional HRM intervenes in order to increase the productivity of individuals working in the factory and/or office order, to increase their commitment to the job and the organization, and their job satisfaction. In the new working environment dominated by the gig economy and new technologies, it is not possible to achieve the desired goals with traditional HRM tools because the concepts of employee, work, and employee management lose their traditional meaning (Parry and Strohmeier, 2014, Connelly et al., 2020).

How the company applies or uses technology affects the organizational culture and its behavior towards stakeholders. The application of new technologies used with Industry 4.0 will bring a gradual change in workforce composition. For example, younger, better educated, and more mobile generations that are more technologically experienced will enter companies, possibly bringing new values, attitudes, and concerns and leading to a change within organizations (Foerster-Metz et al., 2018). Unlike the past, organizations are confronted with a group of employees who have grown up with digital technologies, named as concepts such as "digital workers, net generation, generation Y, millennials". It is assumed that the early, deep and lasting interaction established with digital technologies clearly shaped the new generation with different attitudes, qualities, behaviors, and expectations. According to this, based on a permanent interaction with digital technologies and compared to traditional employees, these new employees generally have multitasking capabilities (especially fast and parallel information processing), a networking tendency, an ability to learn by doing, instant satisfaction, and frequent rewards, and show significant differences. Considering the differences between generation X who worked in a more traditional and factory setting and the digitalized generation Y with its mutual cooperation, teamwork, and mutual understanding, etc., there are concerns that problems may arise in these matters. It is important for HRM to react to such changes, align its strategies and activities to this new labor market community and recruit, develop, and remunerate, etc., such "digital workers." Furthermore, it is necessary to seek appropriate ways to integrate these employees with previous generations (Parry and Strohmeier, 2014). Generation Y has complaints that differ from employees in the past. These are lack of purpose and progress in their careers, not being listened to by management, feeling dedicated or loyal to their company. To eliminate these complaints of this new generation of employees, where uncertain and flexible environments are the main determinants and who have to operate in networked, horizontal, and flattened organizational structures, different solutions from the past should be applied. It will be beneficial to follow high-commitment HR practices that provide communication, empowerment, participation, and digital collaboration opportunities, and encourage teamwork (Larkin, 2017).

Space and time flexibility brought by new technologies is not only the work done individually; it also deeply affects interdependent works. Information flow and simultaneous communication require teamwork in interdependent jobs. In this period where knowledge and creativity gain more importance, teamwork, communication, and the cooperation of teams come to the fore for idea development and implementation. In this sense, it will be important to build the organizational culture in a way that includes agility, learning, innovation, cooperation and communication, and a culture in which employees are constantly improved (Schwarzmüller et al., 2018). The democratic leadership and decision-making process are to provide a direct channel to the management committee for employees to raise concerns, share their opinions, and potentially add or make changes to a company's strategy (Larkin, 2017). What's more, with digital technology for better collaboration that will allow cross-functional partnerships to become commonplace, teams from around the world will be able to improve each other's work in real time. Employees will share a sense of destiny with the organization's employees all over the world and, in cooperation, will feel like global citizens of their organization (Larkin, 2017).

Ongoing digitalization increases the weight of "knowledge work" while consistently transforming traditional manual and routine tasks into automation. Digital technologies have made possible new forms of work ranging from single virtual workplaces to virtual organizations. Members of such virtual business units are generally remote and anonymous. Managing such members is different from managing traditional employees in many respects; such as motivation, performance feedback, and career development (Parry and Strohmeier, 2014). HR plays a significant role in providing appropriate job designs for all duties in an organization. Job characteristics such as task characteristics, autonomy, and feedback play an important role, as employee engagement cannot be encouraged through face-to-face relationships with managers or long-term employment contracts in the new work setting. Although there are organizational constraints, in terms of the new task content, the ultimate goal is to provide a motivating work environment as much as possible (Connelly et al., 2020). HR managers also have important roles in managing the balance between temporary and permanent job types in the organizational working environment, where the ratio of internal and external labor is getting narrower. HR departments should monitor the ongoing (continuous) use of non-employees. Depending on the roles in a large organization, it may be more efficient to hire a permanent employee rather than a set of (different) employees. Depending on the organizational structure, the HR department can facilitate the transition of some employees to more traditional contract work or permanent employment (Connelly et al., 2020).

All new types of working and the gig economy pose challenges for the current theory and practice of HR. Established knowledge and findings of organizational behavioral issues such as leadership, culture, identity, commitment, and engagement might not be easily implemented into an emerging, modular and anonymized workforce that is decontextualized, dispersed and asynchronous. In this context, concerning the new working order, on recruitment and staffing, employee motivation and engagement, and formal and informal relationship management, etc., there is limited research on what motivates employees in the digital age, ways to construct the meaning of work, and what flexibility means for career development (Connelly et al., 2020). The new technologies provide employees with opportunities to manage their time more effectively, to choose the place they want to work, and to establish a better work-life balance (Schwab, 2017). Nonetheless, the form of employment that comes with digitization also causes a number of problems. Due to technology, the concept of "workplace" and rules regarding occupational health and safety also become irrelevant and make it difficult for the person to determine the beginning and end of the workday. The fact that employees always prepare themselves for work causes a blurring of the separation between family and working life, and an increase in work-related stress, and in the degree of employee connectivity through communication technologies. Therefore, as a result of the discussions, some legislative changes have started to be seen; for example, firstly in France, the "right to disconnect" was enacted based on the acceptance that the distinction between professional and private life is a right (Seghezzi and Tiraboschi, 2018). Due to the problems caused by stress, the intertwining of the concepts of work and rest, burnout, sleep problems, problems in family life, not being paid additional wages for overtime, etc., it is also seen that some labor unions have started to put special provisions on these issues in contracts (Yankın, 2019). A subject of great debate is the continuous monitoring of employees through digital tools, and in such countries as the USA, Sweden and England, through the chip implants that are beginning to be worn for the purposes of even opening doors to the employees of some companies, photocopying, running machinery, driving company cars, etc. For now, this technology, which is based on volunteerism and transformed into passive technology outside the company, is worrying in that it will lead to dire consequences, such as exposure to violations which are confidentiality of private life, privacy, stress and anxiety disorders caused by constant monitoring, data passing into the hands of undesirable people, harassment of employees, and discrimination. In addition, it will be inevitable that this technology, which is currently based on volunteerism, will become "mandatory" in the future in order for employees not to lose their jobs or even to be employed. As a matter of fact, in this respect, it is seen that some politicians in the USA have made law proposals to make this type of technology completely voluntary. At this point, it is obvious that regulations will be needed due to the many violations of rights that will occur in the future on these issues all over the world (Metz, 2018, Blue, 2018, Gelecekburada, 2020).

One of the problems that will arise in this new period is employees' engagement and commitment to the organization. It will be inevitable that individuals working remotely or digitally will have problems of alienation and depersonalization after a while. In particular, managing the relationship and distance between manager and subordinate will be taken to a different dimension with electronic performance evaluation and monitoring tools. For this reason, it is aimed to manage the behaviors of individuals at work and outside of work through programs such as artificial intelligence supported programs, second life or virtual environment supports, and gamification activities (Stone et al., 2015).

As time passes, it will be possible to see new practices regarding the new ways of working, such as work engagement programs, a work-life balance, and the protection of employee health. As the expected abilities in the digital business environment differ, it will be inevitable for new HRM practices and techniques to emerge in the context of motivation and empowerment. Undoubtedly, individuals in the digital business environment will need to be motivated differently from employees of classical organizations, and different tools will be used in job design. With the increase of robots in production, robot-human relations, behavioral problems caused by continuous work with robots, the relationships of individuals with their colleagues and supervisors in the robotic working environment, and the establishment of a work-family balance in the working environment that becomes more flexible stand out as important areas of struggle.

With the digital transformation, the work-life order, the relationship between work and private life continues to change radically in the context of spatial and temporal flexibility. Although there are offices in the workplaces of the future, a company building is not always required for these offices, and personal households will become more accepted as home-office mechanisms with the most modern technologies. Therefore, a physical presence in the workplace is less guaranteed for many employees. Finishing essential projects in the evenings or at weekends becomes more familiar, and working hours lose their meaning. The job is no longer defined by usual working hours but takes place within 24 hours with breaks in traditional core times. With this approach, "results" become more important. However, this situation brings some consequences. On the one hand, this situation also takes into account the special needs of employees such as childcare; they can benefit from a better work-life balance, such as being able to work whenever and wherever they are available. However, on the other hand, the ability of employees to access work-related materials from anywhere, to be accessible at all times, and to remain in constant connection can create the norm. This situation may cause the problem of never-ending overtime. Employees will need to organize their break times according to this newly formed working norm in their minds, and take care of their health by taking their minds away from work from time to time. Besides, it will be important for company executives to create a respectful digital freedom environment without exploiting digital unlimited accessibility and without turning it into an excessive workload. Work stress caused by space and time flexibility in employees can be reduced by behaviors such as not making work-related requests on weekends or outside working hours, for example not waiting for an e-mail or phone to be answered except in a truly exceptional situation (Schwarzmüller et al., 2018).

In the Industry 4.0 period, attracting and retaining core employees, who are golden for organizations, will be much more important in terms of sustainable innovation and competition. Studies show that one of the most important reasons for voluntary turnover is that the demands of the job cannot be matched with the demands of the family. In the upcoming period, creating more family-friendly workplaces where employees can balance their work and family responsibilities, which are considered to be one of the most important determinants of work engagement, will constitute one of the important HR strategies in this regard (Torrington et al., 2014).

Bush and Balven (2018) examined the factors that affect gig workers' work engagement. In order to ensure the sustainability of HR practices in this type of new working order, Crowdworker has presented eight proposals as the precursors of engagement. These are listed as follows (Bush and Balven, 2018: 11):

HRM may promote crowd worker engagement by

- *enhancing perceptions of task meaningfulness.*
- *highlighting the values, mission, and goals of the organization.*
- *enhancing the worker-task fit and worker-organization fit*
- *the utilization of more challenging task assignments.*
- *timely feedback and interaction opportunities.*
- *Participation.*
- *creative reward structures.*

The tools available in existing digital technologies that HR can benefit from are diverse. These range from tools that enable employee-level goal management and completion, participation management, employee location management applications, and real-time employee appreciation, to health and awareness tools (Larkin 2017). It is possible to encounter a wide variety of business applications to facilitate working life in the digital environment. One of these is the website named "voice of colleagues" which has started to present voices consisting of typical office noises so that people who have started working from home due to coronavirus can feel they are in a work environment. In this way, it is aimed to focus individuals as if they were in the office while working from home (Channel24, 2020). One of the suggested ways to increase employees' engagement in organizations dominated by digitalization is gamification. As employees increasingly become "digital natives" and desire to enrich their workplaces with more digital technologies, these new forms of gamification can help employees in their applications to become more engaged in their jobs proactively and rapidly (Küpper et al., 2019). Küpper et al. (2019) discuss the psychology of this kind of engagement and how a gamified workplace experience can be an easy way of promoting learning. For this purpose, they put forward an adaptation of the theory of emotional events and claim that gamification can increase work engagement by leading to better learning outputs and higher overall satisfaction with work at the same time. However, they argue that the success of gamification depends on the effective design of gamified experiences and some personality factors such as achievement mindedness because real-time performance monitoring tools provide important data in terms of motivation, learning, and development (Stone et al., 2015). Besides, gamified career development will establish that employees are motivated within regular periods. With the technology that makes this possible, employees will fulfill their duties and roles more efficiently than ever before, as if they had an HR department in their pocket. Through personalized intranets and information channels, ICT technologies, and continuous real-time career development monitoring, they will be more dedicated, more career-oriented, and more informed (Larkin, 2017). According to Larkin (2017), the future employee will digest the information from her/his employer digitally, on a mobile device usually on the go, in an easy-to-digest video/audio format, or as user-friendly articles. Whether it's a company's financial reports, CEO's message, or changes to the company's social benefits program, such content will be consumed in a similar way to content flows on today's social networks, and will be liked, shared, and interacted with in the use of social media within the organization. For generation Y employees born with the internet, this will be similar to their experiences in social media, online shopping and the entertainment providers that they are accustomed to using daily, the software they use in their environment, intranet, etc. It is expected that applications will be designed in a personalized and attractive way. Young people can get bored with pages that do not open within a few seconds and feel the desire to see new things by refreshing the page. The shape, format, and attractiveness of the page constantly keep a focus on social media and online applications. Similarly, it will be significant to ensure that with these habits, generation Y will focus on the job and engage in work for a long time, utilizing an attractive and focus-increasing technology design. Learning and development opportunities will undergo a similar transformation. This modern learning and development approach will grow up in a digital HR environment. Fixed-layout computers, paper-pencil, and classroom-based applications will be eliminated and replaced by augmented reality and artificial intelligence supported applications (Larkin, 2017). Providing personalized information specific to employees with augmented reality is facilitated by applications such as machine learning and data mining. These support systems will be easily adapted to individual talents and benefit from the employee potential at a high level. Electronic support systems play a role that facilitates organizational learning and train employees ranging from bottom-level employees to top managers with smart and adaptable software. With adaptive learning, training can be arranged according to the individual progress of the employees (Schwarzmüller et al., 2018).

As a result of using new technologies in HR functions, human bias can be minimized. By using data-driven algorithmic technologies, future performance, the competency-talent gap, and the intention to quit can be predicted through statistical models. While adopting this type of approach has clear consequences that are readily detectable, more subtle and complex relationships such as *conscientiousness and professional success* can be predicted through previously unused and unstructured data (Stone et al., 2015, Stone and Deadrick, 2015, Cheng and Hackett, 2019).

Due to the widespread use of electronic monitoring (e.g., internet, telephone, video, location sensing technologies) in a wide variety of business types, technology has become part of corporate control systems. Employees' acceptance of the use of digital technologies especially for auditing and monitoring employee performance is important for the success and sustainability of the system. Technology-mediated relationships are now almost ubiquitous in the workplace, so it is important to consider how business decisions and policies can affect perceptions of justice (Ryan and Wessel, 2015). According to Ryan and Wessel (2015: 6), organizations should pay attention to some issues regarding the use of digital technologies that may affect employees' perceptions of justice. Accordingly, in order to monitor private life and to eliminate privacy and confidentiality concerns, it is necessary to clarify which non-work-related information will be monitored through organizational technologies and what should be the expectations of employees regarding privacy. In subordinate-superior relations redesigned through technology, managers and employees should be educated about the limits of when, how, and in what style to use digital technologies.

Conclusion

Since the change and transformation that organizations face in the age of Industry 4.0 are of a revolutionary nature, this situation should be managed much more carefully than usual. In times of change and transformation, as employees will suddenly find themselves with a completely different job and working conditions, the psychological contract between themselves and the organization can be damaged. Employees under these conditions show more cynicism, frustration, anger, and distrust, hiding information, attempting sabotage, etc., so they may show counterproductive behavior. It is the main responsibility of HRM to manage such behaviors and prevent violation of the psychological contract. To achieve success, it is necessary to prepare employees for continuous change and transformation, to provide the necessary information, to equip them with the necessary training, to overlook mistakes and create learning opportunities, and to take their ideas while updating job descriptions.

The interaction of human-artificial intelligence in managing mental processes will attract more and more researchers' attention. With the increasing effect of Industry 4.0 and digitalization, the strategic use of big data management and artificial intelligence in the management of human capital resources can be beneficial in terms of HR planning and understanding current employee needs and expectations in a timely and accurate manner (Garcia-Arroyo and Osca, 2019, Hamilton and Sodeman, 2020). However, these practices eliminate the boundaries between employees' working and living spaces, violate the privacy of private life, can lead to unethical practices, etc. There are various concerns that this will cause problems. In our opinion, using these tools sufficiently without violating the rights of employees is the biggest challenge that awaits HR managers and strategists.

Industry 4.0 is not the last stage of technological change, nor is it an end for the business world. Acknowledging the impact of technological developments on organizational structure and culture from the outset and proactively managing this situation are essential for sustainable competitive advantage and organizations to extend their lives.

Keywords: *HRM, Industry 4.0, digitalization, human labor, human behavior*

References

Barney, J., Wright, M., & Ketchen Jr, D. J. (2001). The resource-based view of the firm: ten years after 1991. *Journal of Management*, 27(6), 625-641. http://dx.doi.org/10.1177/014920630102700601

Blue, V. (2018, November 16), *More companies are chipping their workers like pets*. https://www.engadget.com/2018-11-16-employee-microchip-security-orwell.html

Boxall, P., & Purcell, J. (2000). Strategic human resource management: where have we come from and where should we be going? *International Journal of Management Reviews*, 2(2), 183-203. http://dx.doi.org/10.1111/1468-2370.00037

Bruce, K., & Nyland, C. (2011). Elton Mayo and the deification of human relations. *Organization studies*, 32(3), 383-405. http://dx.doi.org/10.1177/0170840610397478

Bush, J. T., & Balven, R. M. (2018). Catering to the crowd: An HRM perspective on crowd worker engagement. *Human Resource Management Review*. doi:10.1016/j.hrmr.2018.10.003

Chang, W. J. A., Wang, Y. S., & Huang, T. C. (2013). Work design–related antecedents of turnover intention: A multilevel approach. *Human Resource Management*, 52(1), 1-26. http://dx.doi.org/10.1002/hrm.21515

Channel24 (2020, July 17), *This website makes you feel like you're back at the office by recreating the sound of colleagues* https://www.news24.com/channel/music/news/this-website-makes-you-feel-like-youre-back-at-the-office-by-recreating-the-sound-of-colleagues-20200717-2

Cheng, M. M., & Hackett, R. D. (2019). A critical review of algorithms in HRM: Definition, theory, and practice. *Human Resource Management Review*. http://dx.doi.org/10.1016/j.hrmr.2019.100698

Collins, C. J. (2020). Expanding the resource based view model of strategic human resource management. *The International Journal of Human Resource Management*, 1-28. http://dx.doi.org/10.1080/09585192.2019.1711442

Connelly, C. E., Fieseler, C., Černe, M., Giessner, S. R., & Wong, S. I. (2020). Working in the digitized economy: HRM theory & practice. *Human Resource Management Review*, 100762. doi:10.1016/j.hrmr.2020.100762

Evans, P. A. (1999). HRM on the edge: A duality perspective. *Organization*, 6(2), 325-338. http://dx.doi.org/10.1177/135050849962010

Foerster-Metz, U. S., Marquardt, K., Golowko, N., Kompalla, A., & Hell, C. (2018). Digital Transformation and its Implications on Organizational Behavior. *Journal of EU Research in Business*, 30, 1-14. http://dx.doi.org/10.5171/2018.340873

Fry, L. W. (1982). Technology-structure research: Three critical issues. *Academy of Management Journal*, 25(3), 532-552. http://dx.doi.org/10.5465/256078

Garcia-Arroyo, J., & Osca, A. (2019). Big data contributions to human resource management: a systematic review. *The International Journal of Human Resource Management*, 1-26. http://dx.doi.org/10.1080/09585192.2019.1674357

Gelecekburada, (2020, July 1). *Bilim kurgu filmi değil: Çalışanlara Takılan Çipler Yaygınlaşıyor.* https://www.gelecekburada.net/bilim-kurgu-filmi-degil-calisanlara-takilan-cipler-yayginlasiyor/

Guest, D. E. (1987). Human resource management and industrial relations. *Journal of management Studies*, 24(5), 503-521. http://dx.doi.org/10.1111/j.1467-6486.1987.tb00460.x

Hamilton, R. H., & Sodeman, W. A. (2020). The questions we ask: Opportunities and challenges for using big data analytics to strategically manage human capital resources. *Business Horizons*, 63(1), 85-95. http://dx.doi.org/10.1016/j.bushor.2019.10.001

Hartley, N. T. (2005). The 7 hidden reasons why employees leave. *Journal of Applied Management and Entrepreneurship*, 10(4), 80.

Helfat, C. E., & Martin, J. A. (2015). Dynamic managerial capabilities: Review and assessment of managerial impact on strategic change. *Journal of management*, 41(5), 1281-1312. http://dx.doi.org/10.1177/0149206314561301

Heneman, H. G., Schwab, D. P., Fossum, J. A., & Dyer, L. D. (1989). *Personnel Human Resource Management*, Irwin.

Huy, Q., & Zott, C. (2019). Exploring the affective underpinnings of dynamic managerial capabilities: How managers' emotion regulation behaviors mobilize resources for their firms. *Strategic Management Journal*, 40(1), 28–54. http://dx.doi.org/10.1002/smj.2971

Juarez Tarraga, A., Santandreu Mascarell, C., & Marin Garcia, J. A. (2019). What are the main concerns of human resource managers in organizations?. *Intangible Capital* 15(1):72. http://dx.doi.org/10.3926/ic.1342

Kehoe, R. R., & Collins, C. J. (2017). Human resource management and unit performance in knowledge-intensive work. *Journal of Applied Psychology*, 102(8), 1222–1236. http://dx.doi.org/10.1037/apl0000216

Küpper, D. M., Klein, K., & Völckner, F. (2019). Gamifying employer branding: An integrating framework and research propositions for a new HRM approach in the digitized economy. *Human Resource Management Review*. 31(1). 2021. http://dx.doi.org/10.1016/j.hrmr.2019.04.002

Larkin, J. (2017). HR digital disruption: the biggest wave of transformation in decades. *Strategic HR Review*, 16(2), 55–59. doi:10.1108/shr-01-2017-0006

Mahoney, T. A., & Deckop, J. R. (1986). Evolution of concept and practice in personnel administration/human resource management (PA/HRM). *Journal of Management*, 12(2), 223-241. http://dx.doi.org/10.1177/014920638601200206

Marin-Garcia, J.A. (2013). What do we know about the relationship between High Involvement Work Practices and Performance?. *Working Papers on Operations Managemen*t, 4(2), 1-15. https://doi.org/10.4995/wpom.v4i2.1552

Metz, R. (2018, August 17). *This company embeds microchips in its employees, and they love it*. https://www.technologyreview.com/2018/08/17/140994/this-company-embeds-microchips-in-its-employees-and-they-love-it/

Munsamy, M., & Telukdarie, A. (2019, December). Digital HRM Model for Process Optimization by Adoption of Industry 4.0 Technologies. In 2019 *IEEE International Conference on Industrial Engineering and Engineering Management (IEEM)* (pp. 374-378). IEEE. http://dx.doi.org/10.1109/IEEM44572.2019.8978726

Parry, E., & Strohmeier, S. (2014). HRM in the digital age–digital changes and challenges of the HR profession. *Employee Relations*. Vol. 36 No. 4. http://dx.doi.org/10.1108/ER-03-2014-0032

Ryan, A. M., & Wessel, J. (2015). Implications of a changing workforce and workplace for justice perceptions and expectations. *Human Resource Management Review*, 25(2), 162–175. http://dx.doi.org/10.1016/j.hrmr.2015.01.001

Schwab, K. (2017). *The fourth industrial revolution*. Portfolio Penguin, UK.

Schwarzmüller, T., Brosi, P., Duman, D., & Welpe, I. M. (2018). How does the digital transformation affect organizations? Key themes of change in work design and leadership. *Mrev Management Revue*, 29(2), 114-138. http://dx.doi.org/10.5771/0935-9915-2018-2-114

Seghezzi, F., & Tiraboschi, M. (2018). Italy's industry 4.0 plan: an analysis from a labour law perspective. *E-Journal of International and Comparative, Labour Studies*, Volume 7, No. 1, January 2018

Sony, M., & Naik, S. (2020). Industry 4.0 integration with socio-technical systems theory: A systematic review and proposed theoretical model. *Technology in Society*, 101248. http://dx.doi.org/10.1016/j.techsoc.2020.101248

Spreitzer, G., Cameron, L., & Garrett, L. (2017). Alternative work arrangements: Two images of the new world of work. *Annual Review of Psychology and Organizational Behavior*, 4, 473–499. http://dx.doi.org/10.1146/annurev-orgpsych-032516-113332

Stone, D. L., & Deadrick, D. L. (2015). Challenges and opportunities affecting the future of human resource management. *Human Resource Management Review*, 25(2), 139-145. http://dx.doi.org/10.1016/j.hrmr.2015.01.003

Stone, D. L., Deadrick, D. L., Lukaszewski, K. M., & Johnson, R. (2015). The influence of technology on the future of human resource management. *Human resource management review*, 25(2), 216-231. http://dx.doi.org/10.1016/j.hrmr.2015.01.002

Torrington, D., Hall, L., Taylor, S., & Atkinson, C. (2014). *Human Resource Management*. Harlow, England: Pearson.

Trist, E. (1981). The evolution of socio-technical systems. *Occasional paper*, 2(1981), 1981.

Yankın, F. B. (2019). Dijital Dönüşüm Sürecinde Çalışma Yaşamı. *Trakya Üniversitesi İktisadi ve İdari Bilimler Fakültesi Dergisi*, 7(2), 1-38.

Yıldız, E. (2013). İnsan Kaynakları Yönetiminde Davranış Boyutu ve Bir Örnek Olay. *Öneri Dergisi*, 10(40), 103-113.

CHAPTER NINE

THE IMPACT OF THE COVID-19 PANDEMIC ON HUMAN RESOURCES MANAGEMENT AND DIGITAL HUMAN RESOURCES MANAGEMENT PRACTICES

SELMA KILIÇ KIRILMAZ

Introduction

The COVID-19 outbreak spread all over the world shortly after it broke out in China. The World Health Organization declared this outbreak as a pandemic on March 11, 2020 (WHO, 2020). This outbreak has become the biggest epidemic threatening the health of all people in recent years. During the COVID-19 pandemic, changes have been experienced in the stress, anxiety and depression levels of people. The growing threat of the epidemic, the disruption of travel plans, social isolation, overexposure to pandemic-related information in the media and the purchase of essential necessities during a panic have led to an atmosphere of global anxiety and depression (Potcovaru, 2020: 89).

The COVID-19 pandemic has had a profound impact on businesses and employees. According to Papagiannidis, Harris and Morton (2020: 4), COVID-19 is the first major epidemic in the digital era, but it is unlikely to be the last. Businesses are required to find novel and creative solutions that can maintain social distance for months in order to cope with this outbreak. In a short time, the majority of businesses had to switch to teleworking systems. HR departments played a fundamental role in the management of the pandemic process in businesses. They were actively involved in the organization of issues such as working order, communication with employees and continuation of works. They made use of digital technologies in the management of all these processes and also played a role in adapting employees to teleworking conditions and preventing loss of motivation.

The digital transformation accelerated with the pandemic, while digitalization is on the agenda of businesses. During the pandemic period, businesses were able to sustain themselves by doing many jobs thanks to digital technologies. The pandemic increased the use of digital technologies by HR units as well. Cloud technologies, artificial intelligence, analytical programs, etc., can be named among the digital technologies most used by HR units.

In this study examining the impact of the COVID-19 pandemic on human resources management and digital human resources management practices, firstly, there is a focus on the effects of the COVID-19 pandemic on human resources management. Secondly, the subject of digital transformation and its reflections on human resources management is discussed. Lastly, the impact of the COVID-19 pandemic on human resources management and digital human resources management practices is assessed. In this section, teleworking, well-being, digital applications, personnel procurement and selection, online training and online orientation, employee competencies, performance management and the wage system are discussed.

The Impacts of the COVID-19 Pandemic on Human Resources Management

COVID-19, which broke out in Wuhan, the capital of China's Hubei region in December 2019, turned into a world-wide outbreak (Aslan, 2020: 39) and was declared a pandemic by the World Health Organization (WHO, 2020) on March 11, 2020. Governments around the world took strict crowd control measures, including border closures and business shutdowns (excluding essential services) in order to control the rapid spread of the COVID-19 virus. In addition, they established rules of isolation and social distance that restrict people's close physical contact (Chadee, Ren, & Tang, 2021: 1).

The COVID-19 crisis has turned into an economic and labor market shock affecting both the supply of goods and services produced and the demand for consumption and investment. COVID-19 has had a profound impact on the labor market. Along with concerns about the health of employees and their families, the economic shocks experienced after the emergence of the virus affect the business world in three main dimensions: 1) The amount of work in terms of both unemployment and underemployment; 2) The quality of work issues such as wages and access to social protection; and 3) The impacts on vulnerable groups who will be more affected by adverse labor market outcomes (ILO, 2020a: 2-3).

Hecklaua et al. (2016: 2) defined human resources management as "a strategic approach to employing and developing a highly qualified workforce effectively to achieve the objectives of the enterprises." The importance of HR departments in businesses increased along with the COVID-19 outbreak. This is because all businesses were affected by this epidemic and had to carry out all the coordination between employees and business managers. In addition, HR departments had to regulate changing business conditions and ensure that employees adapted to these conditions.

With the COVID-19 outbreak, health and safety issues have become top issues and HR's role in protecting the health and safety of the international workforce has increased (Caligiuri et al., 2020: 700). Employees and managers felt panic and fear due to the uncertainty and virus threat that they experienced immediately after the COVID-19 outbreak. Soon after dealing with the feeling of panic and fear that came with the COVID-19 virus, managers had to make many decisions which included; who would be laid off and who would continue to work, where and how employees could work in the digital field, the priorities of their businesses and how these priorities could be best explained to employees, etc. (Caligiuri et al., 2020: 697).

According to *The Economist*, "The duties of Human Resources Managers look critical during the pandemic process. Because these managers have to keep employees healthy, maintain their morale, control their teleworking experience and consider whether employees will be laid off and, if so, when and how employees will be laid off while firms practice economy" (The Economist, 24 March 2020).

The COVID-19 outbreak has created a difficult environment for human resource management (HRM). Managers were not only helping employees to adapt to radical changes in the business and social environment, but also to adapt quickly to the "unknown unknowns". For example, employees who had previously spent all or most of their time working in the workplace now had to adapt to remote work (Carnevale and Hatak, 2020: 183). Therefore, the role of HR becomes crucial during a crisis like the COVID-19 outbreak. In cases of crisis, HR tries to meet the health and organizational needs of workers. Another HR role is to establish a relationship between employees and leaders. Employees are required to raise business concerns and propose solutions to leaders and leaders should listen to their employees in times of crisis and provide employees with psychological empowerment and control assistance. In addition, it is very important that they keep employees up-to-date and inform them about the current status of the job (Dirani et al., 2020: 383).

The COVID-19 outbreak showed that to ensure rapid corporate decisions are taken, employers should consider building an "outbreak response team" to keep up with the latest developments in the situation, formulate emergency response plans and clarify internal responsibilities. HR or the response team can notify employees of the latest situation with the correct information, inform employees about the corporate plans and security measures taken and actively respond to employees' concerns with corporate communication tools (Xu, Liu and Yin, 2020: 10).

Due to the COVID-19 outbreak, businesses had to face the problem of managing their employees in different regions with unprecedented technical, physical and socio-economic challenges (Carnevale and Hatak, 2020: 183). The COVID-19 pandemic forced many employees, who were already stressed out about the health risks, to work from home. Many managers had to lead teleworking teams for the first time in this period along with this stress factor (Caligiuri et al., 2020: 698).

According to Provino (2020: 31), the health of employees should be a high priority for HR departments as the majority of the labor force is now working at home during the COVID-19 pandemic. It should be ensured that employees are as happy as possible while working away from their offices because the performance of employees depends on employee well-being and motivation. If this motivation and well-being cannot be achieved, the success of the work conducted may be at risk. During the process of COVID-19, teleworking can negatively affect those who live alone and meet their social interaction needs at the office. HR and HR managers should be aware that new projects or learning activities may be needed to prevent these employees from losing their motivation. As the majority of the labor force is now working from home, employee health should be a high priority for HR departments everywhere. It's all about keeping employees as happy as possible while working away from the office (Jones, 2020: 39).

Another important problem faced by employees during the COVID-19 outbreak is that the conflict between work and family is more likely than ever to occur. In addition to the problems of maintaining telework, especially for those who are not used to working from home, it is necessary to pay attention to increased childcare concerns as well as the health and safety of family and friends. Consequently, protecting the boundaries between work and family has become much more difficult for employees than ever before (Carnevale and Hatak, 2020: 184). Therefore, HR departments need to develop effective strategies for resolving potential conflicts.

Another important subject for HR departments is to produce solutions for managing the work and employees after the pandemic. Regarding this issue, Deloitte pointed out in the report titled "Workforce Strategies for

Post-COVID-19 Recovery" that workforce-related strategies can best be organized with five critical actions in the new normal period. These strategies are reflect, recommit, re-engage, rethink and reboot. These topics can help organizations to return to normal in the aftermath of the crisis (Deloitte, 2020: 8).

Businesses participating in the research conducted by Mercer listed the importance of the emergency action plan/crisis management plan, business continuity plan, digitalization and effective management and the possibility of teleworking and flexible working among the lessons learned from the COVID-19 outbreak (Mercer, 2020). It can thus be argued that businesses will tend towards digitalization and make use of more digital applications in the fulfillment of HR functions after the pandemic.

Digital Transformation and Reflections on Human Resources Management

Digitization is defined "as a social and technical process that takes place in individual, organizational, social and global areas and in all sectors. Digitization refers to the use of tools that transform analog information into digital information and involves a complex set of technologies". Digitalization refers to the use of web-based applications to facilitate remote access and collaborative work, such as cloud computing, in its current form for workplaces (ILO, 2020b: 8). Digital transformation describes the changes imposed by information technology (IT) to (partially) automate the tasks. Digital transformation has special importance in the business world because it requires and ensures that corporates operate in changing markets (Legner et al., 2017: 304).

Digital transformation is also "the idea of going 'paperless' that allows people to solve traditional problems with digital technologies or influence businesses and everyone else". Digital transformation refers to the use of digital technology in all business areas and digital transformation delivers customer value by fundamentally changing the way that businesses operate. Digital transformation elements include customer experience, operational agility, culture and leadership, workforce enablement and digital technology integration (Singh, 2019: 16). According to Betchoo (2016: 2), with smart and mobile connectivity, the digital world forces companies to renew and develop their technological infrastructure. This "technology network" makes businesses stronger in critical digital dimensions such as products, services, customer experience, operations and workforce with social media, mobility, analytics, cloud and internet of things (SMACI) technologies.

There is a transformation in the way that HR services are delivered and managed by businesses along with the advancement of technology. Technology in HR aims to make the work paperless and the resources efficient and flexible. Transferring HR practices from desktop computers to laptops and then to smartphones and tablets enabled mobility and convenience for employees. Technology in HR increases the competitive abilities of companies. A technologically enhanced HR department makes a significant difference in delivering more value to the corporate (Bhatia, 2016: 37).

Technology can be a blessing for HR practitioners. However, the HR specialist should be aware of both the benefits and the entrapments of technology solutions (Dickson and Nusair, 2010: 92). As digitalization advances, data resources are becoming more accessible to human resource (HR) professionals, allowing them to better analyze the complexity of their decision-making process related to the workforce. The opportunities for digital technologies to provide big data seem almost limitless (Dahlbom, Siikanen & Sajasalo, 2018: 120).

Human resources departments are severely constrained as they also have to deal with employees' operational problems and daily routines. In the future, these activities will largely be self-service or performed by digital assistants. At the same time, HR departments will help leaders to build perspectives on human resource issues through analytics and artificial intelligence (AI). These developments will enable human resources departments to obtain the time and tools they need for turning to more qualified jobs (DiRomualdo, El-Khoury & Girimonte, 2018: 235).

The employee selection and recruitment process is the most important factor in the HR department's adoption of digital technologies. It is a common practice to use social media for identifying potential employees and communicating with them. Besides this, the use of video tools, artificial intelligence and mobile access in job application processes is increasing as well (DiRomualdo, El-Khoury and Girimonte, 2018: 235). The use of technology makes HRM functions easier to perform, but digitalization affects HRM more than that. Among the functions affected by digitalization are performance management, HR planning, recruitment and selection, employee relations, reward management, health and safety and job design. However, digitalization has also introduced the responsibility of HR functions to ensure that the human capital within the organization is in line with the strategic requirements of the digital age (Fenech, Baguant, & Ivanov, 2019: 168).

There are many digital applications and technologies used by the HR departments of businesses. Artificial intelligence, cloud technologies and mobile applications have an important place among these applications and technologies. In the research conducted by Kilic Kirilmaz (2020: 197-198), the fundamental digital HRM practices of businesses were determined as follows:

- The use of chatbots in answering questions addressed to human resources departments,
- The complete execution of recruitment processes in a digital environment,
- Conducting video and online interviews during recruitment processes,
- Pre-elimination to be performed by artificial intelligence in recruitment,
- Making job applications by filling out an application form with a QR code or a link created on the internet,
- Enabling employees to fulfill their requests such as annual leave and e-payroll via a mobile application,
- Performing recognition and reward processes on a digital platform,
- Transferring all HR processes to mobile applications,
- Conducting orientation training with mobile application assistance,
- Carrying out digital education programs,
- Implementing digital rewarding systems,
- Providing online feedback to employees with mobile application assistance,
- Data-based analysis and reporting via Dashboard,
- Making staffing calculations and reporting in the digital environment,
- Carrying out online entire business processes in career management such as performance management, promotion, appointment and cease of employment, etc.,
- Instantly performing the analyses and assessments of performance and employee commitment with mobile solutions,
- Carrying out the online internship program,
- Quick delivery of business-related information and announcements to employees via mobile applications,
- The ability to share projects and mentoring opportunities as well as works within the organization thanks to the artificial intelligence-enabled platform.

Assessing the Impact of the COVID-19 Pandemic on Human Resources Management and Digital Human Resources Management Practices

"Digital human resources" is a digital process involving the reconstruction and implementation of relationships between businesses, suppliers, customers and service-providing employees (Gökçe Parsehyan, 2020: 216). The fact that economies and regions were put under lockdown for long periods due to the pandemic has made it necessary for many employees to use digital technologies. Besides, employees had to perform interaction tasks with colleagues, customers and suppliers by working from home. Using digital technologies to continue teleworking was seen as a magic tool that could save industries from total collapse in the early stages of COVID-19 (Chadee, Ren & Tang, 2021: 5).

Technology is the only component of transformation because communication with employees, customers and stakeholders changes not only in terms of equipment but also in terms of method and content thanks to the technology. Therefore, businesses need to offer additional opportunities for employees to communicate with each other so that the social aspect of the office environment can be assured. It is also critical to be alert to the data security risks that teleworking can pose (Ilie, Ilie & Marin, 2020: 668). Digital technologies turned into an important tool in enabling large sections of society to function during the COVID-19 pandemic (Chadee, Ren & Tang, 2021: 1).

Before the pandemic, businesses were also making efforts to digitize their HR practices; however, digitization has accelerated more during the pandemic. Overall, the COVID-19 outbreak appears to have accelerated the integration of digital technology into all aspects of public and private life, despite its side effects (Papouli, Chatzifotiou & Tsairidis, 2020: 1109).

An accelerated digital transformation is an important condition that is imposed on the business world by COVID-19 in general. COVID-19 has increased the use of technology by businesses. Some of the advantages brought about by more intense digitalization during the pandemic period may include (Kudyba, 2020: 286):

- More consistently structured collaboration (online digital meetings with agenda items which can easily be scheduled between participants),
- More usage of analytics (e.g., more focus on existing analytics reporting),
- More participation in the meetings compared to the pre-pandemic period due to negative organizational variables and lack of travel arising from physical distance,
- More efficient overall work outcomes could be achieved because of the reduction of distractions in the office,
- The transfer of more informational content (e.g., asynchronous) is ensured by recording digital collaboration,

- A more comprehensive use of existing systems and technologies that reduce learning curve thresholds for effective technology use is enabled.

The pace of digitization has increased since the beginning of the epidemic and the adoption of digital technologies by businesses has allowed employees to work from home. Digitization has led to significant changes in the form of employment, skill requirements and labor standards. However, with the lack of internet connectivity and available ICT tools, etc., digitalization does not spread evenly around the world. For example, in countries where regular power cuts and poor internet connectivity make emailing difficult, remote work is practically impossible without the support of employers in terms of purchasing hardware and providing broadband (ILO, 2020b: 8).

It is explained above that the HR departments of businesses have been benefiting more from digital applications since the beginning of the pandemic. In the next section, HR practices, where digitalization is most effective in the pandemic process, will be explained. These practices include teleworking, well-being, digital applications, employee selection and recruitment, online training and orientation, employee competencies, performance management and wage systems.

Teleworking

Teleworking refers to performing work tasks by using information and communication technologies such as tablets, laptops and desktop computers outside the offices provided to employees by their employers. In other words, teleworking means the work carried out with the help of information and communication technologies outside the employer's principal office (ILO, 2020b: 1). Teleworking has been one of the most transformative workplace practices attributed to COVID-19. Before COVID-19, it was observed that the number of teleworking employees gradually increased, while, the pandemic caused a record increase in terms of teleworking (Akingbola, 2020: 17).

According to Iansiti and Richards (2020: 3), a fourth pandemic dimension was added to digital operating models: teleworking. Today, the teleworking model digitalizes the relationship between the company and the employee, rather than only digitalizing the relationship between the company and the customer. Consequently, office spaces are becoming less important and teleworking is becoming both possible and favored. More and more companies are switching to teleworking every day. For example,

Amazon, Facebook, Google and Microsoft, among the most important companies in the US, switched to teleworking in early March 2020. The most important reason for this was that the test results of those working in the Seattle offices of these companies were positive (Maurer, 2020). Due to the COVID-19 outbreak, many workers had to work from home. This situation has turned into a challenge for HRM to deal with. A survey was conducted with HR managers of 800 global businesses in March 2020, revealing that 88% of businesses encouraged or mandated employees to work from home during the COVID-19 crisis (Caligiuri et al., 2020: 701).

"Teleworking" is not a recent topic that has just begun to be discussed, it has been discussed in the business world for more than 10 years. However, the COVID-19 outbreak has caused a record increase in the number of people working from home. The COVID-19 epidemic has turned teleworking into a driving force rather than a preference (Kaushik and Guleria, 2020: 14). During the COVID-19 pandemic, organizations have experienced teleworking styles in various ways. Some organizations were already used to teleworking and adapted much more easily. Others, on the other hand, did not have teleworking experience, so they had difficulty in adapting to teleworking in terms of process and technology. The inability of employees to have the hardware and software technology they needed while performing their jobs also increased the difficulties (Deloitte, 2020).

According to the outcome of the research conducted by Mercer; it is determined that 71% of businesses contributed to their employees' needs on "digital solutions and their usage" in order to accelerate the adaptation to teleworking during the COVID-19 pandemic. Among the practices of businesses on "digital solutions and their usage", the following are listed: organizing informative materials and training sessions on Zoom, teleworking, working-at-home ergonomics; increasing the internet quotas and covering the relevant costs by the corporate; organizing mailing and webinars; training of basic programs needed for teleworking (VPN, Teams, SharePoint, Workday, etc.) and broadcasting user groups; providing online training on the effective use of communication channels and remote leadership; and creating applications where employees could have a pleasant time with their families and children and improve themselves in their home environment (Mercer, 2020).

Although teleworking is a key factor in ensuring business continuity, it has led to difficulties in managing work-private life conflicts by causing an increase in the number of people present at home (İlhan, 2020: 295). According to the results of the research conducted by Eurofound in April 2020, at the peak of the COVID-19 outbreak; it was found out that participants, especially women with children under 12, had trouble balancing their work and personal lives (Eurofound, 2020: 21).

According to the research outcome conducted by Mercer; "Employee motivation, employee performance management process, communication, lack of technological infrastructure and the difficulty of working while children are present" are listed among the biggest challenges of teleworking during the COVID-19 pandemic process (Mercer, 2020). According to Mateescu, Muscalu and Baleanu (2020: 420), many employers will prefer teleworking to reduce costs even after the pandemic.

Well-being

There is an often-overlooked aspect of teleworking that has been highlighted by the COVID-19 outbreak; loneliness and isolation. If teleworking is to become widespread over time, companies will have to find ways to overcome these problems. The use of innovative technology can assist to some extent. The weekly video-calling culture is a great option for team members to log in remotely so they can meet with their colleagues. Managers can ensure that employees' significant days such as birthdays and anniversaries, as well as business achievements, are shared and celebrated with everyone in the team (Kaushik and Guleria, 2020: 11-12).

According to the results of the research conducted by Mercer; it is determined that 59.9% of the businesses are working on or planning to do studies with the aim of supporting the mental health/resilience of employees during the COVID-19 pandemic. These practices include providing online psychologist support, holding collective sessions; organizing online seminars; a coaching service; organizing mindfulness and well-being training; providing online sports training; and sharing webinars and e-learning on emotional resilience (Mercer, 2020).

According to the research conducted by Akbaş Tuna and Çelen (2020: 2737), it is found that HRM managers carried out social-distanced activities in order to increase staff morale and motivation during the COVID-19 period and these efforts included the use of online talks, therapy and internet communication. It is also determined that these efforts contributed to the employees being able to cope more easily with the pandemic period.

Digital Applications

Technology initiatives all around the world have taken action with the reflex of "What can we do against the virus?" to bring together technology and human resources. It is observed that cloud platforms and recruitment software play an important role in human resources process management in the COVID-19 process. Cloud platforms ease the burden of professionals in storing/managing big data. Thanks to today's new technologies and recruitment software, human resources are able to use data in every process such as recruitment, workforce turnover, backup and training planning. Technological recruitment software and artificial intelligence, which are among the applications that minimize human intervention and therefore error, provide companies with great convenience in terms of optimization and targeting (PERYÖN, 2020: 6).

During the pandemic process, artificial intelligence provides support in the process to recruit the right employee needed by the organization, which is one of the most basic duties of HR departments. Recruitment processes have become much faster, more efficient and easier thanks to artificial intelligence. On the other hand, new methods have been developed in recruitment processes thanks to artificial intelligence. These include conducting interviews with candidates through artificial intelligence-aided chatbots and performing sentiment analysis by evaluating the data obtained through artificial intelligence. It is believed that artificial intelligence applications will conduct direct interviews with candidates during the recruitment process in the near future. The rate of interviews conducted in the digital environment is also increasing (PERYÖN, 2020: 7).

Employee Selection and Recruitment

During the COVID-19 pandemic, businesses had to switch to practices such as online recruitment, employee selection and training instead of face-to-face practices. Online applications can attract and retain employees in the corporate in a different way to traditional face-to-face applications (Carnevale and Hatak, 2020: 184). As the traditional methods remain impossible during the pandemic period, the use of electronic information systems is increasing rather well. Companies make use of the internet to procure the workforce they need and perform processes such as assessment and interviews via the internet as well (Akbaş Tuna and Çelen, 2020: 2751).

According to the outcome of the research conducted by Mercer; it is determined that 59.9% of the businesses decided to continue their recruitment processes in the virtual/online environment and that 32.3% of the businesses decided to continue with assessment center applications in the digital environment during the COVID-19 pandemic (Mercer, 2020). For instance, Amazon, one of the largest companies in the US, canceled most of the face-to-face interviews and set up virtual interview portals for candidates so they could connect with recruitment specialists, fill in the required documents and participate in interviews through the company's video-conferencing software, Amazon Chime (Maurer, 2020). Google advised candidates that interviews would be conducted on Google Hangouts or by using the BlueJeans video-conferencing service. LinkedIn offered job seekers the option to conduct their interviews through BlueJeans or informed candidates that they could re-arrange the timing of their interviews until face-to-face interviews are possible again (Maurer, 2020).

The majority of participants in the study conducted by Akbaş Tuna and Çelen (2020: 2734) explained that technological communication tools would be commoner than conventional methods in employee selection and that they should also be widespread after the COVID-19 process. During the COVID-19 pandemic, digital platforms have gained importance in terms of both health and safety in employee selection.

Online Training and Online Orientation

After the outbreak of the COVID-19 pandemic, businesses had to transfer their training practices to the online environment to a large extent. Before the pandemic, businesses that valued digitalization had already transferred some of their training practices to online environments; however, providing training online became a necessity along with the pandemic process. Some businesses also organize online orientation training for newly recruited employees due to the pandemic. According to the research conducted by Mercer, 71.3% of the businesses decided to continue their 2020 training sessions online during the COVID-19 pandemic (Mercer, 2020). Therefore, it can be expected that the training will mostly be held in digital environments after the pandemic process as well.

On some days during the pandemic period, people cannot leave their homes because of lockdown. Some businesses see this lockdown time as an opportunity for the training and improvement of their employees. According to the research conducted by Akbaş Tuna and Çelen (2020: 2735), it is determined that HRM managers turn to distance education activities for employees so they can use their lockdown time efficiently for both themselves and the business.

Employees' Competencies

The talent pool is also changing together with the COVID-19 crisis. This talent pool is expanding and being restructured. The pandemic revealed gaps in core competencies, both individually and in general and also introduced new capabilities (Caligiuri et al., 2020: 704-705).

Frankiewicz and Chamorro-Premuzic (2020: 9-10) state that, according to popular belief, digital transformation is more about technology, but in reality, digital transformation is more about people. Technologies can be easily purchased, but to adapt to digitalization, it is necessary to develop next-generation skills, balance the talent supply and demand and train all employees according to their future competency needs. During the COVID-19 pandemic, remote workers make more self-learning efforts to learn, thrive and demonstrate their talents. For instance, LinkedIn distance-learning courses have been requested three times more often since the start of stay-at-home calls. In a period when employees want to learn, develop and increase their skills, companies that offer their employees online training opportunities or pay the fees for these training courses will clearly have a win-win opportunity. This training will provide the development of skills and an increase in the motivation of employees (Caligiuri et al., 2020: 700).

It can be ensured that the online courses that employees will take for improving their skills are aimed at the qualifications that businesses will need when these employees return to work after the pandemic. These online courses may include; managing teams, artificial intelligence, machine learning, working with robots, HR analytics and updated employment regulations for HR, etc. HR departments can be a regulatory body to provide such skill training (Jones, 2020: 39-40).

Performance Management

Electronic applications play an important role in assessing the performance of employees during the pandemic process. Electronic performance systems enable the recording of various data such as the amount of work done, the errors that take place and the time spent to perform the work. Thanks to the relevant system, managers can analyze the behaviors of their subordinate personnel and also avoid the loss of time that occurs while assessing performance. Therefore, the relevant system is extremely effective in receiving fast feedback (Akbaş Tuna and Çelen, 2020: 2750-2751).

According to the research conducted by Mercer; 33.5% of the businesses stated that digital applications should be developed for the effective monitoring of business results during the COVID-19 pandemic. In respect of the research study in question, 74.3% of the businesses stated that they would revise their year-end performance targets together with their business targets (Mercer, 2020). Concerning the research conducted by Akbaş Tuna and Çelen (2020: 2750-2738), it is determined that many enterprises will provide flexibility in performance assessment processes depending on the reduction and/or cessation of their activities and will intensely benefit from the internet and technological developments in the assessment criteria.

Wage System

Following the COVID-19 outbreak, "short-term employment allowance" support was provided by the government to businesses in Turkey. Within the scope of the aforesaid support, the state covers a certain amount of the wages to be paid to employees of the businesses by imposing a dismissal ban. This support also introduced a new wage policy. The objective of this support is to enable both employees and businesses to overcome the COVID-19 pandemic process more easily.

Most of the businesses participating in the research conducted by Mercer stated that they focused on the options of applying for a short-term employment allowance for wage management, using the accumulated annual leave, giving employees non-paid annual leave and continuing the teleworking model in case the pandemic process is prolonged (Mercer, 2020).

Conclusion

In this study examining the impact of the COVID-19 pandemic on human resources management and digital human resources management practices, firstly, the effects of the COVID-19 pandemic on human resources management are discussed. Thereafter, the subject of digital transformation and its reflections on human resources management are discussed. And lastly, the impact of the COVID-19 pandemic on human resources management and digital human resources management practices is assessed with the subheadings of teleworking, well-being, digital applications, employee selection and recruitment, online training and online orientation, employee competencies, performance management and the wage system.

The fact that COVID-19 started in China at the end of 2019 and spread all over the world, transforming into a pandemic within a short period of three months, had considerable impacts on both businesses and employees. Many businesses, especially those operating in the service industry, had to reduce the volume of their work or completely shut down their operations. However, those working in mask manufacturing, hygiene products, as couriers, etc., had to work more. Some businesses, on the other hand, had to lay off their employees. In a Fortune survey conducted in the second week of June 2020, 59% of private-sector CEOs stated that their businesses chose to freeze hiring processes to reduce their losses in the first place (Sines, 2020: 10).

Businesses experienced a crisis due to uncertainty in the first days of the pandemic. After overcoming the first shock of the crisis, some measures were taken and efforts were made to sustain the works. Among the first measures taken was establishing the necessary hygiene and distance rules to protect employees. Apart from this, a vast majority of white-collar workers had to work from home during the COVID-19 pandemic.

HR departments mostly benefited from digital technologies while managing the pandemic process. Digitalization was a preference for businesses in the pre-pandemic period, whereas, it became a necessity after the pandemic outbreak. Employees who had to carry out their work from home due to the pandemic were able to adapt to this process thanks to digital technologies. HR digital technologies that businesses have resorted to in the process of working from home include cloud computing, artificial intelligence applications, analytics programs and recruitment software. Apart from these, activities such as zoom meetings, webinars, online training, etc., have facilitated the workloads of HR departments thanks to the internet.

The importance and workload of HR departments of businesses increased with the COVID-19 pandemic. The reason for this is that HR units have to manage the whole process during the pandemic, enable all communication and ensure coordination between business management and employees. However, HR departments played a significant role in the adaptation of employees to the new process.

One of the most important issues that HR departments have had to manage during the pandemic is teleworking. Teleworking refers to employees performing their work outside of the office thanks to technologies such as computers, the internet, etc. While some businesses allowed their employees to work from home on certain days of the week before the pandemic, many did not favor this way of working. On the other hand, almost all businesses had to switch to a mode of teleworking after the pandemic outbreak. Businesses with teleworking experience in the pre-pandemic period were able to manage this process more easily. According to the outcome of the research conducted by Mercer; it is determined that 71% of businesses have contributed to their employees' needs on "digital solutions and their usage" in order to accelerate the adaptation to teleworking during the COVID-19 pandemic.

Teleworking is an important solution to continue work, however, new problems have also arisen with working at home. Employees' difficulties in maintaining the balance between work and private life are the greatest challenge. According to the results of the research conducted by Eurofound in April 2020, at the peak of the COVID-19 outbreak; it was found that participants, especially women with children under 12, had trouble balancing their work and personal lives. According to the outcome of research conducted by Mercer, "Employee motivation, employee performance management process, communication, lack of technological infrastructure and the difficulty of working while children are present" are listed among the biggest challenges of teleworking during the COVID-19 pandemic process (Mercer, 2020).

HR departments play a significant role in overcoming the problems caused by teleworking. Psychosocial problems experienced by employees had to be resolved. According to the results of the research conducted by Mercer; it is determined that 59.9% of the businesses are working on or planning to do studies to support the mental health/resilience of employees during the COVID-19 pandemic. Practices that businesses have or plan to have to support the mental health/resilience of employees include: providing online psychologist support, holding collective sessions; organizing online seminars; a coaching service; organizing mindfulness and well-being training; providing online sports training; and sharing webinars and e-learning on emotional resilience (Mercer, 2020). All these events are organized by HR departments. Digital platforms also play a key role in the organization of these events.

The pandemic also had an important impact on one of the main functions of HR: the procurement and selection of personnel. Businesses' utilization rate of digital technologies for personnel recruitment and selection increased with the pandemic process. Interviews, mostly conducted face-to-face before the pandemic, began to take place almost entirely on digital media with the effect of the pandemic. Similarly, the use of online platforms also increased for receiving applications and performing personality and skills tests. For instance, Amazon canceled most of the face-to-face interviews and set up virtual interview portals for candidates so they could connect with recruitment specialists, fill in required documents and participate in interviews through the company's video-conferencing software, Amazon Chime (Maurer, 2020). Furthermore, according to the research outcome conducted by Mercer, it is determined that 59.9% of the businesses decided to continue their recruitment processes in the virtual/online environment and that 32.3% of the businesses decided to continue the assessment center applications in the digital environment during the COVID-19 pandemic (Mercer, 2020).

The COVID-19 pandemic also had significant effects on education, which is one of the important practices of HR departments. The vast majority of businesses transferred their training to online platforms.

According to the research conducted by Mercer; it is determined that 71.3% of the businesses decided to continue their 2020 training sessions online during the COVID-19 pandemic (Mercer, 2020). Digitalization played a significant role in the organization of these training activities. Some businesses, on the other hand, conducted their orientation training online. It can be expected that businesses will carry out most of their training activities online after the pandemic.

As employees started working outside of the office due to the pandemic, this led to some changes in terms of their competencies. Digital and technological competencies gained importance upon switching to teleworking. HR departments had to find solutions to fulfill these competencies needed in employees. The fact that businesses turned to online training along with the pandemic process helped businesses to increase the competencies of their employees. According to Jones (2020: 39-40), businesses should ensure that their employees spend the pandemic taking courses on subjects such as managing teams, artificial intelligence, machine learning, working with robots, HR analytics, updated employment regulations for HR, etc., because these competencies will be needed more after the pandemic.

During the COVID-19 pandemic, digital performance systems have been significant in the monitoring of employee performance. For instance, thanks to digital systems, managers can analyze the behaviors of their subordinate personnel and avoid loss of time while evaluating their performance. Therefore, the relevant system is extremely effective in receiving fast feedback (Akbaş Tuna and Çelen, 2020: 2750-2751). The monitoring of performance becomes easier when using digital technologies, however, performance expectations should be amended due to the extraordinary situation of employees. For example, according to the research conducted by Mercer; 74.3% of the businesses stated that they would revise their year-end performance targets together with their business targets (Mercer, 2020).

The COVID-19 pandemic also affected the wage policies of businesses. Businesses benefited from the "short-term employment allowance" supported by governments. This wage system aims for the state to cover some part of the wages to prevent employees from becoming unemployed. By this means, both employees and businesses were able to get rid of the negative effects of the pandemic to some extent.

During the COVID-19 pandemic, both businesses and employees are experiencing an extraordinary time. HR departments and digital HR practices play an important role in helping businesses and employees to survive this difficult period. According to Risley (2020: 658), it is possible to overcome the challenges of the COVID-19 outbreak with a growth mindset. Businesses should increase their resilience as they face uncertainties, challenges and changing economic prospects. The circumstances that we are going through may be unusual, but agile thinking will always bring success. Businesses need to attach more importance to digital HR practices so they can improve their agility.

Keywords: *Human resource management (HRM), COVID-19, pandemic, digitalization*

References

Akbaş Tuna, A. & Çelen, O. (2020). İşletmelerin insan kaynaklari yönetimi uygulamalari üzerinde covid-19 pandemisinin etkileri. *OPUS Uluslararası Toplum Araştırmaları Dergisi*, 16(30), 2710-2759.

Akingbola, K. (2020). COVID-19: the prospects for nonprofit human resource management. *ANSERJ*, 11(1), 16-20.

Aslan, R. (2020). Tarihten günümüze epidemiler, pandemiler ve covid-19. *Ayrıntı Dergisi*, 8 (85), 35-41.

Betchoo, N. K. (2016). Digital transformation and its impact on human resource management. *IEEE International Conference on Emerging Technologies and Innovative Business Practices for the Transformation of Societies (EmergiTech)*: 1-6.

Bhatia, P. (2016). Racing ahead with technology: digital hr through smartphones. *The IUP Journal of Information Technology*, 22(4), 36-47.

Caligiuri, P. et al. (2020). International hrm insights for navigating the covid-19 pandemic: implications for future research and practice. *Journal of International Business Studies*, 51, 697-713.

Carnevale, J. B. & Hatak, I. (2020). Employee adjustment and well-being in the era of covid-19: implications for human resource management. *Journal of Business Research*, 116, 183-187.

Chadee, D., Ren, S. & Tang, G. (2021). Is digital technology the magic bullet for performing work at home? lessons learned for post covid-19 recovery in hospitality management. *International Journal of Hospitality Management*, 92, 1-8.

Dahlbom, P.; Siikanen, N. & Sajasalo, P. (2018). Big data and hr analytics in the digital era. *Baltic Journal of Management*, 15(1), 120-138.

Deloitte (2020). Navigating the now: how hr leaders are responding to covid-19. April 2020.

Deloitte (2020). COVID-19 workforce strategies for post-covid- recovery.

Dickson, D. R. & Nusair, K. (2010). An hr perspective: the global hunt for talent in the digital age. *Worldwide Hospitality and Tourism*, 2(1), 86-93.

Dirani, K. M. et al. (2020). Leadership competencies and the essential role of human resource development in times of crisis: a response to covid-19 pandemic. *Human Resource Development International*, 23(4), 380-394.

DiRomualdo, A., El-Khoury, D. & Girimonte, F. (2018). HR in the digital age: how digital technology will change hr's organization structure, processes and roles. *Strategic HR Review*, 17(5), 234-242.

Eurofound (2020). Living, working and covid-19, covid-19 series, publications office of the european union. Luxembourg.

Fenech, R., Baguant, P. & Ivanov, D. (2019). The changing role of human resource management in an era of digital transformation. *International Journal of Entrepreneurship*, 22(2), 166-175.

Frankiewicz, B. & Chamorro-Premuzic, T. (2020). Digital transformation is about talent, not technology. *Harvard Business Review*, May 06.

Göktaş, P. & Baysal, H. (2018). Türkiye'de dijital insan kaynaklari yönetiminde bulut bilişim. *Süleyman Demirel Üniversitesi İktisadi ve İdari Bilimler Fakültesi Dergisi*, 23(4), 1409-1424.

Harvard Business Review Home, https://hbr.org/sponsored/2020/05/workforce-strategies-for-post-covid-19-recovery?utm_source=feedburner&utm_medium=feed&utm_campaign=Feed%3A+harvardbusiness+%28HBR.org%29, Accessed: 29.11.2020.

Hecklaua et al. (2016). Holistic approach for human resource management in industry 4.0. *Procedia CIRP*, 54, 1-6.

Iansiti, M. & Richards, G. (2020). Coronavirus is widening the corporate digital divide. *Harvard Business Review*, March 26, 2-4.

İlhan, U. D. (2020). Covid-19 ile mücadelede insan kaynaklari yönetimi uygulamalarinda ihtiyaç duyulan aksiyonlarin belirlenmesine yönelik örgütsel müdahale yöntemi önerisi. *Gaziantep University Journal of Social Sciences*, Special Issue, 288-307.

Ilie, M.; Ilie, C. & Marin, R. (2020). Human resources and communication management after changes due to covid 19 pandemic, *"Ovidius" University Annals, Economic Sciences Series*, 20(1), 665-669.

ILO (2020a). COVID-19 and the world of work: impact and policy responses. Geneva: *ILO*, 18 March 2020.

ILO (2020b). Teleworking during the covid-19 pandemic and beyond: a practical guide. *Geneva: International Labour Office*, July 2020.

Jones, K. (2020). HR in the time of covid-19. *Feature*, 2nd Quarter, 38-40.

Kaushik, M. & Guleria, N. (2020), The impact of pandemic covid -19 in workplace. *European Journal of Business and Management*, 12(15), 9-18.

Kilic Kirilmaz, S. (2020). Digital transformation in human resources management: investigation of digital hrm practices of businesses. *Research Journal of Business and Management (RJBM),* 7(3), 188-200.

Kudyba, S. (2020). COVID-19 and the acceleration of digital transformation and the future of work. *Information Systems Management*, 37(4), 284-287.

Legner, C. et al. (2017). Digitalization: opportunity and challenge for the business and information systems engineering community. *Business & Information Systems Engineering*, 59(4), 301-308.

Mateescu, M., Muscalu, M. & Baleanu, D. (2020). Human resource dynamics in the context of the pandemic. *"Ovidius" University Annals, Economic Sciences Series*, 20(1), 415-421.

Maurer, R. (2020). Job interviews go virtual in response to covid-19. *Society for Human Resources Management*, March 17, 2020.

Mercer (2020). Covid-19 salgininin türkiye'de çalişma hayati üzerine etkileri anketi. Nisan.

Papagiannidis, S., Harris, J. & Morton, D. (2020). WHO Led the digital transformation of your company? a reflection of it related challenges during the pandemic. *International Journal of Information Management*, 55, 1-5.

Papouli, E., Chatzifotiou, S. & Tsairidis, C. (2020). The use of digital technology at home during the covid-19 outbreak: views of social work students in greece. *Social Work Education,* 39(8), 1107-1115.

Parsehyan, B. G. (2020). İnsan kaynaklari yönetiminde dijital dönüşüm: ik 4.0. *Turkish Studies-Applied Sciences*, 15(2), 211-224.

PERYÖN (2020). Covid-19: ik'nin teknolojiyle sinavi, Nisan 2020 Özel.

Potcovaru, A. (2020). The impact of organizational stress on the human resources from the health system during covid-19 pandemic, *Business Excellence and Management*, 10(Special Issue 1), 88-97.

Provino, J. (2020). HR should not waste the covid-19 crisis. *HR Future* · May, 30-31.

Risley, C. (2020). Maintaining performance and employee engagement during the covid-19 pandemic. *Journal of Library Administration*, 60(6), 653-659.

Sines, D. (2020). How lean hr teams can find success beyond covid-19. *HR News Magazine,* November, 10-11.

Singh, A. (2019). Role of hr in digital transformation. *HR Future*, April 2019, 16-17.

The Economist. The coronavirus crisis thrusts corporate hr chiefs into the spotlight. https://www.economist.com/business/2020/03/24/the-coronavirus-crisis-thrusts-corporate-hr-chiefs-into-the-spotlight, Accessed: 23.11.2020

WHO (2020). WHO director-general's opening remarks at the media briefing on covid-19.11 March 2020, https://www.who.int/director-general/speeches/detail/who-director-general-s-opening-remarks-at-the-media-briefing-on-covid-19---11-march-2020, Accessed: 12.12.2020.

Xu, A., Liu, D., & Yin, E. (2020). HR management during public health crises: learning from the covid-19 outbreak. *China Briefing*, 189, · March, 10-12.

CHAPTER TEN

A SECTORAL ANALYSIS OF THE REFLECTIONS OF DIGITAL TRANSFORMATION IN BUSINESSES TO HUMAN RESOURCES (HR)

EBRU AYKAN AND YASEMIN HARMANCI

Introduction

The complexity of our lives is increasing day by day. As complexity increases, our needs change accordingly and our expectations of the products we purchase or the services we get change according to our changing needs. Businesses desiring to meet the needs of customers try to adapt their products or services by considering the expectations of their customers.

In the ever-changing and developing information age businesses have to keep up with all kinds of competitive conditions. One of the most effective ways to achieve this is to invest in information and communication technologies. Today, businesses prefer to perform their business processes using technology infrastructures rather than traditional methods. This is because the different units or structures they establish in their bodies have changed the forms of business processes (Calp & Doğan, 2019: 387).

The era in which we live is called the "digital age". The whole world is in transformation with various changes in economic, cultural and social areas. Naturally, this transformation changes behaviors in the workplace and the organizational process. It is seen that, in this transformation process, human resource management (HRM) of organizations has changed by integrating with technology. It is observed that many HR practices are planned and implemented through technology, and plans, policies, rules and regulations are changing thanks to technology. Both working conditions and ways of doing business have begun to change especially with the increased use of computers, the internet and intranet. Now HRM departments in organizations use computers, networks, the internet and intranet; in short, they benefit from electronic platforms while performing their activities. Today, internet technology enables a faster and easier execution of all HRM functions from selecting and finding a workforce to training, from job evaluation and performance measurement to pricing, and from morale and motivation to industrial relations (Aksel et al., 2013: 75).

While all stages of the business world from production to marketing and sales, from finance to logistics, and from the collection of revenues to service delivery are digitalized, the automation of business processes reduces the need for manpower and the roles of working people change. In parallel with the role changes, the expected competencies in employees are redefined and research studies in different countries of the world focus on 21st-century competencies (Yamamoto et al., 2019: 2) and HRM practices. From this point of view, this study will discuss digital HRM practices on a sectoral basis by explaining the changes, the need for change, digital transformation and the role of HRM in this transformation (digital HRM).

The Need for Change and Transformation

The phenomenon of change and transformation in the world in the 2000s has become one of the most discussed issues affecting businesses. Businesses are directly affected by the social, cultural, economic and physical changes occurring in their surroundings. Change has accelerated especially with the effect of globalization and the development and spread of communication-information technologies today. The need for change is reemphasized, the roadmaps to be followed are redetermined and the rules are rewritten in the global competition which becomes crueler day by day. At this point, the rules and methods used for centuries are no longer sufficient in the global competitive atmosphere.

Many businesses in the world today are going through a change process that will force them to change their working methods. Each change leads to an interaction and as a result businesses have to change their business methods, technology and group structures and make significant changes to current relationships, habits, ways and methods (Yeşil, 2018: 308).

While the key elements of an agricultural society focused on fertile lands and demographic structure, the industrial society focused on mechanization and strong capital stock with the use of steam power in production (Sezgin & Uçar, 2019: 85). Information and information-producing individuals, and individual-technology harmony, stand out in the information society and especially in Industry 4.0 practices. The introduction of computers in all areas of life, the ever-developing and widespread communication technology, and rapid developments in internet technology have become the drivers of competition in terms of quality, speed and flexibility for businesses. Internet-information-communication systems have brought with them the phenomenon of digitalization.

While the term digital is defined as the use of binary digits, digitization involves the adoption of this technology and the transformation of physical data into a digital format. Digitization refers to the integration of digital technologies into daily life by digitizing everything that can be digitized, i.e., to make digitalized information available to you (Bhatnagar, 2017: 12).

Digitalization is considered to be a destructive innovation, the main reason being that it not only creates new professional and social opportunities but also challenges traditional business design. This challenge necessitates change in both individuals and businesses. It forces employees to create new competencies and abilities based on technological expertise, data analysis, and social, emotional and creative skills (Parsehyan, 2020: 215). As a result, businesses feel the pressure of digitalization and have to redesign their structures and processes (Kane et al., 2016: 16). At this point, businesses seek to achieve a digital transformation without lagging behind any innovative and digitalizing competitors and new entrepreneurs.

Digital Transformation

The industrialization process, starting with the first industrial revolution in the eighteenth century, enters a new era today. Following the industrialization process emerging with water- and steam-powered machines, the second phase, Industry 2.0, started with the use of electricity and mass production systems in the 20th century. The third phase was Industry 3.0, announced with the use of electronic and information technologies in the 1970s, and finally the term Industry 4.0 (creating added value by specializing in qualified jobs and automating jobs requiring unqualified labor) was used for the first time during the 2011 technology fair in Hanover, Germany (Zhou, Liu, & Zhou, 2015: 2147; Kosif, 2019: 3). Industry 4.0 can be called the digital transformation, the digitalized industry, the fourth industrial evolution and the digital era (Kosif, 2019: 3). The common characteristic of these concepts is that they express an approach for business practices, customer interactions and employee behaviors (Sharma & Shukla; 2013: 66).

Digital transformation is the transformation of business activities, processes, competencies and models by harmonizing them with the changes and opportunities in digital technology (Betchoo, 2016: 148). Similarly, according to Corejove et al. (2016), it refers to an organizational change in which digital technology and business models are used together in order to increase organizational performance. According to Clohessy et al. (2017), digital transformation includes the harmonization of business models, products, organizational structures or process automations with technology, leading to changes in a business. At this point, digital transformation is defined as technology-driven change in the many levels of businesses that includes both the use of digital technologies to improve current processes and the discovery of digital innovation (Parsehyan, 2020: 216). Therefore, digital transformation includes activities to manage change in businesses by harmonizing business, business processes and internet-oriented technology.

Systems and individuals produce huge amounts of data due to the rapid introduction of technology into our lives and the fall of internet prices, the increase in mobile device usage and the widespread use of social media. The produced data can easily be saved, analyzed and transformed into valuable information today. Managers who realize the added value of valuable data for an organization get into the process of digitally transforming business processes and production methods. Although this process called digital transformation is thought to be the effective use of technology in institutions, the use of technology in a business is not included in the definition of digitalization. Digital transformation refers to involving business employees in this process, their ability to use the system and their ability to manage the transformation process in a way that affects the business of the organization (Kosif, 2019: 4).

Digital transformation has three forms: customer-based, organizational development-based and technology-based (Hrustek et al., 2019: 1306). In this transformation, which aims to ensure the harmony of the structure and processes within the business with customer satisfaction and technology; *customer-based digital transformation* occurs in accordance with the wishes and desires of customers. With this transformation, it is possible to reach prospective customers with the technology used while targeting existing customer satisfaction. *Organizational development-based digital transformation* is the innovative organizational ideas developed by focusing on the targets to increase profitability, reducing costs and ensuring productivity (Parsehyan, 2020: 7). Kumar (2016) expressed the need to provide customers with content, commerce and collaboration in an understandable, personalized, contextual and cost-effective manner anytime and anywhere. *Technology-based digital transformation* includes the changes and opportunities caused by digital technologies.

Digital transformation changed the relationship between employees and machines/equipment. Many unqualified work tasks performed by employees began to be performed by machines. Costs were thus reduced and qualified employees became more effective and productive in their work. Digital transformation also changed the time and place of work and new business design methods (smart working, agile working and new virtual productions, etc.) occurred. Businesses enable large working groups to work together more harmoniously and more productively and set clearer goals to ensure non-stop development and motivation and provide real-time feedback through these methods (Sonnentag et al., 2008: 681).

HR in Digital Transformation (Digital HR)

The introduction of computers to all fields of our lives and gradually developing and spreading communication technologies brought remarkable changes and effects especially to business life. Rapid developments in internet technology also changed the understanding and processes of HRM. Now businesses use digital HRM systems when operating HRM functions. In today's business world of rapid change and fierce competition, businesses need qualified HRM, which is one of the strategic resources providing them with competitive advantage in order to achieve their goals.

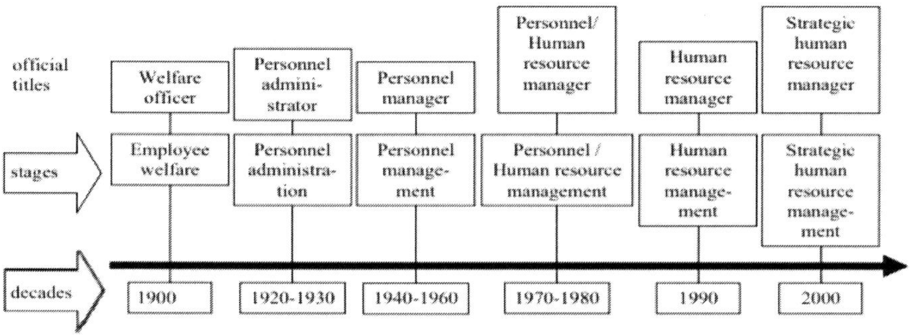

Figure 10.1: Evolution and Development of HRM (Itika, 2011: 7)

When the historical development of HRM is examined, the industrial revolution, which started in the second half of the 18th century and then spread to European countries and America, is actually one of the important milestones of manpower and labor management, and it is important in many ways. Small-scale and irregular production in houses gave way to the factory system and people started to work in factories collectively with the industrial revolution turning a new page in production, savings and employment relations. The focus of employers' interest changed and shifted from production to marketing with the use of various machines in production in this revolutionary process requiring muscle power. However, although very long working hours, heavy physical work and poor working conditions in the early period of the industrial revolution caused fatigue, occupational accidents and various diseases, employees had to accept those conditions. This is because employees had to earn money and they were worried that if they left their jobs, they would not find another. In addition, there were no laws to protect their rights so they knew that even if they found another job, conditions would not be better there.

At the end of the 19th century and the beginning of the 20th century the labor movements became decisive and welfare and the trade union movement became important. As a result of this movement, a welfare officer position was initiated, which had the responsibility of providing cultural, educational and recreational benefits for employees as well as financial, medical, accommodation aid, etc. The welfare officer (social or employee health and occupational safety officer) was the beginning of personnel management understanding (Tosun, 2014: 1).

After the First World War, from the 1920s to the mid-1930s, the process of "personnel management" was effective and the need for HRM to increase production capacities was recognized. The need to manage functions such as employment, training, keeping personnel records, motivation of personnel and control and development of employees had an effect on the emergence of personnel management (Itika, 2011: 7). In addition to the welfare officer, various types of personnel specialists were employed in businesses and these employees were considered to be a cost element.

Although manpower/the labor force literally means "all the physical and intellectual abilities a person has to activate in order to produce useful things", this is a definition belonging to early periods of the industrialization process in which production was rather based on human labor and muscle power. Regarding this, these individuals who were defined as the workforce and used their skills for businesses started to be used as general managers, managers, officers and everyone dealing with paperwork, except for the owner or owners of businesses, within the concept of personnel (Demirkol & Tis, 2018: 536). The changing way of business due to the rapid growth in the world in the 19th century led to the emergence of personnel management. The transition from personnel management, which was based on job definitions and considered as an approach with restricted personnel affairs and business law, to HRM was not easy and took a long time. The change began in the first years of the 20th century in HRM depending on the relationship between employee productivity and working conditions. In parallel with the speed of change in the world, the motivation and commitment of employees have been regarded as one of the important factors along with the increase in the value given to people and the investments made in corporate life (İSO, 2011: 10). The process of conducting activities for the purpose of increasing labor productivity, such as employing qualified personnel at the right place and time, ensuring motivation and job satisfaction by reducing the costs of the business and increasing its profitability, is called as HRM. This concept covers all employees from the top executives to the lowest level employees within the company and includes the workforce outside the business that can potentially be utilized (Demirkol & Tis, 2018: 537). From this perspective, HSM regards humans as a resource to be developed, not a cost element when presenting a conceptual framework about how HRM will be provided, employed and directed along with other resources.

Organizational restructuring continued in the 1980s and 1990s. Especially in the early 1980s, HR managers started to participate in the strategic planning process of organizations and the SHRM approach could be implemented in organizations. The association of HR policies and practices with organizational goals and strategies brought up the concept of SHRM. Thus, HRM was freed from the characteristic of being a department only responsible for a standard set of policies and processes, and gained a more strategic and political character. At this point, HRM had a serious position for businesses in breaking equality in the competitive environment created by globalization. Globalization, which caused change in the production and cost-saving ways of businesses, forced the change in HRM, and SHRM was adopted. On the one hand, SHRM businesses focused on the effective and productive use of current production resources by making long-term plans, and on the other hand, technological developments also affected strategic HRM. SHRM followed personnel management and HRM and refers to an approach that emphasizes the strategic role of HRM in achieving business objectives (Cingöz, 2011: 32-33). It includes approaching HRM with a strategic perspective, creating and implementing proactive HR policies and practices that provide human capital, and contributing to achieve the objectives of the organization (Huselid et al., 1997: 171; Wan et al., 2002: 33).

In the 21st century, the order of businesses is to realize digital transformation and maintain their competitive power in the global market. Therefore, human sciences seek to understand which competencies HRM should have to realize digital transformation. When we look at the recent literature, concepts such as HR 4.0, Electronic HRM (E-HRM), Virtual HRM, Information Systems in HRM, Web-based HRM Management, HRM Information Systems (HRIS), Information Technology-based HRM, HRM Management Information Systems (HRMIS) and E-Transformation in

HRM are used to define the changing dimensions of HRM (Aksel et al., 2013: 73).

The widespread globalization trends in the world and the rapid spread of innovations in the field of information and technology day by day have made the use of technological innovations a prerequisite for businesses to compete in the market mechanism. As artificial intelligence, machine learning and deep learning become widespread, working styles change and the need for manpower in economic activities decreases. Businesses need to re-plan their short- and long-term labor force. Databases and applications that can be accessed with cloud technology, meetings that can be held with audio, video, virtual reality and even holographic participation have gradually made online working without going into an office a more common and economical option. As the delivery methods of goods and products change, it is expected that online working methods will be preferred in more sectors (Yamamoto et al., 2019: 367).

Businesses should primarily prepare their HRM for use of the technology required for their production and emphasize openness to innovation among the values shared within the business culture. Technology and internet- and web-based technologies are indispensable for HRM in terms of both use and self-improvement. At this point, digital HRM is defined as the use of web-based technologies in HRM practices and policies (Ruel et al., 2007: 280). Similarly, Strohmeier (2020) expresses digital HR as the process of digitization of HRM and the transformation of analog HR information to digital HR information.

The effect of information and internet technologies on HRM functions is outlined in Figure 10.2. The process starting with computer-aided wage and payroll preparation systems shifted from wage management to HR-oriented corporate resource planning technologies such as employment, organizational design and reward systems. One-step ahead, integrated talent management technologies were used including appropriate decision-making and management practices. HR cloud technologies are used in the stage of planning for talented personnel to carry the organization towards a future, global labor force and the integration of these employees with businesses. In the last stage, it is observed that the coordination of talented employees is ensured with agile and flexible HR practices within the framework of the requirements of the job and there is a change towards a technology in which skills are not only supported, but also managed.

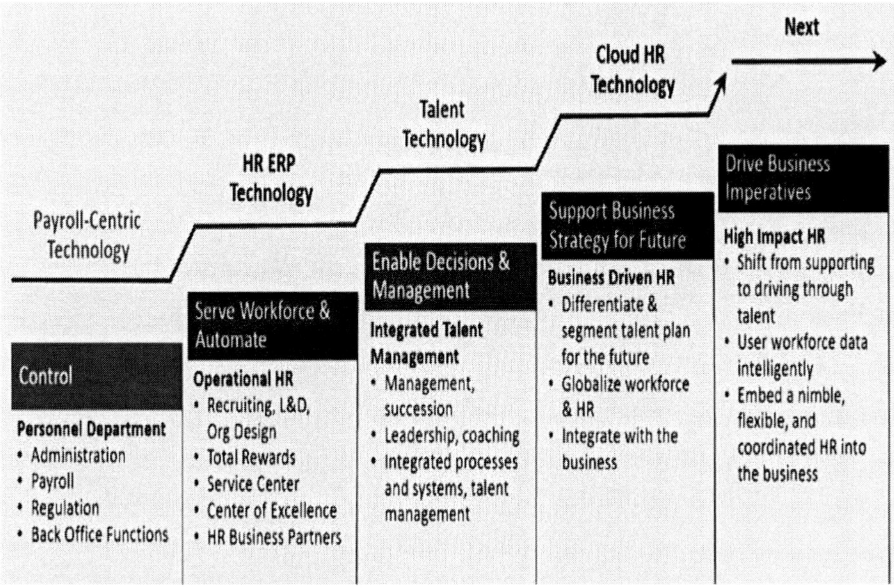

Figure 10.2: Development of HRM with the Use of Information Technologies (Schmidt, 2015: 1)

Digital HRM practices contribute to businesses in some issues such as reducing costs, increasing (increasing the efficiency of time and profits and reducing workload) productivity, management quality, ensuring HR flexibility and the effectiveness of reducing bureaucracy, employee motivation, informing employees and organizing working relations on communication quality. However, failure to ensure information security, a lack of appropriate skills, the inability of current digital HR tools to meet the potential of the business and the difficulties of employees in the use of new technologies are disadvantages for businesses (Maria, 2020: 13).

Internet and information technologies changed the traditional business methods and techniques in business life. This change deeply affected HRM producing values as a means of competitive advantage of businesses. The effect of digital transformation on HRM is outlined in Table 10.1. HR is experiencing a rapid and radical change. While HR in businesses is often considered as a support unit, today HR is expected to lead the digital environment. This leadership is expected to occur in three areas and by answering the questions below (Volini et al., 2017: 87);

- **Digital labor force**: How can businesses direct new management practices (such as a set of skilled practices facilitating the new network-based organization or an innovation and sharing culture called “digital DNA”)?
- **Digital working environment:** How can businesses establish an organizational structure to provide productivity by using modern communication tools (such as Slack, Workplace by Facebook, Microsoft Teams, etc.)?
- **Digital HR:** How can businesses change the HR function itself to run digitally? How can they use digital tools and applications to present solutions? How can they continuously experiment and make innovations?

Table 10.1: HR Projection of Digital Transformation

<table>
<tr><th colspan="2">Digital Labor Force</th><th>Digital Platform</th><th colspan="2">Digital HR</th></tr>
<tr><td rowspan="2">Professions change</td><td>Socio-Economic/ Demographic Change</td><td rowspan="9">Communicational Solutions for Digital Business</td><td rowspan="6">Change in HR Functions</td><td>E-HRM Planning</td></tr>
<tr><td>Technological Change</td><td>E-Supple and Selection</td></tr>
<tr><td rowspan="3">Digital Skills Gap</td><td>Hard Skills</td><td>E-Education and Development</td></tr>
<tr><td>Soft Skills</td><td>E-Career Management</td></tr>
<tr><td>Digital Roles</td><td>E-Performance Management</td></tr>
<tr><td colspan="2">Labor Force with Digital DNA</td><td>E-Salary Management</td></tr>
<tr><td colspan="2" rowspan="3">Innovation and Sharing Culture</td><td colspan="2">Digital Tools and Applications</td></tr>
<tr><td colspan="2">Constant Trial</td></tr>
<tr><td colspan="2">Innovation Culture</td></tr>
</table>

Source: Adapted from Volini, E., Occean, P., Stephan, M., Walsh, B. (2017): 87; Erkmen (2018): 44-67

Traditional HR dynamics change radically in this process. Innovation and experience are the fundamentals of digital HR. Using alternative approaches (Hackathons, rapid design groups, prototyping, etc.) is recommended for piloting HR practices. Design-oriented thinking and integrated local practices are featured by updating business processes. Similarly, instead of the traditional career model, a career journey map is preferred. Digital technology expertise is among the main competencies required from HR experts in this period. Cloud-based HR systems are inadequate and digital designing teams developing HR programs according to the special needs of businesses using the cloud technology as a platform are required. Forms of HR software also change and are based on mobile applications, artificial intelligence and customer experiences. Fast decision-making, coaching, mentoring and relationship development practices and proactive management approaches can be implemented through these tools (Erkmen, 2018: 49-53). As a result, traditional HR practices and functions have also changed and developed. The expected qualities of digital HR functions are as follows:

E-Hrp: Computers and electronic media are used in the stages of the HRM planning process, which are pointed out as data collection and status analysis, an estimation of labor demand and supply, a determination of HRM needs, the development of action plans to meet HRM needs and evaluation. Information and data to facilitate managers in the planning process to make predictions and decisions can be presented online to managers in more accurate, fast and various formats. Computers can create judgmental and numerical methods used for determining labor force demands. Computers can help managers to make the right decisions by providing a large information pool in judgmental methods such as manager estimation, the Delphi technique, scenario analyses and comparison. Computers considerably accelerate transactions in numerical methods that require more complex and mathematical calculations as compared to judgmental methods. Numerical methods such as trend analyses, regression-correlation analyses and ratio analyses are finished in a very short time using computer programs without the need for calculations on paper. Numerical calculations, such as for actual personnel, reserve personnel, additional personnel needs and total workload required, determining these needs, absenteeism analyses, and workforce turnover rate are also performed more accurately and quickly through computers. In addition to these calculations, the opportunity to save the obtained information and data on an electronic platform enables the changes to be seen by year and to be easily compared (Doğan, 2011: 54-55).

E-Supply and Selection: Employment is critical in HR. It is based on finding and assigning the right person for the right time and right place. At this point, the best talent for the business is the target. The point here is ensuring the harmony of this ability between the task, team and business culture (Thite, 2019: 15). Technologies used in employment and selections are as follows (Sharma & Shukla, 2013: 69):

a) Internet Job Boards: Job boards are prepared for employers to publish job advertisements on the internet and job seekers can make appropriate applications on this platform by the touch of a button.
b) CV Databases and Applicant Tracking Technology: The businesses using this application by creating a web-based CV uploading platform can select candidates with appropriate qualifications from the applicants uploading CVs to the system.
c) Online Tests and Assessments: Businesses can define the skills and personality of a candidate by using online tests and assessments.
d) Combined Technologies to Help the Employment and Selection Process: Some technologies use combined softwares to limit the candidate pool for getting, following, testing and assessing the applications of candidates. In this stage, the information of applicants is reviewed by the organization. This technology facilitates the processes for businesses and saves time and money.

E-Training and Development: Now organizations use various technologies to train employees. These e-learning processes range from online educational materials and course content to the use of more advanced technologies to encourage the participation of course attendees in learning processes (Celep & Fındıklı, 2018: 67). Electronic learning processes in organizations have online and offline forms. Online learning means learning by using a corporate network, i.e., an intranet or using the internet and this is defined as web-based training/learning. Offline learning refers to learning by using a CD-ROM and computers, i.e., computer-based training/learning) (Doğan, 2011: 60).

E-Career Management: The internet radically affected the accessibility of career counselors and individuals receiving career-counseling services to career-related information. In addition, the internet completely changed the career-counseling process by allowing instant communication between organizations and employees and/or counselors and customers. Organizations and employees and/or counselors and customers can now communicate online with each other through e-mails, web page records and video-conferencing (McCarthy et al., 2003: 368). With reference to the benefits of the internet for career counseling, web-based career support systems are also developed. Web-based career support systems are offered via the internet or intranet. These systems offer a combination of the main points of career counseling and the career support function on the electronic platform. These main points can be stated as providing assessment support by making personality and skill assessments, and personal feedback about them, informing users by advising appropriate career paths, providing ancillary support through web-based employment and electronic or web-based learning opportunities and providing social and emotional support through online forums and discussion groups administered by them (Doğan, 2011: 65).

E-Performance Management: Electronic performance management can be expressed as the use of electronic tools such as audio, visual and computer systems to collect, store, analyze and report the performance data of individuals and/or groups. The transfer of HR functions to the electronic environment enables performance evaluation to be conducted simultaneously and online as a whole (Bayarçelik, 2020: 72). The main purpose of using technology in performance assessments is to improve individual performance and therefore, organizational performance by offering employees information, techniques and methods and support systems that are required to do the job (Doğan, 2011: 63).

E-Compensation Management: One of the important issues in HRM management is compensation management. Since compensations are income items for employees, but cost items for institutions, they are important for both employers and employees. This module models the salary increase by considering employee performance, the budgeted salary increase and sector benchmark rates for each business. In addition, the system works on the principle of managing salaries within a specific band by limiting the recommended increases of paid employees even if they are performing well and recommends the increase in salaries of employees getting insufficient wages. E-compensation implements performance-based increases, manages sectoral salaries, deals with overpaid and underpaid employees, and covers the salary budget. In addition, the importance of this function is compensation planning. E-compensation is used for purposes such as developing and providing benefits in the implementation of salary balancing systems and assessing the effectiveness of the system (Celep & Fındıklı, 2018: 67).

Sectoral Analysis of Digital HR

While the effects of digitalization are experienced in many areas all around the world, organizations also make investments in HRM. There are many organizations that want to save time and cost by carrying their HRM practices on the digital platform. Digitalization leads to changes and transformations. It is the function of HRM that will manage this change process and guide employees and other business functions.

While it took an average of 20 years for businesses to reach a certain value in the past, today's digital initiatives can reach those values in a few steps. How businesses can attract the right digital talents to the business, keep and improve them under these conditions is among the issues that digital HRM focuses on. Zappos, an online clothing retailer, believes that the best ideas and decisions are taken from bottom to top (World Economic Forum, 2016) and emphasizes that all employees from the bottom to the executives in organizations can contribute to this process.

The digital transformation of the sectors became a current issue with a project initiated by the World Economic Forum in 2015. Digital transformation offers unique opportunities to create values such as increasing profits, creating new revenue models and gaining access to global markets.

Industry 4.0. and digital transformation take business models in various sectors to very different dimensions. One of the problems faced with the adoption and use of digital technologies such as sensor technologies, artificial intelligence and robotics in some sectors is the lack of appropriate skills in the labor force. This has some reasons such as lack of coordination and control in the education department and lack of communication between sector players and universities that are labor force suppliers (Fachrunnisa & Hussain, 2020: 1). The processes concerning HRM practices such as the digital employment process, reward systems, digital training programs, and performance and career management are transferred to the digital platform. Digital HRM practices are not only affected by the size, organizational structure, opportunities and environmental characteristics of organizations, but also, they can be affected by the sector in which the organizations operate. In this part, digital transformation is discussed in terms of HRM practices with the perspective of different sectors.

Health

Since healthcare is one of the complex organizations in which minor negligence can result in loss of human life, the system to be established in this service would have to be properly designed. The development of information and technology enabled better functioning in hospitals (Tüfekçi, Yorulmaz & Cansever, 2017: 143-144).

The use of digital technologies in service delivery by healthcare institutions is important in terms of expanding service areas, increasing patient satisfaction and employee productivity, reducing operating costs, improving medical decision-making processes and using the resources within the institution more effectively. Digital technologies allow many work tasks done by people to be autonomous. More work tasks can be done by employing fewer people. However, a growing healthcare economy with digitalization also brings along various extra employment opportunities. For this reason, health institutions develop strategies to bring new skills and abilities to the people they employ or will employ in the field of health in the digital transformation process (Işık, 2019: 17). Digital hospitals to advantage the system began to exist by using high technologies in hospitals today. Digital hospitals are fully integrated hospitals in which all kinds of technological, financial and administrative management elements such as digital archiving systems, hospital information management systems, information communication technologies, drug tracking systems, smart building systems, digital medical record systems, multimedia technologies, telemedicine, tele-education, consultancy, quality management and HRM are used together. It is a hospital model where all kinds of communication tools and medical devices are integrated with each other and other information systems coming from a hospital where information technologies are used at a minimum level in administrative, financial and medical processes and healthcare professionals and patients exchange data from inside or outside the hospital with telemedicine and mobile applications (http://dijitalhastane.saglik.gov.tr). Along with digitalization, data and analytical applications are used extensively in the healthcare sector. Therefore, experts in these fields are required.

Manufacturing

Industry 4.0 and digitalization have a significant effect on the production sector and this effect will continue exponentially in the future. Digitalization will allow increasing productivity by revealing new types of advanced production and industrial processes for machine-human cooperation and symbiotic product realization (Yıldız, 2018: 554). The complexity and requirements in the production sector are gradually increasing. Factors such as increasing international competition, changes and uncertainties in markets, the demand for highly individualized products, and the shortening of the product life cycle are serious problems for businesses. Current approaches to value creation are not suitable to meet these requirements. While the requirements in the manufacturing sector increase, rapid technological changes create a series of new business potential and opportunities (Hoffman & Rüsch, 2017: 23).

Industry 4.0 allows developed countries to withdraw their investments in Asian countries and developing countries due to the low wage advantage. This will make the west a production center again, reduce unemployment in developed countries, improve foreign trade balances and contribute to sustainable economic development (Bağcı, 2018: 144). Therefore, the balances concerning employment and unemployment around the world will also change. In addition, many processes such as the use of raw materials, storage, production planning and process, the supply chain, logistics, and quality management in the production sector are affected by digitalization. People, objects and systems at the new level to be achieved with digital transformation will be widely and effectively connected. For this reason, companies desiring to increase their competitiveness in the future have to reflect the change in production processes and use technologies such as smart robots, cyber-physical systems and cloud-based production (Yıldız, 2018: 554). One of the important points here is to have a labor force to use these technologies.

Logistics

Cooperation between suppliers, manufacturers and customers can be achieved through coordination, transparency, digitization and process automation throughout the product lifecycle. This makes the contribution of Industry 4.0 applications important in the field of supply chain control. Companies realizing this in various industries have especially digitalized their supply chain operations. Digitalization enables companies to react, take measures and adapt much faster in the supply chain. Logistics is an important part of the supply chain. It especially provides the integration of materials, information and financial assets among different partners by fulfilling logistic processes such as shipping, storage and distribution (Aylak, Kayıkcı & Taş, 2020: 99).

The digital transformation realized with Industry 4.0 will create a database that makes it smarter, more transparent and efficient at every stage from determining customer needs considered as the first and last point of the supply chain to the delivery of the product to end users. In this context, logistic companies playing active roles in the entire supply chain are highly important (Saatçioğlu, Kök & Özispa, 2018). Digitalization contributes to the blurring of boundaries between sectors, accelerating the innovation cycle, and creating new levels of relationships between suppliers, manufacturers and customers (Plekhanov & Netland, 2019: 2). From a logistics point of view, the communication between suppliers, warehouses, market shelves, vehicles on the road and smart factories and the inclusion of all stages of the supply chain in the process will be achieved thanks to Industry 4.0. Thanks to instantly shared data in the logistics process, productivity and efficiency will once again be effective and coordinated (Saatçioğlu, Kök & Özispa, 2018).

Logistics represents a suitable application area for Industry 4.0. The integration of CPS and the internet of things into logistics promises the real-time monitoring of material flows, providing better shipping operations and an accurate risk (Hoffman & Rüsch, 2017: 24). Supergrid logistics, autonomous logistics, robotics and automation, the internet of things, cloud logistics and big data are among the digital trends in the logistics sector. However, the size of the qualified labor force to manage the applications created by these trends is not sufficient (Aylak, Kayıkcı & Taş, 2020: 100-102). The qualified labor force required by digitalization draws attention as a common problem of other sectors. Training the labor force is of great importance.

Media

Rapid advances in communication technologies today have led to many new concepts, such as new media, the internet, social media, social networks, and the virtual world, to be included in the media literature (Başlar, 2013). The media sector in which newspapers and magazines stood out until 1950 has been under the influence of visual communication tools such as radio, television and the internet since 1950. With the development of technology, the media sector started to take a digital form. The tools covered by the media sector are managed over the internet in the period we are currently in, also known as the age of mass media. With the increasing use of computers and the internet in the media, the media sector entered a process of structural change (Akgül & Ayer, 2018: 2319). These new organisms brought about changes and transformations in sociological, cultural and economic fields. They transformed analog media into a digital representation by bringing radical changes to the field of new media communication. The internet makes it possible to access any data at equal speed, digitally encoded data can be reproduced limitlessly and different media types can be displayed on the computer (Başlar, 2013).

New media technologies and the internet are not only considered as a means of communication. In social media, people not only interact with other people, but they also advertise or sell their products to them. Not only do they play games in the visual world, which is one of the new media areas, they improve their level and sell their accounts or purchase various features for their avatars from the site. Users encounter advertisements on all the pages they visit according to their interests. Considering everything, it is observed that new economic areas have emerged thanks to the networks established with new media technologies (Başlar, 2013).

Banking

Banking is one of the leading sectors in which digitalization occurs. Competition, productivity and rapid reply to customer needs are among the reasons for digitalization (Bakırtaş & Ustaömer, 2019). It is observed that the biggest expenses of banks in their balance sheets are personnel and rent expenses following interest expenses. Banks primarily aim to reduce these costs when trying to create customer satisfaction in their digitalization efforts. It is stated that with digitalization in the banking sector, the branch structures and business models of banks change (Özçelik & Akçay, 2019), faster and easy-to-use services and products occur; and therefore, the number of branches and employees decreases (Bakırtaş & Ustaömer, 2019). Branches become small and the number of personnel decreases. It is aimed to reach more customers by opening small branches in more regions. In this new business model routines performed by the cash desk and operational units are performed by ATMs and robots developed by artificial intelligence. Employees having marketing and sales skills and the knowledge to consult customers are in an advantageous position in this new business model. A manager will also be needed for each branch (Özçelik & Akçay, 2019). The number of ATM and credit card, internet and mobile banking users is increasing day by day (Bakırtaş and Ustaömer, 2019). Thanks to digitalization, banking applications especially mobile banking are developing. It is possible for customers to access the products and services offered by the banks from anywhere at any time. The internet of things, open banking, big data and blockchain technologies are more used today and these developments change the way that banking services are provided (Akın, 2020: 22-23).

Marketing

Fierce global competition, new generation consumers and rapid technological developments accelerated digitalization in the marketing sector. With digitalization in marketing, consumer marketing continues to be at the center of marketing; however, marketing activities are carried out by using new generation technologies such as RFID, NFC, cloud technologies and the internet of things. As a result of advancements in information technologies, traditional trade first transformed to e-trade and then to m-trade. Thus, in this period, cyber technologies were central to life and caused radical changes in the marketing mix elements (Başyazıcıoğlu & Karamustafa, 2018). The demands and expectations of customers changed in the new process. Customers not only look for products meeting their basic needs, demands, interests and desires, but these also need to satisfy their creativity and values. Moreover, they want to be part of the production process (Vassileva, 2017: 49).

Digitalization brings great advantages to the marketing industry. Big data management enables the data of each consumer to be read for the prediction of the potential behaviors of consumers and to develop responses accordingly. Consumer behaviors and purchasing decision models are changing. Issues such as digitalization of the brand, digitalization of consumption, digital marketing channels, social media and e-trade are associated with the digitalization of marketing. Internet use has an important place in daily life and the shortening of the product life cycle has also affected the marketing strategies of companies. Employees in marketing and sales fields should receive training on the issues brought up by digitalization, improve themselves and fight against the time pressure caused by the speed of change, and businesses should pay attention to talented management.

Skilled management should cover qualified analysts, data specialists, customer experience officers, content officers, data storytellers, data scientists, and multi-channel campaign managers. These skills play a key role in the digitalization of marketing (Vassileva, 2017: 49).

Education

Educational applications and application methods are one of the fields most affected by digitalization. With digitalization in education, individuals can access information whenever they want, wherever they want. This leads to equal opportunities in education. However, digital education does not develop with the same speed and prevalence in all countries. Factors such as cultures, development levels, educational levels, technological possibilities, national incomes and social characteristics of countries affect digitalization in education (Parlak, 2019).

Developments in the education sector run parallel with the transformations from Industry 1.0 to Industry 4.0. Industry 1.0 was expressed by mechanization, water power and steam power concepts; Education 1.0 was expressed by agriculture, lectures, concepts and traditional environment concepts. The changes with Industry 2.0 and Industry 3.0 also affected the education sector. Computer networks, the internet of things, artificial intelligence and cloud software represent Industry 4.0 and these are reflected in education as innovation, visuals, lifelong learning, collaboration and global problem-solving and therefore, the domains related to Education 4.0 were created with coding, robotics, electronic design, entrepreneurship, global awareness, leadership and digital literacy (Ergin, 2019: 560).

Transformations in the education sector affected the education and teaching strategies of educational institutions. There have been changes such as a transition to educational platforms in which digital culture is widespread, innovation-based education programs, multi-disciplinary education programs, the use of new educational technologies, distance education technologies and the application of new computer-based learning processes (Öztemel, 2018: 29). The adaptation process to these changes is related with both teachers and students. Personalized education, elective courses, project-based learning, practical training, data generation and interpretation are essential. Based on student-centered education, mentor teaching stood out instead of the traditional authoritarian teacher as students prepare and manage their own programs (Ergin, 2019: 561). Therefore, the qualifications of employees in the education sector especially the teachers also changed.

Education policies aiming to meet the demand for Industry 4.0 skills should not only focus on technical skills (digital competence, data analytics, engineering, management, mathematics, language, etc.), but also on soft skills (networking, problem-solving, sustainable mindset, conflict-solving, process understanding, etc.). Changes in the education system should be constantly renovated and adapted to current changes to develop a more sustainable society. According to the report of the Digitalization Strategies in Industry Workshop (2017), a digital inclination should be emphasized in the early stages of the formal education process. It should be considered that the labor force working together with learning robots in their working life should be introduced to these technologies at an early age, and these should be included in all learning outputs. In addition, it should be ensured that some concepts required by digital transformation are part of the curriculum from the first steps of formal education. Software literacy and the ability to write code are parts of the curriculum in some countries from the first years of primary education.

Energy

The increasing population and economy throughout the world lead to a great demand for energy resources. Due to the limited resources, the issue of electrical energy demand becomes a more serious problem. The demand for electricity is growing enormously all over the world. In addition, current network infrastructures are becoming old. It is thus time for change. Renewable energy resources and green and smart energy can be solutions for all those difficulties (Satuyeva et al., 2019). Digitalization in the energy sector involves the processing of large amounts of data generated at all stages of the energy supply chain, through the creation and use of computerized information (Küfeoğlu et al., 2019: 1). IoT applications such as smart meters and smart grids especially in the energy sector can revolutionize the entire energy industry. Smart grids provide electricity to consumers using IT in the distribution network (Satuyeva et al., 2019).

Using high technologies is possible with the achievement of smart and ubiquitous energy management. Smart solutions based on technologies such as information technologies, smart systems, smart grids and digitalization are usually needed in order to obtain such energy management. Although it is relatively possible to achieve these solutions in large-scale businesses, it is not always possible to gain this knowledge and expertise in small- and medium-sized businesses. The main obstacle to the use of high technologies in small- and medium-sized businesses is HRM (Mohammadian & Rezaie, 2020: 1610).

Insurance

Developments such as the increase in internet use, the use of social media and getting services easier from the internet led the insurance industry to make digital applications. The role of digitalization is greater than in other sectors, as it is desired to reach many people in the insurance sector (Yurdakul & Dalkılıç, 2016: 65).

Digitalization affects the faster operation of the structure in financial systems and therefore affects the life styles and expectations of the insurees. It is expected that for traditional policies it will be possible to make changes/additions in short-term periods, perhaps expressed in days, according to the demands of the insurees. Systems that people can easily access with their smart phones should be established and the demands of the insurees should be included in the scope of the policies. However, these possible developments also necessitate regulations in legal processes and the question as to who will be responsible in cases of possible damages should be clarified. Leaving the legislative regulations to the higher institutions, and rather to the public, reveals the necessity of making many different regulations at the same time and the processes progress slowly. In addition, legislative regulations of different institutions force insurance companies to operate on a constantly changing platform. These conditions require insurance companies to approach events in a very systematic manner and to be prepared for many scenarios that may arise as a result of reflecting different aspects of new practices in insurance transactions. While using the digital platforms, insurance companies need information pages that will ensure the trust of potential policyholders, contain understandable and simple expressions and are equipped with accurate information. Questions on the system should not be answered by insurees during the transaction. The introduction of new sales channels with smart phones should not create a question mark for agencies and ways should be sought to turn change into opportunities. Especially the introduction of digital agencies can also increase the number of new insurees in the sector. These rapidly changing conditions can be expected to increase the need for personnel with different qualities according to their own working systems. It is highly important that both undergraduate and associate degree departments, which provide education in the field of insurance, follow these changes closely, add new courses to the schedules for students in these departments and create awareness about these changes in the sector (Baştürk, 2019: 327). Thanks to the widespread use of data with digitalization in the insurance sector, mobile applications, vehicle tracking systems and social media campaigns, not only in the sector but also its sub-branches, are developing.

Public

Digitalization brought changes not only to organizations in the private sector, but also to the structure and functioning of public organizations, and concepts such as reducing bureaucracy, increasing service quality, governance, more citizen participation, and e-government began to be emphasized. More transparent and participatory administrative structures that are faster and less costly, more closely allied to the citizens, were established with e-state applications. The advantages of the e-state not only contribute to the citizens, but also to the rational implementation of HRM practices such as career planning, performance evaluation, training, promotion and discharge. E-registry applications help the organization to not lose talented employees by giving an idea about the best performers. Web-based performance management contributes to the rapid realization of processes and a reduction of costs (Karatepe & Karaman, 2017). We see a change from the traditional printed and manual annual performance assessment to the continuous performance feedback system that supports employees from their first day of employment and throughout their career (Adekunle, 2018: 63-64). Opportunities are thus created for improvement by revealing employees' successful aspects and their shortcomings or weaknesses. In addition, these applications contribute to organizational memory and organizational flexibility (Karatepe & Karaman, 2017). Therefore, as in the private sector, public employees should also be informed about digital technologies and develop themselves in this field. The abilities and training of the potential labor force who want to be public employees should be appreciated in terms of digitalization.

Conclusion

All sectors operate in an increasingly competitive and international market. Digitalization affects the methods that businesses use to interact with their current customers and reach new groups by eliminating the borders between businesses and customers. Businesses need a labor force with digital literacy in order to benefit from opportunities. Businesses need digital skills to allow them to increase their working capacity and take advantage of new and emerging markets and world supply networks (Fachrunnisa & Hussain, 2020: 2-3). Digitalization of HRM is important for reducing process intensity and increasing productivity. However, current employees must get used to the technology introduced by digitalization and need to be trained to use it in their work (Mohammadian & Rezaie, 2020: 1607). Digitalization creates new structures based on decision-making, coordination, control and support services in a complex environment. Also, there is a need for coordination between the virtual and the real. Overall, this gives more meaning to the workforce in terms of the ability to manage complexity and solve problems. Employees are expected to act more on their own initiative, to be able to organize their own work and to have excellent communication skills (OECD, 2017: 109). Intercultural skills, leadership and language skills and social and personal competencies are necessary to create successful businesses. Training and development have a significant role in the adaptation of HRM to digitalization (Mohammadian & Rezaie, 2020: 1607). In addition, in order to be among the leading businesses in the digital age, it is necessary to distribute the power by developing teams consisting of people from different genders, cultures, educational backgrounds and ethnic origins. A trust-based culture should be established for employees to make ethical technological decisions (Bechtel, Briggs & Buchholz, 2020). Understanding the labor force is important in this process. There should be a good analysis of the employees, what skills these people bring and whether these skills are sufficient or not. The new skills and behaviors of future employees should be emphasized in order to move the business to a leading position in innovation.

While there are uncertainties about the effect of digital transformation on jobs, its effects on wages and working conditions are also a concern. Digitalization has significant potential for employment in different fields. Employees can be trained so they can improve their digital knowledge and skills. Apart from employees, the potential labor force and young people can also be trained (World Economic Forum, 2016).

Digitalization makes radical changes to working life. Businesses and international organizations (OECD, 2019; ILO, 2019) carry out activities and make predictions on the "future of work". HRM management is the focus of this search. It is claimed that HRM will undergo a structural change by taking advantage of technological opportunities in this transformation process. How this change will happen is important for organizations. According to current estimates the workforce will be redistributed by sector according to structural and technological requirements and the importance of structures meeting basic requirements, such as digital competencies, problem-solving and human-machine interaction, will increase in the process of change (Başaran, 2020). HRM strategies are key factors for both the labor force and the digital transformation of organizations. Changing conditions create some requirements for employees. One of these requirements is the increase in digital competencies of employees. Based on the new requirements, an HRM management strategy should be created as part of the corporate strategy and put into practice, and an individual development plan should be created for each employee (Sorko, Rabel, & Richter, 2016: 130).

As a conclusion, HRM should be considered as a strategic value in digital transformation. Organizations should take proactive measures that can adapt to this transformation for HRM while trying to seize the trends concerning digitalization. Although the effects of digitalization change in terms of a sectoral perspective, the common point is what can be done for HRM that will adapt to this change. Some recommendations for practitioners and researchers are ensuring the workforce will gain new knowledge and skills through periodic training, considering the strategic role of HRM in the process of integrating technology and organizational goals and including them in the integration process, strategic talent management, redefining workplaces different from the traditional workplace definition, identifying the characteristics of the new generation labor force and creating suitable working conditions and methods for them. It is important for individuals to have leadership, self-discipline, crisis management, communication, digital literacy and emotional intelligence skills. If the qualified labor force that digitalization necessitates cannot be trained, the unemployment rate increases; however, the open positions that require qualification but cannot be covered will increase. Policies regarding training and HRM planning should be established and implemented. Training is crucial in this process. The need for a labor force with interdisciplinary skills increases. A labor force with the characteristics mentioned above will help to meet the needs of all sectors, not just one or specific sectors.

Keywords: *Digital Transformation, Human Resources, Human Resources Management*

References

Adekunle, A.A. (2018). Digital HR, Public Service and Sustainable Governance, *Journal of Humanities and Social Science*, 23(12), 61-65.

Akın, F. (2020). Dijital Dönüşümün Bankacılık Sektörü Üzerindeki Etkileri, *Balkan and Near Eastern Journal of Social Sciences,* 6 (2), 15-27.

Aksel, İ, Arslan, M. L., Kızıl, C., Okur, M.E. & Şeker, Ş.E. (2013). Dijital İşletme, Cinius Yayınları, Türkiye.

Aylak, B.L., Kayıkcı, Y., Taş, M.A. (2020). Investigation of Digital Trends Operating in the Logistics Sector in Turkey, *Journal of Yasar University*, 15(57), 98-116.

Bağcı, E. (2018). Endüstri 4.0: Yeni Üretim Tarzını Anlamak, *Gümüşhane University Electronic Journal of the Institute of Social Sciences*, 9(24), 122-146.

Bakırtaş, T., Ustaömer, K. (2019). Türkiye'nin Bankacılık Sektöründe Dijitalleşme Olgusu, *Ekonomi, İşletme ve Yönetim Dergisi*, 3(1), 1-24.

Başaran, A. (2020). Dördüncü Sanayi Devrimi (Endüstri 4.0) ve İnsan Kaynakları Yönetimi, Global Transformation and Differentiation II, InGlobe Academy Publications, Conference Paper, 187-189.

Başlar, G. (2013). Yeni Medyanın Gelişimi ve Dijitalleşen Kapitalizm, Akademik Bilişim 2013-XV. Akademik Bilişim Konferansı Bildirileri, Antalya, 775-784.

Baştürk, F.H. (2019). Sigortacılık Sektöründeki Dijitalleşme Süreci ve Sigortacılık Eğitimine Yansıması, ERPA International Congresses on Education, Turkey.

Başyazıcıoğlu, H.N., Karamustafa, K. (2018). Marketing 4.0: Impacts of Technological Developments on Marketing Activities, *Kırıkkale University Journal of Social Sciences*, 8(2), 621-640.

Bayarçelik, E.B. (2020). *Dijital Dönüşümün İnsan Kaynakları Yönetimi Üzerine Etkileri*. (Edit. D. Akçay, E. Efe), Dijital Dönüşüm ve Süreçler & Digital Transformation and Processes, İstanbul Gelişim Üniversitesi Yayınları.

Bechtel, M., Briggs, B., Buchholz, S. (2020). Tech Trends 2020, https://www2.deloitte.com/content/dam/Deloitte/pt/Documents/tech-trends/TechTrends2020.pdf.

Betchoo, N. K. (2016). Digital Transformation and Its Impact on Human Resource Management: A Case Analysis of Two Unrelated Businesses in The Mauritian Public Service. In 2016 IEEE International Conference on Emerging Technologies and Innovative Business Practices for the Transformation of Societies (EmergiTech) (147-152).

Bhatnagar, H. (2017). Demonetization to Digitalization: A Step Toward Progress, *Management and Economics Research Journal*, 3, 11-15.

Calp, M. H., Doğan, A. (2019). İnsan Kaynakları Yönetiminde Dijital Dönüşüm, Ubak Uluslararası Bilimler Akademisi, Sosyal Bilimler Tam Metin Kitabı, 387-400.

Cingöz, A. (2011). Stratejik İnsan Kaynakları Yönetimi ve Stratejik İnsan Kaynakları Yönetiminin Örgütsel Performans ve İç Girişimcilik (Girişimsel Performans) Üzerindeki Etkileri: Kayseri İmalat Sanayinde Bir Araştırma. Doktora Tezi, Erciyes Üniversitesi, Sosyal Bilimler Enstitüsü, Kayseri.

Clohessy, T., Acton, T., Morgan, L. (2017). The Impact of Cloud Based Digital Transformation on ICT Service Providers' Strategies. *International Journal of Cloud Application and Computing*, 7(4), 1-19.

Čorejová, T., Rovňanová, A., Genzorová, T., Valica, M. (2016). Digital Transformation and Its Impact on Brand. in Marketing Identitiy Part 2, Conference Proceedings from International Scientific Conference, 54-65.

Demirkol, N., Tis, G. (2018). Endüstri 4.0'ın İnsan Kaynakları ve İnsan Kaynakları Yönetimine Etkisi, IV. International Caucasus-Central Asia Foreign Trade and Logistics Congress, 7-8 September, Aydın/Türkiye, 535-547.

Doğan, A. (2011). Elektronik İnsan Kaynakları Yönetimi ve Fonksiyonları, *İnternet Uygulamaları ve Yönetimi Dergisi*, 2(2), 51-80.

Dumansızoğlu, N. (2020). İK'da Dijital Dönem, Capital, https://www.capital.com.tr/yonetim/insan-kaynaklari/ikda-dijital-donem Date of Access: 28.11.2020.

Ergin, İ. (2019). Endüstri 4.0'dan Eğitim 4.0'a, *Turkish Studies Information Technologies and Applied Sciences,* 14 (4), 553-568.

Erkmen, B. (2018). Dijital Dönüşüm ve Dijital İK, Dijital Dönüşüm ve Dijital İK (slideshare.net) Date of Access: 05.12.2020.

Fachrunnisa, O., Hussain, F.K. (2020). Blockchain-Based Human Resource Management Practices for Mitigating Skills and Competencies Gap in Workforce, *International Journal of Engineering Business Management*, 12, 1–11.

Göktaş, P., Baysal, H. (2018). Türkiye'de Dijital İnsan Kaynakları Yönetiminde Bulut Bilişim, *Süleyman Demirel Üniversitesi İktisadi ve İdari Bilimler Fakültesi Dergisi*, 23, 1409-1424.

Hoffman, E., Rüsch, M. (2017). Industry 4.0 and The Current Status as Well as Future Prospects on Logistics, *Computers in Industry*, 89, 23-34.

Hrustek, L., Tomicic Furjan, M., Pihir, I. (2019). Influence of Digital Transformation Drivers on Business Model Creation. *2019 42nd International Convention on Information and Communication Technology, Electronics and Microelectronics (MIPRO),* 1304-1308.

Huselid, M.A., Jackson, S.E.,Schuler, R.S. (1997). Technical and Strategic Human Resource Management Effectiveness as Determinants of Firm Performance, *Academy of Management Journal*, 40(1), 171-188.

Işık, T. (2019). Türkiye'de Sağlık Kurumlarında Dijital Dönüşüm Adımları, içinde Sağlık Hizmetleri Uygulamalarında Dijital Dönüşüm, Ed. Elgiz Yılmaz Altuntaş, Eğitim Yayınevi, Konya.

Itika, J. (2011). Fundamentals of Human Resources Management: Emerging Experiences from Africa. African Public Administration and Management Series, Vol. 2, African Studies Centre, Leiden.

Kane, G.C., Palmer, D., Phillips, A.N., Kiron D. & Buckley, N. (2016). Aligning the Organization for Its Digital Future, MIT Sloan Management Review and Deloitte University Press, July 2016, 3-17.

Karatepe, S., Karaman, E. (2017). Türkiye'de Kamu Çalışanlarının Dijital Ortamda Değerlendirilmesi: E-Sicil Modeli, *Süleyman Demirel Üniversitesi İktisadi ve İdari Bilimler Fakültesi Dergisi*, C.22, Kayfor 15 Özel Sayısı, 2275-2289.

Kumar, B.N. (2016). Digital Transformation and Its Impact on Human Resource Management: A Case Analysis of Two Unrelated Businesses in The Mauritian Public Service, *International Journal of Novel Research in Interdisciplinary Studies,* 3(5), 1-10.

Küfeoğlu, S., Liu, G., Anaya, K, Pollitt, M.G. (2019). Digitalisation and New Business Models in Energy Sector, Cambridge Working Papers in Economics: 1956, University of Cambridge, https://www.repository.cam.ac.uk/bitstream/handle/1810/294125/cwpe1956.pdf?sequence=3 Date of Access: 1.1.2021.

Maria, M. (2020). Digitalization of: A Study of Success Factors and Consequences in The Last Decade, Master Thesis, University of Twente. Hollanda.

McCarthy, C. J., Moller, N., & Beard, L. M. (2003). Suggestions for Training Students in Using the Internet for Career Counseling, *The Career Development Quarterly*. C:LI, 4, 368-382.

Mohammadian, H.D., Rezaie, F. (2020). The Role of Ioe-Education in the 5th Wave Theory Readiness & Its Effect on SME 4.0 HR Competencies, IEEE Global Engineering Education Conference (EDUCON), Portugal.

OECD (2017). Key Issues For Digital Transformation In The G20, https://www.oecd.org/g20/key-issues-for-digital-transformation-in-the-g20.pdf Date of Access: 1.1.2021.

Özçelik, M., Akçay, V.H. (2019). Bankacılık Sektöründe Dijitalleşmenin Kariyer Platosu ile İlişkisi, *The Journal of Turk & Islam World Social Studies*, 6(22), 150-163.

Öztemel, E. (2018). Eğitimde Yeni Yönelimlerin Değerlendirilmesi ve Eğitim 4.0, *Journal of University Research,* 1(1), 25-30.

Parlak, B. (2019). Bir Kamu Hizmeti ve Politikası Alanı Olarak Eğitimde Teknolojik Gelişimin İzlerini Sürmek ve Dijital Eğitim, *Turkish Journal of TESAM Academy*, 6(1), 77-95.

Parsehyan, B. G. (2020). İnsan Kaynakları Yönetiminde Dijital Dönüşüm: İK 4.0. *Turkish Studies - Information Technologies and Applied Sciences,* 15(2), 211-224.

Phillips, T. N., Isenhour, L. C., Stone, D. (2008). The Potential for Privacy Violations in Electronic Human Resource Practices. Technology, Outsourcing & Transforming HR. ed. Graeme Martin, Martin Reddington, Heather Alexander, Burlington, USA, Elsevier, Ltd., 193-230.

Plekhanov, D., Netland, T.H. (2019). Digitalisation Stages in Firms: Towards a Framework, 26th EurOMA Conference 2019, Helsinki. https://www.researchgate.net/profile/Dmitry_Plekhanov/publication/334064152_Digitalisation_stages_in_firms_towards_a_framework/links/5d14db3e458515c11cfd6c28/Digitalisation-stages-in-firms-towards-a-framework.pdf Date of Access: 1.1.2021.

Saatçioğlu, Ö.Y., Kök, G.T., Özispa, N. (2018). Evaluation of Industry 4.0 and Its Reflections of Logistics Sector: A Case Study, *Suleyman Demirel University the Journal of Faculty of Economics and Administrative Sciences,* 23, Special Issue on Industry 4.0 and Organizational Change, 1675-1696.

Satuyeva, B., Sauranbayev, C., Ukaegbu, I.A, Nunna, K. (2019). Energy 4.0: Towards IoT Applications in Kazakhstan, *Procedia Computer Science*, 151, 909-915.

Schmindt, R. (2015). Evolution of HR, https://www.linkedin.com/pulse/evolution-hr-ralf-schmidt. Date of Access: 06.12.2020.

Sharma, H. & Shukla, S. (2019). Human Resource Management in Digital Age: Trends in Indian Corporate HR Practices. *IRC's International of Multidisciplinary Research in Social & Management Sciences*, 1(3), 66-77.

Sezgin, O.B. & Uçar, Z. (2019). Dijital Çağın İnsan Kaynakları Yönetimi Üzerindeki Etkileri. Aydın, E. & Uğur, U. (Ed.). İşletmelerde Dijital Dönüşümün Yansımaları içinde (pp. 85-104). Detay Yayıncılık, Türkiye.

Sonnentag, S., Binnewies, C. & Mojza, E.J. (2008). Did You Have a Nice Evening? A Day-Level Study on Recovery Experiences, Sleep, And Affect, Journal *of Applied Psychology*, 93(3), 674-684.

Sorko, S.R., Rabel, B.&Richter, H.M. (2016). The Future of Employment-Challenges in HRM Through Digitalization, *International Scientific Journal "Industry 4.0"*, 1(2), 128-131.

Strohmeir, S. (2020). Digital Human Resource Management: A Conceptual Clarification, *German Journal of Human Resource Management*, 34 (3), 345-365.

Tosun, E. (2014). İnsan Kaynakları Yönetimi, Açık Öğretim Fakültesi Yayınları, Eskişehir.

Tüfekçi, N., Yorulmaz, R., Cansever, İ.H. (2017). Digital Hospital, *Journal of Current Researches on Health Sector*, 7(2), 143-156.

Vassileva, B. (2017). Marketing 4.0: How Technologies Transform Marketing Organization, *Óbuda University e-Bulletin*, 7(1), 47-56.

Wan, D., Kok, V., Ong, C.H. (2002). Strategic Human Resource Management and Organizational Performance in Singapore, *Compensation and Benefits Review*, 34 (4), 33-42.

World Economic Forum (2016). Digital Transformation of Industries, https://www.accenture.com/t00010101t000000z__w__/ru-ru/_acnmedia/accenture/conversion-assets/dotcom/documents/local/ru-ru/pdf/accenture-digital-transformation.pdf Date of Access: 28.11.2020.

Yamamoto, G.T., Zümrüt, N., Altun, D. (2019). Dijital Dünyada Analog Kalmamak İçin İnsan Kaynaklarının Dönüşümü, Proceedings of the International Congress on Business and Marketing, Maltepe University, Istanbul, 13-14 Haziran, 360-370.

Yeşil, A. (2018). Örgütlerde Değişimin Önemi ve Değişim Yönetimi Üzerine Kavramsal Bir Değerlendirme. *Uluslararası Akademik Yönetim Bilimleri Dergisi*, 4(5), 307-323.

Yurdakul, M., Dalkılıç, N. (2016). Sigortacılık Sektöründe Dijital Çağ, *Dumlupınar Üniversitesi Sosyal Bilimler Dergisi*, Sayı:50, 49-67.

Zhou, K., Zhou, T., Zhou, L. (2015). Industry 4.0: Towards Future Industrial Opportunities and Challenges. IEEE Xplore Digital Library, 44-49.

Dijital Hastane, http://dijitalhastane.saglik.gov.tr Date of Access: 05.12.2020.

Sanayide Dijitalleşme Stratejileri Çalıştayı (2017). Sabancı Üniversitesi, http://research.sabanciuniv.edu/34507/1/Taslak_Rapor_v3.pdf Date of Access: 06.12.2020.

What Is Strategic HR for State Government? National Association of State Personnel Executives, https://www.cpshr.us/documents/whitepapers/strategichr_NASPE.pdf Date of Access:05.12.2020.

CHAPTER ELEVEN

THE IMPACT OF DIGITIZED BUSINESS MODELS ON EMPLOYMENT IN THE COVID-19 PERIOD: AN EVALUATION OF THE TOURISM SECTOR

SEDA KARAGÖZ ZEREN

Introduction

Business models consist of business strategies that create value, drive, and include business processes (Slowinski et al., 2013). There is an attempt to create business models by adapting to the digital transformation process with a holistic approach in businesses that use and process information. With the existence of technological developments and advances in information technologies, the concept of digital transformation has emerged. Ismail et al. (2017) defined the digital transformation process as the use of multiple digital technologies in order to gain a competitive advantage in the business processes used in the activities of the enterprises. Lucas et al. (2013), on the other hand, expressed digital transformation as a complete change in the traditional way of doing business in the existing skills, processes, and relationships of businesses. Deloitte (2018) emphasized that digitally transformed businesses create new business models using new technologies. The use of appropriate technologies in businesses to carry out activities that will create value for them, and the integration of these technologies into systems enable digital transformation in businesses. This digital transformation leads to the formation of new business models in businesses. The digital transformation that takes place in business activities is not only limited to the application of new and suitable technologies in business processes but also requires integration with the technology of each process that deals with the business in a holistic approach by affecting the organizational structure and culture. In digital transformation, answers are sought as to how to integrate human resources and business processes with technology in organizations (Tutkunca, 2020). In the digital transformation process, businesses that manage human resources and business processes in the best way, and organizations that create their business models according to these processes can achieve a competitive advantage. Digital transformation has positive effects in businesses with effective management in the form of an acceleration of business processes, an increase in the motivation of employees, the effective management of consumer-business communication, and a reduction of costs. In businesses and business environments where the digital transformation process cannot be organized effectively, negative effects are also observed such as decreased employment, loss of competitive advantage and on consumer relations.

The novel coronavirus (Covid-19) epidemic, which emerged for the first time in 2019 in Wuhan, China, has been declared a pandemic, affecting human health and causing deaths in many countries. Countries have taken various measures in order to reduce the spread of this pandemic. Among these measures are curfews, travel restrictions, closing the borders of countries, stopping business activities for a certain period, and conducting business activities online via remote access. These restrictions experienced during the pandemic process caused negative effects in the tourism sector, as seen in many other sectors. With the introduction of travel restrictions, especially by countries, the demand for tourism enterprises has gradually decreased and even the tourism enterprises themselves have decided to stop their activities within a certain period. The tourism sector has also been affected during the pandemic process due to the inability to stop the spread of the virus with travel restrictions, the decrease in consumer confidence in tourism and travel businesses, economic difficulties, coordination problems between countries, decreased in-flight services, and other reasons. According to the UNWTO World Tourism Report (2020), in July and August, when most tourism activities take place, huge changes were experienced compared to the previous year. Compared to 2019, the rate of international arrivals plunged by 81% in July and 79% in August. The decline to August 2020 represents 700 million fewer arrivals compared to the same period in 2019. Besides, it was determined that there was a loss of USD 730 billion in export revenues from international tourism. This loss is 8 times more than the loss experienced during the global economic crisis in 2009 (UNWTO, 2020). The total number of visitors between January and September 2020 in the tourism sector in Turkey has experienced a decrease of 71.3% compared to the same period in 2019. Considering the same period, there was a 64.4% decrease in tourism revenues compared to the previous year (T.C. Kültür & Turizm Bakanlığı, 2020). With these measures taken in the tourism sector and as a result of the decrease in tourism activities, unemployment rates increased and this situation caused a decrease in the employment rate. Also, businesses engaged in tourism activities have changed their business models and started to apply the services offered through online access or tried to offer solutions to the employment problem in the form of a temporary transfer of workers to different sectors.

This research aims to determine the use of digital business models by tourism enterprises as a result of the measures taken in tourism activities after the outbreak of the Covid-19 pandemic and to determine the effect of these applications on employment in the tourism sector. The research attempts to contribute to knowledge of the employment problems experienced in tourism enterprises during the pandemic period. Besides, this research provides a platform for further studies in this field.

Digitalized Business Models in the Tourism Sector

The structure showing the methods used by an enterprise to create value, the ways taken to deliver this value to the consumer, and the acquisition of income with this value is called a business model (Ostelwalder and Pigneur, 2010). The increase in technological innovations, changes in customer expectations and demands, and the acceleration of digital transformation together with changes in the business market structure cause changes to business models and enable the use of digital business models. For a business model to be called a digital business model, digital technologies must be used in the business and generate revenue for the business in order to radically change the business (Veit et al., 2014). Digital business models have emerged with the use of the internet of objects called digital technologies, virtual reality applications, artificial intelligence, smart sensors and devices, nanotechnologies, augmented reality, 3D technologies, smart robots, smart cities, smart hotels, wearable technologies, quantum computing, and blockchain technologies in business models. With the use of these technologies in different structures in the tourism sector, the formation of technological stages in this sector has been realized. Atar (2019) examined these in four stages shown in Table 11.1.

Table 11.1: Technology Phases Occurring in the Tourism Sector with Digital Technologies

Technological Phases	Definition	Specification
Tourism 1.0	This is the period that begins with the acceleration of the transition to urban life and the travel of households outside of natural places	The emergence and development of the concept of tourism for everyone
Tourism 2.0	With the development of oil-based internal combustion engines, tourism activities are realized as individual or group tours with technological tools other than individual vehicles	This has enabled easier, more widespread transportation in tourism activities, and the development of the communication network
Tourism 3.0	This is the period of automation and innovation, developed to facilitate the life of tourists and tourism personnel, in which the communication network of the tourism sector is faster with the rapid development of telecommunications	The development of the internet and the communication network with the concept of sustainable tourism, the formation of innovation and automation in tourism, the existence of green hotels
Tourism 4.0	This is tourism supported by the initiative provided at the destination to collect "data obtained from human minds" regarding physical infrastructure, social connections, government agencies, and businesses	Virtual reality, smart hotel management systems, smart card system, smart remote video monitoring system, smart tour guide system, smart travel agency system, and similar applications

Source: Adapted from Atar, 2019

The concepts of smart systems, smart management systems, smart applications, smart cities, smart tourism, and smart tourist have emerged at the stage of the birth of smart systems and smart tourism by integrating the digital technologies called Tourism 4.0, which are discussed in Table 11.1, with customer expectations and demands. With the application of these technologies by tourism businesses, the digitalized business model in tourism has emerged as a new business model. The digitalized business model in tourism can be defined as the use of digital technologies in these processes by radically changing all business models and processes used in the conduct of tourism activities. The concept of smart tourism is emerging with the formation of digitalized business models in tourism and the development of different digital applications. While the concept of smartness in tourism was first addressed within the scope of the destination and smart city, it was discussed with the concept of smart tourism, which has a wider scope, with the development of technology (Cabi and Erbaşı, 2019). On the other hand, Gretzel et al. (2015) stated that the purpose of smart tourism is to facilitate product/service innovation, to improve information and communication opportunities, to provide an effective tourist experience, and to increase the appeal to all segments. Many different applications are used within the scope of smart tourism in the tourism sector. Among these applications, smart hotels, smart cities, smart door/card/ticket systems, systems integrated with smart devices, and smart management systems can be cited as examples. A compilation of different smart application examples used by tourism enterprises is shown in Table 11.2.

Table 11.2: Smart Applications in the Tourism Sector

Application Fields	**Organization Name/Application Name**	**Service Type**	**Job Description**
Hotel and Accommodation	Starwood Aloft – A.L.O./ Boltr, Henn Na Hotel-Andrew, Cosmopolitan, M SocialSngapore, Yotel Hotel-Yobot, McLean Hotel in Virginia Hilton-Connie, Crowne Plaza-Dash, The Hotel EMC2 in Chicago-Cleo and Leo, Royal Caribbean Hotel Bionic Bar Robot, Savioke Relay robot hotel floor manager	Service Robots	Welcome Communication Robots, Robot Bellboy, Robot Waiter, Robot Chef

Hotel and Accommodation	Hilton, Loews, Marriot, Peninsula, Henn Na Hotel, Hotel Zetta (San Francisco)	Smart Rooms	Personalized room features with infrared sensors with a tablet, mobile application, and artificial reality
Tourism	Singapore-SARA, Malta, Blockchain-Based Smart City-Smart Dubai/Phnom Penh in Cambodia	Smart City	Information data usage to increase customer experience and access more information, virtual auto-answer assistant
Airports	Tokyo Haneda Airport, Miami International Airport, Blockchain-Based Pegasus Airlines Application in Sabiha Gokcen Airport, Turkey, Thomas Cook, and Samsung Gear Corporation about "Try Before You Fly" artificial reality, China Airport-Sanbot	Smart Airport and Applications	Direction finder application adapted with guidance, Blockchain-based baggage tracking system
Restaurant	Many restaurant chains like Royal Palace Restaurant in Netherland-Rosey, KFC in Russia, Qingdao in China-Tete, Chennai-Robot, Drink and Spice Magic Restaurant in Dubai-Ruby, Naulo Restaurant in Nepal-Ginger, The Gran Caffe Rapallo in Liguria/Italy, An Afghanistan Restaurant-Timea Nickname Nazo, The Two Panda Deli in Pasadena, California, USA-Tanbo R-1 and Tanbo R-2	Smart Food	Recommendations and personalized menus created by virtual cashiers, robot waiter, a robot chef, an artificial reality application with the ability to know each customer

Destination/ Tour Applications	Hyper-Reality in Disneyworld Team Park, Florida, USA, Smart travel planning system of Village Spa Resort, Smart Tour Packages-YourTour, Tokyo-Junko Chihira android robotic	Smart Tour Planning System	Making tour plans with realistic experiences of travelers
Management and policy	Many actors in tourism	The smart corporate resource planning system, smart employment management	Use of effective and efficient management systems

Sources: Adapted from Emir and Karagöz Zeren, 2020; Atar, 2020; Kabadayi et al., 2019; Sünnetçioğlu, 2019; Mil and Dirican, 2018; Yalçın Kayıkçı and Kutluk Bozkurt, 2018; Jiang, 2016; Gökalp and Eren, 2016; GuinnessWorld, 02.12.2020; Lyons, 02.12.20; Social Tables, 02.12.2020; Scycanner, 02.12.2020

These smart applications are seen in the tourism sector. The possibility of integrating tourists into tourism business processes, enabling cooperation with partners, networking, reaching customers through social media and similar new channels, the development of internet usage, additional pricing methods, and developments in income streams, is effective in the development of business models in the tourism sector (Verma and Varma, 2003). Grant Thornton's global technology leader Steven Perkins stated that a technological transformation in the tourism sector is the basis of a business strategy and emphasized that there should be three radical changes in the hotel sector to redesign business models expressed as follows (Grant Thornton, 02.12.2020);

- New partners and new expectations,
- Impressing guests at every stage,
- Smarter pricing.

Examples of digitalized business models in the tourism sector can also be considered as follows (Bağıran Özşeker et al., 2018);

- The Hilton, Starwood, and InterContinental Hotels Group has partnerships with Uber, an American international transportation

network company based in San Francisco, California. Guests of the Hilton Hotel can access the "Hilton Honors" application via Uber, perform check-in transactions, and obtain digital keys. Also, by accessing "Local Scene" information, they can evaluate travel experiences.
- Marriott International offers a reservation service through "Alitrip", an e-commerce site of Alibaba.
- The Accor Hotels Group has established its distribution platform called "AccorHotels.com" and offers "the augmented concierge" application developed with the digital personalization of a luxury hotel concierge service.

It is seen that digitalized business models in the sector are realized in applications with the effect of developing technologies in the tourism sector, according to different customer demands and expectations, providing a competitive advantage, and another reason. With this digital transformation in the sector, the creation of new business models is also effective in the management of employee relations in the sector. In addition, the creation of an effective employee relationship with human resources management and the presence of employees who adapt to digital transformation processes together with the digital business model can be both the cause and solution of employment problems in the tourism sector. While it may be possible for the workforce in the tourism sector to decrease with the presence of digital technologies, it may also be seen that less labor is wasted with the changes in the way that employees do business. In order to use digital business models effectively in tourism enterprises, employees should especially be able to provide training on the use of digital technologies and employees should be willing to use these technologies. This process can be carried out with effective human resources management.

Human resources management, which deals with the establishment of business objectives, the determination of strategic decisions, and the provision of personnel management, has become a digital human resources management in which the human resources management in the enterprise is carried out with internet technologies due to the globalizing world and technological innovations (Göktaş and Baysal, 2018). Jones (1997) examined the forces driving the emergence of digital human resources management in six parts:

- **Information Technology:** Digital human resources have become essential with the increase in information age technologies and decreasing costs.

- **Re-Planning and Organizing the Process:** Basic business processes should be rescheduled and improved with digital business processes.
- **High-Speed Management:** Businesses must act smarter and faster to gain a competitive advantage.
- **Network Organizations:** Businesses should try to be more efficient with a less bureaucratic structure.
- **Knowledge Workers:** The task of knowledge workers in learning organizations is to reduce costs and obtain job opportunities by using information. Information workers are obligatory in terms of digital human resources.
- **Globalization:** Businesses should gain a competitive advantage by determining their global strategies.

Digitalized human resources management within the scope of digital business models ensures rapid recruitment and talent management, flexible working solutions, and increased employee satisfaction, increases the accessibility of information and facilitates opportunity analysis, ensures the efficient use of time and faster performance evaluations. One of the digital technologies used in digitalizing human resources management is artificial intelligence. This is a digital technology that performs various activities of a robot based on a computer or computer control in the way of humans (Sas, 03.12.2020). In PwC's (2018) "Artificial Intelligence Forecasts" report, employees in Turkey are reported to be willing to work with artificial intelligence. According to the report, 78% of the employees stated that they could work with an artificial intelligence manager that balances workloads, 65% could get rid of boring and routine work thanks to artificial intelligence technology, 64% could get new business opportunities with artificial intelligence, and 50% who were effective and efficient were willing to use artificial intelligence for business administration (Akduman, 2019).

Digitalized Business Models and Employment in Tourism During the Covid-19 (The Novel Coronavirus) Period

Epidemics, which have an impact on more than one continent and a wide range of the world, are called pandemics (BBC News, 2020). The novel coronavirus epidemic (Covid-19 or 2019-nCoV), which was seen in Wuhan, China in December 2019, spread across continents and had an effect all over the world. It was declared a pandemic by the World Health Organization in March 2020 (WHO, 02.12.2020). Coronavirus is a pandemic that negatively affects human health by showing symptoms of the common cold and even leads to death. According to the data of December 3, 2020, this pandemic was seen in 220 different countries around the world, with 63,719,213 cases and 1,482,084 deaths (WHO, 03.12.2020).

Countries have had to take various measures due to the rapid spread of the coronavirus pandemic and the increase in mortality rates. These measures include the need to maintain social distance between individuals, the use of masks, and personal hygiene rules. Since the pandemic is transmitted due to close contact between individuals and the rate of increase in the epidemic has not decreased or even increased despite these measures, every country has started to apply additional measures. These measures include closing countries' international borders, terminating airline and sea transport for a certain period, initiating curfews for certain periods, closing schools at all levels for certain periods and carrying out educational activities through online education, and temporarily suspending the activities in restaurants, hotels, beauty salons, and similar businesses. These measures have not only affected certain sectors directly or indirectly but have also affected the tourism sector negatively. The fact that tourism activities cannot be implemented for a certain period, the closure of restaurants and cafes, the cancellation of hotels and accommodation, and the suspension of flights have caused employment problems in the tourism sector – one of the drivers of the international economy – the closure and inability of tourism businesses, and serious problems in national economies. With the measures implemented, the global pause at the point of the spread of the pandemic and the new process called the normalization process have been initiated, and the continuation of tourism activities with certain measures, the lifting of travel bans and the restriction of travel in certain ways, the reopening of the countries' borders, etc., are allowed according to countries' own decisions. The cross-continental spread of the Covid-19 pandemic is continuing, and while studies are ongoing to treat the disease, additional restrictions and measures are taken by nations when the pandemic's course is upward. With these measures, businesses operating in the tourism sector should apply new methods to ensure their sustainability. Following the social distance rules that must be applied to prevent the spread of the pandemic, some tourism activities are offered by digital technologies, and digital business models are formed in tourism enterprises.

Fleisch et al. (2015) state that digital business models formed with the effect of digital technologies develop in three stages (Klein, 2020). These stages are stated below (Fleish et al., 2015):

- Internet-influenced business models,
- Business models created by the influence of social media,

- Business models created by the effect of the internet of things.

In Figure 11.1., three phases of digital business models are discussed.

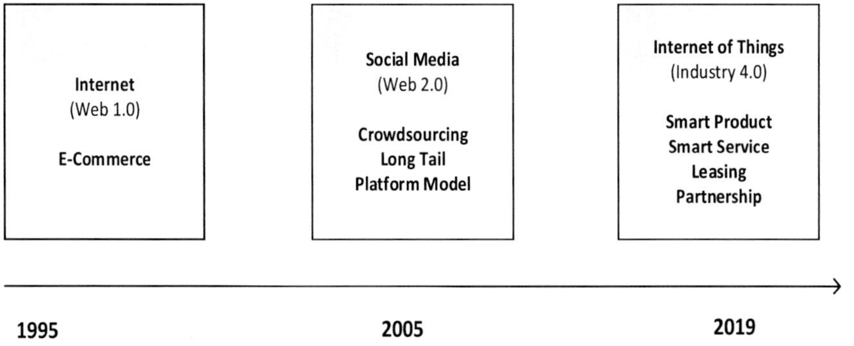

Figure 11.1: The Phase of Digitalized Business Models (Fleisch et al., 2015: 452)

In Figure 11.1, the first phase of digital business models is the phase of Web 1.0 e-commerce applications starting with the use of the internet. In the second phase, Web 2.0 applications with the effect of social media take place in three ways. First, there are crowdsourcing applications where customers are included in the product development process within the network with the idea that collective intelligence will produce better solutions than individual intelligence. Secondly, there are longtail applications that are formed by the transformation of mass markets into small niche markets with digital technologies. Thirdly, there are online store platform models where businesses can market their products. In the third phase, with the Industry 4.0 process, there is the use of the internet of things concept and the digital business model where smart product, smart service, leasing, and partnership business models are formed (Klein, 2020). Business models that are created by the Covid-19 pandemic can be added to these business models. In the Covid-19 pandemic process, digital business models can be expanded to include all three phases, with many restrictions, including maintaining social distance and curfews. This model is shown in Figure 11.2.

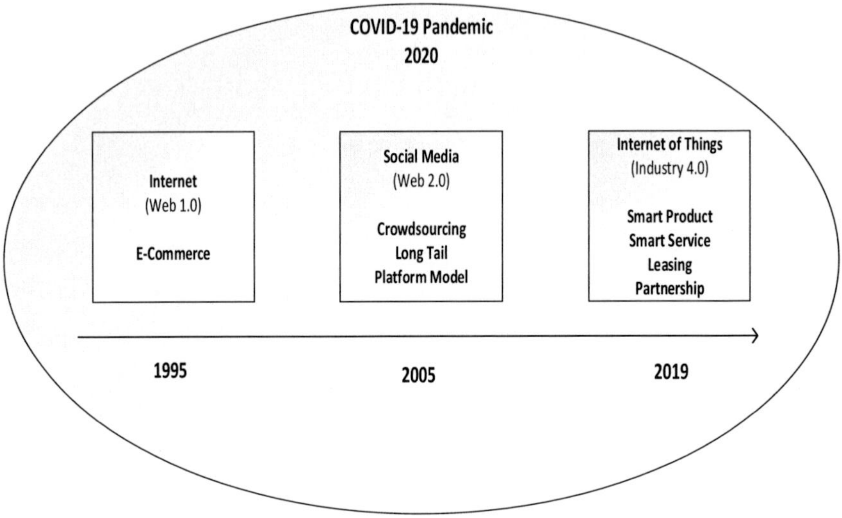

Figure 11.2: Digitalized Business Models During the Covid-19 Pandemic (The Author, self-archive)

In the model discussed in Figure 11.2, smart products and services offered by businesses can be presented on social media and certain platforms through e-commerce activities. In terms of the tourism sector, it has been determined that there may be different applications when digital business models are considered during the Covid-19 pandemic period. For example, a hotel business can differentiate its service in this period and carry out marketing activities on digital platforms. In order to indicate that it is different from its competitors, it can carry out its marketing activities in this direction by obtaining a "Covid-19 Free Certification", which indicates that the safe tourism activity is realized. In service delivery, customers can use online artificial intelligence, virtual reality, blockchain, etc. It can shape the demands by including its applications. A restaurant or cafe business can reflect the use of digital technologies in business models by moving its service to online media.

The digitalization experienced in the business models of businesses operating in the tourism sector also affects the number of employees and the rate of employment. According to 2019 data, the tourism sector is responsible for 330 million jobs in the world, so one out of every 10 jobs globally is in the tourism sector. Also, the tourism industry acts as an economic catalyst, accounting for 10.3% of the global GDP, approximately USD 8.9 trillion (World Travel and Tourism Council and Global Rescue,

2019). The tourism sector plays an important role in reducing poverty, increasing welfare, and ensuring equal opportunity. According to the data of 2019, 54% of the workforce working in the tourism sector are women and more than 30% are young people (World Travel and Tourism Council, 2020). The economic depression in the tourism sector along with the Covid-19 pandemic caused an increase in unemployment rates. According to the International Labor Organization (ILO) data, approximately 15.3 million workers (6.4 million female employees and 8.9 million male employees) in the tourism sector are at risk (ILO, 2020). When the economic impacts of the pandemic on the tourism sector are examined, it is determined that as of the first three-quarters of 2020, there were 142.6 million job losses globally (43% decrease), a decrease of USD 3,815 billion in GDP (43% decrease) and decreases in international (65%) and domestic (33%) global arrivals. In Africa, these rates are determined as 12.4 million job losses (51% decrease), a USD 87 billion GDP loss (51% decrease), and decreases in international and domestic global arrivals, at 63% and 33% respectively. America experienced 19.8 million job losses (44% decrease), a USD 1,074 billion GDP loss (43% decrease) and decreases in international and domestic global arrivals, at 70% and 34% respectively. In Asia, where the Covid-19 pandemic started, this situation was seen as 87.4 million job losses (48% decrease), a USD 1,475 billion GDP loss (50% decrease) and decreases in international and domestic global arrivals, at 71% and 31% respectively (World Travel and Tourism Council, 04.12.2020). According to ILO (2020) data, the pandemic process has affected 144 million workers in the accommodation and food services sector, and more than half of these affected workers are women. The sectoral-based economic effects of the pandemic process are discussed in Table 11.3.

Table 11.3: A Sectoral Perspective of Workers at Risk in Covid-19

Economic Sector	Current Impact of Crisis on Economic Output	Baseline employment situation (global estimates for 2020 before Covid-19)			
		Level of employment (000s)	Share in global employment (%)	Wage ratio (av. monthly sector earning/av. total earnings)	Share of women (%)
Education	Low	176560	5.3	1.23	61.8
Human health and social work activities	Low	136244	4.1	1.14	70.4
Public administration and defense; compulsory social security	Low	144241	4.3	1.35	31.5
Utilities	Low	26589	0.8	1.07	18.8
Agriculture; forestry and fishing	Low-Medium	880373	26.5	0.72	37.1
Construction	Medium	257041	7.7	1.03	7.3
Financial and insurance activities	Medium	52237	1.6	1.72	47.1
Mining and quarrying	Medium	21714	0.7	1.46	15.1
Arts, entertainment and recreation, and other services	Medium-high	179857	5.4	0.69	57.2
Transport; storage and communication	Medium-high	204217	6.1	1.19	14.3
Accommodation and food services	High	143661	4.3	0.71	54.1
Real estate; business and administrative activities	High	156878	4.7	0.97	38.2
Manufacturing	High	463091	13.9	0.95	38.7
Wholesale and retail trade; repair of motor vehicles and motorcycles	High	481951	14.5	0.86	43.6

Source: International Labour Organization (ILO), (2020, 05 07), ILO Monitor: Covid-19 and the world of work. The second edition, updated estimates and analysis. Retrieved on 04.12.2020 from https://www.ilo.org/wcmsp5/groups/public/---dgreports/---dcomm/documents/briefingnote/wcms_740877.pdf

When Table 11.3 is analyzed, it is seen that the global accommodation and food services sector is highly affected in terms of the economic effects of the pandemic. Globally, the tourism sector has been one of the most affected sectors during the pandemic due to the high employment rate compared to other sectors. Global improvement plans should be implemented in terms of the tourism sector.

Methodology

Document analysis is a qualitative data analysis method used to examine and evaluate all printed and electronic documents. This requires the analysis and interpretation of data in order to make sense and create an understanding of a subject, and to obtain empirical information (Kıral, 2020). Document analysis helps to classify the data subject to research by organizing them into main themes, categories, and case examples through content analysis (Labuschagne, 2003). Among the advantages of the document analysis are efficiency in terms of time use, an ability to adjust the sample size, its usability, low cost, and an ability to be used again and again, which require individuality and originality, precision, broad time and scope, a lack of responsiveness, easy access to data, and data that reflect the nature of the subject (Kıral, 2020).

Within the scope of the research, the digitalized business models in the tourism sector during the Covid-19 pandemic period and their effects on employment were investigated. During the Covid-19 pandemic process, scientific articles, reports, and internet and newspaper news published in 2019 and 2020 were compiled, and document analysis, a qualitative data analysis method, was applied to these documents. Since the Covid-19 pandemic process first covered the month of December 2019, the materials examined cover the year 2020. It was attempted to obtain data by using the Boolean operators "or, and, not" in the databases of "Google, Google Scholar, Web of Sciences, Scopus". The keywords "1-) tourism and 2-) Covid-19 or coronavirus or 2019-ncov or sars-cov-2 or cov-19 and 3-) digital business model" have been searched in related databases. The analysis was applied to a total of 100 scientific articles, reports, and internet and newspaper news, including three key headings. 60 of the 100 publications examined consist of internet news, periodicals, and newspaper news. 40 publications include reports and scientific articles. The Maxqda 2020 program was used in order to apply content analysis to the 100 publications examined. Relevant publications were transferred to the program and a document-based content analysis was applied. A total of 100 publications were categorized by publishing type, publication year, number of publishers, keywords, research methodology and subjects, research region, sector, company or application, and research results, and a total of 2080 codings were carried out.

Results

In order to determine the business models that became digital during the Covid-19 pandemic period in the tourism sector and to investigate the effect of this process on employment in the tourism sector, content analysis was applied to a total of 100 publications by scanning databases. The demographic findings obtained from the documents examined are shown in tables and figures, respectively. In Figure 11.3, a graphic representation of 100 documents obtained by scanning with keywords in databases is performed according to the type of publication.

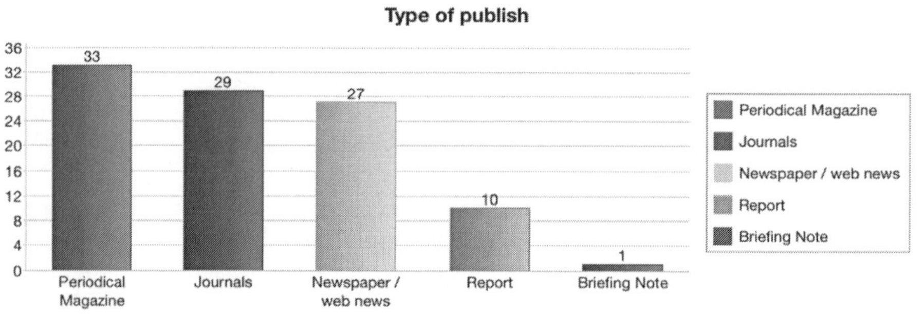

Figure 11.3: Document-based Frequency Graph Regarding Publishing Type Codes in Examined Documents (the author, self-archive)

When Figure 11.3 is examined, 60 of the 100 documents analyzed consist of newspaper and internet news, while 40 are scientific publications. Of the 60 newspapers and internet news, 33 were obtained from periodical magazines and 27 were obtained from the internet and daily newspaper news. 40 scientific publications were examined and the types of these publications were 29 scientific articles, 10 international reports, and 1 briefing note.

Table 11.4: Document-based Frequency Regarding Codes for the Number of Publishers in Examined Documents

Number of Authors	Number of Publishing
Single Author	50
Organization	26
Two Authors	9
Three Authors	8
Four Authors	4
Ten Authors	2
Five Authors	1
Number of Coded Documents	100
Number of Uncoded Documents	0

Source: (the author, self-archive)

In Table 11.4, the frequency information of analyzed documents is shown according to the number of publishers. 50 of the documents were handled by a single author and 26 by an institution, organization, or committee. These findings are followed by the fact that 9 documents have two authors, 8 documents have 3 authors, 4 documents have 4 authors, 2 documents have ten authors, and one document has 5 authors.

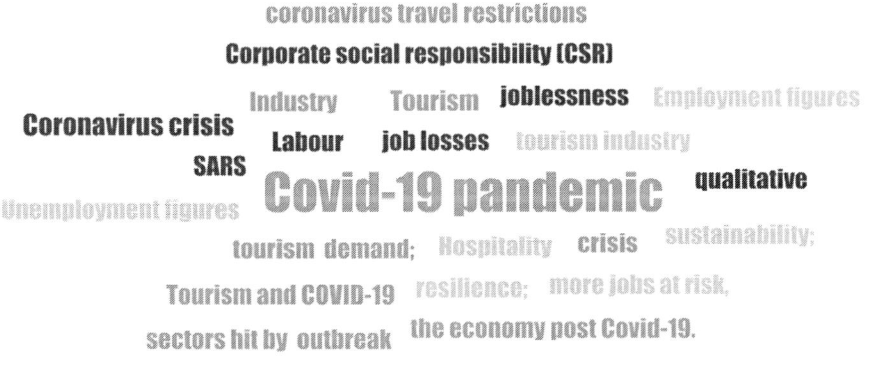

Figure 11.4: Code Cloud Related to Keyword Codes in Examined Documents (the author, self-archive)

Figure 11.4 shows the code cloud of keywords used in examined documents. The code cloud offers a more visual expression to the reader regarding the codes in documents that are analyzed content. While the concept "Covid-19 pandemic", which is mostly mentioned in the keywords of the documents examined, is located in the center of the visual, other concepts are positioned around the center according to the frequency values.

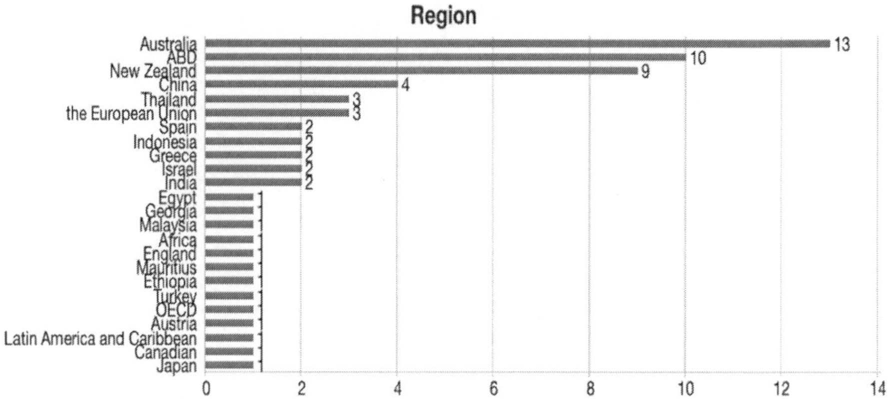

Figure 11.5: Document-based Frequency Graph Regarding Region Codes in Examined Documents (the author, self-archive)

In Figure 11.5, while 13 of the analyzed documents provide information about the situations experienced in the tourism sector during the Covid-19 pandemic in Australia, 10 of them provide information about the situation in the USA. Other regions and countries in the analyzed documents are shown in Figure 11.5. In 37 publications, no region was mentioned and the situations experienced in the tourism sector during the pandemic period were expressed.

Figure 11.6: Code Cloud for Research Methodology and Subject Codes in Examined Documents (the author, self-archive)

In Figure 11.6, a code cloud is shown regarding the research methodology codes in the analyzed documents. The most used research method and subject in the documents examined are to make a general literature review of the issues related to the "coronavirus crisis". This finding is followed by the qualitative research method used to determine this rate about the subject of "the unemployment rate after Covid-19".

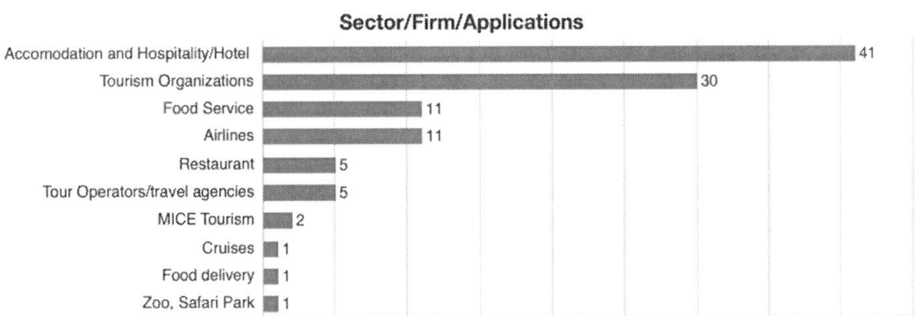

Figure 11.7: Document-based Frequency Graph Regarding Sector/Firm/ Application Codes in the Examined Documents (the author, self-archive)

Figure 11.7 is a visual of the 100 analyzed documents by areas, applications, or businesses in the tourism sector. In 27 of the 100 documents analyzed, no company, application, or area restriction was specified in the tourism sector. In 41 documents, information is provided on the effects of the Covid-19 pandemic process in accommodation and hospitality/hotel businesses.

Figure 11.8: Code Cloud for Results Codes in Examined Documents (the author, self-archive)

Figure 11.8 displays the results presented in the form of a code cloud of the analyzed documents regarding the business models and employment digitalized in the tourism sector during the Covid-19 pandemic. The subject of "The distribution (%) of the losses in employment per sector" is mostly discussed in the analyzed documents.

Conclusion

The Covid-19 pandemic has adversely affected the health of individuals all over the world and has also had negative effects in social and economic terms. Individuals' living conditions and ways of doing business have changed with the pandemic period. In this process, nations have taken various measures in order to reduce the spread of the pandemic. In order to control the pandemic, recommendations are offered to avoid close contact and unhygienic situations, to comply with social distancing rules, to use masks, and to pay attention to hygiene rules. With these rules, new restrictions have been imposed, such as suspending the activities of various businesses for a while and imposing full or certain curfews; the closing of national borders for a certain period; the suspension of each level of education for a certain period or moving education online; the suspension of flights and ships; and the suspension of all kinds of organizations, celebrations, weddings, hotels, cafes, restaurants, and similar events. One of the sectors most affected by these restrictions has been the tourism sector. The existence of travel restrictions, along with the curfews of individuals, and the closure of international borders, has caused many tourism businesses to terminate their activities and even go bankrupt in the sector.

During the pandemic process, digital solutions started to be implemented in business models, and online services were used in order to restrict the activities of businesses and to ensure social distancing. In this process, many businesses in the tourism sector have reflected the use of digital technologies in their service delivery to their business models. With the pandemic, those who wanted to benefit from services due to the cancellation of flights made their cancellation and postponement transactions through online services. Those who made plans to stay in hotels had to cancel or postpone their reservations via digital channels. Travel agencies had to manage processes by focusing on online services. Digital menu services were introduced in cafe and restaurant businesses. Taking advantage of internet of things' devices, the activities of tourism businesses were organized as QR codes, smart systems, and smart applications. Besides, digital technologies in human resources management were handled and recruitment processes were carried out online in this process. Along with the restrictions, the decrease in the employment rate in the tourism sector is among the issues that need to be addressed both nationally and internationally. Although in many countries there has been an increase in the rate of dismissal of workers in tourism enterprises during the pandemic process, different measures have been taken to control this situation in some countries. A business in Australia has pioneered the shifting of those working in tourism businesses to the food supply and logistics sectors, and business lines that are more active during the pandemic process. Since people could not leave their homes during the pandemic process, the provision of basic food was carried out through online services and delivery to the door. One of the business types offering the most employment areas is supermarkets, markets, etc., that have been in this process. It has been ensured that those working in tourism enterprises work in this service sector temporarily so that these employees are not victims. In this period, internet-based job search sites such as "JobSeeker" and "JobKeeper", which offer online services to job seekers, also increased their services.

Since the tourism sector is one of those sectors that are effective in the economic development of nations, it should be evaluated in terms of the negative effects of the pandemic process in the sector and a recovery plan should be made accordingly. With the formation of digital societies in the digitalized age, the pandemic process shows that the activities of tourism businesses should be more integrated with digital technologies. It is thought that these technologies should be included in all processes of enterprises. Digitalized employment creation and business plans can be realized with digitalized business models. Internet of things' devices and services offered by tourism businesses can be integrated and delivered to more customers. In tourism enterprises, planning can be done using digital technologies to find solutions to the working time and employment problems of workers.

Keywords: *Digitalized business model, employment, Covid-19, tourism, the novel coronavirus*

References

Akduman, G. (2019). Dijital İşe Alım: Dijial Dünya'nın İnsan Kaynakları İşe Alım Fonksiyonuna Etkisinin Kavramsal ve Uygulama Örnekleriyle Değerlendirilmesi. *International Journal of Arts & Social Studies (ASSTUDIES), 2*(3), 24-44.

Atar, A. (2019). Dijital Dönüşüm ve Turizme Etkileri. In M. Sezgin, Ö. S. Akgül , & A. Atar, *Turizm 4.0-Dijital Dönüşüm* (pp. 100-111). Ankara: Detay Yayıncılık.

Atar, A. (2020). Gelenekselden Dijitale Turizm Sektörü. *Journal of Turkish Tourism Research, 4*(2), 1640-1654.

Bağıran Özşeker, D., Kurgun, H., and Kurgun, O. A. (2018). The Innovation Radar is a Strategic Approach to Business Model Innovation in Hotel Businesses: The Case of Swissotel Büyük Efes İzmir. *Journal of Tourism and Gastronomy Studies, 6*(3), 133-170.

BBC News. (2020, 02 24). *Pandemi nedir, ülkeleri nasıl etkiler? - Dünya Sağlık Örgütü koronavirüsü pandemi ilan etti.* Retrieved 12 02, 2020, from https://www.bbc.com/turkce/haberler-dunya-51614548

Cabi, A., and Erbaşı, A. (2019). *Akıllı Turizm Bağlamında Akıllı Otel İşletmesi Endeksi ve Uygulaması.* Konya, Turkey: Sami Billur Yayıncılık.

Deloitte. (2018). *Digital Enablement Turning Your Transformation into A Successful Journey.* Retrieved 11 12, 2020, from https://www2.deloitte.com/content/dam/Deloitte/ie/Documents/Technology/IE_C_HC_campaign.pdf

Emir, O., and Karagöz Zeren, S. (2020). Turizmde Blockchain Uygulamaları. In O. Emir, and E. O. Aksöz, *Turizmde Güncel Yaklaşımlar* (pp. 195-217). Eskişehir: Anadolu Üniversitesi Açıköğretim Fakültesi Yayınları.

Fleish, E., Weinberger, M., and Wortmann, F. (2015). Geschäftsmodelle im Internet der Dinge. *Schmalenbachs Z betriebswirtsch Forsch, 67*(4), 444-465.

Gökalp, E., and Eren, E. (2016). Akıllı Teknolojilerin Turizm ve Otelcilik Sektöründe Uygulanması. In V. Tecim, Ç. Tarhan, and C. Aydın, *Smart Technology & Smart Management: Akıllı Teknoloji & Akıllı Yönetim* (pp. 278-287).

Göktaş, P., and Baysal, H. (2018). Türkiye'de Dijital İnsan Kaynakları Yönetimine Bulut Bilişim. *Süleyman Demirel Üniversitesi İktisadi ve İdari Bilimler Fakültesi Dergisi, 23*(4), 1409-1424.

Grant Thornton. (02.12.2020). *The Power of Personalisation: Hotels' Roadmap to 2020.* Retrieved from https://www.grantthornton.com.vn/globalassets/1.-member-firms/united-kingdom/pdf/publication/2016/the-power-of-personilsation-uk.pdf

Gretzel, U., Sigala, M., Xiang, Z., and Koo, C. (2015). Smart Tourism: Foundations and Developments. *Electronic Markets, 3*(25), 179-188.

GuinnessWorld. (02.12.2020). *First restaurant with robot waiting staff.* Retrieved from https://www.guinnessworldrecords.com/world-records/first-restaurant-with-robot-waiting-staff

ILO. (2020). *Thematic Brief: COVID-19 and employment in the tourism sector: Impact and response in Asia and the Pacific.* UK: Regional Office for Asia and the Pacific Regional Economic and Social Analysis Unit.

International Labour Organization (ILO). (2020, 05 07). *ILO Monitor: COVID-19 and the world of work. The second edition Updated estimates and analysis.* Retrieved 12 04, 2020, from https://www.ilo.org/wcmsp5/groups/public/---dgreports/---dcomm/documents/briefingnote/wcms_740877.pdf

Ismail, M. H., Khater, M., and Zaki, M. (2017). *Digital Busines Transformation and Strategy: What do we know so far?* Retrieved 11 12, 2020, from Cambridge Service Alliance: https://cambridgeservicealliance.eng.cam.ac.uk/resources/Downloads/Monthly%20Papers/2017NovPaper_Mariam.pdf/view

Jiang, I. (2016). *Take a look at 20 of the cutest and creepiest robots in stores and restaurants today*. Retrieved 12 02, 2020, from https://www.businessinsider.com/cute-and-creepy-robots-in-retail-stores-restaurants-2020-7#in-kabul-afghanistan-a-japanese-robot-named-timea-that-serves-patrons-of-times-fast-food-has-earned-the-nickname-nazo-or-beautiful-in-the-dari-language-19

Jones, J. W. (1997). *Virtual HR: Human Resources Management in the Information Age.* USA: Crisp Publications.

Kıral, B. (2020). Nitel Bir Veri Analizi Yöntemi Olarak Doküman Analizi. *Siirt Üniversitesi Sosyal Bilimler Enstitüsü Dergisi*(15), 170-189.

Kabadayi, S., Faizan, A., Choi, H., Joosten, H., and Lu, C. (2019). Smart Service Experience in Hospitality and Tourism Services: A Conceptualization and Future Research Agenda. *Journal of Service Management, 30*(3), 326-348.

Klein, M. (2020). Digital Transformation in Business and Its Drivers. *Journal of Business in the Digital Age, 3*(1), 24-35.

Labuschagne, A. (2003). Qualitative research: Airy fairy or fundamental? *The Qualitative Report*(8), 100-103.

Lucas, H. C., Clemons, E. K., Sawy, O. A., and Weber, B. (2013). Impact Research On Transformational Information Technology: An Opportunity to Inform New Audiences. *MIS Quarterly, 37*(2), 371-382.

Lyons, K. (02.12.2020). *A restaurant in the Netherlands is using creepy robot waiters for social distancing*. Retrieved from https://www.theverge.com/2020/5/31/21276318/restaurant-netherlands-robot-waiters-social-distancing-pandemic

Mil, B., and Dirican, C. (2018). Endüstri 4.0 Teknolokileri ve Turizme Etkileri. *Journal of Multidisciplinary Academic Tourism, 1*(3), 1-9.

Ostelwalder, A., and Pigneur, Y. (2010). *Business Model Generation: A Handbook for Visionaries, Game Changers, and Challengers.* United States of America: John Wiley and Sons, Inc.

Sünnetçioğlu, S. (2019). Turizmde Dijital Dönüşüm ve Turist Yerli Halk İlişkileri: Eleştirel Bir Yaklaşım. *The Third International Congress on Future of Tourism: Innovation, Entrepreneurship and Sustainability* (pp. 610-616). Mersin/Turkey: Mersin University Publications.

Sas. (03.12.2020). *Yapay Zeka Nedir? Neden Önemlidir?* Retrieved from https://www.sas.com/tr_tr/insights/analytics/yapay-zeka-nedir.html

Scycanner. (02.12.2020). *The World's Most Hi-tech Hotels*. Retrieved from https://www.skyscanner.net/news/inspiration/the-worlds-most-hi-tech-hotels

Slowinski, G., Hummel, E., Sagal, M. W., Matthews, S., and Gilmont, E. R. (2013). Business Models for Collaborative Research. *Research Technology Managements, 53*(6), 124-128.

Social Tables. (02.12.2020). *Robots in Hotels: 6 Hotel Brands Leading the Way*. Retrieved from https://www.socialtables.com/blog/hospitality-technology/hotel-brands-robot/

T.C. Kültür ve Turizm Bakanlığı. (2020). *Turizm İstatistikleri Ocak-Eylül 2020.* T.C. Kültür ve Turizm Bakanlığı Yatırım ve İşletmeler Genel Müdürlüğü Araştırma ve Değerlendirme Daire Başkanlığı.

Tutkunca, T. (2020). İşletmelerde Dijital Dönüşüm ve İlgili Bileşenlerinin Analiz Edilmesi Üzerine Kavramsal Bir Araştırma. *Çağ Üniversitesi Sosyal Bilimler Dergisi, 17*(1), 65-75.

UNWTO (World Tourism Organization). (2020, 10). *UNWTO World Tourism Barometer 2020* (Vol. 18). Madrid, Spain: World Tourism Organization. Retrieved 11 13, 2020, from https://www.e-unwto.org/doi/epdf/10.18111/wtobarometereng.2020.18.1.6

Veit, D., Clemons, E., Benlian, A., Buxmann, P., Hess, T., Kundisch, D., . . . Spann, M. (2014). Business Models - An Information Systems Research Agenda. *Business & Information Systems Engineering, 6*(1), 45-53.

Verma, D., and Varma, G. (2003). On-line pricing: Concept, Methods and Current Practices. *Journal of Services Research, 3*(1), 135-155.

WHO. (02.12.2020). Retrieved from https://www.who.int/emergencies/diseases/novel-coronavirus-2019.

WHO. (03.12.2020). *Coronavirus Disease (Covid-19) Pandemic*. Retrieved from https://www.who.int/emergencies/diseases/novel-coronavirus-2019

World Travel and Tourism Council. (04.12.2020). *Recovery Scenarios 2020 & Economic Impact from COVID-19*. Retrieved from https://wttc.org/Research/Economic-Impact/Recovery-Scenarios

World Travel and Tourism Council. (2020). *G20 Saudi Arabia 2020 Rıyadh Summit: 100 Million Jobs Recovery Plan Final Proposal.* London, United Kingdom: World Travel and Tourism Council.

World Travel and Tourism Council and Global Rescue. (2019). *Crisis Readiness: Are You Prepared and Resilient to Safeguard Your People & Destinations?* World Travel and Tourism Council and Global Rescue.

Yalçın Kayıkçı, M., & Kutluk Bozkurt, A. (2018). Dijital Çağda Z ve Alpha Kuşağı, Yapay Zeka Uygulamaları ve Turizme Yansımaları. *Sosyal Bilimler Metinleri, 1*(1), 54-64.

CHAPTER TWELVE

DIGITAL TRANSFORMATION AND EDUCATION: ORGANIZATIONAL, CULTURAL AND SOCIOLOGICAL REFLECTIONS

GÖKHAN DEMIRHAN

Introduction

The expressions on the emergence and evolution of organizations that have occupied an important place in our lives for the last three centuries attribute to two main elements with a general trend (almost all): industrialization and modernization, as a result. In accordance with this trend, starting with a characteristic example of the attempts to explain the revolutionary emergence journey of modern organizations will probably be a good choice.

> *Industrialization presages major changes in all societal sectors. A rise in educational standards and achievements, the spread of political consciousness, secularization, the rapid growth of science, the decline of the family, and increase in social mobility: all are associated with industrialization. We refer to all these related changes as modernization.*
> (Etzioni, 1964: 105)

The closely related areas of change that are mentioned in this excerpt in relation to the structuring of modern organizations and other related phenomena, industrialization and modernity, continue to be of great importance today (despite the past 60 years). Many factors such as developments in educational services offered to individuals and society, political awareness and activism that have taken a rather different form thanks to social networks, secularization, the dizzying speed of scientific progress, and the phenomenon of "family", which has been redefined and designed by individuals thanks to the high level of virtual correlativity and both physical and virtual social mobility reaching incredible levels –

although it has been interrupted in the last period – deeply affect the structure and organizational behavior of today's organizations. However, there is an important difference compared to 60 years ago; today, industrialization, which is the basis of the mentioned change, seems to have undergone a major change compared to the version that emerged after the industrial revolution. The expressions Industry 4.0 and even Industry 5.0 are attributed to the new versions of today's industrialization. The most commonly used keyword of this "new industrialization" seems to be "digitalization". The digitalization process strongly affects all organizations regardless of the sector, goals and target audience, and organizations for public services such as education are not exempt from this situation. Recently, educational organizations and policy makers across the world have made significant attempts to keep pace with the digital transformation. However, due to the pandemic that we had to face in the first quarter of 2020, this preparation process seems to have left its place to some kind of emergency action. It may be too early to discuss the consequences of the global reactions of educational organizations to this emergency. However, discussing – albeit theoretically – the structural and behavioral effects of this situation on organizations and the cultural and sociological reflections of these organizations on society as their target group is very important as an early feedback mechanism for the course of the process and this is exactly the main purpose of this chapter.

Digitalization of Education and Organizational Reflections

When the results of studies on the organizational effects of digitalization are evaluated together, it is seen that the relevant literature focuses on organizational learning, digital innovations included in the organizational structure, the ability of organizations to react quickly to change, the ability to adapt to the new ecosystem and new organizational structuring processes (Kuusisto, 2017). Taking a closer look at these domains and understanding what they mean in an organizational context will be a good start.

Organizational learning is one of the most important reflexes that enable organizations to adapt and survive in high-motion periods and environments (Popper & Lipshitz, 2000). It is impossible for organizations that cannot operate information processing to keep up with the times, fulfill their functions and survive in today's world, in which information generation and speed of spread have reached a tremendous level. In this context, educational organizations should also actively participate in the digitalization process in education that continues at an increasing rate globally. Many higher education institutions across the world have digitized a variety of their education and certification programs. Information consumption habits concentrate on accessibility and widespread impact factors as in all issues of today's society. Considering these factors, as well as the awareness of organizations about this digital transformation process and their motivation on the change, their innovation and integration speed is also very important because it is obvious that 21st century society does not tolerate waiting for anything. A tiny gap in the digitalization attempts of prestigious and well-established educational organizations dating back centuries will result in a private or corporate enterprise that is fully organized on the internet to quickly meet the needs of the society in this respect. For instance, the leading enterprises of digital transformation in education such as Udemy, Coursera, MasterClass and Edx deliver hundreds of thousands of digitized educational services today for millions of students; and without the need for any traditional form of organization! It seems that the digitization process necessitates important changes in the current conventional and organizational structures. It should be remembered that there are some public educational organizations that can innovate themselves in accordance with the trends of digital transformation in education such as Harvard, MIT and the Open University.

An important dimension of the digitalization of organizations is the integration of digital technologies, which can be defined as both the drivers and results of digital transformation, into organizational systems. Of course, digital transformation does not only include the transfer or use of new technologies. Moreover, this reaction is a form of follow-up and it is far from being sustainable in the long run because the aging rate of the technologies available today is higher than ever. In the long view, with the integration of technology into the organizational system, digitizing the structure of the organizational system, and making organizational expectations and needs the main component in determining the development direction of digital technologies will be the key to a healthy digital transformation. Success in digitalization seems to belong not only to organizations that closely follow and use technology, but also to demanding and innovative organizations that lead and mediate the development of technologies in accordance with their organizational objectives and needs.

Even when there is no problem in awareness and motivation towards digitalization in education in countries with largely centralized and unitary educational systems such as Turkey, it seems to be quite difficult for these extremely large and hierarchically structured systems to react on time. In addition to this difficulty, which can be called cumbersomeness, it should not be ignored that centralism and unitarism are contrary to the spirit, nature and philosophy of digital transformation. Digitalization is a process that focuses on individual expectations and needs, which makes the debate on locality-globalism meaningless. It is a great mistake to think that devolution of authority and partial decentralization tendencies will provide an advantage in the digitalization process for central structures that address the whole society or consider regional characteristics. The nature and philosophy of digitalization in education necessitate a specific learning/teaching strategy for schools, classrooms and even for all teachers. It is not possible to develop these strategies with formulas to be presented by the regional authorities, which can be called central or distant central authorities. Conventional educational organizations center on two main principles: to raise citizens in accordance with the official ideology that is the building block of nation states and modern pedagogy principles with several centuries of experience. Apart from the discussions and concerns about the survival of nation states and raising citizens in line with macro goals/principles, updating modern pedagogical principles and educational contents that constitute the scientific aspect of education in accordance with the spirit of digital transformation is also as important as individualized strategies. More clearly, digital transformation forces us to look at the questions we have been asking over the last few centuries from a different aspect and search for new answers;

What do we want to obtain with education?
Which skills do we have to teach children?
How can we make learning/teaching activities more efficient and effective?

There are many factors affecting our approaches and answers to the questions above. One of the most important of these factors is the structural features of educational organizations. Almost all educational organizations tend to solve digital transformation by making small changes in existing traditional structures or by adding to the existing structure. It is obvious that we need to keep more in step with the modern education approach and digital transformation in which the phenomenon of school is questioned. For instance, one of the important characteristics of conventional education systems is educational outputs, certificates and diplomas. However, are those as important as in the past in today's rapidly digitizing business world? When a company operating in any field needs to employ more than one mechanical engineer, does it expect standard skills and competencies from all of them? Or is it beneficial and necessary for the company that they all have the same diplomas and certificates? If we think that the answers to all these questions are "no", we should not ignore the potential to provide diversity in learning outputs that is one of the most important advantages of the digital transformation in education. The adaptation of large-scale public educational organization structures to a digital transformation will be possible by developing the potential of offering flexible education options designed according to the (individual and market) preferences, expectations and needs of private sector initiatives.

The emergence of a new ecosystem is inevitable with the digital transformation process. Equipping schools with the necessary technology in the digitalization process, redesigning and reorganizing school buildings, introducing students to new skills required by digital transformation, raising the awareness of parents to their new roles and habits in their children's education, updating teacher training systems, and raising assistant professionals who will be needed for teaching, are the elements of the developing new ecosystem. The unity of purpose, principle and philosophy between these elements is extremely important for the harmony and health of the developing ecosystem.

Specific to Turkey, on behalf of digital transformation in education the Ministry of Education began building the new ecosystem through teacher training and structuring/equipping schools. Within the scope of restructuring educational faculties, departments of computer and instructional technologies education (CITE) were opened in many educational faculties in 1998 with the inclusion of educational technology content in almost all teacher training fields. This attempt, which is one of the important milestones of digital transformation in education, can also be considered as the beginning of important changes in organizational structure. Considering the main objectives of CITE departments, in addition to meeting the need of information technology teachers for schools as a result of the use of computer and internet technologies becoming widespread before the millennium, what stands out are the topics of supporting educational programs at all education levels and in all educational fields with computer and internet technologies and developing digital learning contents and tools. Although the CITE departments are mostly in danger of closure due to the limited employment opportunities today (especially in newly-established provincial universities), they have become a current issue again due to the various problems and urgent needs in the distance education process engaged in the pandemic period. The main reason for this situation is that the CITE departments, opened in 1998 as a strategic need, and the educational organizations with different powers and responsibilities throughout the country could not create a consensus on the nature and philosophy of digital transformation and could not coordinate to show reflexes.

One of the important milestones of digital transformation in the educational organizations of Turkey is the FATİH project (Movement of Enhancing Opportunities and Improving Technology Project). Planning of the FATİH project, which is one of the most comprehensive and the largest budgeted education projects in the world, dates back to 2010. The general objectives of the project, which began to be piloted in 2012 and is still ongoing, are indicated as providing high-level accessibility to digitalized educational platforms, ensuring more efficient use of resources, contributing to ensure equal opportunity in education, founding a process-based evaluation system and achieving high quality educational outputs (MEB, Fatih Projesi, 2020). Concrete structural transformations such as establishing a high-speed and secure internet infrastructure in the central organization and schools, equipping schools with technological tools such as computers, interactive boards, etc., training teachers and other teaching assistant staff, creating curriculum-based and reliable digital educational contents and activities through the EBA (Educational Informatics Network), and creating a kind of educational social network platform for all stakeholders of education have been realized within the scope of the project.

In order to meet the urgent need for distance education created by the closure of schools as in many countries during the pandemic process, the EBA platform established in 2012 within the scope of the FATİH project has been redesigned according to the needs in 2020 and has an infrastructure that can provide services throughout the country. In addition to the EBA web platform, TRT EBA TV channels were opened for each educational level as a result of cooperation with TRT, and contents prepared by field experts and instructional designers were made available through TV programs. The EBA platform is among the most obvious examples of the digital transformation of educational organizations (it should be noted that this is an emergency reflex). According to the statistics announced by MEB (2020), the EBA platform became the world's most visited educational website with over 10 billion clicks between March 23 and November 27, 2020, mobile applications of the platform were downloaded more than 26 million times and it was used by 13.2 million students and approximately 1.2 million teachers. During this period, 62 million lesson hours of synchronous lessons were performed at all educational levels via the EBA platform. 13,650 EBA support points and 133 mobile devices delivered a service in disadvantaged areas where internet access and device support are heavily needed. In addition to live online lessons, the EBA platform can be considered as an example of comprehensive and worldwide educational digital transformation with in-service training for teachers, dynamic assessment and monitoring facilities for parents to follow the development and condition of their children, artificial intelligence-based student monitoring, and evaluation and academic guidance systems at some grade levels.

One of the moves of the education system in Turkey in the pre-pandemic period in organizations in terms of digital transformation was the Educational Vision Document 2023, published in 2018 (MEB, 2018). In this document, under the titles of Digital Content and Skills-backed Transformation of the Learning Process and Data-based Management with Learning Analytics Tools, the fields of digital transformation, which are among the targets to be achieved in the 100th anniversary of the foundation of the Republic, have been explained in detail in the Turkish National Education System. The focal points of this vision document as a national-level digital transformation target in education have been determined as creating the National Digital Content Archive, training teachers in this context and implementing the necessary legal regulation for transformation and local/regional/national organizations (Akgün, 2019).

In the early periods of digital transformation, the majority of attempts to ensure technological integration in schools resulted in computer laboratories. However, there is little knowledge of how to use these effectively and efficiently and they are hidden behind high security steel doors as "window decorations" (Bakioğlu & Şentuna, 2001). This result was mainly due to the fact that school managers and teachers were "digital immigrants". With the spread of computer and internet technologies, these locked steel doors have also started to be opened to students, to the target group, but technology in education has solely been used as computer lessons for millions of students who do not have access to computers and the internet in their homes and their immediate surroundings. This seems normal as an initial stage when compared to the spreading stages of any innovation. However, if this situation continues in this way, this is a sign of an anomaly. Along with many technical problems and malfunctions (such as turning schools into hardware garbage, a lack of electrical infrastructure and internet connections suitable for digital technologies, the lack of knowledge and skills of teachers regarding the use of these technologies, and the inability of teachers to receive sufficient institutional and organizational support for the creation of digital educational content), the failure of technology integration attempts in education at the classroom level is closely related to reasons such as the insistence on maintaining traditional educational practices (such as an insistence on traditional classroom management practices and the perception of technology-supported courses as frivolous) and a negative attitude towards information technologies (Yıldız, Sarıtepeci, & Seferoğlu, 2013).

Digitalization of Education and Cultural/Sociological Reflections

As in all other fields, the effects of digital transformation in education have been different in every society. One of the most important reasons for this difference is, of course, culture. On the fundamentals of the concept of culture, there are ways of thinking and behavioral habits acquired through the socialization process from childhood that are difficult to change or abandon after settling down (Hofstede, Hofstede, & Minkov, 2010). Based on this argument, we can conclude that culture is a factor that affects our reactions to new situations that we experience individually and socially and our attitude towards change. In the study, which is considered to be one of the most important cultural classification studies worldwide, Turkish culture is largely defined as a multi-active culture type. When the characteristics of a multi-active culture determined by Lewis, and also the main defining characteristics of Turkish culture are analyzed in general terms, a human- and communication-oriented profile emerges that is not anxious and uncomfortable in times of chaos, uncertainty and change and that can quickly transform plans and adapt quickly to new situations (2006). Thanks to our cultural adaptation skills and the ability to organize rapidly since the early stages of digital transformation, all stakeholders of the Turkish Education System have rather experienced few problems in terms of the spread and use of innovation. It would be appropriate to evaluate the facilitating effect of cultural characteristics on the digitization process in terms of stakeholders.

Especially during the pandemic period, teachers have managed the crisis period beginning with the closure of schools very well by producing creative, effective and efficient solutions that could sometimes be considered odd, even though many of them do not have enough training in integrating technology into education. In addition to the digital education content, which has been studied by the Ministry for a long time, it has been observed that there is a high level of participation in the in-service training sessions, which were quickly put into service by the Ministry, and teachers have rapidly increased their experience and skills in digital course content acquired from interactive boards in schools. The characteristics of communication and people-orientation, which also have a cultural background, have been effective for teachers to take the initiative in this chaotic process and exhibit a special and valuable example of responsibility that can be called “taking the bull by the horns” with the effects of sacrifice and altruism values, two of the most prominent qualities of the teaching profession in our country. In accordance with the guidelines established by the Ministry to ensure high and quality participation in distance education, teachers have collected in a very short time critical information such as access to distance education (computers, tablets, hardware, internet access, etc.) related to each student and family support status and have taken care of disadvantaged students.

In our country, it is known that parental participation is very low regardless of the public or private sector. This is due to the fact that parents accept the existence of an institutionalized structure responsible for the education of their children and likewise, the school managers and teachers are not very happy to see parents at the school, with similar acceptances (Şimşek & Tanaydın, 2002). However, during the crisis period, school and family cooperation was provided in a very fast and healthy way for the participation of students in the emergency distance education process. Many families have approached digital transformation, which is a very fast entry to education, with great devotion and a sense of responsibility and have started to be interested in the education process on digital platforms as much as they are not interested in the education of their children at school. It should not be ignored that this is related to the fact that digital transformation practices in education are more accessible to parents than schools with a weakening in the corporate responsibility perception of families regarding education as a result of the closure of schools and the return of children to their homes. In other words, digital transformation has provided the potential to increase family participation in education in societies with high adaptability and low resistance to innovation.

The effect of digital transformation in education on social life can occur in many different ways. In the pre-epidemic period, social perspectives on the integration of digital technologies into education were that these technologies would never provide a holistic education atmosphere; however, they would be useful as additional contents and methods (Hürriyet, 2019). The socialization needs of children were also significant parts of education; however, online practices would not achieve these and even intensive digitalization would be harmful in this aspect (Türe, 2015). As these discussions have gone on, the process of using digital technologies in education has undergone a sudden change in course with the Covid-19 pandemic. As mentioned before, the closure of schools due to the epidemic and the implementation of emergency distance education revealed completely different social reflections of the digitalization process. In the first step, the effectiveness and efficiency of the education children receive at home through online platforms and television programs were discussed. The negative effects of education on children who are trying to study in front of a computer/tablet/mobile phone for a long time have also been included in this discussion. After a while, the status of families who have to work while their children continue their education at home has become the current issue. As the homeschooling process of children was taking longer, it was observed that there was a positive development regarding school and teacher perception in the majority of society. Families who had difficulties in following the education process of their one or two children at home and were left alone with their children's needs such as socializing and play started to express their regret on every platform for their negative acceptance and attitude towards their teachers and the teaching profession. This situation, albeit compulsory, caused families to become more aware of, and to take responsibility for, the nature of their children's education as a result of the digitalization process in education. The positive attitude change in society towards the teaching profession led to a kind of collective empathy, which is rare in the education ecosystem. In the later stages of this process, we witnessed that the effect of emergency distance education at home on families reached the level of anxiety. After this point, a social expectation for the controlled reopening of schools began to be voiced loudly and soon took effect. With the partial opening of schools for some grades, simultaneous online education brought the discussion of hybrid education models into question. Schools became the new center for the spread of the epidemic, as case rates started to rise again and the number of infected teachers suddenly increased. At this point, it was observed that the collective empathy emerging in the education ecosystem in the middle of the epidemic process had been replaced by mutual criticism and even accusations in discussions about the re-closure of schools. While teachers were accused of "avoiding taking responsibility in an emergency situation", the perception that the institutional responsibilities for the education of children were not being fulfilled and the entire burden was on the shoulders of families spread rapidly in the society. In this process, the reactions to the teaching profession and teachers caused by anxiety have been greatly weakened especially with the effect of propaganda by the Ministry that the workload of teachers has not decreased in the emergency distance education process; on the contrary, it has increased much more than before, teachers are not satisfied with continuing the education process at home and want schools to be opened and to meet with children as soon as possible. However, unfamiliar responsibilities about children's education have negatively affected the perceptions of families regarding the digital transformation in education. Scientific researches on education during the pandemic period also emphasized the risk of negative attitudes resulting from problems due to emergency distance education turning into negative views and attitudes towards distance education and therefore digital transformation in education (Bozkurt, 2020).

One of the sociological effects of digital transformation in education is related to social justice and equality in access to education. According to one opinion (Rumble, 2007), distance education, one of the basic tools of digital transformation, has the potential to be one of the most effective tools that can prevent inequalities in access to education. This is based on the thought that disadvantaged groups with limited access to education are likely to receive a much higher quality education than they can access in schools, thanks to the distance education system. At first glance, this idea seems quite logical in many respects such as physical environment constraints, the elimination of difference in qualifications between schools and improved ease of access to qualified educational contents. The potential of greatly digitized education to be a remedy for the social injustice identified by Bourdieu and Passeron (1990) as the various types of capital accumulation of families directly affecting the quality of the education that children receive, thus strengthening and legitimizing the existing social stratification through education and schools, seems promising for all. However, according to another opinion, the cognitive, affective and economic technological and technical support that families can offer to their children in distance education, which started to be implemented during the pandemic process, is more important than ever: therefore, inequalities in access to education are likely to deepen further (Özer, Suna, Aşkar, & Çelik, 2020). This opinion emphasizes that the access to internet infrastructure and advanced technology hardware required during the digital transformation in education and the skills that families need to have in order to support their children during the distance education period will maximize the existing inequality in accessing a quality education between societies and socio-economic classes within society. Of course, time will show which of these two scenarios will be justified. However, such a possible sociological effect of digital transformation is not a spontaneous process like a natural event. There are many measures that states, international communities, NGOs and private sectors can take to prevent the possible inequality (or deepening of the existing inequality). One of these measures is to at least provide internet access and hardware support to disadvantaged groups and individuals in the short term. Specific to Turkey, the Ministry of Education is making a great effort in this regard. After the schools were closed, protocols were signed with GSM operators for students who did not have internet access and the necessary equipment determined by teachers and tablet computers were distributed to the students in need. In addition to these measures, as mentioned before, EBA support units were established in schools both in rural areas and city centers and urgent needs were met. While developed countries have rapidly strengthened their existing infrastructures and offered millions of students access to distance education, many countries have not been able to establish the distance education infrastructure that will be needed at the national level due to economic reasons or because they do not have the necessary qualified manpower. International support may help to prevent the inter-communal inequality.

Conclusion

The administrative, economic, sociologic and cultural effects of digital transformation-based change in education policies and the reactions by educational organizations upon facing a digital transformation are in this chapter focused on the context of the world in general and Turkey in particular during the pre-pandemic and post-pandemic periods.

Elements such as artificial intelligence, machine learning, human-computer interaction and intelligent automation systems that began to appear in science fiction works, sometimes as a utopia and at others a dystopia, have become more concrete day by day and have been in our lives for the last 30 years. Although it is called by many different names, this process is referred to as digital transformation in academic circles. Beyond our daily life practices, digital transformation has also deeply affected the modern institutionalized organizational structures that we have been building for the last 300 years. Even if the organized life style into which we are all born in today's society does not lose its importance with the effect of digital transformation, it undergoes important philosophical and formal changes. The expectations of people and society, from the institutionalized organizations they participate in and interact with to the content and morphology of the services and opportunities offered to people and society through organizations, are undergoing a rapid transformation. Like many public services, on a global scale, the field of education made important attempts to adapt to this digital transformation philosophically, organizationally, structurally, sociologically and culturally. While content and discussions suitable for the new digital world such as interactive educational tools, online courses for teachers and students, and digital materials, were put on the agenda, the sudden pandemic has radically affected the digitalization process in education, which has progressed with a slow and evolutionary process, and caused paradigmatic and practical breaks.

Although this break in the digital transformation process in education caused a crisis atmosphere, it brought some opportunities with it. It seems that digitalized education practices coming into our lives with this compulsory and rapid transition period will be a part of our lives in the post-pandemic period. The statement by both the Ministry and the Council of Higher Education that the experience and skills gained during the pandemic process will be used after the pandemic and that distance education will continue, albeit partially, is one of the most important indicators of this fact.

All stakeholders of education should be properly informed so that the digital transformation in education as a phenomenon in cultural and social terms is not identified with emergency distance education practices and that generalizations of negative feelings and attitudes are prevented. The potential of digitized education practices to eliminate current inequalities in access to education around the world and to help ensure social justice should be fully utilized. Intensive research at individual and institutional levels is required on issues such as cyber security, protection of personal data, ethical problems in digitalized education practices and prevention of abuse, which are seen to be largely ignored in emergency practices.

Keywords: *Digitalization in education, educational organizations, digital transformation in education*

References

Akgün, E. (2019). 2023 Eğitim Vizyonunda Dijital Dönüşüm. *SETA Perspektif, Mart 2019*(233), s. 1-6.

Bakioğlu, A., & Şentuna, T. (2001). İnternet ile eğitimde okul yöneticilerinin görevleri. *Pamukkale Üniversitesi Eğitim Fakültesi Dergisi, 2001*(9), 10-18.

Bourdieu, P., & Passeron, J.-C. (1990). *Reproduction in Education, Society and Culture.* London: Sage Publications.

Bozkurt, A. (2020). Koronavirüs (Covid-19) pandemi süreci ve pandemi sonrası dünyada eğitime yönelik değerlendirmeler: yeni normal ve yeni eğitim paradigması. *Açıköğretim Uygulamaları ve Araştırmaları Dergisi, 6*(3), 112-142.

Etzioni, A. (1964). *Modern Organizations.* New Jersey: Prentice-Hall Inc.

Hofstede, G., Hofstede, G. J., & Minkov, M. (2010). *Cultures and Organizations* (3rd b.). McGraw-Hill.

Hürriyet. (2019, Mart 11). *Yapay zekâ öğretmenin yerini alamaz.* 12 22, 2020 tarihinde Hürriyet Gazetesi Web Sitesi: https://www.hurriyet.com.tr/egitim/yapay-zeka-ogretmenin-yerini-alamaz-41145512 adresinden alındı

Kuusisto, M. (2017). Organizational effects of digitalization: a literature review. *International Journal Of Organization Theory And Behavior, 20*(3), 341-362.

Lewis, R. D. (2006). *When Cultures Collide: Leading across cultures* (3 b.). London: Nicholas Brealey Publishing.

MEB. (2018). *2023 Education Vision.* Aralık 20, 2020 tarihinde meb.gov.tr: https://2023vizyonu.meb.gov.tr/doc/2023_VIZYON_ENG.pdf adresinden alındı

MEB. (2020). *EBA.* Aralık 20, 2020 tarihinde eba.gov.tr: http://covid19.meb.gov.tr/covid19.html?cat=uzaktan-egitim adresinden alındı

MEB. (2020). *Fatih Projesi.* Aralık 20, 2020 tarihinde meb.gov.tr: http://fatihprojesi.meb.gov.tr/en/about.html adresinden alındı

Özer, M., Suna, H. E., Aşkar, P., & Çelik, Z. (2020). Covid-19 salgını dolayısıyla okulların kapanmasının eğitimde eşitsizlikler üzerine etkisi. *İnsan ve Toplum, 10*(4), 217-246.

Popper, M., & Lipshitz, R. (2000). Organizational learning: mechanisms, culture and feasibility. *Management Lerning, 31*(2), 181-196.

Rumble, G. (2007). Social justice, economics and distance education. *Open Learning: The Journal of Open, Distance and e-Learning, 22*(2), 167-176.

Şimşek, H., & Tanaydın, D. (2002). İlköğretimde veli katılımı: öğretmen-veli-psikolojik danışman üçgeni. *Elementary Education Online, 1*(1), 12-16.

Türe, C. (2015). *Bilişim teknolojileri öğretmenlerinin ve öğretmen adaylarının tablet bilgisayarla eğitime ilişkin görüşleri* (Yayımlanmamış doktora tezi) Uludağ Üniversitesi Eğitim BİlimIeri Enstitüsü, Bursa

Yıldız, H., Sarıtepeci, M., & Seferoğlu, S. S. (2013). Fatih projesi kapsamında düzenlenen hizmet-içi eğitim etkinliklerinin öğretmenlerin mesleki gelişimine katkılarının ISTE öğretmen standartları açısından incelenmesi. *Hacettepe Üniversitesi Eğitim Fakültesi Dergisi, Özel Sayı*(1), 375-392.

CHAPTER THIRTEEN

THE EFFECT OF THE COVID-19 PANDEMIC ON INTERACTION BETWEEN DIGITALIZATION AND FINANCIAL LITERACY

ERCAN ÖZEN AND MAIA DIAKONIDZE

Introduction

Economic theory assumes that human needs are infinite and resources are scarce. In such a case, it is necessary to effectively manage scarce resources. Ensuring efficiency in the asset and fund management of individuals and institutions becomes an important requirement for increasing individual and social well-being. Ensuring asset and fund management efficiency requires proper decision-making. Increasing financial literacy can also be enhanced by traditional information sources such as the family and school, as well as digital data sources and data flow supported by social media, the internet and mobile facilities today. In this circumstance, it is necessary to discuss the effects of digitalization and mutual interaction in increasing financial literacy.

After the mid-1990s, financial education or financial literacy gained importance worldwide, especially in developing countries. Almost all countries aimed to improve their citizen's poor financial knowledge to make better decisions. Governments follow a wide variety of policies to increase the financial literacy of individuals in order to achieve sustainable growth and increase public welfare. State-affiliated public institutions and universities, associations and financial institutions also have activities in this direction. Efforts are made to disseminate financial information, to enable individuals to make correct financial decisions and to form the right attitude for future planning. It is argued that the most effective tool in increasing financial knowledge is financial education (Swiecka et al., 2020). On the other hand, it is not possible to say that students and other individuals receive adequate financial education in many schools today. For this reason, using different channels in the dissemination of learning will make it easier to reach the desired goals. In recent years, the effects of digital tools have been observed in gaining the targeted high level of financial knowledge, effective financial behavior and financial attitude. Young people are especially at the forefront of adopting and using new technologies. Since smart phones, tablets and different types of computers are used extensively by young people to follow innovations, the use of digital technologies is spreading faster.

The Covid-19 pandemic that broke out at the beginning of 2020 has led to significant and radical changes in human life nowadays. The fact that people are in the same environment has significantly increased the risk of virus transmission. In the current period, millions of infections have occurred worldwide and hundreds of thousands of people have lost their lives. For this reason, many workplaces have suspended their activities, and educational institutions have had to give up face-to-face training and provide training via television or the internet. Thus, many workplaces have also operated on a home/house office basis. As a result, remote work and training have been driven by an explosion in demand on the internet and the computer industry. Although there has been an intense digital transformation, especially in schools, it has not been possible to distribute this transformation fairly in all segments of the society (Livari, et al., 2020).

While significant changes have been observed in the use of digital technology in global life, the need to evaluate the link between this development, the pandemic, and financial literacy has arisen. Therefore, the study aimed to analyze the links between financial literacy, digitalization and the Covid-19 pandemic using statistical data consisting of examples at global and local levels.

Financial Literacy

Financial literacy consists of three main components: financial knowledge, financial behavior and financial attitude. There are many definitions of financial literacy but, the most preferred one is from the Organisation for Economic Co-operation and Development.

The OECD defined financial literacy as:

> *A combination of awareness, knowledge, skill, attitude and behavior necessary to make sound financial decisions and ultimately achieve individual financial wellbeing. (OECD, 2018: 4)*

If a person understands financial concepts, can use financial tools effectively, can manage his/her personal budget and can make the right investment decision, we can say he/she is good in the field of financial literacy. However, the lack of these skills can be defined as financial illiteracy.

Financial literacy includes fiscal and taxation topics as well. Fiscal literacy requires some knowledge on the main provisions and legislative acts of the budget system. Citizens need to have competence in financial topics and an understanding of the financial structure and financial system (Vovchenko et al., 2018). Thanks to good financial literacy, people can manage their personal finances, make accurate financial decisions and can avoid some financial difficulties (Chen & Volpe, 1998; Kezar & Yang, 2010). To make accurate financial decisions, policymakers promote educational programs in order to improve individuals' decisions (Meier & Sprenger, 2007).

There are many examples of financial literacy on the individual's financial decisions, behavior and attitude. For example, Lusardi & Mitchell (2014: 5) advised that:

> *Financial literacy has been proven to affect both saving and investment behavior and debt management and borrowing practices. Empirically, financially literate people are more likely to accumulate wealth.*

There are three widely accepted main elements of financial literacy: financial knowledge, financial behavior and financial attitude. We want to describe these elements briefly as follow:

Financial knowledge: Financial knowledge refers to the level of learning of individuals about financial instruments, payment methods, interest and budgets. The higher the level of financial knowledge, the more it will be possible for individuals to make more financially appropriate decisions and to increase their well-being.

Financial behavior: Financial behavior is shown by people in a financial event, especially by examining how psychology affects financial decisions. Financial behavior is built on a variety of assumptions and economic behavior patterns.

Financial attitude: Financial attitudes are the tendency of individuals to behave in certain ways due to some of their economic and non-economic beliefs about the consequences of certain behaviors. Financial attitudes are also individuals' states of mind, opinions, and judgments regarding financial matters.

Increasing financial literacy leads individuals to use more financial tools and products and financial access increases. The increase in financial access and the use of financial products and financial technologies (Fintech) have positive effects on economic development. According to Demirguc-Kunt et al. (2018), the increase in financial access has noticeable effects on the services provided by the organizations and the public as well as the individual. These effects trigger economic development. The benefits of increased financial access can be explained as follows (Demirguc-Kunt, et al., 2018: 1-2): (i) People using electronic payment methods save more, their income increases, and poverty decreases (a study conducted in Kenya showed that women paid by mobile increased their savings by more than 20% and poverty decreased by 22%); (ii) Financial services help people manage their financial risks; (iii) Financial services contribute to the lower cost of payment transactions; (iii) Financial services contribute to the lower cost of payment transactions; and (iv) Making payments digitally in public administrations increases efficiency while reducing corruption.

Financial inclusion is financial literacy, which plays a significant role in reducing and, therefore, eliminating poverty from the country. Digital technologies play a key role in financial inclusion, as demonstrated by the meteoric rise of mobile money across developing countries. However, there is still an important gap between access and usage.

Method

The research method is based on obtaining and analyzing different data, such as obtaining traditional and digital financial transaction data, examining the literature, evaluating reports belonging to private and public institutions, scanning internet resources and interviewing. The design of the chapter includes theoretical explanations and empirical evidence (analysis of statistical data) regarding financial inclusion, financial literacy and the usage of digital technologies before and during the pandemic conditions.

A Note on the Financial Literacy Level

Financial literacy needs to be measured and its results compared by year. The OECD determines and publishes the financial literacy scores every year. However, as the selected countries change every year, it becomes difficult to interpret the development in financial literacy and to make comparisons by year.

Table 13.1 shows the financial literacy scores for 2020 published by the OECD. The highest literacy scores of 2020 belong to Hong Kong with 14.8 and Slovenia with 14.7. The lowest scores belong to Italy with 11.1, and Romania and Colombia with 11.2. Some countries' scores for 2019 are also included in the table. Values shown with an asterisk (*) in the table are for 2019. Since countries such as Austria, Croatia, Czech Republic, Hong Kong,

Table 13.1: Financial Literacy Scores 2020

	Number of participants	Financial Literacy Score	Knowledge	Behavior	Attitude
Austria	1418	14,2*/14.4	5.3	6.0	3.1
Bulgaria	1047	12.3	4.1	5.3	2.9
Colombia	1200	11.2	3.8	4.8	2.6
Croatia	1079	12,0*/12.3	4.5	5.0	2.8
Czech Republic	1003	12,6*/13.0	4.5	5.3	3.1
Estonia	1005	13.3	4.9	5.3	3.1
Georgia	1056	12.1	4.5	5.1	2.5
Germany	1003	13.9	5.2	5.7	3.1
Hong Kong, China	1002	14,4*/14.8	6.2	5.8	2.9
Hungary	1001	12,4* / 12.3	4.6	4.5	3.3
Indonesia	1000	13.3	3.7	6.3	3.3
Italy	2036	11.1	3.9	4.2	3.0
Korea	2400	13.0	4.6	5.4	3.1
Malaysia	2818	12.5	3.7	6.1	2.7
Moldova	1074	12.6	4.0	5.5	3.1
Montenegro	1030	11.5	4.1	4.7	2.6
Peru	1205	12.1	4.1	5.1	2.9
Poland	1000	11,6*/13.1	5.0	5.5	2.6
Portugal	1480	14,0*/13.1	4.0	5.9	3.2
North Macedonia	1076	11.8	3.9	5.1	2.8
Romania	1060	11.2	3.5	5.0	2.7
Russia	83478	12.5	4.8	4.9	2.8
Slovenia	1019	14.7	4.8	6.3	3.6
France	2155	-	4,8	-	-
Malta	1013	10,3	2,2	5,2	2,8
Thailand	11129	-	3,9	-	3,9
Average		12,7	4,4	5,3	3,0
Average-OECD-12		13,0	4,6	5,3	3,1

Source: OECD (2020), OECD/INFE 2020 International Survey of Adult Financial Literacy, 15; *Financial Literacy Scores of 2019 OECD, OECD (2019), OECD/INFE 2019 International Survey of Adult Financial Literacy

Hungary, Poland and Portugal have scores for 2019, it can be understood whether there is an improvement in financial literacy levels. According to the table, while the financial literacy score increased in five of these seven countries, the scores of two countries, Hungary and Portugal, declined.

Digital Knowledge Production and Financial Literacy

It is seen that the increase in financial literacy has positive effects on the economic development of countries. One of the factors affecting financial literacy is financial education. Many studies have shown that individuals with higher education levels have higher financial literacy levels.

Therefore, it can be assumed that publications on financial issues around the world will also have a positive effect on financial literacy. Financial knowledge and education can be traditionally taught in books, at school or digitally. Table 13.2 shows the number of academic publications on financial literacy published in different languages in the last 10 years.

The most striking detail when looking at Table 13.2 is that the number of academic publications on "Financial literacy" in English and German is decreasing. The common feature of countries where these languages are spoken is that they are economically developed countries. On the other hand, Turkey, Spain and countries where languages such as Polish (Poland) are spoken are developing countries.

Table 13.2: Number of Academic Publications Including the Word "Financial Literacy"

Year	Turkish	English	Spanish	Chinese	Polish	German
2020-Nov.	866	52600	28400	5160	798	2080
2019	1320	44700	44500	10900	1710	3030
2018	844	57200	51100	14900	2460	3110
2017	736	63000	50600	22100	2790	3160
2016	579	68900	47200	23700	2960	3080
2015	500	63600	44000	23200	3150	3520
2014	409	63900	39600	25900	2790	3230
2013	327	66300	36600	28800	2820	5850
2012	226	63300	32000	24500	2340	3950
2011	254	57100	28000	26800	2030	3590

The reason for the decline in financial literacy studies in developed countries is that the need for such academic publications is now decreasing. These countries have significantly completed their development with the support of these academic studies. However, Turkey, Poland, and countries like Argentina and Mexico are still under development. For this reason, there has been an increase in studies dealing with financial literacy problems and solutions in these countries in the last decade. These studies in the Google Academic database can be accessed on the internet.

It is not always possible for individuals to be interested in and read academic studies. For this reason, it is seen that the results of these studies and different topics related to financial literacy appear on non-academic websites. It is estimated that this information on many internet sites reaches more segments in some way.

Table 13.3 contains the total number of web pages published in different languages with financial literacy content that can be actively accessed. According to Table 13.3, the largest number of internet pages is in Spanish. This is the 4th most spoken language in the world after English, Chinese and Hindi. As of December 2020, the most active web page with the words "financial literacy" is in Spanish (261 million).

According to financial literacy in developing countries such as Turkey, the number of titled news sites should be expected to continue to rise. The number of active internet news sites in Chinese is around 194 million. Therefore, the high savings rate in China can be shown as a result of the high level of financial literacy.

Table 13.3: Number of Web Pages Including “Financial Literacy” (000)

Year	Turkish	English	Spanish	Chinese	Polish	German
2020-Nov.	516	177.000	261.000	194.000	8.820	11.600

Source: Compiled by the authors from Google search results

Table 13.4 contains the number of academic publications in different languages with a title including the word “finance” in the last 10 years. According to the table, there is a decline in the number of academic publications published in English, Chinese and German. However, the number of Turkish, Spanish and Polish publications is on the rise. In this case, contrary to developed countries, the need for academic publications including the word “finance” in the title continues in developing countries.

Table 13.4: Number of Academic Publications Including the word "Finance" in the title

Year	Turkish	English	Spanish	Chinese	Polish	German
2020-Nov.	5050	179000	14800	23200	3210	5290
2019	9600	365000	34000	89900	6050	7320
2018	8350	354000	34700	93300	7390	7720
2017	7820	567000	37800	98000	7370	7180
2016	7140	634000	32000	109000	7080	7970
2015	6200	789000	30200	144000	6730	7980
2014	5420	914000	29700	157000	6120	8060
2013	5330	979000	27300	178000	6830	11400
2012	4990	1060000	24600	161000	5410	8410
2011	4710	1090000	21600	230000	5140	7150

Source: Compiled by the authors from Google Scholar database search results

Table 13.5 shows the number of active internet pages according to different languages with the word "finance". According to Table 13.5, the number of web pages available in English is significantly higher than those in other languages (1.540 million). There are 836 million internet reports in Chinese and 240 million in German.

Table 13.5: Number of Words Including the word "Finance" (000)

Year	Turkish	English	Spanish	Chinese	Polish	German
2020 -Nov.	105.00 0	1.540.00 0	191.00 0	836.00 0	134.00 0	240.00 0

Source: Compiled by the authors from Google search results

Financial Literacy Levels and Financial Product Holding

The development of individuals' computer and internet access facilities enables the rapid spread of information. Access to financial institutions and products is among the factors that increase individuals' financial literacy. Transactions such as opening accounts in banks or other financial institutions, using credit, using credit cards, performing mobile and internet banking transactions, using mobile, internet or contactless credit cards, and automatic payment orders contribute to the increase of financial literacy as individuals increase the possibility of "exposure" to financial services.

Figure 13.1 shows the relationship between financial product use and financial literacy. According to the OECD (2020), the financial literacy score of those who do not use financial products is 46, while the score of those who do use a product increases to 56, and the score of those who use at least two products increases to 66. This reflects the importance of introducing individuals to new financial products.

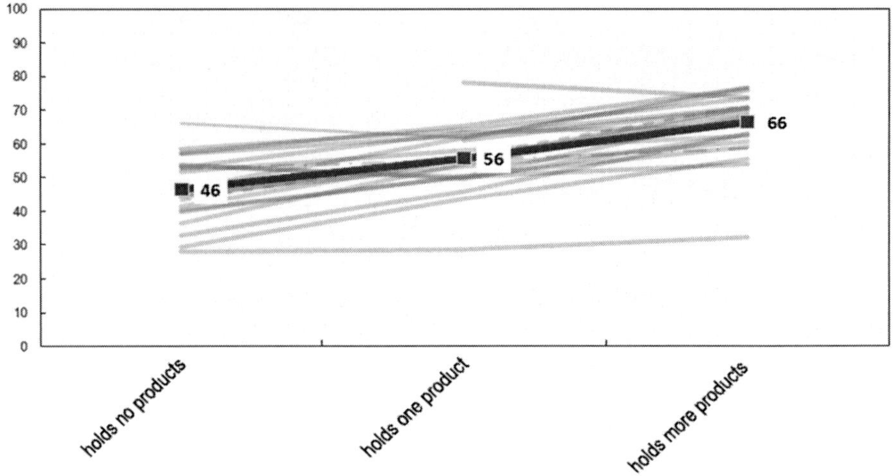

Figure 13.1: Financial Knowledge Levels and Financial Product Holding
Source: OECD-infe-2020, p. 33

The Global Findex database data show that between 2014 and 2017, 515 million adults opened accounts in banks or financial institutions. As a result of this increase, the account ownership rate, which was 62% in 2014, increased to 69% in 2017. While this rate is 94% in developed countries, it is 63% in developing countries. The number of adults who do not have a bank account is 1,7 million. Globally, 52% of adults (76% of account holders) use digital payment methods. While 97% of account holders perform digital financial transactions in developed countries, this rate is 70% in developing countries (Demirgüç-Kunt et al., 2018: 2-7).

Ozili (2018) reported that the World Bank has implemented initiative programs to increase the financial spillover to reduce poverty in developing countries. Policymakers and academics are closely involved in digital finance and financial diffusion to reduce hunger and ensure economic growth because digital finance provides significant benefits to digital finance providers, digital finance users, governments, banks and financial institutions by reducing financial access costs, and poor individuals in accessing finance.

There are few studies in the literature that investigate the relationships between financial literacy and digital financial technology (Fintech) products. Pioneering studies in this area include Morgan and Trinh (2019), Morgan and Trinh (2020), and Swiecka et al. (2021). Morgan and Trinh (2019) in their study used the standardized questionnaire developed by the Organization for Economic Cooperation and Development's International Network on Financial Education (OECD/INFE).

The authors found positive and strong relationships between financial literacy and the level of use of Fintech products in their studies in the Lao People's Democratic Republic (PDR). Morgan and Trinh (2020) conducted a similar study in Vietnam and found positive relationships between financial literacy and the use of many Fintech products.

When there is 1 standard deviation in financial literacy, there is a change in digital borrowing of 5,2%, digital lending by 3 percentage points, digital payment by 3,6 percentage points and digital insurance by 1.6 percentage points. There is a positive relationship between the income level, education level, and Fintech awareness and Fintech adoption. Younger people have a higher likelihood of using Fintech products.

Swiecka et al. (2021), in their study in Poland, determined that despite the significant progress in modern payment methods, cash payments maintain their strong position. Despite the individual characteristics of individuals, financial information is the most important determinant of the choice of payment tools. As financial knowledge increases, the use of Fintech products increases. In their study, Jünger and Mietzner (2020) determined that perceived trust and reliability, transparency and financial literacy have an important effect on accepting Fintech products and services.

Smartphone applications can also have an impact on financial literacy. French et al. (2020) presented one of the first studies on this subject. The authors determined that individuals who use smartphone applications have a 20% higher level of financial knowledge than others. The results of the study indicated that the financial behavior and attitudes of individuals who use these applications designed to support very complex financial decisions change positively. Sebetçi et al. (2018) also investigated the effects of smart phone applications on financial literacy and determined the existence of a positive relationship between the use of mobile applications developed in finance and financial literacy.

While the use of financial products is increasing all over the world, the Covid-19 pandemic has caused some changes in the use of financial products. The fact that both financial institutions and customers prefer contactless financial transactions in order to comply with hygiene rules played a role in this change.

Table 13.6 shows the usage statistics for the first nine months of 2020, and debit cards are shown in Turkey. With a population of about 83 million people, the number of active credit cards in Turkey is 73,9 million and 58% of these have the contactless feature. While the contactless feature rate is 18% in debit cards, the rate of pre-payment cards with the contactless feature is 50%. While the number of terminals where customers can shop is 2.6 million, 53% of these terminals can be used for contactless shopping.

Table 13.6: Bank Cards Number in Turkey as of 2020

Financial Products	Value/Rate	Financial Products	Value/Rate
Credit card number	73,9 million	Debit card number	141,1 million
Contactless rate	58%	Contactless rate	18%
Pre-payment card	40 million	Terminal Number	2,6 million
Contactless rate	50%	Contactless rate	53%

Source: Turkish Banking Cards Center Co., Interim Annual Reports, 2020-III, p. 11

Bank card transaction amounts are shown in Table 13.7. While Turkish individuals use credit cards at the rate of 83.33% for shopping, the debit card usage rate for cash withdrawals is 89.86%.

Table 13.7: Bank Card Transaction Amounts (billion USD)*

	By Credit Cards	By Debit Cards	By Pre-payments Cards	Total
Shopping Amount	97,90 (83,6%)	18,43 (15,75%)	0,76 (0,6%)	117,09
Cash Withdraw	9,73 (9,04%)	96,74 (89,86%)	1,19 (1,10%)	107,66

*We considered 1 USD is 7 TRY on average for 2020-01/2020-9

Source: Turkish Banking Cards Center Co., Interim Annual Reports, 2020-III, p. 11

Rates of change of the Covid-19 period in the use of cards in Turkey are located in Table 13.8. These rates reflect the effects of the crisis environment created by the pandemic period. People who think their income will decrease in the future want to reduce their future payments. For this reason, the rate of using credit cards in shopping remained at 11%, and the rate of using them in cash withdrawals remained low at 9%.

Mr. Canko, CEO of Turkish Banking Cards Center Co., advised that the contactless credit card transaction amount increased by 169% just after the outbreak of the Covid-19 pandemic.[1] The number of card payments in the on-line supermarket/food category increased by 139% and the amount of payments increased by 129% compared to the previous year. According to the statement, 3 million cards were used for the first time on the internet right after the pandemic announcement, and 2.5 million credit cards were used for the first time contactless.

Table 13.8: Growing Rate of Card Usage

	By Credit Card	By Debit Cards	By Pre-payments Cards	Total
Shopping Amount	11%	38%	91%	15%
Cash Withdrawn	9%	10%	25 %	10%

Source: Turkish Banking Cards Center Co., Interim Annual Reports, 2020-III, p. 11

Statistics on the use of credit cards during the pandemic period are included in Table 13.9. According to the table, the amount of credit card usage over the internet is around USD 25.56 million, which constitutes 21% of the total credit card shopping volume. While the number of contactless transactions made with credit cards is around 1.12 billion, the transaction volume is around USD 9.21 billion. The increase in such transactions also contributes to the increase of the financial literacy of individuals.

[1] https://www.bloomberght.com/martta-3-milyon-kart-internet-ile-25-milyon-kart-da-temassiz-odeme-ile-tanisti-2252272 (accessed: 18.12.2020).

Table 13.9: Contactless Card Usage

Payment by Credit Cards over the Internet	$25,56 billion	Contactless Payment Number	1,12 billion
Rate of Credit Card Usage over the Internet	21%	Value of Contactless Payments	$9,21 billion

Source: Turkish Banking Cards Center Co., Interim Annual Reports, 2020-III, p. 11

Development in Digital Technologies and Covid-19 Pandemic

The internet is a network that allows information to be spread all over the world, simultaneously. The increase in people with internet access in the world is effective with a faster spread of financial information that constitutes financial literacy among individuals who gain the appropriate financial attitude and financial behavior.

The internet access rate of the world population is at the level of 63.2% as of September 30, 2020 (Table 13.10). North America (90,3%) and Europe (87,2%) are the continents with the highest reach. The rate in Africa, the least developed continent of the world, is at the level of 47.1%.

Table 13.10: Internet Access in the world

World Regions	Population (2020 Est.)	Population % of World	Internet Users 30 Sept 2020	Penetration Rate (% Pop.)	Growth 2000-2020	Internet World %
Africa	1,340,598,447	17.2 %	631,940,772	47.1 %	13,898 %	12.8 %
Asia	4,294,516,659	55.1 %	2,555,636,255	59.5 %	2,136 %	51.8 %
Europe	834,995,197	10.7 %	727,848,547	87.2 %	593 %	14.8 %
Latin America / Caribbean	654,287,232	8.4 %	467,817,332	71.5 %	2,489 %	9.5 %
Middle East	260,991,690	3.3 %	184,856,813	70.8 %	5,527 %	3.7 %
North America	368,869,647	4.7 %	332,908,868	90.3 %	208 %	6.8 %
Oceania / Australia	42,690,838	0.5 %	28,917,600	67.7 %	279 %	0.6 %
WORLD TOTAL	7,796,949,710	100.0 %	4,929,926,187	63.2 %	1,266 %	100.0 %

Source: https://www.internetworldstats.com/stats.htm (accessed: 18.12.2020)

The internet penetration rate increases significantly over the years. Table 13.11 shows comparatively the internet penetration rates of some countries in 2008 and 2020. According to the table, the country with the highest penetration rate in 2008 was South Korea (70,7%) and the lowest was India (5,2%) and the penetration rates increased significantly in 2020.

South Korea has the highest share in 2020 along with Germany at 96%. India, on the other hand, reached 40,6%. The countries with the highest increase in access rate in the 12-year period were Russia (57,5%), Indonesia (52,1%), Turkey (46,4%), Brazil (45,6%) and India (35,4%).

Accordingly, developed countries are beginning to reach their limits on internet access capacity, while developing countries are closing the gap with developed countries. Closing this gap will increase financial literacy in these countries in the following years, and differences in economic development will tend to decrease.

Table 13.11: Internet Penetration Rates by Selected Countries

	2008	2020	Difference between 2008 and 2020
South Korea	70,7%	96,0%	25,3%
United States	72,5%	89,8%	17,3%
Japan	73,8%	93,8%	20,0%
Germany	63,8%	96,0%	32,2%
Italy	59,7%	92,5%	32,8%
Turkey	36,9%	83,3%	46,4%
Russia	23,2%	80,9%	57,5%
Brazil	25,1%	70,7%	45,6%
China	19,0%	59,3%	40,3%
Indonesia	10,5%	62,6%	52,1%
India	5.2%	40,6%	35,4%

Source: Compiled by authors from Topal & Kayahan, 2009 and https://www.internetworldstats.com/stats.htm (accessed: 18.12.2020)

Digital products are important elements of modern daily life which have a significant impact on the financial sector. Both locally and globally, digitalization is affecting households and businesses: digital financial services/mobile money services are available in almost 2 in 3 of the emerging countries, and this is expected to increase 100% by 2020 (GSMA, 2016). For example, PayPal, one of the technological payment methods, is continuing the growth of active and new registered accounts in 2020, growing by close on 70 million year-on-year. Also, global online payment businesses have been increased and within pandemic conditions become an important part of trading in general. Besides, there is an increasing correlation between the usage of online payment methods and financial literacy.

Vovchenko et al. (2018) stated that even though digital technologies are used worldwide, there are no common terms for them, but there are terms such as: “creative economy”, “e-economy”, “API economy”, etc.

To understand the development of digitalization in human life, it is necessary to analyze the statistical data (2008-2017) of the decade and identify the dynamics of the digitalization of the economies of EAEU states. In order to see the development in digitalization, we should look at the trend in the field of digitalization in relation to worldwide average indicators (Table 13.12).

Based on the foregoing, in a normal social-economic environment, the development of internet technologies in order to improve financial circulation and, therefore, the financial literacy of the population is dynamic and characterized by a positive trend. This process accelerated a little in the year 2019-2020, which can be explained by many factors, but the most important of them is determined by the influence of a global process called the Covid-19 pandemic. Data analysis of the global business data platform shows that Microsoft powers the highest share of the global computer market, with 72,98% of desktop, tablet and console computing devices. There is still a need to expand the computer market as in the United Kingdom, the household computer penetration rate was 52% in 2018, and 64% in the USA.

Worldwide quarterly PC shipments in the period 2009-2020 by vendor (Alsop, 2020) shows that Lenovo shipped 16,2 million personal computers during the second quarter of 2020, exceeding HP's 16,17 million shipments in that same period and it has the leader position in the computer market. The top three vendors in the computer market increased their combined market share. Lenovo, HP Inc. and Dell accounted for a growth of nearly 65% in the last quarter of 2019 (see Table 13.12).

Figure 13.2 contains information on the world computer market before and during the Covid-19 pandemic conditions. Accordingly, computer sales declined in the first quarter of 2020, when the pandemic exploded. During this period, the business community implemented the option of out-of-office work, while educational institutions also focused on the distance education system. For this reason, in the quarters after the pandemic announcement made by the World Health Organization, desktop, tablet and notebook sales increased significantly. With the pandemic, digital business and the digital education period started all over the world after March 2020.

Table 13.12: Worldwide PC Vendor Unit Shipment Estimates for the fourth quarter of 2019 (1000s of units)

Company	**4Q19 Shipments** (1000s of Units)	**4Q19 Market Share (%)**	**4Q18 Shipments** (1000s of Units)	**4Q18 Market Share (%)**	**4Q19-4Q18 Growth (%)**
Lenovo	17,498	24.8	16,418	23.8	6.6
HP Inc.	16,129	22.8	15,301	22.2	5.4
Dell	12,114	17.2	10,805	15.7	12.1
Apple	5,262	7.5	5,425	7.9	-3.0
ASUS	4,062	5.8	4,100	5.9	-0.9
Acer Group	3,994	5.7	3,861	5.6	3.5
Others	11,553	16.4	13,104	19.0	-11.8
Total	**70,612**	**100.0**	**69,014**	**100.0**	**2.3**

Source: Stamford, Conn., January 15, 2020

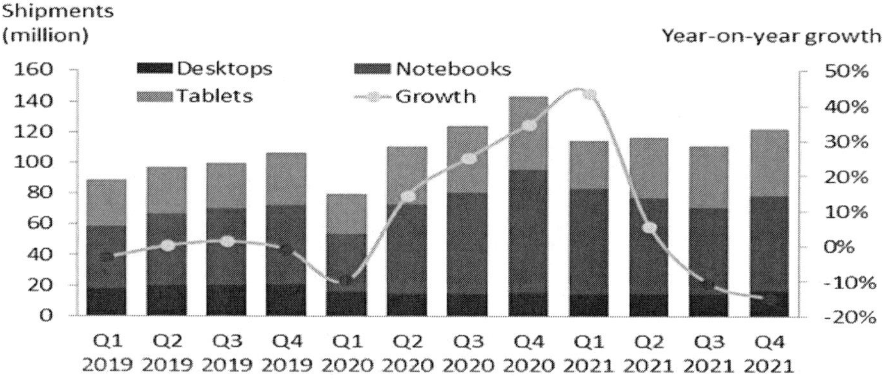

Figure 13.2: Global PC Shipments from Q1 2019 to Q4 2021 (desktops, notebooks and tablets). Note: desktops and notebooks include desktop workstations and mobile workstations, respectively
Source: Canaly estimates and forecast, PC Analysis, November 2020

According to Figure 13.2, computer sales will be second in 2020. During the quarter, they entered a serious upward trend. This upward trend is expected to continue in quarter one of 2021. By the end of 2020, the growth rate is expected to approach 50%. Quarterly computer sales are expected to be around 140 million in the final quarter of 2020. Therefore, as the rate of access of individuals to these digital technologies increases due to this increasing trend, it is expected that they will have a positive impact on financial literacy.

Social Media and Financial Literacy

Social media are one of the leading indicators of digitalization. Individuals will have much more access to information with accounts they open on social media than before. Smartphones are the most important channel for internet access in the world. A significant proportion of young people prefer smartphones when using social media accounts. In this case, it is increasingly easy for society to access financial literacy content as well as other content via smartphones. Many countries provide information transfer from all digital environments due to changing information technologies. Social media accounts are also very important in sharing information today.

Turkey, one of the developing countries, has a significant savings deficit and is one of the countries with a low savings rate. For this reason, it is important for citizens to be more knowledgeable and conscious and to increase their savings by investing correctly. For this purpose, almost all financial public institutions in Turkey, such as the Central Bank of the Republic of Turkey (CBRT), the Capital Market Board (CMB), Borsa Istanbul and Turkish Capital Market Associations, and private financial institutions such as banks and insurance companies share many current financial issues or news on their social media accounts. The most actively used social media accounts in Turkey are YouTube, Instagram, Facebook, Twitter and LinkedIn. Financial institutions can access millions of people through their own social media accounts.

Table 13.13: 2016-2020 Social Media with the Most Users (World)

2016	2017	2018	2019	2020
Facebook	Facebook	Facebook	Facebook	Facebook
QZone	YouTube	YouTube	YouTube	YouTube
Tumblr	QZone	Instagram	Instagram	Instagram
Instagram	Tumblr	Tumblr	QZone	TikTok
Twitter	Instagram	Qzone	TikTok	QZone
Baidu Tieba	Baidu Tieba	Sina Weibo	Sina Weibo	Sina Weibo
Sina Weibo	Baidu Tieba	Twitter	Reddit	Reddit
YY	Pinterest	Baidu Tieba	Twitter	SnapChat
VKontakte	YY	LinkedIn	Douban	Twitter
Pinterest	LinkedIn	Reddit	LinkedIn	Pinterest

Source: https://medyaakademi.com.tr/2020/02/03/2020-sosyal-medya-kullanici-sayilari/ (accessed: 18.12.2020)

Financial Literacy in the Covid-19 Pandemic

We have seen very limited academic publication on financial literacy during the Covid-19 pandemic. The Covid-19 outbreak has affected people financially in different ways and to different degrees and rattled economies worldwide. These effects vary by their financial literacy level. Yuesti et al. (2020) advise that Indonesian people are not equipped to face the economic paralysis during the pandemic because this unpreparedness is partly caused by the lack of people's financial literacy. Low financial literacy results in people not being able to evaluate personal finances and make effective decisions.

Conclusion

As can be seen, the increasing use of computers, financial products and services and internet access is accelerating the upward trend in the digitalization in society. As a result, it is inevitable that a period of rapid growth in the level of financial literacy will be entered.

Some ideas have been proposed about the impact of the global pandemic and the Covid-19 conditions on digitalization to enhance knowledge and improve the skills of financial inclusion, financial literacy and usage digital technologies in terms of adjusting people's core attitudes and beliefs, so that a change in financial behavior can help them to achieve a future of financial freedom and security.

The research results show that digitalization will be effective in spreading financial and non-financial information, forming financial attitudes and making financial decisions more accurately. But with these positive effects, it can also be seen that information attacks aimed at manipulation with the rapid dissemination of information lead to negative consequences for financial decisions. However, these manipulative behaviors will not be dominant enough to negatively affect the level of financial literacy. The study findings provide data supporting the planning work of private and public-based policymakers.

Practical Implications: Specific ideas about financial literacy, digitalization and the impact of global pandemic conditions have been identified.
Originality/Value: This is a first attempt at describing and identifying issues related to the correlation between Covid-19 and digitalization in terms of financial literacy.
Keywords: *Digitalization, financial literacy, financial technology, FinFech, Covid-19, pandemic*

References

Alsop, T., Nov 25, 2020, https://www.statista.com

Demirguc-Kunt, A., Klapper, L., Singer, D., Ansar, S., & Hess, J. (2018). The Global Findex Database 2017: Measuring financial inclusion and the fintech revolution. The World Bank.

French, D., McKillop, D., & Stewart, E. (2020). The effectiveness of smartphone apps in improving financial capability. *The European Journal of Finance*, 26(4-5), 302-318.

Grima, S., & Sammut, S., (2017). A Study on the Impact of the Short Selling Ban on FIBS, *International Journal of Economics & Business Administration (IJEBA)*, 5(1), 18-48.

Haiyang Chen and Ronald P. Volpe, (1998). An Analysis of Personal Financial Literacy Among College Students, *Financial Services Review*, 7(2), 107-128.

Jünger, M., & Mietzner, M. (2020). Banking goes digital: The adoption of FinTech services by German households. *Finance Research Letters*, 34, 101260.

Ivari, N., Sharma, S., & Ventä-Olkkonen, L. (2020). Digital transformation of everyday life–How COVID-19 pandemic transformed the basic education of the young generation and why information management research should care? *International Journal of Information Management*, 55, 102183.

Kezar, A., & Yang, H. (2010). The importance of financial literacy. *About Campus*, 14(6), 15-21.

Lusardi, A. & Mitchell, O.S. (2014). The Economic Importance of Financial Literacy: Theory and Evidence, *Journal of Economic Literature*, 52(1), 5-44.

Morgan, Peter J. and Trinh, Long Q. (2019). Fintech and Financial Literacy in the Lao PDR (March 18, 2019). ADBI Working Paper 933, March 2019, Available at SSRN: https://ssrn.com/abstract=3398235 or http://dx.doi.org/10.2139/ssrn.3398235.

Morgan, Peter. J. and Trinh, Long Q. (2020). Fintech and Financial Literacy in Viet Nam. ADBI Working Paper 1154. Tokyo: Asian Development Bank Institute. Available: https://www.adb.org/publications/fintech-and-financial-literacy-viet-nam.

Meier, Stephan, & Charles Sprenger. (2007). Selection into Financial Literacy Programs: Evidence from a Field Study. *Research Review*, 8, 6–8.

OECD (2018). OECD/INFE Toolkit for Measuring Financial Literacy and Financial Inclusion.

OECD (2019). OECD/INFE International Survey of G20/OECD INFE Core Competencies Framework on Financial Literacy For Adults, Adult Financial Literacy Competencies

OECD (2020). OECD/INFE 2020 International Survey of Adult Financial Literacy

www.oecd.org/financial/education/launchoftheoecdinfeglobalfinancialliteracysurveyreport.htm, (Access: 10.12.2020)

Ozili, P. K. (2018). Impact of digital finance on financial inclusion and stability. *Borsa Istanbul Review*, 18(4), 329-340.

Sebetçi, Ö., Karabıyık, C., & Karabıyık, B. K. (2018). The Impact of Mobile Applications Developed in Finance on Financial Literacy, *Journal of Business Research Turk*, 10(2), 37-55. DOI: 10.20491/isarder.2018.418

Świecka, B., Yeşildağ, E., Özen, E., & Grima, S. (2020). Financial literacy: The case of Poland. *Sustainability*, 12(2), 700.

Świecka, B., Terefenko, P., & Paprotny, D. (2021). Transaction factors' influence on the choice of payment by Polish consumers. *Journal of Retailing and Consumer Services*, 58, 102264.

Stamford, Conn., January 15, 2020, https://www.gartner.com/en/newsroom/press-releases/2020-01-15-gartner-says-global-it-spending-to-reach-3point9-trillion-in-2020, (Accessed: 10.11.2020)

Topal, Y., & Kayahan, C. (2009, June). The Perceptions of Individual Internet Users about E-Finance Applications. In 1. International Symposium on Sustainable Development.

Turkish Banking Cards Center Co., Interim Annual Reports, 2020-III.

Vovchenko, N. G., Galazova, S. S., Danchenko, E. A., Ivanova, O. B., & Kostoglodova, E. D. (2018). Improvement of Financial Literacy as a Crucial Factor of Economic Development, *European Research Studies Journal*, 21(Special Issue 1), 16-24.

Yuesti, A., Ni, W. R., & Suryandari, N. N. A. (2020). Financial literacy in the COVID-19 pandemic: pressure conditions in Indonesia. *Entrepreneurship and Sustainability Issues*, 8(1), 884-898. DOI: 10.9770/jesi.2020.8.1(59), September 2020.

https://globalfindex.worldbank.org/ (Accessed: 14.11.2020).

https://www.canalys.com/newsroom/canalys-global-pc-market-forecasts-2021, (Accessed: 14.11.2020).

https://www.bloomberght.com/martta-3-milyon-kart-internet-ile-25-milyon-kart-da-temassiz-odeme-ile-tanisti-2252272, (Accessed: 14.11.2020).

CHAPTER FOURTEEN

DIGITAL CHANGE AND TRANSFORMATION OF OCCUPATIONAL HEALTH AND SAFETY APPLICATIONS IN THE IMPACT OF COVID-19 PANDEMIC

MUSTAFA TATLICAN AND YILMAZ KARADAŞ

Introduction

Looking at the studies on viral diseases throughout history, it is seen that the flu virus was discovered in 1933. One of the main reasons for the reproduction of and studies on the flu virus, which has been alive for years until today is the increase in industrialization, civilization and socialization by the 20th century. The rapid development in technology, the increase in living conditions and socialization, and the decrease in the number of healthy foods in parallel with the increase in the variety of food and beverages brought many flu-like diseases over time. The Covid-19 virus, which affected the whole world in late 2019 and 2020, is also stated as one of the consequences of these impacts (Ateş, 2020: 162).

Covid-19 is an infectious disease, an acute respiratory syndrome caused by the corona virus, which has a severe impact on the respiratory tract of human beings (Pharmetic, 2020: access date: September 07). Covid-19, which was first seen in Wuhan, China in the last months of 2019, spread to the whole world in a short time and turned into a global pandemic. The World Health Organization (WHO) announced the coronavirus outbreak as a pandemic in March 2020, declaring that it was an international public health emergency (who.org, 03.11.2020: access date: September 07)

With a mortality rate of more than 1% and no effective antiviral therapy or vaccine, the fundamental ground of pandemic therapy is pacification and palliation. The decrease in manual applications with the impact of digitalization played an important role in preventing the spread of Covid-19 disease, which has a high infectious impact. Social areas and industrial enterprises, which are at the centers of production, attract attention as the most crowded places where social distance should be paid the most attention. All over the world, after the Covid-19 outbreak there was an attempt to minimize the manual and contact-oriented applications used before the pandemic process. These applications, which were created with the impact of technology, are also important for occupational health and safety that are fundamental to employee health.

Occupational Health and Safety Applications

The Concept of Occupational Health and Safety

Health is defined by the World Health Organization (WHO) as "not only the absence of diseases and disabilities, but also being in a state of complete physical, mental and social well-being" (Callahan, 1973: 77). With reference to this definition of the World Health Organization, we can define occupational health and safety as being "to aim to ensure that the physical, mental and social conditions of employees are in a sustainable well-being, to eliminate the risks arising from working conditions and to protect the working life and social structure of employees by employing them in occupations suitable for their personal characteristics".

The International Labor Organization (ILO) is the institution that plays the unity and leadership role in occupational health and safety around the world. The International Labor Organization (ILO) identified the targets of occupational safety in 1959 and declared them to all member countries with Recommendation 112. The related targets were determined as:

- To keep the health status of employees at the highest level.
- To prevent interruption of the work due to unfavorable work-related conditions.
- To employ employees in works suitable for their physical and mental status.
- To obtain possible maximum productivity by ensuring the harmony between employees and employers (ilo.org, 09.09.2020: access date: July 14).

Main Principles of Occupational Health and Safety

Occupational health and safety (OHS) refers to a very wide discipline in which many fields, especially technology, economy, physics, ergonomics, engineering and law, interact with each other. Despite various fields related to OHS, it is possible to say that there are some main principles regarding OHS. These main principles are:

1. OHS is a right for employees. Employees should have as many rights as the government and employers to comment on the development and improvement of these rights.
2. Policies suitable for businesses should be developed concerning OHS. All stakeholders of workplaces, especially employees and employers, should exchange views on the regulation, renewal and implementation of these policies.
3. The main purposes of applications and policies prepared for OHS should be protective and preventive measures.
4. Hazard analyses should be done in workplaces and implemented policy results and workplace departments should be observed; therefore, in accordance with the obtained information OHS applications should be updated to be more effective and productive.
5. The main element of occupational health and safety applications should include efforts to improve the physical, mental and social status of employees.
6. Health units that can be a benefit to all employees should be established in the workplace.
7. Improvement services should be established for employees in order to prevent the negative consequences of occupational accidents or diseases.
8. OHS training should be given to employees and employers so they become aware of and understand the importance of OHS systems established to create a healthier and safer working environment.
9. At workplaces, employers are charged with establishing the necessary OHS systems for a healthy and safe working environment, employees are charged with working in accordance with established systems, and those assigned to OHS are charged with establishing a policy on occupational health and safety and updating this policy periodically.

A system that controls the implementation and supervision of OHS policies should be established. OHS policies should be mandatory (Alli, 2008: 17-19).

Historical Development of Occupational Health and Safety

When the historical process of occupational health and safety is examined, we can say that the industrial revolution was an important moment. It can be said that the reason why OHS studies became important after the industrial revolution is due to the industrialization process and the increased risks and hazards.

The industrial revolution that started in England and then spread to the world over time and became important in production led to the emergence of new developments in many areas. The large factories established by using technological developments such as steam engines, railways, weaving machines, etc., caused the people living in rural areas to leave their lands in the hope of a safe job and flock to the factories, and the migration rate to the cities to increase (Abrams, 2001: 41).

The “Apprentices’ Health and Morale Act” of 1802, the “Factory Act” of 1833 and the “Ten Hours Act” of 1847 were some regulations in England that was the leader of the industrial revolution. With another legal regulation in 1842, the employment of children and women under the age of 10 in mines was prohibited and in 1895 it became mandatory to report some important occupational diseases (Abrams, 2001: 43-45).

International studies in the field of occupational health and safety began with the “International Labor Organization” established in 1919 at the Paris Peace Conference. The ILO brought international regulations to working environments by publishing conventions and recommendations with the participation of member countries (ILO, 1996). The World Health Organization (WHO), which was established within the United Nations in 1948, is another significant organization that aids the international examination of occupational health and solutions for the issues (WHO, 2019: access date: May 13).

Covid-19 And Its Impacts on Business Life

A pandemic is a concept used in the meaning of "affecting all people" consisting of the words, "pan" meaning "all" and "demos" meaning "people" in the ancient Greek language. A vaccine was developed for the first time in history for epidemic diseases such as smallpox, plague and rabies in 1796, and a new era began in human and animal health. In this period, important medical successes were achieved in order to make human and animal health sustainable with the discovery of the first penicillin and antibiotic. Before these two treatments were discovered, throughout history human beings and animals experienced pandemics and endemics that caused severe pain and deaths. As a result, they significantly influenced human life and psychology, caused social migration and brought about the collapse of states and the change of rulers. If such outbreaks occurring in the world can be easily transmitted from human to human or from animal to human, and if they occur with a different virus, they directly become a current issue for the World Health Organization (WHO) as a global threat and the WHO decides whether the outbreak is a pandemic. The WHO considers the following three features to declare an outbreak as a pandemic.

- The disease-causing agent should be easily and continuously spread,
- An epidemic disease that has not been exposed before should be emerging,
- The disease-causing agent should infect humans and cause a dangerous disease (Washington Post, 2020; Wang, Ng, and Brook, 2020: 1341; New National, 2020; Coronavirus, 2020; Wall Street Journal, 2020).

Diseases such as Amwas Plague, Black Plague, cholera, Spanish Flu, Hong Kong Flu, Smallpox, Swine Flu and Avian Flu are pandemics in history. Ongoing pandemics are HIV/AIDS and Coronavirus (Covid-19) (Aslan, 2020: 36-41).

What is Coronavirus and How did it break out?

Coronaviruses (CoV) are a family of viruses that includes severe diseases such as severe acute respiratory syndrome (SARS-CoV), the common cold and Middle East respiratory syndrome (MERS-CoV) and causes various outbreaks. The Covid-19 outbreak is different from the coronaviruses above because Covid-19 has many varieties of disease and causes mild infectious diseases in about 80% of the cases. Control of the virus is a little more challenging because it causes mild infectious diseases and some patients do not have symptoms. This outbreak first broke out on December 1, 2019 in Wuhan in the Hubei province of China and began to spread around the world (McKibbin and Fernando, 2020: 3-5). With the spread of the outbreak, the number of Covid-19 cases outside China within two weeks increased 13 times and the number of countries affected by the outbreak increased 3 times. The WHO announced a public health emergency to determine the international situation of the outbreak, and then declared Covid-19 as a pandemic on March 11, 2020, because the number of cases had increased and spread all over the world (Hui et al, 2020: 264-266).

Covid-19: Spread and Symptoms

Covid-19, which entered our lives as a new type of coronavirus, is thought to have a very high rate of spread and, contrary to some suggested ideas, it is not man-made. For this reason, it is possible to say that Covid-19 is a mutated virus. Virus infection can occur by human-to-human and animal-to-human contact and the spread of droplets. There are two important factors for virus infection to occur by contact. It can be said that the first is the holding/touching duration and the second is the humidity in the environment. 10 seconds of contact are required for virus infection under normal conditions. However, if one of the contacting or contacted surfaces is humid, this duration can be reduced to 5 seconds and up to 3 seconds if both are humid. Considering these conditions, it is possible to say that the infection possibility is very low as long as the contact time does not last long in the opening of any door or touching a surface. It is recommended that diseases caused by the Covid-19 virus should be taken into consideration, especially by young people. It is widely believed that young people are not affected by this disease and can easily recover. It should not be forgotten that even if the symptoms of the disease are very mild, the virus causes damage to the lungs or other tissues of infected people regardless of their age (Wall Street Journal, 2020: access date: May 21; USA Today, 2020: access date: April 13). The clinical symptoms of the disease are as follows:

Day 1-3: A sore throat, mild fever and symptoms such as diarrhea and nausea are observed in the case of a weak immune system,
Day 4: Aphonia occurs, the sore throat increases, it becomes difficult to eat and drink and mild headache and diarrhea may be observed,
Day 5: It becomes difficult to move the arms and legs, eating and drinking become painful, joint pains begin, and the sore throat becomes severe,
Day 6: When swallowing and talking, the throat begins to ache, diarrhea and vomiting become severe, a feeling of fatigue and nausea begins, it becomes difficult to breathe and a cough begins,
Day 7: Vomiting becomes severe with the body and head aching, sputum production and cough increase and the fever rises above 38°C,
Day 8: Headache and joint pains have increased immensely, chest pain increases, breathing difficulties begin and the fever rises above 38°C,
Day 9: Symptoms become severe, the body and head ache, vomiting, cough and sputum production become extremely severe, and bruising of the face or lips may be observed.

Afterwards, the disease may result in death depending on people's risk groups. Not all individuals have the same risk of death in this disease. The most endangered group consists of COPD patients, those who use immunosuppressive drugs, cancer patients and those who receive chemotherapy and smokers. The second risk group consists of health care and cleaning employees, those who are malnourished, diabetic patients and those who live and work in a polluted environment (Aslan, 2020: 40).

The Impact of Coronavirus on Business Life

It is thought that some protective measures should be taken in all developed and developing countries in order to control the Covid-19 pandemic, which continues to increase rapidly and gradually around the world. Especially with social isolation and curfews, mandatory measures such as the prohibition of travel all over the world, starting part-time and rotational work in workplaces or closing workplaces brought many sectors to a standstill economically. The ongoing COVID-19 pandemic across the world negatively affects many sectors such as trade, transportation, agriculture, airways and energy markets, industry, finance and banking and as a result causes some businesses to suspend production and others to be completely closed. The macroeconomic impacts of the pandemic on banking and finance, agriculture, the supply chain and the manufacturing industry, aviation and energy sectors are discussed respectively below.

The Impact of the COVID-19 Pandemic on the Supply Chain and the Manufacturing Industry

The manufacturing industry and supply chain sectors are the leading sectors in which the materially and morally negative impacts of the pandemic will be intensely seen. In such an extraordinary situation, it is seen that the supply chain is negatively affected if factories, customers and shipping units are not used. Material insufficiency and delays in orders caused by the decrease in production lead to fluctuations in productivity and service quality and result in a decline in performance (Ivanov, 2020: 2-3). It is known that the pandemic first broke out in China and spread to the world, and China is ranked first place in the world in terms of the supply chain. The fact that the measures taken against the epidemic have not been taken in some regions causes China to be blamed; therefore it is predicted that countries will make some changes in their supply chains in order to avoid such a case in the future. These changes are considered to be some countries making more investments in their own sectors and other countries starting to research different routes for the supply chain. If there is any change in consumer demand, the next step, the manufacturing industry, will also be affected. Accordingly, it is predicted that the Covid-19 outbreak will affect the manufacturing industry negatively (Duran and Acar, 2020: 58). According to a study in the UK, more than 80% of the participants expect a decrease in their turnover in the next two quarters, while 98% stated that they have a negative opinion about the impact of the outbreak in the field of commercial movements (Nicola et al., 2020: 186).

The Impact of the COVID-19 Pandemic on Banking and the Finance Sector

The banking and finance sector is negatively affected by an excessive transaction volume and non-performing loans in economic regression. It is thought that as the impact and spread of the pandemic in the world increases, the possibility of bankruptcy will increase in the developing banking and finance sector. In addition, the outstanding loans provided to the poor in the society during the pandemic affect the financial sector negatively. Situations such as the decrease and cessation of production in many sectors, employees forced to stay at home, the closure of workplaces and the negative decrease in sales affect the payment of debts and most of the loans cannot be repaid. In these periods, central banks and governments should delay the debts of companies, help the SMEs and contribute to the society by providing liquidity in order to avoid problems in the banking and finance sector (Duran and Acar, 2020: 57).

The Impact of the COVID-19 Pandemic on the Agricultural Sector

One of the most important criteria in the pandemic period is that people can continue their lives in a healthy way. Looking at Maslow's hierarchy of needs, the most important needs include shelter and physiological and security needs to ensure vital continuity. Accordingly, people have to meet their basic needs related to shelter, survival and food and drink. As a result of the fact that all people act based on this opinion and some groups in the society stockpile, the agricultural sector and food processing companies have difficulty in satisfying demand due to Covid-19. In addition, there is an increase in product prices due to people who buy more products than they need (Akça and Küçükoğlu, 2020: 73). The measures taken during the Covid-19 pandemic led to an 80% reduction in the rate of eating and drinking outside. Therefore, the demand for agricultural products decreases and the agricultural sector is negatively affected by this situation. It is seen in a study that the global decrease in demand from hotels and restaurants reduces the prices of agricultural products by around 20%. The fact that the shrinkage in sectors such as tourism, finance, energy and education is above 50% indicates that the agricultural shrinkage will be lower (Nicola et al., 2020: 185-186).

The Impact of the COVID-19 Pandemic on the Aviation Sector

Airline transport, used as the fastest means of transportation worldwide, causes intercontinental transportation and leads to the novel coronavirus being transported from different areas and spread over wide territories. For this reason, one of the main reasons that airline transport is at the forefront during the pandemic period is that the number of tourists entering and leaving a country and the human mobility in that region increase the spread and transmission rate of the outbreak. Although airline transport is considerably preferred, it may become a non-preferred means of transportation because it accelerates the spread of the disease (Li et al., 2020: 6; Akça, 2020: 47-49). 25 airport managers participated in a study conducted to explain the impact of the pandemic on airport operations and it was concluded that too many air zone sections were closed in airports. In addition, while 44% of the participants stated that 90% of air traffic decreased around 90% due to Covid-19, 80% stated that the number of employees in airline transport decreased by 80% and employees were taking paid or unpaid leave in order to protect their health (Kaçkın et al., 2020: 1-4).

The Impact of the COVID-19 Pandemic on the Energy Sector

The Covid-19 pandemic brought about a widespread crisis all over the world. The energy sector, one of the important resources of today, is also negatively affected by this crisis. It is observed that oil prices declined as a result of the decrease in demand for coal and other energy products. The news of the first deaths from China on January 1 due to the outbreak, negatively affected many sectors and the price of crude oil declined around 30%. As a result of the rapid spread of the pandemic in all territories, the global demand for oil decreased and this accelerated the reduction in oil prices. The pandemic not only stopped the supply and manufacturing sectors in China, but also accelerated the global cyclical slowdown and reduced industrial production all over the world. Therefore, shrinkage in the energy sector and decreases in oil prices continued (Kouman and Kingsly, 2020: 2-3; Akça, 2020: 54-55).

Digital Transformations in Occupational Health and Safety Applications with Covid-19

Both businesses and employees are affected by the spread of Covid-19 in business life. In order to control the spread of the coronavirus, some businesses were suspended while other businesses were closed. After the businesses were suspended, the financial difficulties of the employees began. However, occupational health and safety measures become more of a current issue due to the necessity of the work and also to the fact that some sectors need to continue to work. As stated in the Occupational Health and Safety Regulation No. 6331, employers are obliged to protect their employees (Ateş, 2020: 164). The measures to be taken by employers in workplaces differ with the current developments and are constantly renewed. In order to protect employees mentally and physically, employers are obliged to take the occupational health and safety measures required by the mind, science and techniques and to monitor whether or not these measures are followed (Sümer, 2017: 105-106). One of the measures that employers should take is to provide employees with some personal protective equipment (mask, gloves, glasses, shoe covers, visors, protective clothing, etc.). Personal protective equipment is of great importance in terms of occupational health and safety, as well as in protecting employees from the pandemic. In addition to personal protective equipment, mass protection measures such as placing information and warning signs at necessary points in workplaces, placing disinfectant where employees can easily reach it, and keeping hygiene conditions at the highest possible level in public areas such as washbasins, dressing rooms and dining halls are also important in order to protect employees from the disease. These measures are recommended by the Ministry of Health for all businesses during the pandemic period. Eleven guidelines for different sectors including the measures to be taken in businesses were published by the Ministry of Health Scientific Committee (Özgenç, 2020: 14). According to these guidelines, the measures to be taken by employers as recommendations, provided that they consider the working conditions of the employees and the requirements of the job, were shared with the public. First of all, it is recommended to disinfect workplaces and to ensure this action is continuous in order to prevent the spread of the virus. In addition, it is recommended to pay more attention to daily workplace cleaning and to provide cleaning employees with hygiene products that can eliminate the virus.

Employers are obliged to make new plans to eliminate risks and determine the measures to be taken in order to prevent or minimize the outbreak. Within the framework of this plan, the physical conditions of workplaces can be changed and the spread risk of the virus can be reduced. Thus, employers should follow the recommendations of the Ministry of Health and the Scientific Committee and put them into practice. Working environments should be constantly ventilated and highly protective filters should be used in order to prevent the virus in workplaces. In addition to personal protective equipment and environmental cleaning in workplaces, digital transformations in businesses have also recently been implemented. Workplaces with a high number of employees started rotational work and thus employees can work online from home under the name of distance working. Announcements that need to be made in businesses are sent to the e-mails of employees who are sure to be more interested in technology. Employees who need to work in businesses have their temperature taken with a temperature measuring device at the entrances and employees with a high fever are sent to the hospital (Ateş, 2020: 167-168). In some companies, customers are accepted through an appointment system which is aimed to prevent potential crowds within a company. Necessary studies are carried out to ensure that only one person can use a device commonly used by employees and the number of devices is increased. In addition, glass partitions become widespread in order to obey social distancing rules and to reduce contact by taking into account the employees' face-to-face interaction with customers. Working behind a glass partition is of great importance, especially for supermarket cashiers, when we consider that thousands of people come to supermarkets daily. Also, it is ensured that customers use contactless devices as much as possible (Tunçomağ & Centel, 2018: 136). In addition, events such as job interviews and meetings are carried out online rather than face to face. HES (Hayat Eve Sığar) code checks are always carried out at the entrances to businesses and the individuals in dangerous groups are directed to hospitals. Also, with the HES code feature, individuals in dangerous groups are identified by defining the HES code on the cards used to get on public transportation vehicles. Cash desks in supermarkets are regularly disinfected, the products that employees buy themselves such as greengroceries and bread are packaged and sold and contact is avoided as much as possible.

Some regulations were also made for cafeterias and services, places where collective use is most common in all workplaces. Some of these regulations are:

- In order to prevent crowds in dining halls, meal durations were extended and tables normally used by 4 people were reduced to 2 users with a cross and distance use.
- During meal purchases, lines were drawn at least 1.5 meters apart on the floor, allowing employees to stay distant. This was applied in the same way to leave plates after the meal.
- The impact of digitalization was observed with the use of sensors, not contact, in hand-washing systems after meals and in the normal process.
- In service buses, employees are constantly checked for masks and the seating is arranged by leaving one seat empty, corresponding to half the number of seats.
- Fever measurement devices were also replaced at the doors of service buses, without contact with the wrist or forehead.
- The police constantly monitor whether control measures are obeyed or not in service buses and impose sanctions on both employees and service officers if someone who does not obey is detected.

Occupational health and safety applications, the most important agents for employees to lead a healthy and safe working life, have brought some innovations in the digitalization process. Some of these innovations are:

- The occupational health and safety training sessions for employees were arranged online, while the necessary training sessions that had been booked were arranged in open areas with at least 1.5 meters of distance between employees.
- The informative videos and visuals prepared by occupational health and safety professionals were continuously broadcast on screens that could be seen by employees at workplaces.
- The informative posters published by the Ministry of Health, including occupational health and safety as well as Covid-19 measures were transferred to the employees in the digital environment.
- All measures to be taken in businesses overall, especially the number of employees suitable for the size of workplaces, are subject to continuous supervision by occupational health and safety professionals and employers are guided to take the necessary measures.

While this type of digitalization is observed in our country, different digitalization types are observed in other countries of the world. If we have a look at these, we can list them as a follow-up system, infection monitoring, communication monitoring, quarantine and self-isolation and clinical methods.

Table 14. 1: Follow-up System

	Functions	Digital technology	Countries	Advantages	Disadvantages
Follow-up System	Following disease activity in real time	Data dashboards; migration maps; machine learning; real-time data from smartphones and wearable technology	China; Singapore; Sweden; Taiwan; USA	Allows visual depiction of spread; directs border restrictions; guides resource allocation; informs forecasts	Could breach privacy; involves high costs; requires management and regulation

Source: Whitelaw et al., 2020: 437

The follow-up method is an important system to monitor the preparations for Covid-19 and see how and to what extent Covid-19 spreads in which country. For example, a platform has been created in Sweden to access the information of healthcare professionals, the number of personal protective equipment items, personnel, the number of Covid-19 patients and other necessary resources. With the information collected through this platform, the status of hospitals was monitored and health equipment supplied and this information was shared with health authorities in the country in order to increase the number of beds in hospitals (Rao, 2020: 149).

Table 14.2: Infection Monitoring

	Functions	**Digital technology**	**Countries**	**Advantages**	**Disadvantages**
Infection Monitoring	Monitoring individuals and populations for disease	Artificial intelligence; digital thermometers; mobile phone applications; thermal cameras; web-based toolkits	China; Iceland; Singapore; Taiwan	Provides information on disease prevalence and pathology; identifies individuals for testing, contact tracing, and isolation	Could breach privacy; fails to detect asymptomatic individuals if based on self-reported symptoms or monitoring of vital signs; involves high costs; requires management and regulation; requires validation of screening tools

Source: Whitelaw et al., 2020: 437

In Iceland, information about symptoms declared by patients is collected using mobile technologies and this information is combined with other information such as genomic and clinical sequencing data to reveal information about the spread of the virus. In Singapore, the body temperature of people is measured at the entrances to public transport vehicles, schools and workplaces. The data from thermometers are monitored and people at risk are detected. Web-based tools are used in China to scan people and direct them to ideal references. In Taiwan, people with a high fever are detected with high performance, infrared thermal cameras installed at airports (Hitelaw et al., 2020: 437; USA Today, 2020: access date: April 13).

Table 14.3: Communication Monitoring

	Functions	Digital technology	Countries	Advantages	Disadvantages
Communication Monitoring	Identifies and tracks individuals who might have come into contact with an infected person	Global positioning systems; mobile phone applications; real-time monitoring of mobile devices; wearable technology	Germany; Singapore; South Korea	Identifies exposed individuals for testing and quarantine; tracks viral spread	Could breach privacy; might detect individuals who have not been exposed but have had contact; could fail to detect individuals who are exposed if the application is deactivated, the mobile device is absent, or wi-fi or cell connectivity is inadequate

Source: Whitelaw et al., 2020: 437

During the pandemic process, Germany launched a smart watch application that measures temperature, sleep patterns and pulse to scan for the symptoms of the virus with a digital monitoring method. Taking measures against the outbreak was accelerated by sharing the data obtained from this smart watch with the authorities in the country. Despite the high number of cases in Germany, the mortality rate was lower than in other countries with digital health examinations and tests (Coronavirus, 2020: access date: September 03). A mobile phone application that can change Bluetooth signals when people do not social distance was launched in Singapore. The application data are recorded for 21 days and if any person is diagnosed with Covid-19, the people in contact with the positive person are determined by the Ministry of Health. Singapore is among the countries with the lowest mortality rate (New National, 2020: access date: April 12). In this process, in South Korea a detailed travel timetable of people is kept and contact is monitored using security camera images, bank card records, GPS and face recognition technology data taken from mobile phones. In the light of these data, emergency text alerts are sent to people who are found to have been in contact with positive people, and they are told to isolate themselves. South Korea is among those countries with a low mortality rate by detecting positive cases early and taking the necessary measures (New York Times, 2020: access date: April 13).

Table 14.4: Quarantine and Self-Isolation

	Functions	Digital technology	Countries	Advantages	Disadvantages
Quarantine and Self-Isolation	Identifies and tracks infected individuals, and implements quarantine	Artificial intelligence; cameras and digital recorders; global positioning systems; mobile phone applications; quick response codes	Australia; China; Iceland; South Korea; Taiwan	Isolates infections; restricts travel	Violates civil liberties; could restrict access to food and essential services; fails to detect individuals who leave quarantine without devices

Source: Whitelaw et al. 2020: 437

In Australia, when tourists returned to the country, hotels were quarantine areas, and tourists returning from Wuhan state were specially quarantined. According to new legislation published, the people who violated the quarantine rules were forced to wear a monitoring device and they were fined (Wall Street Journal, 2020: access date: May 21). Iceland developed a mobile phone system to detect people with Covid-19 and ensure that these people quarantined. In Taiwan, people who isolated themselves in their homes were given mobile phones by the government and these people were monitored electronically (USA Today, 2020: access date: April 13).

Table 14.5. Clinical Management

	Functions	Digital technology	Countries	Advantages	Disadvantages
Clinical Management	Diagnosis of infected individuals; monitors clinical status; predicts clinical outcomes; provides capacity for telemedicine services and virtual care	Artificial intelligence for diagnostics; machine learning; virtual care or telemedicin e platforms	Australia; Canada; China; Ireland; USA	Assists with clinical decision-making, diagnostics, and risk prediction; enables efficient service delivery; facilitates patient-centered, remote care; facilitates infection control	Could breach privacy; fails to accurately diagnose patients; involves high costs; equipment may malfunction

Source: Whitelaw et al. 2020: 437

Virtual maintenance platforms using digital monitoring and video conferencing are used worldwide to prevent the Covid-19 outbreak. In Australia and the USA, digital platforms are used to provide remote care to those with chronic diseases and moderate Covid-19 disease. In Canada, while the video visits to infected individuals by people working in the clinic were approximately 1000 per day in February 2020, this number reached 14000 per day in May 2020. If the virtual care system is used correctly and its use is increased, this system can increase access to healthcare services during and after the outbreak. Equipment malfunctions, misdiagnoses, privacy violations, and healthcare system costs may sometimes occur during the use of this system (Wall Street Journal, 2020: access date: May 21; Caretaker, 2009: access date: May 21).

Conclusion

The Covid-19 outbreak affecting the whole world is one of the biggest epidemics in history. Workplaces and communal areas are at risk of the Covid-19 virus. If adequate measures are not taken and individuals are not monitored, it becomes very difficult to identify how and where people caught the virus. Digital innovations are very important, especially to monitor individuals in business life. In line with these innovations, it is possible to prevent the spread of the Covid-19 virus and similar diseases by minimizing contact between individuals.

There are many measures to be taken and implemented by employers during the pandemic period. These measures are shared by organizations such as the International Labor Organization and the World Health Organization, and especially those measures published by the Ministry of Family, Labor and Social Services. In this respect, the measures to be taken to prevent the spread of the virus in workplaces are the responsibility of employers. Measures to be taken in terms of occupational health and safety in working environments can be listed as the regular disinfection of dormitories, dining halls, elevators, sinks, toilets, showers and working areas. In addition, employees should be informed about the Covid-19 virus and be taught how to take measures against it. Measures such as expanding the order and usage times in accordance with social distancing rules should be taken in areas such as dining halls and workplaces which employees will use collectively at one time. When taking all these measures, the digital measures mentioned in the study should certainly be implemented. Digital measures such as holding meetings online, keeping documents on computer, the widespread use of the e-signature and using face recognition systems instead of fingerprints at entrances play an important role in mitigating and preventing the pandemic process. Up-to-date information about the pandemic process should be followed and technological developments should continue to be implemented. It is not yet known when the pandemic process will end and what effects it will have. Therefore, the measures taken during the pandemic period should be continuously improved and their continuity should be ensured.

Keywords: *Occupational health and safety, Covid-19, digitalization*

References

Abrams, H.K. (2001). A Short History of Occupational Health. *Journal of Public Health Policy*, 22 (1), 34-80.

Akça, M. (2020). The Impact of Covid-19 on the Aviation Industry. *Journal of Eurasian Social and Economic Studies*, 7 (5), 45-64.

Akça, M. and Küçükoğlu, M.T. (2020) Covid-19 and Its Effects on Business Life: Home Work. *International Journal of Management Education and Economic Perspectives*, 8 (1), 71-81.

Alli, B. O. (2008). Fundamental Principles of Occupational Health and Safety Second Edition. Geneva, *International Labour Organization*, 15, 17-19.

Aslan, R. (2020). Epidemics, Pandemics and Covid-19 from History to Present. Details Magazine, 8 (85).

Ateş, Z. G. (2020) The Effect of Covid-19 on the Precautions to Be Taken By the Employer For Occupational Health and Safety. *Istanbul Commerce University Journal of Social Sciences*, 19 (38), 161-179.

Becker. (2020) Https://Www.Beckershospitalreview.Com/Healthcare-İnformation-Technology/Swedish-Health-Services-Taps-Microsoft-To-Build-App-That-Tracks-Covid-19-Patients-HospitalCapacity.Html (Access Date: April 12, 2020)

Callahan, D. (1973). The who Definition of Health. *The Hastings Center Studies*. 1(3), 77-87

Caretaker. (2020) Https://Www.Caretakermedical.Net/Australias-First-Virtual-Hospital-For-Covid-19-Patients-Use-Caretaker-Medical-Wireless-Patient-Monitor-For-Remote-Monitoring-And-Reporting/ (Access Date: May 21, 2020).

Coronavirus. (2020) Https://Coronavirus.Jhu.Edu/Map.Html. (Access Date: April 10, 2020).

Duran, M. and Acar, M. (2020). What A Virus Happens To The World: The Macroeconomic Effects Of The Covid-19 Pandemic. *International Journal of Social and Economic Sciences*, 10 (1), 54-67.

Hui, D. S., Azhar, E.I., Madani, T.A., Ntoumi, F., Kock, R., Dar, O., İppolito, G., Mchugh, T.D., Memish, Z.A., Drosten, C., Zumla, A. and Petersen, E. (2020). The Continuing 2019-Ncov Epidemic Threat of Novel Coronaviruses To Global Health—The Latest 2019 Novel Coronavirus Outbreak In Wuhan, China. *International Journal of Infectious Diseases*, 91, 264-266.,

Ivanov, D. (2020). Predicting the İmpacts of Epidemic Outbreaks on Global Supply Chains: A Simulation-Based Analysis on the Coronavirus Outbreak (Covid-19/SARS-Cov-2) Case. *Transportation Research Part E: Logistics And Transportation Review*, 2-3.

Ilo.Org.Https://Www.ilo.Org/Dyn/Normlex/En/F?P=1000:12100:1630274 1292760::No::P12100_Show_Text:Y: (Access Date: July 14, 2020).

Kara, A. (2010). Swine Flu (Pandemic Influenza 2009, Influenza 2009 H1N1). *Journal of Pediatric Health and Diseases*, 53 (1).

Kouman, H., and Kingsly, K. M. (2020). Economic Implications of Covid-19 and Key Lessons for Policymakers. 2-3.

Li, S., Wang, Y., Xue, J. and Zhao, N. (2020). The İmpact of Covid-19 Epidemic Declaration on Psychological Consequences: A Study on

Active Weibo Users. *International Journal of Environmental Research and Public Health*, 17(6), 2032.

Mckibbin, W. J. and Fernando, R. (2020). The Global Macroeconomic Impacts of Covid-19: Seven Scenarios. 3-5.

New York Times. (2020) Https://Www.Nytimes.Com/2020/03/23/World/Asia/Coronavirus-South-Korea-Flatten-Curve.Html (Access Date: April 13, 2020)

NewsNational (2020). Https://Thenewdaily.Com.Au/News/National/2020/03/19/Singapore-Coronavirus-Temperature-Scans/ (Access Date: April 12, 2020)

Nicola, M., Alsafi, Z., Sohrabi, C., Kerwan, A., Jabir, A.A., Iosifidis, C., Agha, M. and Agha, R. (2020). The Socio-Economic İmplications of the Coronavirus and Covid-19 Pandemic: A Review. *International Journal of Surgery. International Journal of Surgery.*, 185-193

Özgenç, M. https://www.hurriyet.com.tr/galeri-son-dakika-haberi-yeni-hayata-merhaba-hayatimizda-neler-degisecek-41530214 (Access Date: April 12, 2020)

Pharemetic. (2020). Http://Pharmetic.Org/Covid-19 (Access Date: September 07, 2020)

Rao, G. H. (2020). Clinical Evaluation of a Topical Patch For the Management of Acute and Chronic Osteoarticular Pain. *Journal of Medicine and Healthcare*. SRC/JMHC-149, 3.

Sümer, H.H. (2017). Occupational Health and Safety Law. Seçkin Publishing.

Swedish Health Services Taps Microsoft to Build App That Tracks Covid-19

Patients, Hospital Capacity. (2020, November 12). Swedish Health Services Taps Microsoft to Build App That Tracks Covid-19 Patients, Hospital Capacity.

Tunçomağ, K., and Centel, T. (2008). Principles of Labor Law: General Concepts, Service Agreements, Trade Unions, Collective Bargaining Agreements, Mediation and Arbitration, Strike and Lockout. Beta Publishing Distribution.

USA Today. (2020). Https://Www.Usatoday.Com/Story/News/World/2020/04/10/Coronavirus-Covid-19-Small-Nations-İceland-Big-Data/2959797001/ (Access Date: April 13, 2020)

Wall Street Journal (2020). Https://Www.Wsj.Com/Articles/Australias-Coronavirus-Evacuation-Plan-A-Tiny-İsland-1-000-Miles-Away-11580295354 (Access Date: April 18, 2020).

Wall Street Journal. (2020) Https://Www.Wsj.Com/Articles/Hospitals-Monitor-Some-Coronavirus-Patients-At-Home-11586856604 (Access Date: May 21, 2020)

Wang, C. J., Chun, Y., and Brook, R. H. (2020). Response to Covid-19 in Taiwan: Big Data Analytics, *New Technology, and Proactive Testing*. Jama, 323(14), 1341-1342.

Washington Post (2020). Https://Www.Washingtonpost.Com/Opinions/2020/04/10/How-Digital-Data-Collection-Can-Help-Track-Covid-19-Cases-Real-Time/ (Access Date: April 18, 2020).

Whitelaw, S., Mamas, M. A., Topol, E., and Van Spall, H. G. (2020). Applications of Digital Technology in Covid-19 Pandemic Planning and Response. The Lancet Digital Health.

WHO. (2020). https://www.who.int/director-general/speeches/detail/who-director-general-s-opening-remarks-at-the-media-briefing-on-covid-19---11-march-2020 (Access Date: September 07, 2020)

CHAPTER FIFTEEN

REFLECTIONS OF DIGITALIZATION ON HEALTH SERVICES: E-HEALTH LITERACY AND CYBERCHONDRIA

HARUN KIRILMAZ AND KÜBRA ÖZTÜRK

Introduction

The process, which started with the implementation of mechanical production facilities in the 18th century, proceeded with the transition to mass production based upon electricity and the division of labor in the 19th century, and continued with the automation of production processes in the 20th century, has brought a new era in the field of management and organization today, with the effect of digitalization and digital change taking place in the 21st century. This era, which is expressed as Industry 4.0 (Fourth Industrial Revolution) and consists of the internet of things, the internet of services and cyber-physical systems is based on the principles of interoperability, virtualization, autonomous management, real-time capability, service orientation and modularity. Therefore, digitalization, which is the key concept of Industry 4.0, has led to innovations in the production and service industries and in the management processes of organizations.

On the other hand, it is observed that the COVID-19 pandemic, which emerged at the end of 2019, has brought opportunities in many fields, especially in technology, online services and education, as well as its sociological, psychological and economically negative consequences, especially in terms of health. For example, based on the widespread digital learning experience that has been switched to with a rapid adaptation process due to the COVID-19 pandemic, it is predicted that this method will increase in functionality and grow into the main learning structure in the near future with the contribution of digital learning, new technologies and systems (Yamamoto & Altun, 2020: 32-33). Similarly, the COVID-19 pandemic has provided an opportunity for more effective use of digital technologies in health as well. It is believed that the difficulties emerging in health service delivery during disasters and epidemics can be overcome with the widespread use of digital technologies such as tele-medicine (Hollander and Carr, 2020: 1697).

Digitalization, which has gained more prominence in the COVID-19 pandemic, can also lead to some problems. As a matter of fact, it has been demonstrated that social media have played an important role in the spread of information and misinformation during the COVID-19 pandemic. At this point, the presence of insufficient evidence-based data on COVID-19 and the disinformation emerging on social media complicate the rapid and objective management of the process. In general, digitalization has brought forward concepts and practices such as the digital hospital, tele-health, and mobile-health in the field of health; and has enabled technologies such as robotic surgery, wearable technology products, 3D printers, and smart medicine, etc., to be used in the delivery of health care. However, it also has some disadvantages arising from management, organizational structure and human factors. Interaction models revealed in a research study examining the role of social media platforms such as Twitter, YouTube and Instagram in the COVID-19 pandemic demonstrated that each social media platform plays an important role in the spread of information and misinformation, when combined with the characteristics of the audience (Cinelli et al., 2020: 2). The presence of insufficient evidence-based data on COVID-19, which is declared a global epidemic, and the disinformation emerging on social media complicate the rapid and objective management of the process. In this framework, it will be possible to manage and plan the global epidemic in a more effective way, to clarify the current situation and to make clearer projections for the future as the accredited studies gain wide currency (Kakodkar et al., 2020: 15-16).

People are able to gain more access to health information with the increase in digitalization. The internet is superseding traditional methods in accessing this information. The internet provides the opportunity to access hard-to-reach information in a rapid, cheap, easy, and anonymous manner and on equal terms. However, the internet can also be dangerous as it contains conflicting, incorrect, incomplete or unaccredited information. In addition to the disadvantageous characteristics of the internet, the expansion of the online health information spectrum makes it critical for individuals to choose, perceive and manage this information and consequently, e-health literacy comes to the fore as a new structure. Cyberchondria, which is defined as the search for information about health, carried out over the internet to alleviate anxiety, is constantly repeated and causes unfounded distress as a result of the information obtained. As the language, width and quality of information on the internet cannot be separated, cyberchondria may be seen in people who did not have any previous health concerns. The ability to make a critical evaluation is only possible by gaining e-health literacy.

In this section, the correlation between e-health literacy and cyberchondria, one of the reflections of digitalization in the field of health, will be discussed. In this context, first of all, a framework related to these concepts will be set forth. After this, the field research will reveal whether there is relevance between e-health literacy and cyberchondria, whether e-health literacy affects cyberchondria, and whether socio-demographic characteristics create a difference at the level of e-health literacy and cyberchondria.

Conceptual Framework

The Fourth Industrial Revolution, known as Industry 4.0 (Ajmera and Jain, 2019: 130; Rehman et al., 2019: 556), and the information and communication technologies that facilitate this structure, is gradually changing the world of service and production, and the scope is moved to Health 4.0 with the integration of Industry 4.0 to health (Aceto et al., 2020: 1; Ajmera and Jain, 2019: 129; Bause et al., 2019: 888; Mesko, 2020: 20). The objectives of health personalization, virtualization in healthcare services, and improving the technology and healthcare services lie behind the concept of Health 4.0 (Bause et al., 2019: 888). The field of healthcare has undergone various transformations from 1.0 to 4.0 in parallel with the development processes of the industrial revolution. The physician-centered Health 1.0, in which physicians were manually keeping patient records, was followed by Health 2.0, which involved electronic health records. Computerization has dominated the patient-centered Health 3.0 and this era has further progressed to the point where wearable devices are put into service (Hathaliya et al., 2019: 398). The feature that distinguishes Health 4.0 from other eras is that many devices of different types communicate with each other and with individuals; the execution of healthcare activities is driven by the internet of things, the internet of services, and cyber-physical systems (Ajmera and Jain, 2019: 130; Rehman et al., 2019: 557). Health 4.0 is making the healthcare services more predictive, collaborative, and convergent (Ajmera and Jain, 2019: 130; Bause et al., 2019: 887).

It is indicated that the concept of “digital health”, which is the key element of Health 4.0, was created based on the concept of “e-health” (WHO, 2019a: 1), and marks the next stage of e-health, taking into account the technological changes as well (ThinkTech, 2019: 4). E-health is the safe and cost-effective use of information and communication technologies (ICT) with the aim of supporting health and health-related areas, including healthcare services, health literature, health surveillance, and health education, information and research (WHA, 2005: 109). Eysenbach (2001: 1) states that the meaning of "e", which refers to the first letter of the term e-health, is not only "electronic", but also includes a series of "e" concepts as to what e-health is and what it should be (such as efficiency, enhancing the quality of care, evidence-based and empowerment of consumers and patients). E-health, which was previously discussed as an umbrella concept for terms such as tele-medicine, mobile health, and the digital hospital (Kılıç, 2017: 205; ThinkTech, 2019: 5-6) has expanded its scope under the concept of digital health with the development of fields such as the use of computer science (big data, artificial intelligence, genomics, etc.) as well as itself (WHO, 2020). Digital health can be characterized as the integration of various technologies and electronic services with health in order to improve medical care and supervision (Morrison, 2017: 2; von Eiff and von Eiff, 2020: 182). The WHO has comprehensively redefined digital health as "the field of knowledge and practice associated with any aspect of adopting digital technologies to improve health, from inception to operation" in its publication within the framework of the vision of "improving health for everyone, everywhere by accelerating the development and adoption of appropriate digital health solutions" (WHO, 2019b: 2).

Digital health includes elements such as the internet, wireless devices, hardware and software sensors, health information technologies, microprocessors, and mobile networks. Because of these elements, the term is regarded as an umbrella term for many fields such as e-health, mobile health, personalized medicine, telemedicine, telehealth, remote patient monitoring, social networks, digital forums, data analysis at the individual and population level and wearable technologies (Lampariello and Labrique, 2020: 266; Lowery, 2020: 216; Morrison, 2017: 2). While it is emphasized that digital health is important for enhancing the quality and accessibility of health services (Levin-Zamir and Parial, 2020: 1), the mentioned "accessibility" no longer refers to physical access but rather virtual access (Mitchel and Kan, 2019: 114), such that an online health search made by an individual can be considered as a dimension of digital health (Lampariello and Labrique, 2020: 266). Digital health is paving the way towards a future which focuses on real-time, personalized care direct-to-consumer, is able to make consistent decisions, provide preventive measures with a proactive approach, and create value together with the patient (Ajmera and Jain, 2019: 130; Bause et al., 2019: 887; Lowery, 2020: 222).

Based on the literature, Aceto et al. (2020: 5-6) compiled the possible scenarios that Health 4.0 will make possible as follows: monitoring physiological-pathological signals, self-management prevention, monitoring drug intake-smart drug use, personalized health services, development of elements such as cloud-based health information systems, telepathology-telemedicine, assisted living and rehabilitation. Similarly, in other studies, it is stated that digital health will provide ease of access, can save costs and time, enhance the continuity of care and decision-making processes, enable the remote management of chronic illnesses, prevent exposure to infectious diseases, avert unnecessary hospitalization processes and emergency care visits and provide treatment follow-up opportunities for patients who especially live in rural and remote areas or cannot leave their place of residence (Işık, 2019: 1980-1982; Lowery, 2020: 219; von Eiff and von Eiff, 2020: 182). On the other hand, factors such as unreliable online sources, possible misinterpretation of information by patients, concerns about data security-quality-confidentiality, secrecy, lack of training in human resources, legal and administrative problems, technical infrastructure problems, a digital divide that can be experienced according to the differences in development levels of countries and rapidly changing demands can be seen as obstacles to digital health (Dhingra and Dabas 2020: 357; Işık, 2019: 1982; Mesko, 2020: 20; Mitchel and Kan, 2019: 117; Rehman et al., 2019: 559; WHO, 2019b: 4).

Individuals are increasingly having a voice in coping with disease and protecting their health, and their responsibilities are increasing with the digitalization of health (Işık, 2019: 1984). The internet is regarded as the principal source during the search for health information by users (AlGhamdi and Moussa, 2012: 364), digital technologies offer individuals the opportunity to instantly access health information (Chong et al., 2020: 1) and the focus is changing from "patient" to "person", i.e., from passivity to autonomy (Robbins and Dunn, 2019: 154). This is undoubtedly due to the fact that access to health information on the internet is easy, cheap and fast, bureaucratic obstacles are skipped, there is a lack of waiting in queues and the process takes place anonymously (Starcevic and Berle, 2013: 205). However, most of the information existing on the internet can be incorrect, incomplete or out of date, even commercial, confusing and harmful (AlGhamdi and Moussa, 2012: 364). It is considered crucial for individuals to make critical evaluations of the information they have acquired with the expanding range of online health information resources and the increasing number of internet users; the skill sets to harness this information and to cope with the digital health environment are referred to as *"e-health literacy"* (or digital health literacy) (Levin-Zamir and Parial, 2020: 3;

Monkman and Kushniruk, 2015: 542-543; Shiferaw et al., 2020: 2). If the objective of e-health is to improve the health of the public with the services it provides, the gap between the offered e-health resources and the ability to use these resources should be eliminated; this is possible with e-health literacy (Norman & Skinner, 2006a: 1).

E-health literacy is expressed as the integration of "e-health" with "health literacy" and "the ability to search, find, understand, evaluate and use information about health from electronic sources to process or solve a health problem" (Norman and Skinner, 2006a: 2). Bautista (2015: 35-43) stated that this definition is the first step towards functionalization; however, he/she proposed a new definition on the grounds that important factors such as digital technologies are not taken into account: "E-health literacy is the interaction of individual and social factors in the use of digital technologies to search, acquire, comprehend, evaluate, communicate and apply health information in all contexts of healthcare with the aim of maintaining or improving the quality of life throughout life".

Using the metaphor of the lily, Norman and Skinner (2006a: 2) presented the *Lily Model* for e-health literacy. According to this model, e-health literacy refers to the cluster of six basic abilities *(traditional literacy and numeracy, science literacy, information literacy, media literacy, health literacy and computer literacy)*; e-health literacy connects these abilities at the center, while lily leaves represent the literacy. The literacies organized in two types including *analytical* (traditional, media, information) and *contextual* (computer, science, health) are combined to optimize individuals' e-health experiences. Although not all ability types can be mastered, it is important to be moderately competent in order to benefit from e-health resources. Lack of one of the abilities can restrain the utilization of e-health information. In these days when the COVID-19 pandemic still continues, e-health literacy seems more important than ever. As a matter of fact, it is noteworthy that in such times, e-health literacy is not an optional or luxurious approach for the reliable and effective delivery of healthcare services with the internet and related technologies (Shiferaw et al., 2020: 2).

In addition to digital health barriers, the utilization effects of digital health technologies are questioned when there is no disease present or when existing diseases mean small blows, rather than milestones in an individual's life (Mesko, 2020: 23). Indeed, the internet may have the potential to increase health anxiety when it is used as a diagnostic methodology by people without medical education (White and Horvitz, 2009: 1). The phenomenon referring to the search for health-related information, begun on the internet to alleviate anxiety, which is "excessive" or "constantly" repeated and consequently causes greater unfounded distress, is defined as *"cyberchondria"* (Muse et al., 2012: 189; Starcevic and Berle, 2013: 206). Although healthcare professionals have not yet reached a consensus on its definition/scope and there is still terminological confusion existing in the concept, it is becoming popular with the effect of the media (Loos, 2013: 439; Startevic and Berle, 2015: 107; Starcevic et al., 2020: 1).

Cyberchondria is derived from the words "cyber" and "hypochondriasis"; and it refers to a form of hypochondriasis occurring on the basis of internet usage and perhaps even a form caused by internet usage (Starcevic and Berle, 2013: 206). Although not yet certain, it is indicated that the term first appeared in a report of Business Wire in 1996 (Loos, 2013: 439-440); some researchers trace the article of Ann Carrns for this term, which was published in the Wall Street Journal in 1999 (Startevic and Berle, 2013: 206). The concept consists of a multidimensional structure with five components which are also explained as sub-factors in the scale studies regarding cyberchondria. Dimensions are as follows: *compulsion*, which indicates that online health information research will interrupt daily life activities; *distress*, which refers to negative emotional consequences and physiological reactions associated with search behavior; *excessiveness*, which refers to the ever-increasing, time-consuming and repetitive nature of these search activities; *mistrust*, which refers to the internal conflict about whether to trust the information obtained as a result of searching or the physicians; and finally, *reassurance*, which refers to the desire to consult medical professionals and obtain assurance from experts regarding the information acquired after searching (Barke et al., 2016: 596; McElroy and Shevlin, 2014: 263-264; Starcevic and Berle, 2015: 108).

Cyberchondria can occur in an effort to quench the curiosity caused by searching a symptom that a person carries or seeing the title of a "new disease" on any news site. The availability of new medical studies that contradict previous studies, the discovery of dangerous side effects of drugs, or research studies conducted on the unknown risks of routine procedures can trigger cyberchondria (Startevic and Berle, 2015: 113). Although it is stated in many studies that cyberchondria is associated with health anxiety (Barke et al., 2016: 598; Batıgün et al., 2018: 7; Fergus, 2013: 737; Muse et al., 2012: 193; Norr et al., 2015: 61), it is believed that it may occur even in individuals who have not had health concerns before as a result of the abundance, language and quality of information available on the internet (Te Poel et al., 2016: 33). At the same time, the relevant results listed when looking for health information from search engines are not based on accuracy or prevalence; rather, they are listed according to the frequency of visits, popularity of access, and commercial features such as advertising

(Barke et al., 2016: 596). White and Horvitz (2009: 28-29) indicate that people are directed to pages that will result in more serious and rare diseases by searching for simple symptoms online. Negative features of the internet and inadequacies in terms of online health information increase uncertainty regarding health, which may pave the way for cyberchondria for individuals who have difficulty in tolerating uncertainty (Fergus, 2013: 735-736; Uzun, 2016: 12).

In a qualitative research study conducted to comprehend cyberchondria, McManus et al. (2014: 6) state that participants concerned about epidemics cited that the internet is a potential tool in preventing or limiting the disease by obtaining timely and additional information. The widespread use of online health resources makes COVID-19 unprecedented among other epidemics. In unconventional and new situations such as epidemics, it is not easy to make sense of vast amounts of information as contradictory and ambiguous fake news spreads out, and conducting symptom research becomes ordinary. The pandemic environment becomes a fertile ground for cyberchondria with the abundance of unconfirmed and constantly updated online health information and the questionable reliability of this information, and, it is stated that exposure to this information and excessive information overload trigger stress with the inability to assess and process the information and cause cyberchondria (Laato et al., 2020: 3-7; Stracevic, Berle and Arnáez, 2020: 5). In the present pandemic period, the term "infodemic" comes to the fore with the aim of referring to erroneous or unreal information disseminated through different channels on the internet that may cause uncertainty and anxiety; the importance of e-health literacy is being emphasized in crediting accurate, quality and scientific health data (Chong et al., 2020: 1). As a matter of fact, the internet contains a vast amount of uncontrolled health information, which is unfiltered. In the digital age, where the internet is the main resource for health information, the solution to "avoid" doing online research for the prevention and management of cyberchondria is unrealistic. The focus of prevention efforts should be making a critical evaluation, that is, improving e-health literacy (Starcevic & Berle, 2015: 113; Stracevic et al., 2020: 7-8).

Research

The objective of the study is to examine the effect of e-health literacy on cyberchondria. In addition, it is further aimed to determine whether the e-health literacy and cyberchondria levels of the participants differ depending on the socio-demographic variables. The following hypotheses have been built and the research model has been created in line with the determined objectives of the research:

H1: Socio-demographic characteristics of the participants make a significant difference in their e-health literacy levels.

H2: Socio-demographic characteristics of the participants make a significant difference in their cyberchondria levels.

H3: There is a significant correlation between e-health literacy and cyberchondria levels.

H4: E-health literacy has a significant effect at the level of cyberchondria.

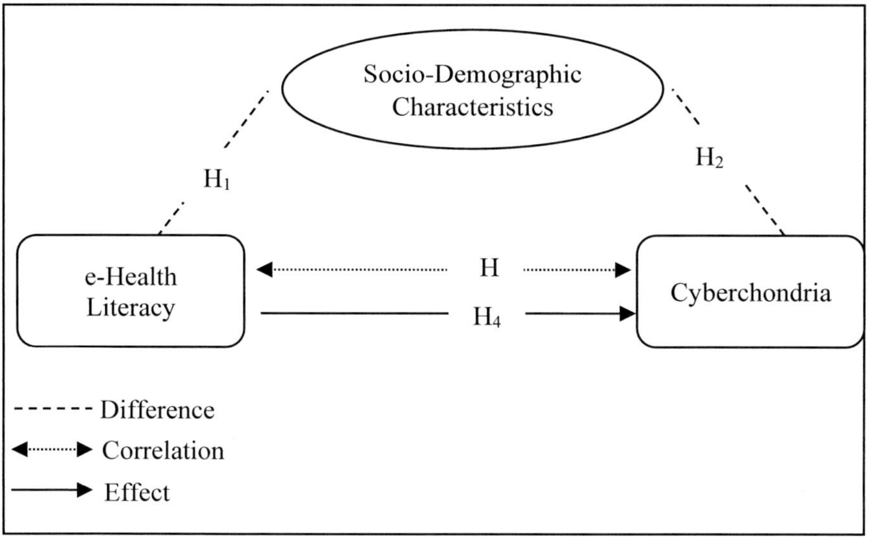

Figure 15.1: Research Model

The research population consists of individuals who reside in Eskişehir province in the Republic of Turkey; they are over the age of 18, literate and have basic internet usage competence. The simple random sampling method is used in the study. The sample size that could represent the research population is calculated as 384 people at the confidence level of 95% (Karagöz, 2014: 15). Data were collected from 407 individuals for the study, and 12 unusable surveys were not included in the study. Accordingly, the sample of the study consists of 395 individuals.

In the study, two different scales and a survey form consisting of socio-demographic characteristics of the participants were used as data collection tools. The *"e-Health Literacy Scale (e-HEALS)"*, which was developed by Norman and Skinner (2006b) and adapted into Turkish by Gencer (2017) after conducting a validity and reliability study, was used in order to measure the e-health literacy level of individuals. The scale is one-dimensional and consists of 8 items. The Cronbach's Alpha value of the scale was determined as 0.88 in the original study (Norman & Skinner, 2006b: 4); and as 0.915 in the Turkish adaptation study (Gencer, 2017: 143). The *"Cyberchondria Severity Scale (SCS)"*, which was developed by McElroy and Shevlin (2014) and adapted into Turkish by Uzun (2016) after conducting a validity and reliability study, was used in order to measure individuals' cyberchondria. The SCS is a 33-item scale consisting of 5 dimensions: reassurance (6 items), distress (8 items), excessiveness (8 items), mistrust (3 items) and compulsion (8 items). The items regarding the dimension of mistrust are inverse. In the original study of the scale, the Cronbach's Alpha value was determined as 0.94 and the sub-dimensions were determined as 0.89 in reassurance, 0.92 in distress, 0.85 in excessiveness, 0.75 in mistrust and 0.95 in compulsion (McElroy and Shevlin, 2014: 262). In the Turkish adaptation study of the scale, the Cronbach's Alpha value was determined as 0.89 and the sub-dimensions were determined as 0.78 in reassurance, 0.84 in distress, 0.86 in excessiveness, 0.65 in mistrust and 0.85 in compulsion (Uzun, 2016: 49). As a result of the exploratory factor analysis conducted, it was stated that the sample size for both scales was sufficient and the data set was suitable for the factor analysis. The scales used are designed in a 5-point Likert structure. The last part of the research survey consists of questions to determine the socio-demographic characteristics of the participants.

In the analysis of the data; descriptive statistical methods, correlation analysis, regression analysis, independent-samples t-test and one-way analysis of variance were used. As a result of one-way analysis of variance, the Scheffe test was implemented in order to determine the difference between groups. Data were analyzed at a 95% confidence level ($p = 0.05$). The IBM SPSS Statistics program was utilized for data analysis.

The Cronbach's Alpha coefficient was utilized to test the reliability of the scales used in the study. According to the results, the Cronbach's Alpha value of the e-health literacy scale was determined as 0. 947. The Cronbach's Alpha value of the cyberchondria severity scale was determined as 0.967 and the sub-dimensions were determined as: 0.890 in reassurance; 0.925 in distress; 0.951 in excessiveness; 0.900 in mistrust; and 0.965 in compulsion. The scales are highly reliable, as the values remain between $0.80 \leq \alpha < 1.00$ (Kalaycı, 2014: 405). Since the Turkish adaptations of the scales used within the scope of the study were made, they were discovered before. For this reason, exploratory factor analysis was not implemented in the study, but confirmatory factor analysis was carried out (X2/ sd: e-HEALS = 1.037 Cyberchondria = 1.908; RMSA: e-HEALS = 0.017 Cyberchondria = 0.048; RMR: e-HEALS = 0.076 Cyberchondria = 0.054; NFI: e-HEALS = 0.998 Cyberchondria = 0.948; CFI: e-HEALS = 0.998 Cyberchondria = 1.974; GFI: e-HEALS = 0.997 Cyberchondria = 0.901; AGFI: e-HEALS = 0.997 Cyberchondria = 0.857). According to the results, it was determined that the values remained within the acceptance range (Meydan and Şeşen, 2015: 37) and the goodness of fit for the scales was appropriate.

Results

In the study, 58.5% (n = 231) of the participants were women and 57% (n = 225) were single individuals. Looking at the age distribution of the participants, it is seen that the largest group at 25.6% (n = 101) is the 18-25 age range, and, the smallest group at 10.7% (n = 42) is the age range ≥56. When the educational status is examined, the largest group among the participants is associate/undergraduate degree graduates with 46.6% (n = 184), while the smallest group is postgraduate degree graduates with 12.2% (n = 48). 81.8% (n = 323) of the participants do not have a chronic illness.

Table 15.1: Distribution of the participants by socio-demographic characteristics

	Characteristics	(n)	(%)
Gender	Female	231	58.5
	Male	164	41.5
Marital Status	Married	170	43.0
	Single	225	57.0
Age	18-25	101	25.6
	26-35	98	24.8
	36-45	91	23.0
	46-55	63	15.9
	≥ 56	42	10.7
Educational Status	Primary/Secondary Education	55	13.9
	High School	108	27.3
	Associate/Bachelor's Degree	184	46.6
	Postgraduate Degree	48	12.2
Chronic Illness	Present	72	18.2
	Not Present	323	81.8

When the mean and standard deviation values of the scales used in the study are examined, the e-health literacy levels of the individuals participating in the study (3.47±0.918) are slightly above the medium; while, cyberchondria severity levels (2.64±0.821) are slightly below the medium. Looking at the sub-dimensions of cyberchondria; it can be seen that participation in the dimensions of reassurance (2.88±0.966), distress (3.15±0.953) and excessiveness (2.69±1.077) is at the medium level. Participation in the dimensions of mistrust (2.28±1.223) and compulsion (2.22±1.028) is at lower levels.

According to the results of the gap analysis presented in Table 15.2, gender and the presence of chronic illness do not make a significant difference in terms of e-health literacy and cyberchondria and its sub-dimensions ($p > 0.05$). The marital status of the participants, on the other hand, creates a statistically significant difference for both variables and their sub-dimensions as well ($p < 0.05$). Participants with a single marital status (3.37±0.874) have lower e-health literacy levels compared to those who are married (3.60±0.961). On the other hand, the severity levels of cyberchondria are higher for the single participants (2.80±0.808) compared to the participants who are married (2.43±0.790). A similar situation is also observed in all sub-dimensions of cyberchondria. Accordingly, it can be reported that single individuals participate less in a positive situation such as e-health literacy; and more in a negative situation such as cyberchondria.

Age groups of the participants do not make a significant difference in terms of e-health literacy ($p > 0.05$). In contrast, there is a statistically significant difference in cyberchondria and its sub-dimensions according to age groups ($p < 0.05$). The difference in the level of cyberchondria stems from the participants in the 18-25 (2.89±0.759) and 46-55 (2.43±0.737) age groups and participants in the ≥56 (2.21±0.588), the 26-35 age group (2.81±0.954) and the ≥56 age group (2.21±0.588). When the sub-dimensions of cyberchondria are examined, the difference in the dimension of reassurance stems from the participants in the ≥56 age group (2.46±0.867) and participants in the 18-25 age group (3.07±0.860) and the 26-35 age group (3.06±1.086). The difference in the dimension of distress stems from the participants in the 18-25 age group (3.43±0.727) and the 36-45 (2.98±0.930) age group and participants in the ≥56 age group (2.83±0.912). The difference in the dimension of excessiveness stems from the participants in the 18-25 age group (2.95±1.070) and participants in the ≥56 age group (2.28±0.830). The difference in the dimension of mistrust stems from the participants in the 18-25 age group (2.59±1.229) and the 46-55 age group (1.94±0.967) and participants in the ≥56 (1.74±0.781), 26-35

(2.59±1.443), 46-55 (1.94±0.967) and ≥56 age groups (1.74±0.781). Finally, the difference in the dimension of compulsion stems from the participants in the ≥56 age group (1.73±0.871) and the 18-25 age group (2.40±1.099) and participants in the 26-35 age group (2.37±1.169). As the age group moves up, it is seen that there is a tendency for a decrease in the averages of cyberchondria and its sub-dimensions. According to this result, individuals' cyberchondria severity increases as their ages decrease.

While the educational status of the participants does not make a significant difference in terms of e-health literacy ($p > 0.05$), it is seen that statistically there is significant difference in cyberchondria and in the sub-dimensions of cyberchondria except compulsion ($p < 0.05$). The difference in the level of cyberchondria stems from the participants who are primary education graduates (2.33±0.735) and associate/bachelor's degree graduates (2.77±0.821) and postgraduates (2.91±0.872); and high school graduates (2.47±0.762) and also associate/bachelor's degree graduates (2.77±0.821) and postgraduates (2.91±0.872). When the sub-dimensions are examined, the difference in the dimension of reassurance stems from the participants who are primary education graduates (2.40±0.916) and associate/bachelor's degree graduates (3.04±0.969) and postgraduates (3.17±0.898); and high school graduates (2.71±0.907) and associate/bachelor's degree graduates (3.04±0.969) and postgraduates (3.17±0.898). The difference in the dimension of distress stems from the participants who are primary education graduates (2.81±1.025) and associate/bachelor's degree graduates (3.33±0.918) and postgraduates (3.34±0.883); and high school graduates (2.94±0.923) and associate/bachelor's degree graduates (3.33±0.918). The difference in the dimension of excessiveness stems from the participants who are primary education graduates (2.43±1.029), associate/bachelor's degree graduates (2.81±1.092) and postgraduates (2.91±1.207); and high school graduates (2.53±0.977), associate/bachelor's degree graduates (2.81±1.092) and postgraduates (2.91±1.207). The difference in the dimension of mistrust stems from the participants who are primary education graduates (1.88±1.035) and associate/bachelor's degree graduates (2.41±1.250) and postgraduates (2.65±1.304). As a result of these findings, it is observed that participants' cyberchondria severity increases as their education levels increase. Based on these findings, the H_1 hypothesis was accepted in terms of marital status; on the other hand, H_2 was accepted in terms of marital status, age and educational status.

Table 15.2: Gap analysis results according to socio-demographic characteristics

Variables	Reassurance	Distress	Excessiveness	Mistrust	Compulsion	Cyberchondria	E-HEL
Gender							
Female	2.85	3.21	2.77	2.34	2.18	2.67	3.39
Male	2.91	3.07	2.58	2.19	2.28	2.61	3.58
	t: -.638	t: 1.436	t: 1.672	t: 1.233	t: -.953	t: .752	t: -1.958
	p = .524	*p = .152*	*p = .095*	*p = .218*	*p = .341*	*p = .453*	*p = .051*
Marital Status							
Married	2.63	2.91	2.50	2.09	2.02	2.43	3.60
Single	3.06	3.33	2.84	2.43	2.37	2.80	3.37
	t: -4.413	t: -4.333	t: -3.136	t: -2.746	t: -3.515	t: -4.614	t: 2.446
	p = .000	***p = .001***	***p = .002***	***p = .006***	***p = .000***	***p = .000***	***p = .015***
Age							
18-25	3.07	3.43	2.95	2.59	2.40	2.89	3.37
26-35	3.06	3.27	2.75	2.59	2.37	2.81	3.37
36-45	2.80	2.98	2.68	2.09	2.16	2.54	3.61
46-55	2.66	2.98	2.46	1.94	2.12	2.43	3.49
≥56	2.46	2.83	2.28	1.74	1.73	2.21	3.59
	F: 4.939	F: 5.188	F: 3.943	F: 7.475	F: 3.929	F: 8.091	F: 1.353
	p = .001	***p = .000***	***p = .004***	***p = .000***	***p = .004***	***p = .000***	*p = .250*
Educational Status							
Primary Education	2.40	2.81	2.43	1.88	2.11	2.33	3.26
High School	2.71	2.94	2.53	2.09	2.10	2.47	3.60
Associate/Bachelor's Degree	3.04	3.33	2.81	2.41	2.27	2.77	3.44
Postgraduate Degree	3.17	3.34	2.91	2.65	2.45	2.91	3.53
	F: 9.336	F: 7.212	F: 3.287	F: 5.214	F: 1.673	F: 7.780	F: 1.784
	p = .000	***p = .001***	***p = .021***	***p = .002***	*p = .172*	***p = .000***	*p = .150*
Chronic Illness							
Present	2.80	3.15	2.68	2.31	2.40	2.67	3.30
Not Present	2.89	3.15	2.69	2.27	2.18	2.64	3.51
	t: -.747	t: .001	t: -.121	t: .224	t: 1.676	t: .247	t: -1.619
	p = .456	*p = .999*	*p = .904*	*p = .823*	*p = .094*	*p = .805*	*p = .109*

Table 15.3 presents the results of the correlation analysis conducted in order to analyze the relations between e-health literacy and cyberchondria and its sub-dimensions. When the table is examined, it is observed that there is a statistically significant correlation between both scales and sub-dimensions. There is a poor negative correlation between e-health literacy and cyberchondria ($r = -0.305$; $p < 0.01$). Similarly, there is a poor negative correlation between e-health literacy and the following sub-dimensions of cyberchondria: excessiveness ($r = -0.248$; $p < 0.01$), mistrust ($r = -0.311$; $p < 0.01$) and compulsion ($r = -0.299$; $p < 0.01$), while there is a highly poor negative correlation between reassurance ($r = -0.195$; $p < 0.01$) and distress ($r = -0.111$; $p < 0.05$).

When the relationships between the sub-dimensions of cyberchondria are considered, it is seen that except for mistrust, other dimensions are in a positive medium/strong correlation with each other. There is a poor positive correlation between the dimension of mistrust and other dimensions. The highest level of correlation is determined between excessiveness and reassurance ($r = 0.753$; $p < 0.01$), on the other hand, the lowest level of relation is determined between mistrust and distress ($r = 0.250$; $p < 0.01$). Based on these findings, the H_3 hypothesis was accepted.

Table 15.3: Correlation between e-health literacy and cyberchondria

	1	2	3	4	5	6
Reassurance (1)	1					
Distress (2)	.659**	1				
Excessiveness (3)	.753**	.635**	1			
Mistrust (4)	.288**	.250**	.364**	1		
Compulsion (5)	.623**	.572**	.752**	.402**	1	
Cyberchondria (6)	.821**	.772**	.877**	.620**	.847**	1
E-Health Literacy (7)	-.195**	-.111*	-.248**	-.311**	-.299**	**-.305****

** Correlation is significant at the 0.01 level (2-tailed)
* Correlation is significant at the 0.05 level (2-tailed)

A summary of the regression models developed in order to test the effects of the correlation between e-health literacy and cyberchondria is presented in Table 15.4. As one can see, e-health literacy has a statistically significant effect on cyberchondria and all sub-dimensions of cyberchondria ($p < 0.05$).

The regression model created in order to measure the effect of e-health literacy on cyberchondria is significant ($F = 40.171$; $p = 0.000$), and e-health literacy has a negative effect (= -0.272) on cyberchondria. However, e-health literacy has an explanatory effect of 9.3% in predicting the severity of cyberchondria. In other words, although e-health literacy is limited, it affects cyberchondria; a possible increase in term of e-health literacy could lead to a decrease in cyberchondria severity.

Models created in order to predict the effect of e-health literacy on the sub-dimensions of reassurance (F = 15.461; p = 0.000), distress (F = 4.906; p = 0.027), excessiveness (F = 25.753; p = 0.000), mistrust (F = 42.163; p = 0.000) and compulsion (F = 38.723; p = 0.000) are also significant. E-health literacy has a negative effect on all sub-dimensions of cyberchondria (reassurance: β = -0.195; distress: β = -0.111; excessiveness: β = -0.248; mistrust: β = -0.311; compulsion: β = -0.299). E-health literacy accounts for the dimension of reassurance by 3.8%; the dimension of distress by 1.2%; the dimension of excessiveness by 6.2%; the dimension of mistrust by 9.7% and the dimension of compulsion by 9%. Based on these findings, the H_4 hypothesis was accepted.

Table 15.4: The effect of e-health literacy on cyberchondria

Dependent Variables	Independent Variable	Unstandardized Coefficients		Standardized Coefficients	t	p	R	R^2	F	p
		B	S.H.	β						
Reassurance	(Constant)	3.586	.187		19.186	.000	.195	.038	15.461	.000
	E-HEL	-.205	.052	-.195	-3.932	.000				
Distress	(Constant)	3.551	.187		19.016	.000	.111	.012	4.906	.027
	E-HEL	-.115	.052	-.111	-2.215	.027				
Excessiveness	(Constant)	3.703	.206		17.986	.000	.248	0.062	25.753	.000
	E-HEL	-,291	.057	-.248	-5.075	.000				
Mistrust	(Constant)	3.720	.229		16.230	.000	.311	.097	42.163	.000
	E-HEL	-.414	.064	-.311	-6.493	.000				
Compulsion	(Constant)	3.386	.194		17.494	.000	.299	.090	38.723	.000
	E-HEL	-.335	.054	-.299	-6.223	.000				
Cyberchondria	(Constant)	3.589	.154		23.379	.000	.305	.093	40.171	.000
	E-HEL	-.272	.043	-.305	-6.338	.000				

Discussion and Conclusion

This study was conducted with the aim of determining the effect of e-health literacy on cyberchondria and revealing whether socio-demographic characteristics make a difference at the levels of e-health literacy and cyberchondria. According to the results of the study, the cyberchondria levels of the participants are slightly below the medium level. When other studies are examined, it is observed that the mean cyberchondria score is lower (Fergus and Russell, 2016: 90; Norr et al., 2015: 61). In this sense, the level of cyberchondria of the participants is higher than the average of the general literature. As digitalization in healthcare is increasing day by day, this may cause individuals to have an increasingly higher cyberchondria level. Different studies conducted support the results of the research study (Elçiyar and Taşçı, 2017: 239; Başoğlu, 2018: 50). The sub-dimensions of cyberchondria are generally at intermediate levels in line with the scale as well. According to another result of the study, the e-health literacy levels of the participants are slightly above the medium level. It is seen that parallel results were also obtained in other studies (Park et al., 2016: 72; Tennant et al., 2015).

The gender of the participants and the presence of chronic illness do not make a statistically significant difference in e-health literacy; and, there is a statistically significant difference between marital status and e-health literacy. Married individuals are more likely to participate in e-health literacy compared to single individuals. It is believed that married individuals tend to search for online health information for themselves, as well as their spouses and children, and that this situation may improve their e-health literacy skills. The age and educational status of the participants do not make a statistically significant difference in terms of e-health literacy. While different studies support the results of the research in terms of gender and the presence of chronic illness; it was concluded that the level of e-health literacy increased as the age decreased and the education level increased (Paige et al., 2017: 56; Tennant et al., 2015: 11-12; Witten and Humphry, 2018: 54). This result is explained as follows: older people may have difficulty in learning new skills with less internet experience; on the other hand, individuals with a higher education level may have more strategic skills in interpreting online information (van Deursen & van Dijk, 2011: 7-8). However, on the contrary, there are also studies stating that education level does not make an additional contribution to internet skills and concluding that age and educational status do not make any difference in e-health literacy (Deniz, 2020: 90; Norman & Skinner, 2006b: 4; Park et al., 2016: 75).

The gender of the participants and the presence of chronic illness do not make a statistically significant difference in terms of cyberchondria and its sub-dimensions. In other studies, it was found that gender (Elçiyar and Taşçı, 2017: 239; Batıgün et al., 2018: 9; Deniz, 2020: 90) and chronic illness (Uzun, 2016: 56) did not make a difference either. Marital status, age, and educational status make a statistically significant difference in cyberchondria and its sub-dimensions. The participation of single individuals in cyberchondria and its sub-dimensions is higher compared to married individuals. At the same time, it was determined that the level of cyberchondria increased as the age decreased and the education level increased. The higher prevalence of cyberchondria in the young population is explained by the higher rate of internet use among this generation and their preference for anonymous access to medical information (Lewis, 2006: 530). It is believed that individuals with a higher level of education may be more aware of different information sources other than health professionals and can access this information more easily; therefore, this may form the ground for cyberchondria. The results obtained by different studies also coincide with the results of the study (Tüter, 2019: 33-35; Uzun, 2016: 55).

According to the results, there is a poor significant negative correlation between e-health literacy and cyberchondria and its sub-dimensions. It can be said that as individuals' e-health literacy level increases, their cyberchondria levels will change in the opposite direction. When the correlation between the sub-dimensions of cyberchondria are examined, there are positive, strong or nearly strong correlations among the dimensions except for the dimension of mistrust. According to this result, it is thought that negative emotions, reactions and behaviors that make up the dimensions foster each other, but the health search activities conducted do not change the individual's confidence in the knowledge of the physician. Similar results were also obtained in different studies (McElroy and Shevlin, 2014: 263; Norr et al., 2015: 61).

According to another important result of the study, e-health literacy has a negative effect on cyberchondria and all its sub-dimensions. There are different studies investigating whether there is a correlation between e-health literacy and cyberchondria, but the effects of the relations have not been tested. In these mentioned studies, a correlation was found between e-health literacy and cyberchondria; however, in contrast to the results of the research, it was determined that this correlation was positive (Beydağ and Güldür, 2019: 375; Deniz, 2020: 92). The researcher states that this case may be related to the time spent on the internet (Deniz, 2020: 92). Internet usage experience can enhance e-health literacy. However, individuals bearing this skill are expected to be able to distinguish between diagnostic information that causes distress and unfounded diagnostic information by accessing accurate and reliable online health resources and filtering the information in accordance with the definition. In the literature, it is stated that individuals' health concerns can be reduced by increasing health literacy (Tüter, 2019: 10), and people who are not competent to assess online health information can make a false diagnosis (Cole, 2014: 10). This is given that distress, the negative correlation found by Beyoğlu (2019: 69) between distress and health literacy may support the result of the study. It is thought that more clear/generalizable results may emerge when the limited number of studies is increased.

The following recommendations are made in line with the results of the study: creating reliable online health information pages with the cooperation of experts from different disciplines; screening and controlling accurate, complete and out-of-date information; carrying out awareness activities in cooperation with stakeholders such as the Ministry of Health, the Ministry of National Education, academic communities and non-governmental organizations in order to adapt the society to digital health and increase the level of e-health literacy; and adding cyberchondria and e-health literacy to the curriculum of education levels in the field of health. The study is important in terms of revealing whether e-health literacy and cyberchondria differ according to socio-demographic variables and also indicating the effect of e-health literacy on cyberchondria.

Keywords: *E-health, e-health literacy, cyberchondria*

References

Aceto, G., Persico, V. & Pescape, A. (2020). Industry 4.0 and health: Internet of things, big data, and cloud computing for Healthcare 4.0. *Journal of Industrial Information Integration, 18*, 1-17.

Ajmera, P. & Jain, V. (2019). Modelling the barriers of Health 4.0-the fourth healthcare industrial revolution in India by TISM. *Operations Management Research, 12*(3), 129-145.

AlGhamdi, K.M. & Moussa, N.A. (2012). Internet use by the public to search for health-related information. *International Journal of Medical Informatics, 81*(6), 363-373.

Barke, A., Bleichhardt, G., Rief, W. & Doering, B.K. (2016). The Cyberchondria Severity Scale (CSS): German validation and development of a short form. *International Journal of Behavioral Medicine, 23*(5), 595-605.

Başoğlu, M.A. (2018). *Investigation of cyberchondria's connection with trait anxiety and psychological well-being in women 15-49 years in Edirne province center.* (Unpublished specialty thesis in medicine). Trakya University Faculty of Medicine, Edirne.

Batıgün, A.D., Gör, N., Kömürcü, B. & Şenkal Ertürk, İ. (2018). Cyberchondria Scale (CS): Development, validity and reliability study. *The Journal of Psychiatry and Neurological Sciences, 31*(2), 148-162.

Bause, M., Khayamian Esfahani, B., Forbes, H. & Schaefer, D. (2019). *Design for Health 4.0: Exploration of a new area.* Proceedings of the

22nd International Conference on Engineering Design (ICED19), Delft, The Netherlands.

Bautista, J.R. (2015). From solving a health problem to achieving quality of life: Redefining eHealth literacy. *Journal of Literacy and Technology, 16*(2), 33-54.

Beydağ, K.D. & Güldür, A. (2019, Nisan). *Health literacy and cyberchondria level of pregnant women with online health seeking behavior.* 3rd International Congress on Woman and Child Health and Education, Trabzon.

Beyoğlu, M.M. (2019). *Examination of the relationship between health literacy, concern and anxiety in adults with diabetes mellitus or hypertension and comparison with individuals without chronic disease.* (Unpublished specialty thesis in medicine). Yüzüncü Yıl University Faculty of Medicine, Van.

Chong, Y.Y., Cheng, H.Y., Chan, H.Y.L., Chien, W.T. & Wong, S.Y.S. (2020). COVID-19 pandemic, infodemic and the role of eHealth literacy. *International Journal of Nursing Studies*, *108*, 1-2.

Cinelli, M., Quattrociocchi, W., Galeazzi, A., Valensise, C.M., Brugnoli, E., Schmidt, A.L., … Scala, A. (2020). The COVID-19 social media infodemic. *Sci Rep, 10*(16598), 1-10.

Cole, A.W. (2014). *College student lay health information mediary behavior: An examination of eHealth literacy and unrequested health advice.* (Unpublished PhD Thesis). The University of Wisconsin-Milwaukee, USA.

Deniz, S. (2020). A Study on the e-Health Literacy and Cyberchondria Levels of Individuals. *İnsan&İnsan Journal of Science, Culture, Art and Thought, 7*(24), 84-96.

Dhingra, D. & Dabas, A. (2020). Global strategy on digital health. *Indian Pediatrics, 57*, 356-358.

Elçiyar, K. & Taşçı, D. (2017). Application of Cyberchondria Severity Scale to the students of Anadolu University Communication Faculty. *Abant Journal of Cultural Studies, 2*(4), 231-244.

Eysenbach, G. (2001). What is e-health?. *Journal of Medical Internet Research, 3*(2), e20, 1-2.

Fergus, T.A. (2013). Cyberchondria and intolerance of uncertainty: Examining when individuals experience health anxiety in response to internet searches for medical information. *Cyberpsychology, Behavior, And Social Networking, 16*(10), 735-739.

Fergus, T.A. & Russell, L.H. (2016). Does cyberchondria overlap with health anxiety and obsessive–compulsive symptoms? An examination of latent structure and scale interrelations. *Journal of Anxiety Disorders, 38*, 88-94.

Gencer, T.Z. (2017). Analysis of validity and reliability of Norman and Skınner's e- health scale literacy for cultural adaptation. *Istanbul University Journal of Communication Sciences, 1*(52), 131-145.

Hathaliya, J.J., Tanwar, S., Tyagi, S. & Kumar, N. (2019). Securing electronics healthcare records in Healthcare 4.0: A biometric-based approach. *Computers & Electrical Engineering, 76,* 398-410.

Hollander, J.E. & Carr, B.G. (2020). Virtually perfect? Telemedicine for Covid-19. *The New England Journal of Medicine, 382*, 1679-1681.

Işık, T. (2019). Digital Perception and Its Importance in Terms of Usage in the Context of Health Communication. *Atatürk University Journal of Social Sciences Institute, 23*(4), 1979-1994.

Kakodkar, P., Kaka, N. & Baig, M.N. (2020). A Comprehensive literature review on the clinical presentation, and management of the pandemic coronavirus disease 2019 (COVID-19). *Cureus, 12*(4), e7560.

Kalaycı, Ş. (2014). *SPSS applied multivariate statistical techniques* (6th Edition). Ankara: Asil Publishing.

Karagöz, Y. (2014). *SPSS 21.1 applied biostatistics.* Ankara: Nobel Academic Publishing.

Kılıç, T. (2017). e-Health, Best Practices; Netherlands. *Gümüşhane University Journal Of Health Sciences, 6*(3), 203-217.

Laato, S., Islam, A.K.M.N., Farooq, A. & Dhir, A. (2020). Unusual purchasing behavior during the early stages of the COVID-19 pandemic: The stimulus-organism-response approach. *Journal of Retailing and Consumer Services*, *57*, 1-12.

Lampariello, R. & Labrique, A.B. (2020). Digital health: Is the glass half-full or half-empty?. *Health Policy and Technology, 9*(3), 266-267.

Levin-Zamir, D. & Parial, L.L. (2020). Digital health. İçinde D. Gu & M. Dupre (Eds.), *Encyclopedia of Gerontology and Population Aging.* Springer, Cham.

Lewis, T. (2006). Seeking health information on the internet: Lifestyle choice or bad attack of cyberchondria?. *Media, Culture and Society, 28*(4), 521-539.

Loos, A. (2013). Cyberchondria: Too much information for the health anxious patient?. *Journal of Consumer Health on the Internet, 17*(4), 439-445.

Lowery, C. (2020). What is digital health and what do i need to know about it?. *Obstetrics and Gynecology Clinics of North America, 47*(2), 215-225.

McElroy, E. & Shevlin, M. (2014). The development and initial validation of the Cyberchondria Severity Scale (CSS). *Journal of Anxiety Disorders, 28*(2), 259-265.

McManus, F., Leung, C., Muse, K. & Williams, J.M. (2014). Understanding 'cyberchondria': An interpretive phenomenological analysis of the purpose, methods and impact of seeking health information online for those with health anxiety. *The Cognitive Behaviour Therapist, 7*(21), 1-13.

Mesko, B. (2020). Digital health technologies and well-being in the future. *IT Professional, 22*(1), 20-23.

Meydan, C.H. & Şeşen, H. (2015). *Structural equation modeling AMOS applications* (2nd Edition). Ankara: Detay Publishing.

Mitchell, M. & Kan, L. (2019). Digital technology and the future of health systems. *Health Systems & Reform, 5*(2), 113-120.

Monkman, H. & Kushniruk, A.W. (2015). eHealth literacy issues, constructs, models, and methods for health information technology design and evaluation. *Knowledge Management & E-Learning, 7*(4), 541-549.

Morrison, C. (2017). Emerging technologies blog series part 2: A definition of digital health. *Digital Helath & Care Institute,* 1-4.

Muse, K., McManus, F., Leung, B., Meghreblian, C.B. & Williams, J.M. (2012). Cyberchondriasis: Fact or fiction? A preliminary examination of the relationship between health anxiety and searching for health information on the internet. *Journal of Anxiety Disorders, 26*(1), 189-196.

Norman, C.D. & Skinner, H.A. (2006a). eHealth literacy: Essential skills for consumer health in a networked world. *Journal of Medical Internet Research, 8*(2), e9, 1-10.

Norman, C.D. & Skinner, H.A. (2006b). eHEALS: The eHealth literacy scale. *Journal of Medical Internet Research, 8*(4), e27, 1-7.

Norr, A.M., Allan, N.P., Boffa, J.W. & Raines, A.M. (2015). Validation of the Cyberchondria Severity Scale (CSS): Replication and extension with bifactor modeling. *Journal of Anxiety Disorders, 31*, 58-64.

Paige, S.R., Krieger, J.L. & Stellefson, M.L. (2017). The influence of eHealth literacy on perceived trust in online health communication channels and sources. *Journal of Health Communication, 22*(1), 53-65.

Park, H., Cormier, E., Gordon, G. & Baeg, J.H. (2016). Identifying health consumers' eHealth literacy to decrease disparities in accessing eHealth information. *Computers, Informatics, Nursing: CIN, 34*(2), 71-76.

Rehman, M.U., Andargoli, A.E. & Pousti, H. (2019, Aralık). *Healthcare 4.0: Trends, challenges and benefits.* 30th Australasian Conference on Information Systems, Perth, Australia.

Robbins, D. & Dunn, P. (2019). Digital health literacy in a person-centric world. *International Journal of Cardiology, 290*, 154-155.

Shiferaw, K.B., Tilahun, B.C., Endehabtu, B.F., Gullslett, M.K. & Mengiste, S.A. (2020). E-health literacy and associated factors among chronic patients in a low-income country: A cross-sectional survey. *BMC Medical Informatics and Decision Making,* 20(181), 1-9.

Starcevic, V. & Berle, D. (2013). Cyberchondria: Towards a better understanding of excessive health-related internet use. *Expert Review of Neurotherapeutics, 13*(2), 205-213.

Starcevic, V. & Berle, D. (2015). Cyberchondria: An old phenomenon in a new guise?. İçinde E. Aboujaoude & V. Starcevic (Eds.), *Mental health in the digital age: Grave dangers, great promise* (ss. 106-117). New York: Oxford University Press.

Starcevic, V., Berle, D. & Arnáez, S. (2020). Recent insights into Cyberchondria. *Current Psychiatry Reports, 22*(56), 1-8.

Te Poel, F., Baumgartner, S.E., Hartmann, T. & Tanis, M. (2016). The curious case of cyberchondria: A longitudinal study on the reciprocal relationship between health anxiety and online health information seeking. *Journal of Anxiety Disorders, 43*, 32-40.

Tennant, B., Stellefson, M., Dodd, V., Chaney, B., Chaney, D., Paige, S. & Alber, J. (2015). eHealth literacy and web 2.0 health information seeking behaviors among baby boomers and older adults. *Journal of Medical Internet Research, 17*(3), e70, 1-14.

ThinkTech STM Teknoloji Düşünce Merkezi. (2019). *Advanced health technologies II: Comparative analysis of the digitalization process in the Turkish health system.* https://thinktech.stm.com.tr/uploads/raporlar/pdf/2352019164719686_stm_ileri_saglik_teknolojileri_1.pdf (Accesed: 20/09/2020).

Tüter, M. (2019). *Evaluation of cyberchondria level and related factors in patients presented to family medicine clinic.* (Unpublished specialty thesis in medicine). University of Health Sciences / Okmeydanı Training and Research Hospital, İstanbul.

Uzun, S.U. (2016). *Cyberchondria levels and contributing factors among Pamukkale University employees.* (Unpublished specialty thesis in medicine). Pamukkale University Faculty of Medicine, Denizli.

van Deursen, A.J. & van Dijk, J.A. (2011). Internet skills performance tests: Are people ready for eHealth?. *Journal of Medical Internet Research, 13*(2), e35, 1-11.

von Eiff, M.C. & von Eiff, W. (2020). The digitalisation of healthcare. *Health Management, 20*(2), 182-187.

WHA (World Health Assembly, 58). (2005). *Fifty-eighth World Health Assembly*. Geneva: World Health Organization. https://apps.who.int/gb/ebwha/pdf_files/WHA58-REC1/english/A58_2005_REC1-en.pdf (Accesed: 22/09/2020).

White, R.W. & Horvitz, E. (2009). Cyberchondria: Studies of the escalation of medical concerns in web search. *ACM Transactions on Information Systems, 27*(4), 1-37.

WHO. (2019a). *WHO guideline: recommendations on digital interventions for health system strengthening.* https://www.who.int/publications/i/item/978924155050-5 (Accessed: 15/09/2020).

WHO. (2019b) *Global strategy on digital health. 2020-2024.* https://extranet.who.int/dataform/upload/surveys/183439/files/Draft%20Global%20Strategy%20on%20Digital%20Health.pdf (Accessed: 20/09/2020).

WHO. (2020). *Digital health,* WHO Regional Office for Europe. https://www.euro.who.int/en/health-topics/Health-systems/digital-health (Accesed: 22/09/2020).

Witten, N.S.K. & Humphry, J. (2018). The electronic health literacy and utilization of technology for health in a remote Hawaiian community: Lana'i. *Hawai'i Journal of Medicine & Public Health, 77*(3), 51-59.

Yamamoto, G.T. & Altun, D. (2020). The coronavirus and the rising of online education. *Journal of University Research, 3*(1), 25-34.

CHAPTER SIXTEEN

DIGITALIZATION AND DATA SECURITY IN HEALTHCARE

HÜSEYİN ASLAN

Introduction

Technological development continues in health services, as in other fields, by their interaction with each other in both direct medical application fields and the fields supporting these services. In parallel with the development of computer technology and internet networks, digitalization starting with the use of computer technologies and electronic recording systems in healthcare institutions has progressed and continues to progress in accordance with the developing technology. Medical records include the identity information given directly by patients, the medical information conveyed by patients and the patient information revealed in healthcare institutions. The development of digital technology, e-health, m-health, wearable health technologies, etc., has brought the emergence of new technologies. Digitalization in the field of health services has brought some problems along with its advantages. One of these is the problem of privacy, confidentiality and security for patient data.

For patients, knowing that their personal information is not revealed and their confidentiality and security are ensured makes them feel safe and have trust in the healthcare institutions in choosing healthcare institutions and giving accurate information. Service providers have to determine and implement the necessary administrative, physical and technical information security policies in accordance with the legal legislations of countries to ensure the confidentiality and security of patient information.

Privacy, confidentiality and security issues will be discussed in this chapter. First, the concept of medical records and electronic patient records will be defined. Then, information about the benefits and risks of digitalization in healthcare services will be given. Later, there will be an attempt to explain the concept of ownership of patient data, and then privacy, confidentiality and security concepts will be explained. The legal background to the privacy, confidentiality and security of patient information will be discussed under the next title. Finally, ensuring data confidentiality and security and some practices for these will be explained.

Medical Records

Data belonging to patients on both electronic platforms and paper are qualified as medical records. Briefly, these can be defined as outpatient and inpatient health service records that are prepared and documented during the delivery of health services (Harman et al., 2012). In addition to detailed identity information, these data may also include detailed medical data and very private or highly confidential information. Data such as patients' examination information, diagnostic information, consultation information, laboratory test information, radiology information and image records, treatments, doctor notes, surgery notes, and nurse treatment information can be considered as medical data. In addition to the medical data, descriptive identity and demographic information such as birth date, gender, address, etc., is non-medical patient data. Recording these medical and non-medical data leads to the occurrence of big data in healthcare. Both data diversity and data size increase with digitalization (Gopal, G. et al., 2019) (Tresp et al., 2016) (Lv & Qiao, 2020). The types of patient data may vary. While patients' demographic data are obtained during registration at health institutions, medical data are obtained both directly with the declaration and documentation of patients and with patient data emerging directly or on medical devices recorded by healthcare professionals in the period from the time they start receiving health services to the end of follow-up and treatment. There are different types of data in imaging services and doctor reports/notes or laboratory test data or demographic data. The types and size of data bring some challenges in data collection and storing and reusing/putting these data in service (Volker et al., 2016). These data recorded in digital platforms belonging to inpatients and outpatients are called patient data or electronic healthcare records. Regardless of how they are recorded, medical records directly affect service quality, effectiveness, productivity, clinical decision processes, research, legal protection and educational activities (Harman et al., 2012) (Gopal, G. et al., 2019) (Zhang & Liu, 2010). The transfer of patient data records from paper to the digital platform positively affects the benefits of these effects.

Advantages of Digitalization in Healthcare Services

Digitalization, which is an important stage of technology, reduces the information asymmetry in healthcare services due to access to more information via the internet and the widespread use and development of devices for that purpose (computers, phones, tablets, etc.) (Gopal, G. et al., 2019). The development of digitalization in the field of healthcare services has also brought advantages such as time and cost. The time advantage in accessing information has especially created great benefits for both patients and institutions. We can also mention the many advantages, such as increasing more effective research activities, ensuring more active use of decision support systems and increasing service quality. It is known that digitalization increases productivity in healthcare institutions. It also appears to be facilitative in ensuring and protecting the accuracy of data which is necessary in the current technological environment. Besides the problems of storage and classification in paper media before the use of digital technology, problems due to access taking too long have disappeared and have now begun to be replaced by problems with the confidentiality and security of data in the digital environment (Choi et al., 2006) (Lv & Qiao, 2020) (Liang et al., 2018). The ability to collect and store more information with digitalization in healthcare services also increases the amount of information in this field. It is known that digitalization has positive effects on costs and patient care quality. Although the increase in the amount of data brings the reuse of data and other advantages, the fact that it becomes more complicated is among its challenges (Gopal, G. et al., 2019). As the data increases, it becomes difficult to ensure access control (Kim et al., 2013) (Lv & Qiao, 2020). In addition, applications such as wearable technologies, m-health and e-health have begun to be used more frequently in the field of health with the acceleration in digitalization. Although the widespread use of the internet and such technologies provides great advantages for patients and healthcare institutions, it brings great problems and responsibilities in terms of privacy, confidentiality and security (Meingast et al., 2006) (Liang et al., 2018). This information in the digital platform can be used by healthcare professionals and relevant institutions within the framework of access authorizations, as well as by others as a violation of privacy, confidentiality and security rules in the case of security gaps.

Data Ownership

What first comes to mind in data collection and storage is data ownership. In general, the owner of data/information is called the producer, i.e., the creator of the data/information. Data ownership is related with the question of who is responsible for recording and storing the data. Is the data owner the patient him/herself, the institution providing the service or the insurance institution? Who decides with whom a patient's data will be shared, the owner individual/patient, the institution providing the service or the insurance institutions? (Zhang & Liu, 2010) (Meingast et al., 2006). Although the practices in this issue are usually flexible and vary between countries, the general rule is that the institutions copying and storing the data and providing healthcare services, the insurance institutions and the individuals who are the sources of data have rights in accordance with legislation in the country. The main sensitivity in data confidentiality and security is for the individuals to whom the data is provided. The greatest responsibility for recording, storing and organizing patient data, ensuring internal and external sharing security, and the accuracy, safety and reliability of the data provided by the individuals for the institution and the data produced in the institution, belongs to the institutions providing the service and producing the patient data. Institutions may use digital programs specific to the institution, joint programs with other institutions or WEB-based programs to record, store and reuse the personal and medical information of individuals. Electronic health records are interactive and have lots of users (Harman et al., 2012) (Kostkova et al., 2016). The data produced in all digital platforms can be shared with healthcare professionals (in the case of authorization and assignment) in order to be used in accordance with their purpose, both internally and externally. Data about the healthcare services of patients from institutions, their details and healthcare bills can also be shared with supreme institutions and insurance institutions (Zhang & Liu, 2010). While all these processes occur in digital platforms, security hazards increase and security problems, such as possession of the data by malicious people and data corruption, become the current issues. If the patient data records are made only on paper, the security problem is limited to the place where the data is and the people present there. However, if data records are made in the digital environment, it is likely to be attacked by anyone with malicious intent due to security vulnerabilities.

The Concepts of Privacy, Confidentiality and Security

The concepts of privacy and confidentiality are often confused with each other and security is a different concept again. “Privacy is the right of individuals to control the acquisition, use, and disclosure of their definable data. Confidentiality refers to the obligation of the information recipients to respect the privacy interests of the data owners. Security refers to physical, technological and administrative security measures or tools used to protect health data from unfair access or disclosure” (Cohn, 2006). Privacy is defined as an interest in individuals' personal and health data in healthcare to identify those who have access to these data or to limit access to data by unrelated individuals. In other words, on the one hand, limiting the persons who have access to data is one dimension of privacy; and on the other hand, limiting the access of the data subject is the other dimension (Kahn & Sheshadri, 2008). Ensuring privacy, confidentiality and security is under the responsibility of the institution recording the data. The relevant institution is obliged to make the necessary arrangements. However, privacy, confidentiality and security problems are too important to be left to the initiative of individuals and institutions and they are supported by legal regulations. The confidentiality issues are the protection of the privacy interest of patient data, ensuring their proper use and not sharing with third persons without permission. It is a process beginning with ensuring security accuracy. It can be said that the physical, administrative and technological activities carried out to ensure data integrity and usability, to prevent unauthorized access to data and prevent corruption are the subjects of data security.

The Legal Dimension of Data Confidentiality and Security

Data security is as important in healthcare as in other fields and in some cases even more so. It is obligatory to use legislation to determine the responsibilities of individuals and institutions in the confidentiality and security of health data. All countries have legislation on privacy, confidentiality and security despite their being different from each other. Karim Abouelmehdi et al. (2018) investigated the legislation in some countries regarding data confidentiality and security, reported as: the Data Protection Directive to protect the privacy rights of people within the scope of fundamental rights and freedoms in the European Union, the Personal Information Protection and Electronic Documents Act, which includes the right to collect the personal data of individuals and to know the reasons in Canada, the Health Insurance Portability and Liability Act, the Patient

Safety and Quality Improvement Act and Health Information Technology for Economic and Clinical Health in order to ensure standardization in electronic health transactions in the United States of America, the Constitution to Protect Privacy, Dignity, Private Life and Image and protect from material and moral damages arising from their violation in Brazil, the Data Protection Act in the UK (Abouelmehd et al., 2018) and the Protection of Personal Data Act to ensure data security and confidentiality in Turkey. The purpose of these laws is ensure the confidentiality of private life, protect the fundamental rights and freedoms and regulate the liabilities of natural and legal persons who own and process personal data and the procedures and principles to be followed (KVKK, 2016).

It is possible to increase the number of country examples related to legal regulations on data confidentiality and security. However, what is meant to be stated here is to indicate that, in almost all of them, the basis of legal regulations regarding data confidentiality and security is personal rights and freedoms and privacy rights. Personal rights and freedoms necessitated the privacy and confidentiality rights, data confidentiality and security to be determined by legal regulations. The development of digital technologies did not eliminate the necessities in this issue, but brought about the increase in confidentiality and security problems in physical records. Confidentiality and security problems increase with reasons such as the increase in data diversity and size of electronic patient records, intranet and internet roaming, and the increase in the number of data users due to technological opportunities. For these reasons, countries are now trying to close the legal gaps in confidentiality and security by adding legal regulations on electronic information security to their current legal regulations. The ever developing technology for electronic records brings the necessity to keep up with the developing technology in terms of confidentiality and security.

Ensuring Data Confidentiality and Security and Some Applications

As a result of the development of computer and internet technologies and the increase in their use in healthcare services, patient data recorded on paper in the past are now recorded in the electronic platform. The electronic recording system not only increases the content of data, but also provides great advantages to increase data quality and to be more convenient in data analysis and decision support (Choi et al., 2006) (Volker et. al, 2016). The diversification and increase in data with the development of digital technologies also brought about problems such as recording and managing the data, transforming them into an appropriate format for analysis, using and sharing them with partners, privacy, confidentiality and security. The problems that existed during the periods when patient records were made physically (on paper) changed their shape and size with digitalization (Abouelmehdi et al., 2018).

Issues such as preventing patient data collected in the digital platform from being possessed by others except for the use of service providers, masking out personally identifying information of the data or medical data for people, protecting the data against deletion and corruption and efforts to prevent them being possessed by others (including exposure to cyber-attacks) are the most important data confidentiality and security issues in electronic patient records (Volker et al., 2016) (Abouelmehdi et al., 2018). Wireless network systems, intranet and internet network systems, cloud information systems, health record sharing systems, malware threatening information security, and poorly constructed and poorly managed electronic record systems increase the risks to information security and confidentiality (Houlding, 2011).

Huge amounts of patient data should be safely recorded against improper use and illegal digital theft, stored in accordance with medical evaluations and decision support analyses and be available for use in accordance with data privacy, confidentiality and security whenever necessary (Xu et al., 2014). Data storage is an important issue in data confidentiality and security. There can be some alternatives such as institution databases, central databases and interconnected databases in data storage. In addition, confidentiality and security issues such as which data will be stored and how they can be shared with whom also become very important at this point (Meingast et al., 2006) (Choi et al., 2006). Ensuring the security and confidentiality of the data in all these processes is crucial for both institutions and the owners of personal data. Proper use of patient data, not giving the data to others and institutions without permission, the right to protect patient data against other individuals and institutions and the authority to decide which data can be seen by whom are covered in the confidentiality issues (Xu et al., 2014). Institutions have to ensure confidentiality and security by using techniques such as encoding, firewalls and masking against the dangers derived from the digital networks and devices they use (Abouelmehdi et al., 2018). While ensuring the confidentiality and security of big digital data, the benefit of data should also be protected. Data corruption, loss, replacement, unauthorized access and sharing risks are among the security problems that apply to all processes such as obtaining, saving, storing, and reusing, making them suitable for analysis (Xu et al., 2014).

All activities to ensure data security are important in all the processes mentioned above. Activities to ensure data security can be listed as protecting the used devices and the facilities they are in, administrative security activities such as training personnel in accordance with legal liabilities for data confidentiality and security, data collection, technical security activities such as security, technology and access in all processes, activities arising from institutions holding the data and the relevant documentation requirements and activities arising from the legislation on this issue (WEDI, 2004).

Administrative security activities start with the relevant assignment in accordance with data confidentiality and security policies. It is necessary to establish a technical and administrative team to ensure data confidentiality and security. It is necessary to establish the required management and employee team for user updates and follow-up, monitoring and implementing the changing and developing security technology, determining possible risk factors and carrying out such activities. The sensitivity of management on data security and the emphasis on this issue are the most important determinants indicating how serious the institution is on this issue (Choi et al., 2006).

Primarily, activities to limit physical access are used in order to ensure data security and confidentiality. Preventing access to physical platforms where patient data can be accessed, preventing data from being viewed on a computer and preventing the capture/recording of information by audio and video can be considered as highly effective physical measures in ensuring information confidentiality and security (Choi et al., 2006).

The intensive use of digital technology caused data confidentiality and security risks to increase in number in the digital platform. The ability to view patient data/information over intranet computer networks or internet networks by healthcare professionals and institutions that are legally required to share is one of the processes that can endanger confidentiality and security. In order to prevent such risks, the security of digital devices, security measures for sharing networks such as the intranet and internet, technical measures for storage devices, taking technical measures such as back up, etc., became highly important for the accuracy, confidentiality and security of data. Filters, firewalls, and anti-virus software programs for data protection are the leading technical measures (Choi et al., 2006). By ensuring access to the system only by relevant persons, access security is ensured with technical protection activities related to information confidentiality and security, and transmission security is ensured against the risks that may occur during the transmission of data to the relevant person, institution or devices (Kahn & Sheshadri, 2008).

Limiting Access

Data in digital platforms can appear as passive data, often produced by systems during applications, and can also appear as active data through direct transfer from data owners to data collectors (Xu et al., 2014). Data should be protected against some dangers such as unauthorized access to information systems and data in the course of the data collection stage, manipulations, data theft, disclosure and changing or copying of the data, and corruption or destruction (deleting) of the data (Abouelmehdi et al., 2018). A patient's declaration of data such as name, surname, id number and other identity information and addresses during registry to the institution can be given as an example of the direct collection of data. The medical data of individuals produced in healthcare services such as policlinics, clinics, laboratories and imaging services can appear as passive data in the system. Health service providers may use documents instead of voice communication in order to prevent others from hearing while obtaining personal information from individuals through their employees. Data confidentiality and security can be ensured through physical measures that will prevent being followed and heard during registry in the stage of active data collection. However, with developing digital technology, individuals do not only actively transfer data in this way. They can also transfer data in ways such as digital demand, registry, inquiry, etc., on internet platforms. Institutions should take the necessary measures against harmful software while collecting active personal data in digital platforms. Extensions, scripting and ad-blockers for preventing digital media tracking and encryption methods provided by different means of communication between institutions and individuals (such as mail or phone messages) can be used (Xu et al., 2014).

After collection, the data are classified and filtered in the digital platform according to certain properties. The collected data are stored digitally by providing transformations to be reused for the necessary analysis and decision support systems in order to share with external stakeholders such as higher institutions and reimbursement institutions and provide medical services to individuals again. Since all data collected from or on behalf of individuals will not be required at all times or in all cases, they should be properly classified. Sorting out and arranging missing data, repetitive data, and the data called data pollution are very important for reliable data and data security. It is also necessary for the reuse of data, such as in legal, medical and analysis procedures, decision support systems and the generation of new data based on these data. It is recommended to use data configurations to ensure data security and to eliminate security gaps in these stages (Abouelmehdi et al., 2018).

The issue of confidentiality and security, how much of the data or what kind of data will be made available to whom and who can see the data, is of great importance while re-using the data stored in digital platforms. Access to data other than by relevant or unrelated users and data seen, disclosed, and leaked by others during the re-use process and intermediate processes can be confidentiality and security problems. In addition to data actively received from patients or passively generated during medical processes, new information can be generated through system analysis and evaluations based on these data. While all these data are re-used, data confidentiality and security can be ensured by using techniques such as firewalls, authentication and encryption to prevent the data from being obtained directly or digitally by others (Abouelmehdi et al., 2018).

The rapid spread and development of the use of digital technology in the field of health services and the size of obtained data in this field also accelerated efforts to ensure privacy, confidentiality and security in all data-related processes. Abouelmehdi et al. (2018) listed the methods used for this purpose as authentication, encryption, data masking, access control and monitoring and auditing (Abouelmehdi et al., 2018).

***Authentication*:** This aims to verify users and ensure that user data are correct in order to secure access to corporate networks. It is the process to ensure that correct transactions are carried out in corporate networks and transactions are performed in a way to ensure accuracy (Abouelmehdi et al., 2018) (Xu et al., 2014). Different methods such as electronic signature and digital authentication can be used in authentication (Zhang & Liu, 2010). Authentication should include authorizations regarding which data can be seen by whom as well as for what purposes, when and how the data can be used. Data confidentiality and security should be ensured using passwords after authentication (Smaradottir, 2017).

Data Encryption: All data appearing in the healthcare sector should be protected by ownership-controlled encryption. Data encryption means authorization of access to sensitive data in terms of privacy and security. It is known that this is an effective way to secure access in cases such as personal use devices of persons authorized with encryption falling into the hands of others. Institutions should also provide the necessary ease of use in order to ensure its effective use and expand the use of this method, which has a clear impact on data security (Abouelmehdi et al., 2018) (Zhang & Liu, 2010).

Data Masking: Instead of blocking access to prevent data from falling into the hands of others, giving digital data thieves access to the wrong data can be a solution for data security. Therefore, creating data dummies, creating data pollution in the case of abnormal data flow in digital platforms and using mask data instead of real data can be listed among these ways (Xu et al., 2014). Since mask data are not revealed by transforming real data, mask data cannot be transformed into real data. Masking is considered as an advantageous method in that it reduces additional security needs and reduces data security costs (Abouelmehdi et al., 2018) (Choi et al., 2006).

Access Control: Data management systems used in healthcare institutions include the personal medical information of patients and this information does not only apply to the doctor examining the patient. Patient data are associated with different services with different service roles such as administrative services, pharmacy services, laboratory services, radiology services, etc. (Win, 2005). Data access authorization should not mean that everyone can access any data at any time. The units in healthcare institutions and healthcare professionals working within these units or employees affiliated to the support team should be able to access the data in accordance with the intended use. Regulations about who can access which data include advanced authorizations for activities such as accessing permission to permitted data, assigning tasks through the system (consultation, laboratories, etc.) caused by business flows and processes and group management (Abouelmehdi et al., 2018).

Monitoring and Auditing: These include monitoring the actions/activities in the digital network. In the course of this monitoring activity, unauthorized or illegal activities are attempted to be identified by monitoring entries and interventions to the data (Abouelmehdi et al., 2018). Monitoring and auditing can be considered as an essential part of the data security process for detecting security gaps and taking further measures. Monitoring and auditing also help to identify and prevent potential data security vulnerabilities.

Conclusion

The rapid development of computer and internet technologies accelerates digitalization in healthcare services. Patient data, which used to be recorded on paper in the past, are now recorded in digital platforms. Obtaining patient data via both internal and external technological devices during the delivery of healthcare services and the emergence of data diversity and big data due to the ease of use of electronic patient record systems bring some risks besides the advantages of digitalization in healthcare services. One of the most important risks is patient data confidentiality and security. Constant developments and changes in digitalization in healthcare services create new confidentiality and security risks.

The confidentiality and security of patient data are primarily the responsibility of the service providers that record the data. Health service providers need to determine data confidentiality and security policies in such a way to protect the privacy rights of individuals, as required by the relevant legal regulations on data confidentiality and security. For this purpose, institutions need to take administrative, physical and technical data confidentiality and security measures. The first step in ensuring data confidentiality and security is to identify a manager and team to manage and take responsibility for this issue within the organization, to prepare the necessary documentation procedures and to determine the processes. With increasing digitalization, it is also necessary to determine how and where computers and connected devices will be physically located, who will be given responsibility, how to ensure their physical security (against fire, falls, flood, etc.), what kind of devices will be stored in the data and where these devices are installed, etc. Since confidentiality and security gaps are rather seen in digital platforms in parallel with the developing technology, technical measures such as limiting access to patient data in digital platforms, using encryption and masking techniques, ensuring access control, using authentication methods, determining and authorizing stakeholders, using anti-virus software against harmful electronic software, following data and user updates and using monitoring and auditing techniques are required to be taken. Administrative, physical and technical methods are complementary and interwoven activities that support each other in ensuring the confidentiality and security of patient data.

Keywords: *Data privacy, data confidentiality, data security, patient information, digital data*

References

Abouelmehdi, K., Beni-Hessane, A., & Khaloufi, H. (2018). Big healthcare data: preserving security and privacy. *Journal of Big Data*, *5*(1), 1–18. https://doi.org/https://doi.org/10.1186/s40537-017-0110-7

Choi, Y. B., Capitan, K. E., Krause, J. S., & Streeper, M. M. (2006). Challenges Associated with Privacy in Health Care Industry: *Implementation of HIPAA and the Security Rules. J Med Sys*, 30(1), 57–64. https://doi.org/10.1007/s10916-006-7405-0

Gopal, G., Suter-Crazzolara, C., Toldo, L., & Eberhardt, W. (2019). Digital transformation in healthcare – architectures of present and future information technologies. *Clinical Chemistry and Laboratory Medicine (CCLM)*, 57(3), 328–335. https://doi.org/https://doi.org/10.1515/cclm-2018-0658

Harman, L. B., Flite, C. A., & Bond, K. (2012). Electronic health records: privacy, confidentiality, and security. *The Virtual Mentor : VM*, 14(9), 712–719. https://doi.org/10.1001/virtualmentor.2012.14.9.stas1-1209

Houlding, D. (2011). Health Information at Risk : Successful Strategies for Healthcare Security and Privacy. Retrieved from https://www.digitalhealthnews.eu/images/stories/pdf/successful_strategies_for_healthcare_security_privacy.pdf

Kahn, S., & Sheshadri, V. (2008). Medical Record Privacy and Security in a Digital Environment. *IT Professional*, 10(2), 46–52. https://doi.org/10.1109/MITP.2008.34

Kim, S.-H., Kim, N.-U., & Chung, T.-M. (2013). Attribute Relationship Evaluation Methodology for Big Data Security. In International Conference on IT Convergence and Security (ICITCS) (pp. 1–4). https://doi.org/10.1109/ICITCS.2013.6717808.

Kişisel verileri koruma kanununu, KVKK (2016). Turkey: Gazete, Resmi. Retrieved from https://www.resmigazete.gov.tr/eskiler/2016/04/20160407-8.pdf

Kostkova, P., Brewer, H., de Lusignan, S., Fottrell, E., Goldacre, B., Hart, G., … Tooke, J. (2016). Who Owns the Data? Open Data for Healthcare. Frontiers in Public Health, 4(February). https://doi.org/10.3389/fpubh.2016.00007

Liang, X., Zhao, J., Shetty, S., Liu, J., & Li, D. (2018). Integrating blockchain for data sharing and collaboration in mobile healthcare applications. IEEE International Symposium on Personal, Indoor and Mobile Radio Communications, PIMRC, 2017-October, 1–5. https://doi.org/10.1109/PIMRC.2017.8292361

Lv, Z., & Qiao, L. (2020). Analysis of healthcare big data. *Future Generation Computer Systems*, 109, 103–110. https://doi.org/10.1016/j.future.2020.03.039

Meingast, M., Roosta, T., & Sastry, S. (2006). Security and Privacy Issues with Health Care Information Technology. In International Conference of the IEEE Engineering in Medicine and Biology Society (pp. 5453–5458). https://doi.org/10.1109/IEMBS.2006.260060

Smaradottir, B. F. (2017). Security Management in Health Care Information Systems — A Literature Review. In 2017 International Conference on Computational Science and Computational Intelligence (CSCI) (pp.

1742–1746). Las Vegas, NV. https://doi.org/10.1109/CSCI.2017.303
Tresp, V., Overhage, J. M., Bundschus, M., Rabizadeh, S., Fasching, P. A., & Yu, S. (2016). Going Digital: A Survey on Digitalization and Large Scale Data Analytics in Healthcare. Proceedings of the IEEE, 104(11), 2180–2206. https://doi.org/10.1109 / JPROC.2016.2615052
WEDI, W. for E. D. I. (2004). Security Policies and Procedures White Paper: A Resource Document.
Win, K. T. (2005). A review of security of electronic health records. *Health Information Management*, 34(1), 13–18. https://doi.org/10.1177/183335830503400105
Xu, L., Jiang, C., Wang, J., Yuan, J., & Ren, Y. (2014). Information Security in Big Data: *Privacy and Data Mining. IEEE Access*, 2, 1149–1176. https://doi.org/10.1109/ACCESS.2014.2362522
Zhang, R., & Liu, L. (2010). Security Models and Requirements for Healthcare Application Clouds. In IEEE 3rd International Conference on Cloud Computing (pp. 268–275). https://doi.org/10.1109/CLOUD.2010.62

CHAPTER SEVENTEEN

THE CITY HOSPITALS AND THE PANDEMIC SCIENCE COMMITTEES IN TURKEY IN THE CONTEXT OF META-GOVERNANCE AND DIGITALIZATION

YELİZ POLAT AND MERYEM KARTAL

Introduction

Epidemic diseases (smallpox, measles, etc.), which are dense population diseases, have spread among people and societies for hundreds of years and caused mass deaths. The development of technology after the industrial revolution, the increase in transportation facilities and the increase in the rate of urbanization have further accelerated the spread of such epidemics in the urban area and caused them to rapidly turn into a global problem. Finally, the COVID-19 epidemic also tends to spread rapidly in areas where urbanization is intense. According to the world urbanization expectations of the United Nations Department of Economic and Social Affairs in 2018, it is predicted that the level of urbanization worldwide will increase from about 68% to 86% in Turkey in 2050 (www.population.un.org). This prediction requires the development of more effective and rapid solutions in cities against diseases of dense population. This phenomenon requires the use of digitalization tools and meta-governance practices in coordination with the management of cities.

Meta-governance is concerned with the role of self-organizing forces and action forms in the realization of political and economic goals and strategies and it is defined as a method of negotiation and decision-making (Jessop, 2001: 17). One of the most important tools of meta-governance, the "public-private partnership" is the models that are accepted as a public service, where the state does not completely withdraw from the service provision, and the private sector participates in services that the private sector cannot do without the state and the solution of the financing problem in the provision of public service is realized. In short, the public-private partnership is the collaboration of public and private sectors with a corporate contract for the public offering of a public service. The public-private partnership, which began to be implemented in the UK and the USA in the 1990s for the first time in the world, has also been a new approach in Turkey in recent years in infrastructure, transport, health, airports, electricity, energy, etc., as it has often been used in areas of service delivery as a public service delivery model.

COVID-19, which emerged for the first time in China in December 2019 and turned into a global epidemic, has also become a major problem in cities since March 11, 2020. In the study, "pandemic science committees" as a form of meta-governance and "city hospitals" as a tool of meta-governance, are problematized at the urban scale and effectively organized in the fight against the epidemic; these ensure the rapid implementation of decisions regarding the epidemic.

The main purpose of this study is to examine the meta-governance practices in the field of public health, strengthened by digitalization opportunities during the COVID-19 pandemic. For this purpose, within the framework of meta-governance, the development of public-private partnership in the health sector in Turkey (city hospitals-integrated health campuses) and "science committees" on a local scale at national and provincial levels created during the pandemic, was first resolved.

In this context, the basic assumption of the study is to bring together actors to facilitate cooperation and mediation in the resolution of disputes and support decision-making. Pandemic science boards established in Turkey and city hospitals established in public-private partnership have turned into a successful meta-governance implementation with the opportunities provided by digitalization, as a meta-governance model that stands out in processes such as the implementation of solutions reached by negotiation.

In other words, city hospitals created by public-private partnership in Turkey were implemented in a predictable manner before the pandemic. The rapid creation of "pandemic science committees" in the COVID-19 process at both national and provincial levels and the effective implementation and isolation measures by using the advanced digital infrastructure in the pandemic process are an important result of the functioning of meta-governance practices in Turkey in coordination with digitalization. Thus,

a) The executive power in Turkey is making efforts to coordinate meta-governance practices with digitalization in the COVID-19 pandemic. This effort ensures that the public is informed quickly and does not experience "lack of information" during the pandemic process. The pandemic process is effectively managed with the Hayat Eve Sığar (HES) application implemented during the pandemic period with information applications such as E-Pulse, Spatial Business Intelligence (MIZ) and "Public Health CBS" implemented by the Ministry of Health since 2015.

b) In Turkey, with the understanding of meta-governance, the state follows an intermediary and supervisory path in bringing together actors, facilitating cooperation between actors and resolving disputes. This pushes forward the supervisory and guiding function of the state beyond being solely an implementer.

c) "Pandemic science committees" consisting of public health experts, convened under the chairmanship of the Ministry of Health on the COVID-19 pandemic were established, and the health minister informed the public about the course of the pandemic every day. This practice ensured the trust of the public in the management of the pandemic process and the public's support was provided in the implementation of the measures. In addition, "recommendation decisions" taken by pandemic committees were quickly implemented by the presidency and local governments.

d) "Provincial pandemic committees" have been established locally. In these committees, local public health experts and the mayor come together under the chairmanship of the governor and develop solutions to problems identified on a local scale and contribute to the management of the process by working in coordination with the central administration.

For the purpose of the study, the theoretical dimension of meta-governance is primarily explained. The contribution of the digitalization process to meta-governance is then put forward and finally, the practices in the pandemic process in Turkey and the city hospitals and pandemic committees conducted in public-private partnership are examined. For the purpose of the study, documents are analyzed in a literature review and decisions announced by the Ministry of Health on corporate web pages during the COVID-19 process are assessed. Applications made on the axis of meta-governance are examined during the COVID-19 pandemic which first appeared in China in December 2019 and has affected Turkey since March 11, 2020.

A Theoretical Overview of Meta-Governance

In recent years, the political identity of states has been demanded to be at the forefront of "new governance" models (Zhang, 2015: 380). In this context, some scientists argued in the past two decades that there should be a transition from the hierarchical governance model dominated by governments to non-hierarchical governance models (market and network governance). This has often been observed in the rise of the "new governance" literature as public sector reform in developed countries since the 1980s (Rhodes, 1996 transferring; Zhang, 2015: 379). The increasing multi-layered structure of many interdependent actors in the governance process has been emphasized with the policy network approach. While policy networks had an autonomous management to some extent, how these networks would be directed and managed sometimes caused some problems (Sørensen, 2006; transferring Roy, 2014: 53). Governance theories for the emerging problems emphasize the dominance and leading role of governments by focusing on meta-governance (Rhodes, 2012; transferring Roy, 2014: 54).

Meta-governance is a concept that brings up questions concerning how values, norms and principles will support the governance systems and management approaches (Kooiman and Jentoft, 2009: 818). Meta-governance refers to a concrete governance process in which states shape, organize and transform the economic and social life. The main concern of meta-governance is to focus on existing and potential failures among actors and to eliminate the democratic gaps among networks. Thus, meta-governance can also be defined as "the art of managing interactive governance" in general. In addition, meta-governance is a governance model that is applied when exchanges are necessary in the market, coordination between actors must be ensured and heterarchical governance fails. Meta-governance is a new governance model with the idea of "re-engaging the government" instead of "governance without government" (Sorensen and Torfing, 2009: 245-246).

Meta-governance is due to the failure of networks to manage or maintain the processes that serve for public purposes regularly and steadily. Therefore, meta-governance serves for purposes such as assuring the coordination between and the combination of various governance actors and actors, achieving effective political goals and developing cooperative approaches (Sobacı and Köseoğlu, 2015: 244). Meta-governance focuses on the relationship between markets, hierarchy and networks. However, meta-governance emphasizes the need to reconstruct political controls in the governance process (Peters, 2010: 37).

The main difference between governance and commodity governance is that governance draws attention to processes that separate political organization from the government and state; however, meta-governance explicitly focuses on the practices and procedures that secure government impact, command and control in governance regimes. In addition, it is argued that meta-governance provides a way to explore new articulations of state power, particularly in the transition from top-down management to more collaborative governance (Whitehead, 2003; transferring Roy, 2014: 55).

Meta-governance pertains to managing and "combining" the positive aspects of networks and finding the proper way to manipulate them without destroying the dynamics of network governance. The meta-governance approach is used in order to strengthen the ability of elected politicians and chief executives to promote, direct and manage networks to democratically provide public goods and important services to citizens. In this context, the majority of the discussions on current governance in the literature are on the role and position of political institutions in governance (Wilson, Morrison and Everingham, 2017: 189). "The purpose of meta-governance is to create a form of coordination, coherence and integration in fragmented network governance without harming autonomy, participation and self-regulation in governance networks. Through meta-governance it becomes possible to make regulations without using traditional government techniques such as hierarchical orders, bureaucratic rules, control and detailed regulations" (Sørensen, 2006; transferring Lund, Sehested, Hellesen and Nellemann, 2012: 617).

Meta-governance is based on the dialogue, interaction and sharing of resources among the actors within the principles of responsibility, accountability and sustainability. The coordination of relations is one of the underlying factors in creating meta-governance in complex and mutual relations in the sharing of regional resources, location, and scale among the participating actors. Meta-governance refers to an inter-institutional network design as a result of the generation of visions that can facilitate the arrangement of different organizations under a common roof. In this context, decisions are made by negotiating different and multiple goals among organizations (Albareda and Waddock, 2016: 9-11).

In conclusion, meta-governance, in fact, focuses on the relationship between hierarchy, market and networks. In addition, in meta-governance, the government's authority over the organizations involved in the governance process must be acknowledged by these organizations. However, meta-governance tries to control public sector actions instead of directly controlling the relevant actions. If the public administration faces a difficult situation, meta-governance tries to control the action indirectly through legal regulations (Peters, 2010: 37).

Digitalization and Meta-Governance

The widespread use of the internet, the transition to the information age and the period defined as the information society, and the way of providing public services have also undergone an important change and transformation with the developments in information and communication technologies in the last decades. The classical understanding and presentation of public service can generally develop under the influence of various factors such as ideologies, governance styles and cultures of states, and economic and political systems. The way public service is delivered differs according to internal and external dynamics. Global developments are also changing the way that public services are delivered. As the borders of states become uncertain with the globalization process, the use and sharing of information also change. The globalization process that makes the boundaries of states uncertain, the information society and information age in which ways of using and sharing information change, and trends and understandings such as Web 2.0 and Industry 4.0 that emerge as a reflection of these factors, are the most important examples of these global developments. With the development of information technologies in the 21st century, the development of technology in the information age that we are in, the rapid spread of internet use in countries, and the "learning machines" and "smart devices" developed to make things easier depending on the developing technology to be used in service delivery, have all attracted the attention of both private and public sectors. In the information age, central governments, local governments and public institutions have started to offer citizens a digitalized public service with e-government applications since the 2000s (Göçoğlu, 2019: 615-616).

Since the 1990s, there has been a transformation from the traditional state model in developed countries to the electronic state model (e-government), where services are largely carried out via electronic media. Information technology (IT) was used as an important tool in the restructuring of public administration in the United States in 1993. In addition, EU countries aiming to lead the wave of information technologies started the e-Europe Project in Lisbon on March 23, 2000 (Aydın, 2007: 295-299).

Table 17.1: New Opportunities Offered by IT Applications in Public Services to Individual and Social Life

E-Democracy	E-Government	E-Health	E-Business
Online Voting	Payments	Electronic Health Services	Working From Home
Organizing Political Campaigns Online	Interactive Public Services	Health Information Networks	Computer Aided Design and Production
Public Opinion Poll	Video Conferencing	Remote Scan	Online Shopping and Banking Services
Communication between Politicians and Citizens	Interoperability of Public Databases and Data Sharing	Video Consultation	Electronic trade
Monitoring the Legislative Process on the Internet	Cost Gain by Regulating Public Procurement on Online	Preventive Health Services	Remote Interaction after Sales

Source: (Aydın, 2007: 301)

Developments in information and communication technologies affect nation states economically, politically, socio-culturally and socially and force them to change. In this process of change, states also benefit from information and communication technologies in the formulation of public policies. These technologies are also effective on public policies. Acceleration in the provision of public services over the internet in recent years has made the effect on public policies multidimensional (Kırışık and Sezer, 2015: 199).

Today, classical management systems are being restructured within the scope of digitalization and governance, as if "tectonic plates change valleys and hills". Questions challenge the classical understanding, such as, Who has the power? Who makes the decisions? How will multiple actors make their voices heard in the face of the current monopoly? Who will be accountable, and how? However, it is aimed to change these classic perspectives, which cannot have knowledge of where power is dispersed, and where accountability and responsibility are needed. For this purpose, information and communication technologies are used for change and factors of "digital governance" are rapidly becoming widespread. Thanks to the understanding of digital governance, citizens are provided with direct access to information and services through technological tools. With this new understanding of governance, states envisage accepting citizens as partners in government affairs, rather than simply serving them as clients (Özer, 2017: 460). In other words, digital governance is used as a method of meta-governance.

In the process of the COVID-19 pandemic, the implementation of curfews, the imposition of national or international travel bans and the introduction of distance education methods as a result of the interruption of education increased even more the willingness to benefit from digital technologies in 2020. Thus, information governance as a method of meta-governance gained an important place in the fight against the pandemic.

Meta-Governance and Practices in Turkey

As in many countries of the world in recent years, there are some practices within the scope of meta-governance in Turkey. In this part of the study, the development of public-private partnership in Turkey, which is primarily considered to be one of the tools for implementing meta-governance, is discussed. In the following parts, the transformation of the health sector and the implementation of public-private partnership (KÖO) as a meta-governance tool in the field of health are discussed. Finally, the practices implemented within the scope of meta-governance in the COVID-19 process, which has influenced Turkey since 11 March 2020, are discussed.

The Development Process of Public-private Partnership as a Meta-Governance Tool in Turkey

The transformation of the understanding of limiting the role of the state in the economy in the way that public services are provided and funded in the world also affected Turkey. The liberalization and privatization policies that started with the decisions of 24 January 1980 and continued in the 1990s formed the fundamentals of public-private partnership (KÖO) practices in Turkey (Tokatlıoğlu and Şen, 2019: 227). In neoliberalism, which has been developing since the 1980s, various methods such as limiting the economic activities of the state, using private sector business methods and capital in public investments, and privatization and concession practices have become prominent (Uysal, 2019: 877). The PPP model in Turkey with the EU's influence became widespread. Concrete regulations and funds allocated for the provision of infrastructure services by EU member states with this model, and especially the private sector's initiatives in 2003, required concrete steps to be taken in this regard as a state (Özer, 2016: 28).

In 2012, Turkey's first Public Private Partnership Special Commission was established within the 10th Development Plan under the leadership of the Ministry of National Development (Ministry of Development, 2016: 14). In Turkey, the most serious arrangement for the PPP model was in 2013 with Law No. 6428 about Building, Renewal and Service Procurement of Facilities with the Public-Private Partnership Model and the Amendments in Certain Laws and Decree-Laws by the Ministry of Health (Boz, 2013: 279). According to this law, health facilities with the PPP model are built by real persons or private law legal entities to be determined by tender on the immovables belonging to the Ministry of Health, within the framework of the preliminary project to be given and the basic standards to be determined, for a certain period and price. The Ministry of Finance establishes the right of construction free of charge on the immovables belonging to the Treasury in favor of real persons or private law legal entities and thus the immovables are transferred. The private sector undertakes the construction and presentation of the product or service as a construction phase and a term operation phase. The state, one of the parties of the PPP model, pays rent to the private sector with a payment plan that spans many years (Özer, 2016: 31). "City hospitals" established in cities in Turkey are implemented by this method. During the pandemic period, most of these hospitals were effectively used in the fight against the COVID-19 epidemic. Thus, the progress in the health sector is based on raising and improving the health level of the population – the ultimate goal of health policies –, minimizing health risks – one of the strategic objectives – and protecting the society from these risks.

In recent days, from this point of view and within urban transformation, transformation in health and PPP, many applications such as a "health city or health campuses" have begun to be put into practice in Turkey (Acartürk and Keskin, 2012: 45).

Methods Applied in Public-private Partnership as a Meta-Governance Tool in Turkey

In Turkey, the future viability of the PPP model is directly associated with the creation of the legal infrastructure. Privatization in Turkey and the PPP model, the ideological approach to service delivery methods in general, and the cancellation of legal texts issued by the legislative and executive bodies by the judicial body restrict the implementation of these models (Acartürk and Keskin, 2012: 37).

In Turkey, PPP is realized by sharing investments and services on the basis of a contract, costs, risks and returns for the project between the public and private sectors. In this context, various methods such as concession, asylum, build-operate-transfer, build-operate, and transfer of operating rights are applied in the provision of public services within the scope of PPP (Özer, 2016: 28).

According to the data of the Presidency of the Republic of Turkey's Strategy Development Department in January 2020, from 1988 to 2020, a total of 252 projects in 12 different areas including 97 energy, 41 highways, 23 customs, 23 port, 18 health, 18 airport, 18 marina and tourism, 8 mining, 2 solid waste, 2 industrial, 1 railway and 1 cultural and tourism facility were carried out with PPP. Only three of the 252 projects were implemented in 2020, while most projects were implemented in 2013 with 31 applications. Of the 252 projects, 120 were carried out by build-operate-transfer, 109 by transfer of operating rights, 18 by build-lease-transfer and 5 by the build-operate method (www.koi.sbb.gov.tr).

The "build-operate" model is used in electric power production in Turkey. With this model, the private sector is given permission and ownership to build and operate thermal power plants and the electricity generated is purchased by the state. At the end of the contract, the facility remains in the ownership of the private sector. In the "build-operate-transfer" model, the private sector is granted the right to build facilities for public service on public land. The risks of the project in question are shared between the private and public sectors and the private sector operates the facility for a certain period of time, performs maintenance and repair and at the end of the contract period, the facility becomes the property of the public sector. This model can be applied in various areas from bridges and tunnel constructions to nature parks and wholesale state construction. In the "build-rent-transfer" model, the private sector is obliged to build the plant, provide its physical equipment, operate the plant in accordance with the contract for the specified period of time and eventually transfer the plant to the public sector (Strategy and Budget Presidency, 2019: 25).

Although Turkey was one of the first countries in the world to implement some public-private partnership models, and considering the nearly 30-year period in which PPP has been implemented, it is stated that private sector participation is not at the desired levels and the projects implemented have problems due to various reasons, especially risk sharing (Eroğlu, 2018: 53). PPP has been widely applied mainly in the energy and airline transportation sectors in Turkey and has been more successful in these sectors (Uz, 2007:

1176). In addition, about 10,5 million dollars were invested in city hospitals under the social state policy; health institutions maintained their sustainability during the pandemic period and prevented the collapse of the health system.

City Hospitals and Pandemic Science Committees in the Context of Meta-Governance and Digitalization in Turkey

The transformations in the health sector and city hospitals built via PPP and the establishment of national and local scientific boards during the COVID-19 epidemic are analyzed in this section.

Meta-Governance and Transformation of Health Sector in Turkey: City Hospitals

With the acceleration of neoliberal policies in the last quarter of the 20th century, there have been changes in economic and social policies. One of the most effective areas in which this change has occurred is the health sector. Since the 1980s, health services have been restructured in the axis of different economic concepts such as profitability, cost, efficiency and performance-based pricing (Erol and Özdemir, 2018: 118; Yeşiltaş, 2020: 15).

In Turkey, the Fundamental Law of Health Services No. 3359 introduced in 1987 is regarded as the first serious step in the framework of qualifications and the organization of services. Outsourcing practices in the health sector that started with Numune Hospital in 1988, extended project implementation areas after the constitutional amendment in 1999 (Acartürk and Keskin, 2012: 46).

In order to restructure the Turkish health sector, the Ministry of Health has been using the PPP model in health services in terms of organization and financing. Some reform studies have been carried out to regulate the health system since the 1980s and the Health Transformation Program, which was set in train in 2003, is considered to be the most comprehensive of these reform practices (Çınar, Türkoğlu and Tütünsatar, 2017: 221-223).

The PPP implementation in the health sector in Turkey began with the affixation of an additional article to the fundamental Law of Health Services No. 5396 which was passed in 2005 (Karasu, 2011a: 223). In 2013, it continued with the adoption of Law No. 6428 about the Construction, Renewal and Service Procurement by the Public-Private Sector Partnership Model and the Amendment of Certain Decree Laws by the Ministry of Health (Kerman, Altan, Aktel and Eke, 2012: 11). With this regulation in the mentioned law, PPP private sector initiatives are expected to comply with terms and conditions such as, constructing health facilities in return for the costs they will receive from the Ministry of Health, allocating facilities to the Ministry, providing core health services by using public personnel and other support services by private sector entrepreneurs, and endorsing the facility to the Ministry at the end of the contract period (Sözer, 2014: 218). Special financing support has been provided to overcome the budgetary limits in the organization of public services through the use of the PPP model in the health sector. In addition, the innovative operating capacity and techniques of the private sector are used significantly in service delivery. With PPP, the private sector got the opportunity to make a profitable investment with huge potential for up to 49 years under state guarantee (Karasu, 2011a: 220-223).

The first legal regulation for the use of the build-lease-transfer (YKD) model in the healthcare sector was made in the period 2005-2006 via the addition of Annex 7 of the Fundamental Law of Health Services No. 3359 with the Ministry of Health's Build-Rent-Transfer (YKD) Regulation on Health Services Construction (Ayhan and Önder, 2018: 115).

With this YKD model, which is considered to be a sub-model of PPP, it is aimed to make very serious changes and to implement the conversion of the health sector coverage of infrastructure and health services, and the quality of the service delivery type and format in Turkey (Uysal, 2019: 877). With the YKD model, the private sector is generally obliged to build the facility, provide and operate the physical equipment and transfer the facility to the public administration at the end of the contract period. In response to these activities, the public sector regularly pays rent to the private sector every year (Ministry of Development, 2018: 21). The lease terms given to the private sector are long for hospitals and the private sector is obliged to provide services other than the "basic service" (Yeşiltaş, 2020: 19). The contract period made within the context of the PPP model is extended to 49 years in Turkey (Karasu, 2011b: 179), even though there are examples of up to 67 years, such as in England. In the PPP model, the demand risk is undertaken by the state, not by the private sector. However, the most important features of the hospitals built with PPP are considered to be the fact that the hospital is a state hospital, the medical core/medical services are provided by the public sector and there is a widespread beneficiary group (Karasu, 2011a: 244-245). Integrated health campus and city hospital applications to enter the Turkish health system with YKD projects have come to prominence in the provision of health services in cities in recent years (Ayhan and Önder, 2018: 115).

State hospitals in some provinces of Turkey have been transformed into the PPP model by merging under the name of "Integrated Health Campuses", "Health Cities", "Regional Hospital", or more commonly "City Hospitals" on one campus (Yılmaz, 2019: 101). The new period starting with the opening of many city hospitals especially in 2017, is called the "City Hospitals Period" (Uysal, 2019: 892).

Table 17.2: City Hospitals Built with Public-private Partnership and Under Construction

Project Name	Bed Capacity	Targeted Completion Date
Adana City Hospital	1550	In Service
Mersin City Hospital	1.294	In Service
Bursa City Hospital	1335	In Service
Isparta City Hospital	755	In Service
Yozgat City Hospital	475	In Service
Kayseri City Hospital	1.607	In Service
Manisa City Hospital	558	In Service
Elazığ City Hospital	1.038	In Service
Ankara Bilkent City Hospital	3.711	In Service
Eskişehir City Hospital	1.081	In Service
İstanbul Başakşehir City Hospital	2682	In Service
Konya Karatay City Hospital	1250	In Service
Tekirdağ City Hospital	480	In Service
Kocaeli City Hospital	1210	Under Construction
Kütahya City Hospital	610	2021
Ankara Etlik Şehir Hastanesi	3624	2021
Gaziantep City Hospital	1875	2021
İzmir Bayraklı City Hospital	2060	2021

Source: (www.sygm.saglik.gov.tr)

Meta-Health Governance in Turkey in the Context of Digitalization

City hospitals and integrated health campuses, equipped with high-tech facilities built with the PPP model, have enabled faster decisions to be made in diagnosis, and all users can access health information without time and space limitations with the internet-based Health Information Management System (SBYS) application created by the Ministry of Health. It can be accessed from all hospitals of the Ministry. With the e-Nabız application, the patient can manage personal health information.

Except for those belonging to universities and the Ministry of National Defense of Turkey, incorporation of all public institution hospitals into the Ministry of Health in 2005, is regarded as an application made to be taken within the scope of integration policy (Karasu, 2011a: 237-239).

Since 2008, new regulations and databases have been created by the Ministry of Health and affiliated organizations in order to use registration information systems in accordance with e-government applications, which is the first step of digitalization in the provision of public services. E-Pulse, one of the most important regulations made in line with this purpose, has been developed as a personal health system managed by the citizens themselves since January 1, 2015. With this system, personal health data collected by citizens' healthcare institutions are protected in terms of intimacy, integrity, privacy and security, and citizens can check their health history via mobile devices or the internet. The E-pulse system is a personal health record that manages all the health information of citizens, regardless of where techniques and treatments are performed (Yorulmaz, Odacı and Akkan, 2018: 2-3).

With the E-Pulse system, the increase in the quality and speed of the diagnosis and treatment of health problems facilitates the establishment of a strong communication link between the citizen and the medical attendant. Besides, as the patient-related examinations are prevented again, the treatment of the patient can be carried out simultaneously in a different place. In addition, the system reduces costs by controlling the patient, the doctor and the hospital's operation.

In the course of the COVID-19 pandemic, coronavirus test results are also served through the E-pulse system. Those who have tests in city hospitals during the COVID-19 pandemic can instantly find out their test results by entering the ID number and barcode number given by the hospital through this system (enabiz.gov.tr).

The Ministry of Health is authorized as the main actor in PPP practices in the field of health. PPP is a suitable model for the regulatory-supervisory role envisaged for the Ministry of Health. With the changeover to this model, the structure of the Ministry of Health, the way it organizes health services and its relationship with the organizations that carry out this service take the form required by the contractual relationship (Karasu, 2011a: 236), and the Ministry plays this supervisory role via informatics applications such as "Spatial Business Intelligence" (MIZ) and "Public Health GIS".

Organization includes integrating the data collected in the central and provincial units of the Ministry of Health with MIZ via Spatial Business Intelligence, establishing common information pools for other public institutions and organizations within the scope of GIS (sbsgm.saglik.gov.tr), with spatial statistics and analyses, analyzing and interpreting data according to geographical location collected by public and private healthcare providers, and enabling policy-makers to take effective decisions. In addition, spatial analyses are made according to certain diseases, diagnosis groups and epidemic diseases and service delivery is accelerated (envanter.kaysis.gov.tr). The contact tracing teams, which play a very important role in the fight against COVID-19, have become stronger with the MIZ application. The contact tracing teams immediately turn to the positive cases and contacts that are apparent on the map and the coordination between the teams is provided quickly.

Geographic information systems (GIS) are generally used for viewing and managing information related to a specific location and analyzing spatial relations. The vast majority of data in the field of public health has a spatial component. In addition, database operations such as querying and statistical analysis of data, geographic analysis and visualization on the map are performed with GIS technology (Danacıoğlu, 2019: 99). Public health GIS provides modeling and mapping for the realization of objectives such as surveillance and monitoring of cases, fulfilment of needs, and strengthening communication during the pandemic process. These maps provide the necessary information to intervene in cases during the pandemic process and help reduce the spread ratio of the disease.

MIZ and public health GIS applications have become important in the effective control of the spread of the epidemic, reducing the risk of transmission, making forward-looking predictions and decision-making during the pandemic process. Especially with the estimation program, artificial intelligence and big data analysis, it is easier to make predictions and then make decisions accordingly, such as how many people will die as a result of the spread of COVID-19 and how much medical material will be required for effective treatment (Kara and Karanfiloğlu, 2020: 91).

Hospitals built with the PPP model also share a common information system in coordination with family physicians. During the pandemic period, university hospitals were included in this data-sharing system and the information of patients or contacts diagnosed with COVID-19 is directly shared with the Ministry of Health and processed into the HES code application. Citizens carrying out transactions in public institutions are admitted to the institution after it is determined whether or not the HES code has been introduced to the system about the contact risk, and these persons comply with the isolation measures.

Pandemic Science Boards of Turkey in the Context of Digitalization and Meta-Governance

On December 31, 2019, a new coronavirus called COVID-19 emerged in Wuhan city, in China's Hubei province (Hongzhou, Charles and Yi-Wei, 2020: 401). Subsequently, the World Health Organization (WHO) made important warnings and recommendations to all states by declaring that COVID-19 is an international emergency related to public health. Accordingly, the WHO emphasized the importance of correctly defining internal and external factors in determining effective strategies to minimize risks and fight COVID-19. In this process, a variety of strategies to prevent the virus from spreading in Turkey began to be put in practice (Çınar and Oğuz, 2020: 1).

In Turkey, in January 2020, the Minister of Health "Fahrettin Koca" held meetings with various bureaucrats and a "Science Board" of 26 people was established before COVID-19 was declared a pandemic by the WHO in March 2020.

In the following period, the number of members of the Scientific Committee was increased to 38. With the progress of the pandemic, the Scientific Committee held online meetings regularly. The board takes combative decisions to reduce the impact and spread of the epidemic. While the Committee announces its decisions to the public through various media organs, it also undertakes duties to inform citizens about non-scientific information and recommendations through social media, television and newspapers (Şengül and Ünal, 2020: 168). The Scientific Committee is not a final decision-making body, but is essentially an advisory board that carries out all processes in consultative terms regarding preventive, protective, diagnostic and medical processes for public health and communication (Babacan, 2020: 422). Although the decisions taken by this committee are advisory, the executive takes these decisions seriously and puts them into practice by making the necessary arrangements for the implementation of the decisions.

The Scientific Board, which is one of the important actors in making effective combative decisions against COVID-19, has made recommendations that to date have been important in many respects; these are, the cancellation and prohibition of international flights, the closure of land borders to some countries and therefore, the postponement of the travels of citizens abroad, the 14-day quarantine of those coming from abroad, the introduction of distance education at all educational levels, taking various measures in restaurants, dormitories, hotels and nursing homes, postponing open views in open and closed prisons, and curfews for all citizens over 65, under 20 and with chronic diseases and low immune systems (web.archive.org). Referring to the decisions taken by the Scientific Committee, COVID-19 pandemic management is carried out under the coordination of Turkey's Ministry of Health and in cooperation with the sectors within the scope of the "Pandemic Influenza National Preparation Plan" with the recommendations of the Scientific Advisory Board. In addition, the impact of the COVID-19 measures taken by the central institutions and organizations in the country during the pandemic process is increased by the city-specific evaluations made by the "Provincial Pandemic Committees" (Şengül and Ünal, 2020: 168-169).

For the period of active combat on the outbreak in Turkey, at both the local and national levels the Provincial Councils and Boards of Public Health have been created. Provincial pandemic committees established in the country offer opinions as advisors to take local measures accordingly, by taking the special conditions of the provinces into account. The decisions taken by the provincial pandemic committees are arranged to contribute to the implementation process of the decisions taken at the central level. Other prominent actors in the combative process of COVID-19 are the provincial/district police directors, the provincial/district gendarmerie commanders, the representatives of public institutions and organizations to be determined by the governors/district governors, local administrations, AFAD, Red Crescent and Vefa Social Support Groups, constituted from representatives of the non-governmental organizations that may be needed (Turan and Çelikyay, 2020: 13-14).

During the course of the pandemic, while NGOs played an active role, public-NGO cooperation has been implemented. In addition, from informative transparency and appropriateness to local solidarity networks, social and technological opportunities have been used in coordination. Vefa Social Support Groups in Turkey have worked effectively in the field to identify and help the needy in coordinated moves. A constitution called "Coronathon Turkey Initiative", whose stakeholders are the Industry and Technology Ministry, Turkey Informatics Foundation, TOBB, Bogazici

University, Middle East Technical University and the ITU, has been founded as a structure containing the epidemic process and subsequent technological and innovative path for the coordination model. In the final phase of the governance model, local governments have also been actively involved in the process. In this context, while some municipalities try to support citizens in need in a coordinated manner, they also organize online social activities for those who follow the "stay at home" proposal. Some municipalities carry out crisis desk missions and information, precaution and protection activities established in their medical centers in cooperation with public and non-governmental organizations. The initiative has also been at the forefront of important and acute public services ranging from the production of masks and personal protective equipment for healthcare personnel in their occupational roles to the transportation of employees of the pandemic hospital in the city, to the provision of accommodation, catering, personal cleaning and hygiene materials (Babacan, 2020: 428). In other words, the applications of the municipalities in the field contain remarkable examples in terms of producing effective practices in social service policies at the local level and presenting concrete practices for the understanding of institutional politics through coordination and the partnership mechanism.

In Turkey, during the course of COVID-19, a meta-governance administration consisting of health care, social security, education (teachers, universities, vocational schools), science and technology R & D units (centers, institutes), local governments, quasi-public entities, related areas of private sector organizations, social support units, environmental protection units, religious officials, the agricultural sector, TAF, internal security units, the defense industry, communication channels, transportation and supply institutions, energy organizations, chambers, unions, the CDI, youth centers, nursing homes and non-governmental organizations have been implemented. Turkey has carried out a corporate restructuring with investments in health infrastructure and service capacity, and a public-private sector model that can be operated in a system based on cooperation and coordination between the institutions in this process. The functionality of the coordination model among the Ministry of Health, the Ministry of Industry and Technology, TÜBİTAK, TÜSEB, the private sector and NGOs has been ensured (Babacan, 2020: 425). Although the decisions taken by national and local pandemic committees are advisory, the executive takes these decisions seriously and puts them into practice rapidly by making the necessary arrangements for the implementation of the decisions.

Conclusion

In Turkey, a meta-governance concept was presented during the course of the COVID-19 pandemic that involved a large number of actors, particularly in the health and education sectors, developing under the central government leadership in the consideration and implementation of decision-making. Considering the recommendations made by the Scientific Committee under the Ministry of Health and by the central government and accordingly, making the final decisions to combat the pandemic, the provincial and local government units of the Ministry of Internal Affairs issued circulars to make decisions to facilitate combating the pandemic and the subject of management units producing and implementing policies is the concrete reflection of meta-governance. In this meta-governance process for the epidemic, the opportunities offered by the digital infrastructure and information technologies have effectively been used in the implementation of decisions, and the control, rapid updating and re-evaluation of data. This increases efficiency and productivity in epidemic management and ensures the sustainability of the process of combating the epidemic.

The HES mobile application, created by the Ministry of Health, ensures that citizens have information and guidance on COVID-19, the spread rate of the epidemic and the control of cases; in this way the disease risk is minimized. Besides, the interaction and cooperation between central-local and non-governmental organizations during the pandemic process, enhancing pandemic decisions within the national and local conditions, are carried out more effectively with digital-based applications such as MIZ and public health GIS.

Keywords: *Meta governance, digitalization, COVID-19, city hospitals, pandemic scientific boards*

References

Acartürk, E., and Keskin, S. (2012). Public-Private Partnership Model in the Health Sector in Turkey, *Süleyman Demirel University Faculty of Economics and Administrative Sciences Journal*, Volume: 17, Issue: 3, pp. 25-51.

Albareda, L and Waddock, S. (2016). Networked CSR Governance: A Whole Network Approach to Meta-Governance, *Business & Society*, Volume: 57, Issue: 4, pp.1-40.

Aydın, M. D. (2007). Information Technologies Applications in Public Services: Opportunities and Threats, *H.Ü. Journal of Faculty of*

Economics and Administrative Sciences, Volume: 25, Issue: 2, pp. 295-322.

Ayhan, E. and Önder, E. (2018). Public Private Partnership Model in the Health Sector in Turkey, *Usaysad Journal*, Volume: 4, Issue: 1, pp. 109 -121.

Babacan, A. (2020). "Covidien-19 Aftermath and New Institutional Politics in Turkey", the Global Outbreak Future of Human Anatomy and Society, Editors. Muzaffer Şeker, Prof. Dr. Ali Özer and Dr. Cem Korkut, *Turkey Academy of Sciences*, Ankara, pp. 407-436.

Boz, S. S. (2013). Public Private Partnership (PPP) Model, *İnönü University Faculty of Law Journal*, Volume: 4, Issue: 2, pp. 277-332.

Çınar, N. F., Türkoğlu, Ç. and Tütünsatar, A. (2017). Public-Private Partnership / Collaboration Model and Measuring Service Satisfaction in Health Services Delivery: A Research for Integrated Health Campuses (City Hospitals), *Süleyman Demirel University Journal of Social Sciences Institute*, Volume: 4, Issue: 29, pp. 215-232.

Çınar, F. and Oğuz, M. (2020). Turkey's Covidien-19 Evaluation SWOT Analysis of Strategy for Pandemic, *Health and Social Welfare Research Journal*, Volume: 2, Issue: 2, pp.1-11.

Danacıoğlu, Ş. (2019). Environmental Health and Geographical Information Systems. T. Yılmaz (Ed.), *Health from the Perspective of Psychology, Sociology and Geography*, Berikan Publishing, Ankara, pp. 95-114.

Eroğlu, İ. (2018). Increasing the Role of Private Sector in Environmental Infrastructure Projects, Financial Services Specialization Thesis, Ministry of Environment and Urbanization Strategy Development Directorate, Ankara.

Erol, H. and Özdemir, A. (2018). Conversion and Its Effects on Health Expenditures in Turkey in 1980 Health Policy, *Economics and Business Administration in International Management Magazine*, CEEIK Special Issue, pp. 119-146.

Göçoğlu, V. (2019). Digital Transformation in the Delivery of Public Services: A Study on the Internet of Things, *Manas Journal of Social Research*, Volume: 9, Issue: 1, pp. 615-628.

Jessop, B. (2001). "The social Embeddedness of the Economy and İts İmplications For Economic Governance", F. Adaman and D. Pat (Ed.), *The Socially Embedded Economy* http://www.comp.lancs.ac.uk/sociology/soc016rj.html, (21.05.2020)

Ministry of Development (2016). Developments in the World and Turkey on Public Private Partnership Implementation, Ministry of Development Publications, Ankara, https://www.sbb.gov.tr/wp-content/uploads/2019/05/Kamu-Ozel_Isbirligi_Raporu-2018.pdf (15.04.2020).

Kara, N. and Karanfiloğlu, M. (2020). Digitalization of Communication: Pandemic (COVID-19) and Information Technologies, *AJIT-e: Information Technologies Online Magazine*, Volume: 11, Issue: 42, pp. 87-99.

Karasu, K. (2011a). Public-Private Partnership in the Organization of Health Services, *Ankara University SBF Journal*, Volume: 66, Issue: 3, pp. 217-262.

Karasu, K. (2011b). Public-Private Partnership in the Organization of Health Services, Public-Private Partnership in the Field of Health Symposium, 6-7 May 2011, pp. 164-232. https://www.ttb.org.tr/kutuphane/kamuozel_sempozyum.pdf (12.05.2020).

Kerman, U. Altan, Y. - Aktel, M. and Eke, E. (2012). Public Private Partnership Practice in Health Services, *Süleyman Demirel University Journal of the Faculty of Economics and Administrative Sciences*, Volume: 17, Issue: 3, pp. 1-23.

Kırışık, F. & Sezer, Özcan (2015). The Role of Information and Communication Technologies (Bit) in the Public Policy Making Process, *Journal of Economic and Social Research*, Volume: 11, Issue: 2, pp.199- 215.

Kooiman, J. and Jentoft, S. (2009). Meta-Governance: Values, Norms and Prıncıples, And The Making of Hard Choices, *Public Administration* Volume: 87, Issue: 4, 818-836.

Lund, D., Sehested, K, Hellesen, T. and Nellemann, V. (2012). Climate Change Adaptation İn Denmark: Enhancement Through Collaboration Andmeta-Governance?, *Local Environment*, Volume: 17, Issue: 6-7, pp. 613-628.

Özer, M.A. (2016). A New Service Delivery Model in the Health Sector: Public Private Partnership, *Journal of Social Security*, March 2016, Volume: 6, Issue: 1, pp. 9-38.

Özer, M.A. (2017). From Governance to Digital Governance: The Technological Dimension of Paradigm Change, *HAK-İŞ International Journal of Labor and Society*, Volume: 6, Issue: 3, pp. 428-473.

Peters, G. (2010), Meta-Governance And, Public Management, The New Public Governance, Emerging Perspective on Theory and Practice of Public Governance, Edt. Stephen Osborne, Routladge, Londdon and New York, pp. 37-51.

Roy, S. (2014). Meta Governance: An Assessment, *NU Journal of Humanities, Social Sciences & Business Studies*, Volume: 1, Issue: 1, December 2014, pp. 53-60.

Sobacı, M. Z. and Köseoğlu, Ö. (2015). "Yeni Kamu Yönetişimi: Birlikte Üretmenin ve İşbirliğinin Teorik Çerçevesi", Edt. Özer Köseoğlu and Mehmet Zahid Sobacı, Kamu Yönetiminde Paradigma Arayışları: Yeni Kamu İşletmeciliği ve Ötesi, Dora Publishing, Bursa, pp. 231-248.

Sorensen, E. and Torfing, J. (2009). Making Governance Networks Effective and Democratic through Metagovernance, *Public Administration*, Volume: 87, Issue: 2, pp. 234-258.

Sözer, A. N. (2014). City Hospitals as a Continuation of Health Restructuring (Privatization), *Dokuz Eylül University Faculty of Law Journal*, Volume: 15, Special Issue, pp. 215-253.

Şengül, E. and Ünal, E. (2020). Public Health Management in the COVID-19 Outbreak, *Med Res Rep*, Volume: 3, Issue: 1, pp. 162-171.

Strategy and Budget Presidency (2019). In the world and in Turkey Regarding Public-Private Partnership Practice Development Report 2018, https://www.sbb.gov.tr/kamu-ozel-isbirliginde-gelismeler-yayinlar/ (15.11.2020).

Tokatlıoğlu, M. and Şen, S. (2019). Presentation and Public Private Partnership Model for Financing of Public Service: The European Union and Turkey, *International Journal Of Public Finance*, Volume: 4, Issue: 2, pp. 205-235.

Turan, A. and Çelikyay, H. (2020). Combating Kovid-19 in Turkey: Policies and Actors, *International Academy of Management Journal*, Year: 2020, Volume 3, Issue: 1, pp.1-25.

Uysal, Y. (2019). Public-Private Partnership (Build-Rent-Transfer) Model and the Effects of City Hospitals on Change and Transformation in Health Services, *Eskisehir Osmangazi University Journal of FEAS*, Volume: 3, Issue: 14, pp. 877-898.

Uz, A. (2007). Public-Private Partnership / Publıc-Prıvate Partnership (PPP) (Concept and Legal Framework), *Gazi University Faculty of Law Journal*, Volume: 11, Issue: 1-2, pp. 1165-1182.

Wilson, C., Morrison, T. and Everingham, J. (2017). Linking the 'meta-governance' imperative to regional governance in resource communities, *Journal of Rural Studies*, Volume: 50, pp. 188-197.

Yeşiltaş, A. (2020). Public Private Partnership in Health Sector: An Evaluation on City Hospitals, *Usaysad Magazine*, Volume: 6, Issue: 1, pp. 15-28.

Yorulmaz, M., Odacı, Ş. and Akkan, M. (2018). Digital Health and E-Pulse Awareness Level Determination Study, *Selcuk University Journal of Social and Technical Research*, Volume: 16, pp.1-11.

Zhang, Qian F. (2015) State Political Identity and Meta- Governance: Comparative Analysis of Governance Modes in Vegetable Retail in Urban China, *Journal of Comparative Policy Analysis: Research and Practice*, Volume: 17, Issue: 4, pp. 378-392.

https://enabiz.gov.tr/PcrTestSonuc/Index (5.12.2020).

https://envanter.kaysis.gov.tr/HizmetDetay.aspx?ID=84043 (5.12.2020).

https://koi.sbb.gov.tr/ (5.12.2020).

https://sbsgm.saglik.gov.tr/TR,32359/mekansal-is-zekasi-birimi.html (5.12.2020)

www.sygm.saglik.gov.tr/%20TR,33960/sehir-hastaneleri.html /22.10.2020)

https://web.archive.org/web/20200328185751/https://www.gzt.com/jurnalist/uzmanlari-bir-araya-getiren-bilim-kurulu-nasil-kuruldu-3531656 (24.10.2020).

https://population.un.org/wpp/, United Nations Department of Economic and Social Affairs Population Dynamics, (01.11.2020).

CHAPTER EIGHTEEN

DIGITALIZATION IN THE HEALTH SECTOR

EMINE ÇETIN ASLAN

Introduction

The introduction of the internet and new generation devices that can communicate via the internet has significantly affected both the daily life of people and their way of doing business (Litan, 2008). It is clear that all people or regions are not equally affected by this change. Similarly, this equality also exists among the sectors. It is frequently emphasized that digitalization in the health sector is slower compared to other sectors and it has not yet reached the desired potential (Cisco, 2016; Litan, 2008; Rutkevich, n.d.). The sensitivity and traditional structure of the sector, the concerns about ensuring privacy of records, and also the fact that patients are involved in the production process can somehow explain the slightly distant approach to the change.

It is possible to see the serious terminology in the health sector to express the use of digital technologies. Concepts such as digital health, telehealth, telemedicine, mHealth, and electronic health records have become concepts seen every day. It is necessary to define these concepts that are closely related to each other and sometimes used interchangeably and reveal their common and different aspects. The most common two concepts concerning the use of digital technologies in the health sector are digital health and telehealth. It is possible to express these concepts explained with different expressions by researchers and authorities as to the use of digital technology opportunities in different fields (data collection, collecting health-related records, doctor-patient communication, etc.) of the health sector in the broadest sense (World Health Assembly, 2018). Concepts such as mHealth, telehealth, tele-monitoring, tele-radiology, and tele-psychology have been developed to express the use of digital opportunities in certain fields of the health sector.

In addition, it is possible to say that the latest developments have been remarkable in increasing digitalization in the health sector or the utilization rates from digital opportunities. As telehealth has been around for decades, the rapid evolution of technology and infrastructure over the past few years has combined telehealth with mobile applications (mHealth) and wearable technology and created a new and incrementally growing digital health field (Martin et al., 2018). The biggest share in this development belongs to the expansion of internet network connections and the widespread use of smart mobile phones with a large processing capacity (Topol, 2010). The Covid-19 pandemic, which has continued for about a year, has been a demand-side driving force to increase the digitalization of the last decades. The ability of digitalization to minimize the need for people to be face-to-face has led to its consideration as a rescuer, leaving concerns about digitalization aside. It is thought that it will not be surprising to anyone that future studies on the use of digital technology in the health sector will find that the use of technologies during and after the pandemic has increased significantly as compared to before the pandemic.

This chapter mainly consists of three subparts. In the first subpart, the concepts emerging due to the use of digital technologies in the health sector are presented. In the second subpart, the opportunities to use digital technologies in the health sector are discussed. In the third part, the advantages of digital technologies in the health sector are presented. In the conclusion, the topics mentioned in the text are evaluated in general.

Commonly Used Concepts Concerning Digitalization in the Health Sector

New concepts have developed with the use of digital technologies in different fields of the health sector. Each concept defines the scope of services, the types of technologies, and the methods used for patients to receive telehealth services (American Hospital Association, 2015). Some of these concepts refer to a wide range of applications, while others refer to very specific applications of the sector. Explaining the concepts is useful in terms of both providing language unity and revealing different uses.

The most comprehensive and interchangeable concepts related to digitalization applications in the health sector are digital health and e-Health. E-Health is a concept consisting of the abbreviation of "electronic health" (Van Velthoven, and Cordon, 2019). It is possible to define these two concepts as the use of digital technology opportunities in the health sector in the broadest sense. In other words, e-Health refers to the cost-effective and safe use of information and communication technologies to support health and health-related fields including healthcare services, healthcare surveillance, health literature and health education, information, and research (World Health Organization, 2005).

The two most common concepts seen in daily life are telehealth and telemedicine. Typically, these refer to the use of modern communications to provide a wide range of healthcare services to patients who are far from the service provider (Center for Medicare and Medicaid, 2020; Young et al., 2019; Martin et al., 2018; American Hospital Association, 2015; Litan, 2008). Although they are used interchangeably in most cases, there are some differences between them. Telehealth can be defined as using digital technologies to promote remote clinical health care, patient education, community health, and health management (U.S. Department of Health and Human Services –HHS, 2020; American Hospital Association, 2015). According to another definition, telemedicine is defined as the transfer of medical information from one place to another via electronic communication to improve the health status of a patient. Communications tools such as email, smartphones, and wireless devices, and a variety of applications can be used for this purpose (quoted by; American Hospital Association, 2015).

The main difference between telehealth and telemedicine is that telehealth includes a wider health service that does not always include the services provided by members of the clinic care team (Martin et al., 2018) while telemedicine rather focuses on therapeutic health services. In other words, telehealth includes different types of health services (preventive, therapeutic health services, managed care) as well as elements that are not directly related to health service delivery such as health management and health education.

Another digital technology application that is mentioned more each passing day is mobile health or mHealth. It is seen that mHealth can be defined with different expressions corresponding to the same concept. Each of these definitions emphasizes a different feature of mHealth; for instance, using mobile devices to monitor or identify the biological changes in human bodies (Park, 2016). According to another definition, it is the delivery of health services via mobile devices, also including wearable technologies usually integrated with particular software (Young et al., 2019; Park, 2016). In its shortest form, mHealth can be expressed as health-related services offered through mobile communication devices (Bhavnani et al., 2016; Whittaker, 2012). As stated in the definitions, the main features of mHealth are the use of mobile devices and the collection of biological or health data of distant patients, and wearable health technologies are appreciated within mHealth applications.

The main reasons for mHealth's popularity are its ease of application, the ability to use simple devices that can be sold directly to patients, and the ability to collect a wide range of data. A wide range of products can be used in the mHealth application from wearable electrocardiogram (ECG) monitors to wristwatches with programs and free applications that can be downloaded to mobile phones. Easy access to smartphones, tabs, and other communicative devices is a critical component that enables mHealth to become widespread and easy to be adopted (American Hospital Association, 2015).

In addition to its accessibility, mHealth is a good solution and tool for service providers to collect much information about patient health and vital status. The collected data are evaluated by the family doctor, the doctor treating the disease, or the health center. The units responsible for device management such as clinics or service providers collect data and use them for health care and health status improvement (Park, 2016). The data flow can be synchronous or it is possible to analyze the stored data retrospectively. The use of these devices in treatments allows healthcare delivery to move away from a structure created by health systems and evolve into a structure created by patients (Bhavnani et al., 2016).

It is seen that concepts such as tele-stroke, tele-radiology, tele-ICU, tele-mental health, tele-pathology, cyber-surgery, remote patient monitoring, tele-pharmacy and tele-consultations refer to the use of digital technologies in very specific fields of health services apart from commonly used concepts have entered the medical literature (American Hospital Association, 2015).

Uses of Digital Technologies in the Healthcare Sector

It is possible to list the fields in which digitalization is mostly used in the health sector, especially telehealth, as real-time interviews, store-and-forward, remote patient monitoring, and hospital information systems.

Real-Time Interview

This is a live, two-way interaction between a patient (or caregiver) and the service provider (e.g., doctor) using audio-visual technology. Real-time telehealth services can be used to consult, diagnose, and treat patients. Virtual visits are acknowledged within this scope. The service provider or patient communicates via teleconferencing. It is generally used in tele-psychiatry, tele-homedicine, tele-cardiology, and tele-consultations with specialists, primary care physicians, counselors, social workers, and other health professionals (American Telehealth Association, 2015).

Store-and-Forward

This method, also called asynchronous telehealth, refers to consultations that do not include live (simultaneous) interactions (Young et al., 2019). Clinical data, photographs, laboratory values, culture results and radiographic studies are presented digitally to the specialists, deeply examined and integrated by the physicians and used to generate an expert opinion. The specialist sends a consultation report to the doctor monitoring the patient (Young et al., 2019). The obtained data are used to evaluate a patient's condition, make a diagnosis or in some cases provide a service other than real-time interaction. Store-and-forward technologies have the advantage of access for a long time after the collection of patient data (American Hospital Association, 2015).

This method contributes to the more efficient use of resources, especially when there is local shortage of specialist human resources. For instance, a general practitioner may request a consultation by sharing the recorded ECG results of a patient with a cardiologist. It is also possible to use the store-and-forward method in sharing human resources among countries. For instance, countries with a shortage of radiologists or with high radiologic procedure fees can benefit from reporting MRI, CT, and X-ray results taken by a radiologist in another country. In addition, this method has the potential to save critical patient data for a long time, avoid repeat tests, and contribute to better patient diagnosis and treatment.

Remote Patient Monitoring

This is the collection of the personal status and health data of a patient outside the health institution through electronic communication technologies (American Hospital Association, 2015). Wearable health technologies and mHealth that can be integrated with particular applications are used in this method (Young et al., 2019; Park, 2016). Hardware components can provide clinicians with video, photo and electrocardiography as well as monitored data (Young et al., 2019). Once data are collected, they are transmitted to a healthcare professional in a different location (American Hospital Association, 2015).

Application examples of the method include drug compliance and monitoring of side effects, monitoring disease parameters, and improving chronic disease management (Young et al., 2019). This method allows the healthcare institution to continue monitoring the patient data even after the patient goes home or to another care facility (American Hospital Association, 2015). Since patients can be sent home for follow-up after their acute treatment is completed, their hospital stay can be shortened, or they are monitored at home without the need for hospitalization.

The main advantages of the method are thought to be better understood due to the Covid-19 pandemic process. The use of this method, without the need for patients to go to the health institution and in most cases without contacting healthcare professionals, enabled interventions whenever necessary by monitoring changes in the patients' conditions. Thus, health institutions, which are very busy, were used more efficiently and contact was reduced. Hence, Medicare has announced that it will pay for telehealth services during the pandemic (Centers for Medicare and Medicaid Services, 2020).

Hospital Information Systems

It would not be wrong to say that hospital information systems are one of the most widely used fields of digitalization in the health sector. Hospitals are organizations that contain various administrative and medical services and where big data appear in these processes. Hospital information systems are information processing and storage systems that include computer networks and computer-based applications (Homayounfar, 2012).

In both administrative and medical processes, the use of hospital information systems provides basic advantages such as facilitating communication and information exchange between departments, creating timely and accurate information and reports, increasing the performance of service providers, the quality of health care, patient satisfaction and employee satisfaction, and performance, providing management convenience, enabling cost-benefit evaluations and the use of decision support systems, increasing medical and administrative efficiency and reducing costs (Farzandipour, Nabovati, Zaeimi, and Khajouei, 2018). The correct recording and long-term storage of these data not only contribute to institutional performance, public health, and patient monitoring but also include legal obligations.

In the hospital information system, the socio-demographic and medical information of the patients is recorded and presented to the right users at the right time, at the right place, whenever needed. It contains a wide range of information regarding both administrative and medical processes, compares them, generates new information based on them and ensures that it is transferred to users when necessary (Wendt, Häber, Brigl, and Winter,

2004; Homayounfar, 2012; Haux, 2006). The hospital information system acts as an interface for the applications of hospital and non-hospital users (insurance institutions, higher institutions such as the Ministry of Health, other hospitals, etc.) (Homayounfar, 2012).

Advantages of Digital Technologies for the Healthcare Sector

The healthcare sector is a huge industry consisting of hospitals, nursing homes, home care, pharmaceutical companies, research and development organizations (Rutkevich, n.d). While the widespread use of digitalization in the health sector provides new opportunities with different application fields in terms of digitalization, it contributes to the development of the health sector, enabling a more effective and productive delivery of health services (Park, 2016; Cisco, 2016; Rutkevich, n.d). It is possible to see that every institution in the sector produces solutions to meet their needs with digital technologies.

In fact, the eHealth application exemplifies some of the key features of late modernity: it eliminates distance in communications, reduces wasted time when time is critical, and restructures both the care processes and the labor market supporting them (Andreassen et al., 2018). The advantages of digitalization can be listed as strengthening physician-patient coordination, facilitating management processes, coordinating multiple physicians, increasing data security and facilitating access to health records (Rutkevich, n.d.). The climax of these factors is that they offer unique opportunities to increase patient engagement, lower healthcare costs and improve outcomes (Bhavnani et al., 2016).

The use of digital technologies in healthcare has significantly changed the way things are done (Cisco, 2016). These changes have made significant contributions to particular points of the health system. It is possible to examine the advantages of digitalization in the health sector under the headings of increasing the accessibility of communities with low access to healthcare, reducing costs, ensuring long-term care candidates stay away from institutional care, and obtaining big data.

Increasing the Access

One of the main purposes of health systems is to provide accessible health services to everyone in the society. However, some parts of society continue to remain disadvantaged due to difficulties in accessing services. The most disadvantaged are those who live in rural and outside metropolitan areas. From the beginning, telehealth has been used to deliver healthcare services to consumers in remote locations (Martin et al., 2018; American Telehealth Association, 2015).

In the USA, one-fifth of the population at the age of 65 and over who need health services the most (Onor et al., 2008) live outside metropolitan areas. Elderly people living in metropolitan areas often have problems in accessing primary health care services as well as specialist health services. In addition, those living in the suburbs of big cities also have difficulties in attending hospitals and doctor's appointments (Herman, 2016).

Another obstacle to healthcare access is the seriously long hours spent reaching healthcare services, even if there is no personal problem. These distances bring additional time and cost burdens for users in transportation. Telehealth and virtual care can increase access to care for rural communities, underserved and vulnerable patient populations and individuals who cannot provide face-to-face care and ensure that everyone has access to safe, effective and appropriate care whenever and wherever they need it. Telehealth is an attractive strategy, especially for patients who cannot move on their own, because their transfer is always difficult, time-consuming and expensive (Rees and Bashshur, 2007).

Another important problem for rural areas is the failure to employ particular medical professionals. Telehealth not only improves consumer access, but also expands the geographic access and expertise of doctors and healthcare institutions (American Telehealth Association, 2015). Safe communication technologies allow these rural centers to pass tests such as x-rays to radiologists and other specialists in larger locations. Patient follow-up can similarly be outsourced so that rural hospitals or clinics can take care of special services such as intensive care units and cardiac care units (Litan, 2008). This enables millions of people living in both rural and urban areas to reach safe, effective and proper care when and where needed (American Telehealth Association, 2015; Litan, 2008).

The use of digital technologies helps disadvantaged people to access the healthcare services they need without leaving their homes (Whittaker, 2012). Through video conferences, patients can be examined and monitored remotely and medications can be prescribed (Litan, 2008). Such distribution channels can enable real-time health advice, prompts, monitoring, feedback, personalized support and interventions that were not easily available before mobile phones became so widespread (Whittaker, 2012). To sum up, digital transformation can make long distance installation less costly and easier (Cisco, 2016; Whittaker, 2012). It increases the level of access for those who cannot access critical services for different kinds of needs, particularly in rural areas or traditionally underserved groups (Litan, 2008).

Increasing the Coordination

The use of digital technologies increases the amount of communication and quality of information between patients and caregivers and therefore, contributes to the development of communication. Caregivers have the opportunity to obtain more detailed information on which they can ground treatment decisions. In addition, the participation of a medical team is increased in the long-term care of patients and can increase patients' adaptation to a treatment plan through video conferencing and tele-visits (Litan, 2008). The delivery of care to patients in accordance with their lifestyles is supported with the flexibility created by digital opportunities (Martin et al., 2018). mHealth methods can be used to distinguish the adaptation behaviors and factors affecting the real-time monitoring of the adaptation to treatment (Kumar et al., 2013). Thus, by designing more successful and patient-centered therapies, there can be reduced morbidity, improved quality of life for patients, and reduced hospitalization and other care facilities (Litan, 2008).

Coordination in treatment is more important in chronic diseases that necessitate long-term treatment. Adaptation to treatment in these diseases is of great value in terms of preventing other health problems related to the disease from occurring and reducing the frequency of acute exacerbation of the disease. In addition to the applied treatments, the course of the disease should be monitored and the treatment reviewed periodically. More regular monitoring with remote monitoring; provides an advantage in quickly recognizing the changes in vital signs in patients with chronic diseases and determining the need for medical intervention. Remote monitoring technologies can transfer data to the health care provider, on a regular and real-time basis and prevent hospitalization by detecting problems and reporting negative trends before they reach the crisis stage. Thus, hospitalization can be prevented, hospitalization duration can be shortened and some of the emergency admissions can be prevented (Litan, 2008).

Telemedicine facilitates coordination between physician and physician, caregiver and health professional, and patient and doctor. New developments in the patient's condition can be evaluated with different specialist physicians and the patient can receive better care. In addition, it is expected that the training of informal caregivers and the provision of support whenever necessary will increase the potential of patients to increase treatment success.

Avoiding Institutional Care

One of the areas in which digital health technologies and remote monitoring methods are most needed is the monitoring of individuals who constantly need the surveillance of someone else, especially the elderly. Most long-term care is provided informally, i.e., by the family. The necessary care is provided by children, spouses or partners or other family members (Onor et al., 2008; Spillman and Pezzin, 2000). Institutional care is needed when the care of relatives is not sufficient. Institutional care is provided by healthcare institutions such as hospitals, care centers, and nursing care homes. As a result of the increase in the elderly population in the society and the change in family structures, the current situation seems not to continue in this way. Moreover, institutional care is currently a significant burden on the budgets of reimbursement institutions in many countries. There is concern that this burden will be unrecoverable in the future (Onor et al., 2008).

In addition, due to comorbidities of the elderly, rapid deterioration can be observed in their health conditions. Due to the decrease in biological reserve, the reserves of frail elderly are limited for physiological and psychosocial recovery. Minor health problems have the potential to trigger acute situations. A functional decline leading to re-hospitalization and the worsening of chronic diseases restarts the disease process and causes patients to lose their independence (Onor et al., 2008). The decrease in physical and mental activities when old people lose their independence further increases their vulnerability. Remote monitoring and video visits may prevent diseases from reaching serious levels (Litan, 2008).

Telehealth and mHealth have the solution potential for the surveillance needs of the elderly. These technologies enable individuals in need of care to “age in place” and regularly connect with a provider by supporting access to high quality, safe and appropriate care. They could also contribute to a more efficient use of scarce health resources, lower costs and the benefit of healthcare providers and hospital systems for more people (American Telehealth Association, 2015).

Telemedicine also contributes to the protection of the independence of frail elderly people. The ideal solution for the elderly is home care if possible. Home care is not only significantly cheaper than nursing home care, but patients are more satisfied with staying in their home as well.

However, home care can only be achieved when patients can live independently in their homes (Litan, 2008).

The study results found that the number of emergency admissions in the group supported with telemedicine was 50% less than that of the control group. Emergency admissions should be appreciated as significant data since the hospitalization rates of those elderly with high risks are high. In fact, the number of hospitalizations was found to be half that of the control group and the duration of hospitalization was 54% lower (Rees and Bashshur, 2007). In addition to these positive data in the statistics of healthcare use, the satisfaction of the elderly who receive home care and their relatives with telehealth is very high. While 75.3% of those living in nursing homes and 76.5% of those who went to day care centers were satisfied or very satisfied with the service they received, almost all of the telehealth supported home care recipients (98.5%) stated that they were satisfied or very satisfied (Onor et al., 2008).

Patients with temporary health conditions that require home care or monitoring (e.g., hip fracture, post-operative, Covid-19, etc.) are also excellent candidates for telemedicine (Litan, 2008). These telemedicine interventions not only give better healthcare results, but also the recovery (and therefore the return to work) is faster and it has few effects on the family or other caregivers (Litan, 2008).

Cost Control

Health expenditures are increasing rapidly around the world. Health expenditures increasing faster than national income in the long term is squeezing the budgets of many countries. The increase in health risks in the society and private insurance premiums make it difficult to preserve the market and to achieve actuarial balance in terms of private insurance. At this point, the use of digital healthcare technologies can be regarded as a cost-saving method in terms of being cheaper as compared to face-to-face service delivery in many cases, allowing people with diseases to stay at home instead of in institutional care and providing support for the effective management of chronic diseases (Bhavnani et al., 2016; Herman, 2016; Kumar et al., 2013). Digital technologies could be an alternative to get greater advantages for low-income countries with more restricted resources (Tambo et al., 2016).

Reducing and controlling the costs of healthcare services is one of the strongest motivating factors to finance and adopt digital healthcare technologies (Bhavnani et al., 2016; American Telehealth Association, 2015). More insurance coverage of telehealth services with each passing day (Herman, 2016) supports the belief that digital health services will contribute to the efficient delivery of resources. In real practices, a telemedicine check in most cases requires a lower payment for insurance than an emergency service application (Herman, 2016).

One of the most important areas where digital technologies create cost advantages is their effect on the management of chronic diseases. Especially mobile healthcare applications make positive contributions to the prevention of exacerbation through the close monitoring and control of current chronic patients and therefore reductions in policlinic and emergency applications (Herman, 2016; American Telehealth Association, 2015; Kumar et al., 2013). In addition, enabling patients to take an active role in the care process can encourage them to be more conscious and adopt healthy behaviors. It may contribute to getting better healthcare results and reducing the burden of disease (Kumar et al., 2013). With this aspect, it can be the function of a preventive health service application whose effectiveness is acknowledged by everyone. An exemplary advantage of digitization is that it can increase continuity of care through the better protection of patient medical records (Park, 2016).

The use of digital health technologies can reduce indirect healthcare costs by reducing the transportation time and costs of patients and their relatives in addition to reimbursement institutions (American Telehealth Association, 2015). The savings from patient shares that healthcare users will have to pay due to the use of healthcare services is also a point to be considered. In addition, the fact that more than one institution can benefit from advanced medical expertise, limited in number in many countries, will achieve savings for health institutions with the opportunity that a wide range of society can benefit (American Telehealth Association, 2015).

Creating Big Data

Thanks to digital opportunities, especially mobile healthcare applications, obtaining health data has never been easier than today. Both patients and healthcare institutions can obtain and store data. Again, thanks to technological developments, the collected data can easily be analyzed and put into use.

The obtained data combine with the personal data of other people to create much larger datasets – or big data – that can be combined in almost infinite variations for analysis about community diseases and health-related behaviors. In recent years, great emphasis has been placed on the potential of big data to contribute to medical data, healthcare delivery, health promotion practice and disease surveillance. Institutional actors also consider big data to be important information resources and precious products. Community-based big data make important contributions to determining the prevalence of diseases, reducing medical mistakes, improving patient care, planning medical experiments and early diagnosis and preventive medicine (Lupton, 2018). Healthcare professionals and patients similarly have access to large amounts of medical information via mHealth (Martin et al., 2018).

Researchers and public healthcare employees have also begun using large digital data sets as a form of disease surveillance. Here, the content of other digital data such as social media material and search engine queries is collected again in an attempt to differentiate outbreaks of epidemics. Some platforms and related applications have been created specifically to collect and display information about infectious diseases. They can be used by members to map the disease of the general public who want to control where outbreaks occur, as well as by public healthcare professionals (Lupton, 2018).

The use of healthcare technologies has also made significant contributions to health research. Since many data collected by mHealth can be obtained remotely in real time, data analysis can be performed faster, sometimes simultaneously. This can therefore ensure that studies are terminated earlier than usual (Kumar et al., 2013).

Conclusion

The healthcare sector is not one of the leading sectors in digitalization. Many authors state that this sector does not make enough use of digitalization opportunities. In this case, it is seen that the health sector is subject to strict legal regulations and deals with "vital" activities which make flexibility difficult. Developments in digital technology created significant changes in the way of service delivery in the health sector although these are not at the desired or expected level. Traditional applications turn into a different form due to the use of digital technologies each passing day.

Digitalization has brought significant advantages to the healthcare sector. One of these advantages is that many health services can be provided without the need for the physician and the patient to be in the same physical atmosphere. Healthcare services that can be provided remotely range from monitoring the vital signs of patients to giving examinations and even performing surgical procedures. The fact that many health services can be provided remotely has increased the chance of disadvantaged rural areas receiving similar health services to the metropolitan areas with less cost and effort. Digitalization has also brought significant advantages to healthcare service providers. The healthcare institutions that are small and far from metropolitan areas and have difficulty in employing expert healthcare personnel have the chance to get consultancy and services easily.

Perhaps the most promising application for the healthcare sector is the contribution to the monitoring of chronic diseases. In almost all countries of the world most of the healthcare resources are allocated for chronic diseases. Monitoring patient findings, reducing the exacerbation of diseases and the need for institutional care through early interventions whenever necessary promise to reduce the burden of health systems. In addition, the findings that patient monitoring systems can reduce disease causing risky behaviors are highly promising.

Despite the important contributions of digitalization, it is clear that its potential advantages are not available to everyone and every region. The use of digital technologies at least requires a certain level of infrastructure. However, this infrastructure is not established everywhere. Studies have begun to discuss the concept of "digital inequality" in an environment in which ongoing inequalities in healthcare sector cannot be resolved.

There are some reasons for the limited use of digital technologies in the health sector, apart from infrastructure opportunities. Foremost among them is that newly developing technologies rarely have evidence supported by randomized controlled trials as the sector is accustomed. Therefore, there is concern that the use of these technologies may bring certain risks. Another important reason is that the purchasers of most of the health services produced are not the patients but the public and private insurance organizations. Producing a service that these organizations do not pay for may require financial risk-taking. The most debated and concerning issue about digitalization is data security. Numerous personal data are obtained about patients. There are still concerns about who can see these data, most of which are personal, and to what extent patients' personal rights are protected.

As a result, there are many fields in the healthcare sector in which digital technologies can be used effectively and productively. However, suitable infrastructure, legislation and payment models are needed in order to benefit from these potential advantages. It is thought that the efforts of the countries in this aspect will be rewarded by improvement and savings in public health.

Keywords: *Digital health, digitalization, health sector, e-health*

References

American Hospital Association. (2015). *The Promise Of Telehealth For Hospitals, Health Systems And Their Communities. American Hospital Association*. Washington, DC. Retrieved From Https://Www.Aha.Org/Guidesreports/2015-01-20-Promise-Telehealth-Hospitals-Health-Systems-And-Their-Communities

Andreassen, H. K., Dyb, K., May, C. R., Pope, C. J., & Warth, L. L. (2018). Digitized Patient–Provider İnteraction: How Does İt Matter? A Qualitative Meta-Synthesis. *Social Science And Medicine*, *215*, 36–44. Https://Doi.Org/10.1016/J.Socscimed.-2018.08.036

Bhavnani, S. P., Narula, J., & Sengupta, P. P. (2016). Mobile Technology And The Digitization Of Healthcare. *European Heart Journal*, *37*(18), 1428–1438. Https://Doi.Org/10.1093/Eurheartj/-Ehv770

CISCO. (2016). *The Digitization Of The Healthcare Industry: Using Technology To Transform Care. CISCO*. San Jose. Retrieved From Https://Pdfs.Semanticscholar.Org/2480/F6c0e56ec942aed96db6a9883 1ce2f60033a.Pdf

CMS, C. For M. & M. S. (2020). President Trump Expands Telehealth Benefits For Medicare Beneficiaries During COVID-19 Outbreak. Retrieved From Https://Www.Cms.Gov/Newsroom/Pressreleases/ President-Trump-Expands-Telehealth-Benefits-Medicare-Beneficiaries-During-Covid-19-Outbreak

Farzandipour, M., Nabovati, E., Zaeimi, G. H., & Khajouei, R. (2018). Usability Evaluation Of Three Admission And Medical Records Subsystems Integrated İnto Nationwide Hospital Information Systems: Heuristic Evaluation. *Acta Informatica Medica*, *26*(2), 133–138. Https://Doi.Org/10.5455/Aim.2018.26.133-138

Haux R. (2006). Health İnformation Systems - Past, Present, Future. *International Journal Of Medical İnformatics*, 75(3-4), 268–281. Https://Doi.Org/10.1016/J.İjmedinf.2005.08.002

Herman, B. (2016). Virtual Reality: More İnsurers Are Embracing Telehealth. *Modern Health Care*. Retrieved From Https://Www.Modernhealthcare.Com/Article/20160220/MAGAZINE/ 302209980-/Virtual-Reality-More-İnsurers-Are-Embracing-Telehealth

Homayounfar, P. (2012). Process Mining Challenges İn Hospital İnformation Systems. 2012 Federated Conference On Computer Science And Information Systems (Fedcsıs), 1135-1140.

HHS. (2020). What İs Telehealth? Retrieved December 15, 2020, From Https://Www.Hhs.Gov/Hipaa/-For-Professionals/Faq/3015/What-İs-Telehealth/İndex.Html#:~:Text=The Health Resources And

Services,Professional Health-Related Education%2C And

Kumar, S., Nilsen, W. J., Abernethy, A., Atienza, A., Patrick, K., Pavel, M., Riley, W. T., Shar, A., Spring, B., Spruijt-Metz, D., Hedeker, D., Honavar, V., Kravitz, R., Lefebvre, R. C., Mohr, D. C., Murphy, S. A., Quinn, C., Shusterman, V., & Swendeman, D. (2013). Mobile Health Technology Evaluation: The Mhealth Evidence Workshop. *American Journal Of Preventive Medicine*, 45(2), 228–236. Https://Doi.Org/10.1016/J.Amepre.2013.03.017

Litan, R. E. (2008). *Vital Signs Via Broadband: Remote Health Monitoring Transmits Savings, Enhances Lives*. Retrieved From Https://Docplayer.Net/16910841-Vital-Signs-Via-Broadband-Remote-Health-Monitoring-Transmits-Savings-Enhances-Lives.Html

Lupton, D. (2018). *Digital Health: Critical And Cross-Disciplinary Perspectives* (1st Ed.). London And New York: Routledge Publishing.

Martin, A., Brummond, P., Vlasimsky, T., Steffenhagen, A., Langley, J., Glowczewski, J., Boyd, A., Engels, M., Hermann, S., & Skaff, A. (2018). The Evolving Frontier Of Digital Health: Opportunities For Pharmacists On The Horizon. *Hospital Pharmacy*, 53(1), 7–11. Https://Doi.Org/10.1177/0018578717738221

Onor, M. L., Trevisiol, M., Urciuoli, O., Misan, S., Bertossi, F., Tirone, G., Aguglia, E., & Pascolo-Fabrici, E. (2008). Effectiveness Of Telecare İn Elderly Populations-A Comparison Of Three Settings. Telemedicine Journal And E-Health : *The Official Journal Of The American Telemedicine Association*, 14(2), 164–169. Https://Doi.Org/10.1089/Tmj.2007.0028

Park Y. T. (2016). Emerging New Era Of Mobile Health Technologies. *Healthcare Informatics Research*, 22(4), 253–254. Https://Doi.Org/10.4258/Hir.2016.22.4.253

Rees, R. S., & Bashshur, N. (2007). The Effects Of Telewound Management On Use Of Service And Financial Outcomes. Telemedicine Journal And E-Health : *The Official Journal Of The American Telemedicine Association*, 13(6), 663–674. Https://Doi.Org/10.1089/Tmj.2007.9971

Rutkevich, J. (N.D.). 5 Benefits Of Digitization İn The Healthcare Industry. Retrieved December 15, 2020, From Https://Digitalhealthbuzz.Com/5-Benefits-Of-Digitization-İn-The-Healthcare-İndustry/

Spillman, B. C., & Pezzin, L. E. (2000). Potential And Active Family Caregivers: Changing Networks And The "Sandwich Generation". *The Milbank Quarterly*, 78(3), 347–374. Https://Doi.Org/10.1111/1468-0009.00177

Tambo, E., Madjou, G., Mbous, Y., Olalubi, O. A., Yah, C., Adedeji, A. A., & Ngogang, J. Y. (2016). Digital Health İmplications İn Health Systems İn Africa. *European Journal Of Pharmaceutical And Medical Research*, *3*(1), 91–93. Retrieved From Https://Www.Researchgate.Net/-Profile/Ernest_Tambo2/Publication/291346057_DIGITAL_HEALTH_IMPLICATIONS_IN_HEALTH_SYSTEMS_IN_AFRICA/Links/56a136c708ae2afab8829224.Pdfe2afab8829224.Pdf

Topol E. J. (2010). Transforming Medicine Via Digital İnnovation. Science Translational Medicine, 2(16), 16cm4. Https://Doi.Org/10.1126/Scitranslmed.3000484

Van Velthoven, M. H., & Cordon, C. (2019). Sustainable Adoption Of Digital Health Innovations: Perspectives From A Stakeholder Workshop. *Journal Of Medical Internet Research*, 21(3), E11922. Https://Doi.Org/10.2196/11922

Wendt, T., Häber, A., Brigl, B., & Winter, A. (2004). Modeling Hospital Information Systems (Part 2): Using The 3LGM2 Tool For Modeling Patient Record Management. *Methods Of İnformation İn Medicine*, 43(3), 256–267.

Whittaker R. (2012). Issues İn Mhealth: Findings From Key İnformant İnterviews. *Journal Of Medical Internet Research*, 14(5), E129. Https://Doi.Org/10.2196/Jmir.1989

WHO. (2005). *RESOLUTIONS AND DECISIONS. World Health Organization* (Vol. WHA58.28). Geneva. Retrieved From Https://Www.Who.İnt/Healthacademy/Media/WHA58-28-En.Pdf?Ua=1

World Health Assembly, 71. (2018). Mhealth: Use Of Appropriate Digital Technologies For Public Health: Report By The Director-General. World Health Organization. Https://Apps.Who.İnt/İris/Handle/10665/276430

Young, J. D., Abdel-Massih, R., Herchline, T., Mccurdy, L., Moyer, K. J., Scott, J. D., Wood, B. R., & Siddiqui, J. (2019). Infectious Diseases Society Of America Position Statement On Telehealth And Telemedicine As Applied To The Practice Of Infectious Diseases. *Clinical Infectious Diseases : An Official Publication of The Infectious Diseases Society Of America*, 68(9), 1437–1443. https://doi.org/10.1093/cid/ciy907

CHAPTER NINETEEN

PSYCHOSOCIAL PROBLEMS OF THE DIGITIZED ERA: PSYCHOSOCIAL VIOLENCE AND HARASSMENT IN ORGANIZATIONS

MEHMED ZAHİD ÇÖGENLİ
AND FATİH ULUKAYA

Introduction

Technological developments are gaining momentum day by day. The rapid development and change in technology lead to innovations which will appear in all fields of our lives. The innovation and sustainability efforts of organizations change within the framework of technological developments and accelerate the transition to digital transformation by organizations which are concerned about globalization as a result of the modernization of information and communication technologies.

The rapid development, adoption and use of new digital technologies as well as the emergence of information and digital technologies and the use of information and communication technologies offer organizations a new transformation opportunity. Organizations evolving through digital transformation transition to the use of information communication technologies (ICT), promising great opportunities. These digital technologies provide integration into the functioning of the organization by including virtualization, mobility and analytical systems. Organizations are associations of people or institutions that come together to achieve a common goal. Organizations meeting on common ground form the structural elements. These structural elements constitute the working areas, functioning, control mechanism, division of labor and specialization levels of organizations in the organizational chart.

Organizations working for the transition to digital transformation open the floodgates for radical structural changes. The tech-advanced organizational transformation method in business organizations enables them to make a difference among their partners by providing advantages such as social media, mobile technologies, analytical solutions, cloud technology, etc. These changes give the opportunity to add new departments to the organizational chart and for current departments to evolve through digital transformation. The new generation systems that businesses run based on basic information technologies include different dimensions for the private lives of employees and the relationships between individuals and create fundamental problems in the structure of organizations regarding psychological violence and harassment. Current psychosocial risks that emerged following digital transformation in organizations and the new psychosocial risk issues (information security, cyber-attack, etc.) will be discussed in this part. Security risks that may occur in the private lives of individuals resulting from security vulnerabilities after digital transformation in organizations and the harassment, pressure and violence that may occur in accordance with risks will be evaluated.

Digital Transformation and Organizations

Technological developments are gaining momentum day by day. The fact that the current technological infrastructure in organizations is always open to development and change opens the floodgates for the use of many new methods in the production and service processes of these businesses. The innovation and sustainability efforts of organizations change within the framework of technological developments and accelerate the transition to digital transformation by those organizations concerned about globalization as a result of the modernization of information and communication technologies.

Organizations are associations of people or institutions that come together to achieve a common goal. Organizations meeting on common ground form the structural elements. These structural elements constitute the working areas, functioning, control mechanism, division of labor and specialization levels of organizations in the organizational chart. Organizations working for the transition to digital transformation open the floodgates for radical structural changes. These changes give the opportunity to add new departments to the organizational chart and for current departments to evolve through digital transformation (Eryılmaz, 2020: 109-113).

The rapid development, adoption and use of new digital technologies as well as the emergence of information and digital technologies and the use of information and communication technologies offer organizations a new transformation opportunity. The tech-advanced organizational transformation method in business organizations enables them to make a difference among their partners by providing advantages such as social media, mobile technologies, analytical solutions, cloud technology, etc. Organizations that can integrate science and technology into the business and have built the majority of their organizational management on the grounds of knowledge and technology will be able to fight against other developed or developing competitors more easily in the process by transforming into a structure that is open to positive changes and developments. In order to achieve such goals, significant initiatives such as technology policies, development plans and informatics councils should be among the main policies of the organization (Morakanyan et al., 2017: 428).

Many companies operating at the national and international scale have experienced contractions in trade due to the "Covid-19" outbreak that we fight against as a worldwide pandemic disease today. However, the businesses which continue and transfer their activities to digital platforms and are open to change aim to establish a more active and permanent structure in online services in order to reduce their losses. This period, which we can describe as the digital transformation era, also means restructuring the concept of organizational culture and opening the floodgates for radical change. In order for digital innovations to be integrated into the organization, it should not be forgotten that the concept of "organizational culture" is very important in the organizational structure. In other words, the fact that businesses act in an integrated and highly compatible manner with the concept of "organizational culture" is highly important for them to be faster and more successful in the way of digital transformation. The concept of organizational culture which refers to common values shared by individuals is one of the building blocks in the organizational structure.

Studies today assert that organizational culture is an extreme triggering factor for businesses to reach new information and create innovative ideas. For some business structures, the concept of "organizational culture" poses an important obstacle for the adoption of services in the new digital transformation field. The main reason for this obstacle occurring in organizational structures is the inflexible "rigid" management structure. The easiest way to change this rigid structure in such businesses is to create flexible and agile management systems that are open to change.

Although an organizational structure that is not open to change resists innovative changes, it should not be forgotten that the key words to survive in today's conditions are "agile" and "digital organizational" structures. Businesses with flexible and agile organizational structures that are open to change have flexible structures that may adapt to environmental change and therefore they can adapt to different conditions by changing many important features such as their organizational culture and management structure (Guinan et al. 2019: 717-720).

Organizations evolving through digital transformation transition to the use of information and communication technologies (ICT), promising great opportunities. These digital technologies provide integration into the functioning of the organization by including virtualization, mobility and analytical systems. The technology provided for organizations reveals 3 main opportunities. Virtualization systems provide great convenience and benefit in data storage and the management of organizations. The mobility system enables organizations to be dominant and recognized in the market through social media and internet advertisements. As well as dominance and recognition in the market becoming very precious issues for businesses today, advertisements to be created on social media greatly benefit businesses allowing them to express themselves and reach their goals. Embedded analytical systems enable organizations to analyze their data. Organizations making digital technologies a part of the organization gain significant strategic advantages in their sectors (Loonam et al., 2018: 101-102).

Berman (2012) expresses digital transformation "as a set of values characterized by the creation of new value chains by organizations and consumers, changes in product range and cooperation" with other partners. Digital transformation is a service that adds value to the organization and stands out in the private sector. In terms of the competitiveness of organizations, it is becoming a necessity that the services they offer are both online and offline. This online service transformation method is open to change and regarded as a way to improve organizational automation. One of the main goals of digital transformation in organizations is the changes in the way services are delivered. Organizations make the effort to directly interact through social media with the target group for their current products and services according to changing customer needs. Thanks to technological tools that can actively provide instant data tracking and updating, our digital transformation life has started to take a very important place in terms of strengthening the production chain and service-customer relationship. It is now clear that organizations are changing existing channels and actors for the delivery of new services or current services. For this reason, digital transformation offers broad opportunities to gain new market shares, enter new markets, also gain new customers and reduce the number of items that do not contribute to the financial benefit (Mergel et al., 2018: 1-3).

In the public sector, the transfer of services to digital platforms, smart products in accordance with customer needs, has led to radical changes. The transition from paper-based management to digital government has become a situation that often starts with policy changes and is very easy to adopt. In order to achieve the goal of being fast, transparent and dynamic in the services they provide, state institutions work towards the need to improve the existing service provision and provide a more efficient service. In accordance with these goals, states now focus on providing services to their citizens with the understanding of the digital state, which is called an "e-state". The developing and developed countries are not transferring their services on digital platforms and present innovations for citizens to fulfill their transitions easily (Meijer, 2015: 237-238).

Current Psychosocial Risks after Digital Transformation

It is a fact that not only financial matters are determiners for the satisfaction, motivation and productivity of employees working in organizations existing for many years and growing and developing with digital transformation, but also issues considering the behaviors and psychological conditions of people.

We can basically examine the risk factors occurring in the working environment under five titles: chemical, biological, ergonomic, physical and psychosocial risk factors. Apart from psychosocial risks, the other factors include risks that have long been known in the history of work and there has been a partial attempt at prevention. Psychosocial risks are rather newer concepts than other risk factors. For this reason, it is quite difficult to draw a general framework to define their characteristics and also prevent them. However, especially with the increase in the rate of white-collar employees this issue has become a big problem that cannot be ignored in working environments. Psychosocial risks interrupt workforce productivity and continuity more than other risk factors. For this reason, the measures to be taken against psychosocial risks are important so that employees do not have trouble in terms of professional continuity (Gökgöz, 2017: 22).

Psychosocial risk factors also have economic effects for businesses as well as employees to sustain continuity. The digitalization processes coming with the Covid-19 outbreak process, which the whole world is experiencing and inevitably being affected, brings some factors in terms of psychosocial risks as well as positive contributions for employees. Particularly white-collar employees may be negatively and psychosocially affected by innovations such as rotational work and home working through digital ways.

Identifying Psychosocial Risk Factors

It is harder to identify and analyze psychosocial risks in organizations than chemical, biological and physical risks. One of the main reasons for this is that they are invisible factors that affect employees mentally. For this reason, knowing what the concept of risk means and defining it correctly can be considered as the first step that will facilitate an understanding and identification of psychosocial risks.

Psychosocial risks are important for workplaces and factors that should be prevented can be understood from some definitions of occupational health and safety which are the fundamentals of the protection of employees' health in working life. Gerek (1999) defined occupational health and safety as "maintaining the physical, mental and social well-being of employees in all occupations, ensuring that employees are protected from risks due to working conditions, preventing impairment of their health, employing them in occupations that are suitable for them and ensuring the adaptation of the occupation to the person and the person to the occupation". Çögenli (2019) defined it as "aiming to ensure a sustainable well-being in physical, mental and social conditions of the employees, to eliminate the risks due to the working conditions and to protect the life and social structure of the employees by employing them in occupations suitable for their personal characteristics".

In the light of these definitions, we can define the psychosocial risks as "the risk factors that occur due to factors caused by the working environment or social life, that can be identified by invisible mental states and behaviors and finally, that affect the whole life of employees especially the working life".

Psychosocial risks that have been existing from the very beginning in working life will continue to exist as long as people are in working life. The advancement in technology and the increase in digitalization in workplaces have paved the way for extra psychosocial risks by creating negative effects as well as positively affecting psychosocial risks. Although psychosocial risks usually occur in workplaces, they affect the entire social and family life of employees. With the increase in digitalization, face-to-face working has been reduced in some sectors and the online working system has become widespread. This not only causes psychosocial risks, but also paves the way for the effects especially on the family of employees. It is also observed that digitalization causes such and similar situations to occur and psychosocial risks to increase.

Qualities of Psychosocial Risks

One of the most important steps to identify and detect psychosocial risks is to know their qualities very well. When preventing the identified psychosocial risks and taking measures for them, knowing their qualities and contents is also an important step. It is possible to list the apparent qualities of psychosocial risks as the following:

- The presence of psychosocial risks is newly known compared to other risk groups. Therefore, it is more difficult to identify them compared to other risk groups.
- After identifying the psychosocial risks, new regulations are performed in the legal process. There are still gaps in the legislation in underdeveloped and developing countries.
- The causes of psychosocial risks always vary. The working environment, family and social life of a person should be known well in identifying psychosocial risks.
- Psychosocial risks can usually be identified after the damage occurs. The fact that risks are invisible is the most important reason for this.
- The measures to be taken against psychosocial risks do not always have positive results. For this reason, the measures taken should be constantly checked and, if necessary, renewed in accordance with the conditions.
- Psychosocial risks are often proved by the person who is exposed to them. This causes people with low opportunities and education level to have difficulties in providing proof. Therefore, it would not be possible to exactly prove psychosocial risks in some cases (Levi, 2000: 76-77).

Occupational Reasons of Psychosocial Risks

There are many occupational reasons for psychosocial risks to occur. While some of these identified risks can be completely eliminated, others cannot, but they can be reduced to the possible minimum. The World Health Organization (WHO) stated the occupational causes of psychosocial risks in 2008 as the following and the reasons are still up-to-date today. They are:

Content of Work

- Low variety of work,
- Performing a very small part of the work,
- The work is inappropriate for the abilities of employees,
- High ambiguity about the work.

Work Load and Work Pace

- Overwork and being idle,
- The pressures caused by the production speed,
- Too much time pressure – the pressure caused by deadlines.

Working Programs

- The shift working system,
- The night shift – working programs that are not suitable for flexibility,
- Last minute overwork practices,
- The obligation to work alone for hours.

Control

- No rights for employees to participate in decisions,
- Less frequent controls on work schedules of employees.

Environment and Equipment

- Lack of equipment,
- Adverse physical atmosphere such as voice, insufficient place and illumination.

Organizational Culture

- Lack of communication,
- Lack of institutional support for solving problems,
- Lack of support for personal improvement,
- Company targets that are not known by the employees and not shared with them.

Interpersonal Relations

- Social or physical isolation,
- Breakdown in relations with employees or managers,
- Interpersonal conflicts,
- Less social support.

Tasks in Workplaces

- Role ambiguity,
- Role conflicts,
- Responsibilities for individuals.

Career Development

- Absence or uncertainty of promotions,
- Low salaries,
- Lack of job security,
- Low social value of the job.

Interaction in working life and out of working life

- Non-coordination in working life and family life,
- Less family support,
- Dual career problems.

Prevention of Psychosocial Risk

After the psychosocial risks are identified, it is important to struggle against and prevent them. The prevention of psychosocial risks plays an active role in increasing work performance, regular production and the welfare of social life. In 1981, Bertil Gardell made some recommendations for preventing some psychosocial risks so that the health of employees is protected and sustained. Even though it has been over twenty years, these recommendations are still valid. Some recommendations are as follows (Kompier, 2002: 1-4):

- Working methods should be organized that are suitable for the speed and abilities of employees.
- An employee should appreciate the work and the product to be produced as a whole.
- The working order should be planned in a way that individuals can improve themselves in accordance with the conditions of the age.
- Cooperation and social opportunities in the working environment should be kept at the highest possible level.
- The working pace should be such that a person can fulfill the responsibilities and roles of the work.

The most important emphasis for the mentioned measures is that it is stated that the process begins in the workplace, but it is not limited to the workplace and affects the whole life of the person. It seems that it is an important point to prevent psychosocial risks so that the social unrest caused indirectly by this situation cannot occur.

Psychological Violence and Harassment in Organizations

The historical development of social psychology dates back to the Plato period between 427 and 347 BC. Studies in the field of social psychology beginning with the Plato period analyzed human behaviors psychologically and sociologically until the 1900s. The studies conducted by scientists after the 1900s emphasized that psychology has an important place in the basis of human behaviors. Working conditions are changing and improving in today's conditions day by day. Organizations transition to dynamic, agile and service-oriented structures by performing digital transformations. Based on working conditions, interpersonal behaviors and attitudes in organizations become important. Organizations are places where bilateral relations are at a high level and communication is extremely important. Communication disorders arising among employees in organizations lead to psychological violence and harassment among individuals in time.

Social psychologists deal with behaviors, emotions, thoughts and intentions in interpersonal relationships. According to psychologists, the concept of behavior can be observed and measured. However, since emotions, thoughts, beliefs and intentions cannot be directly observed, they can be expressed by making inferences from behaviors. The concept of social psychology was expressed by Allport (1935: 789-844) as "the scientific study of how an individual's emotions, thoughts and behaviors are affected by the real, imaginary or implicit presence of others".

In developed and developing countries, the information and service sector replaces manpower used in the production and industrial sector and the needs of employees and human behaviors become more valuable along with the digital transformation in organizations. Due to the increased workload of employees, insufficient workplaces, a lack of social conditions in organizations and stress, psychosocial risks in workplaces have become an issue that must be emphasized (Şahan, 2016: 3).

Organizations can be defined as complex structures consisting of individuals with different personality traits who come together to achieve certain goals. For this reason, individuals in organizations strive to achieve their goals and the goals of the organization. Organizations that are mostly structured in a hierarchical order may cause employees to compete for promotion in this order. In this case, some problems arise with the work and roles in organizations, bilateral relations and the organizational structure. These problems lead individuals to apply psychological pressure, violence and harassment to each other in time.

Workplaces may have both positive and negative effects on employees. Organizational support theory, a workload model (demand-control-support) and developmental climate theories provide evidence for the positive effects of support from colleagues and supervisors on health, job satisfaction and other job performance outcomes. The verbal harassment of individuals defined as an interpersonal behavior and the use of violence with the intention of harming other employees in the workplace are negative effects in organizations. It is observed that female employees apply emotional harassment behaviors more frequently than male employees in workplaces (Węziak-Białowolska et al., 2020: 2-3).

The use of online applications and online services in workplaces is increasing with the digital transformation. Online services cause cybercrimes and sexual harassment behaviors to increase in number. This situation which women are exposed to at a high rate is frequently encountered in training sessions, professional studies and personal online accounts within the organization. This leads women to behave insecurely towards organizations and workplaces (Jackson, 2017: 1-3).

Violence in workplaces includes the use of all kinds of physical force against employees which may cause or causes the physical injury of employees, threatening behaviors, harassments, implicit threats and intimidation. The OHSA defines violence in workplaces as violence or violent threats against employees. These threats may happen in workplaces or out of workplaces. The threats happening in workplaces may range from verbal abuse to physical attack and murder. Conducted studies indicate that thousands of employees are exposed to violence in workplaces every day. The OSHA takes violent threats so seriously that in 2011 it issued a "prevention of workplace violence" directive on violence and harassment in workplaces. The US Ministry of Labor recommends that employees should receive education to know themselves and control their anger (Black and Fennelly, 2020: 207-208).

The European Commission defines the violence in workplaces as “the events that employees expose to implicit or explicit harassments, are threatened or attacked in conditions related with their jobs”. This definition is also approved by ILO (International Labour Office) and WHO (World Health Organization). Even the ILO has recently expanded this definition to include behaviors of psychological, physical and sexual violence by clients, colleagues and supervisors, even if they occur outside workplaces (Portoghese et al., 2017: 36-37).

Effects of Psychological Violence and Harassment Problems on Organizations

The concept of psychological violence and harassment is an important social problem that almost everyone around the world can be exposed to or witness through online applications inside or outside organizations. Problems that we experience socially also affect the dynamics of organizations negatively. Distrust among employees creates negative consequences on the productivity and functioning of organizations.

Distrust in organizations will cause stress and psychological problems in employees. The fact that managers and employees are under constant stress can cause a slowdown in productivity and production and increase incompatibility and conflicts between managers. Cognitive and emotional abilities may be damaged in employees within the organization in time. This may cause psychological problems, dissatisfaction and loss of morale in employees. These situations may negatively affect organizations and cause serious financial losses. These problems may cause a decrease in productivity and performance in organizations and an increase in absenteeism, employee turnover rates and occupational accidents that can be appreciated within the scope of occupational health and safety (Yates, 1986: 10).

What actually underlies the psychological pressure and violence among employees in organizations is mobbing. Mobbing is expressed as an emotional attack. It begins when a person is exposed to disrespectful and harmful behaviors. Then, by gathering other people around, they apply psychological violence to the target people through malicious, insinuating and derisive behaviors and ways that will lower social reputation. The target employees begin to experience increasing distress, illnesses and social problems in time. The productivity of employees decreases and their attitude towards the job changes. Employees under pressure and experiencing problems may experience work accidents as a result of lack of attention and concentration on work. It is possible to think of mobbing as a cancer cell for organizations. The cancer cell will grow in time and take over the whole organization and cause serious damages. 45 different mobbing behaviors were discussed by Dr. Heinz Leymann in *Mobbing: Emotional Harassment in Workplaces* written by Cavenport et al. Leymann categorized these behaviors into 5 groups according to their features and structures. According to Leymann, it is not necessary to have all of these behaviors in all mobbing cases. When we consider these behaviors one by one, it is possible to see them as miserable, uncivilized and unacceptable. If these behaviors adopted by individuals are applied consistently, they turn into deliberate harassment against the targets (Davenport et al., 1999: 15-20).

Conclusion

Psychosocial risk factors are extremely important dimensions in organizations. It is possible to say that the human organism is based on balance and as a result of unbalanced events a number of psychological problems can arise as well as physiological problems. Psychosocial problems in organizations such as psychological violence and harassment increase with the digital transformation of organizations. Online services and employee communication have become extremely important issues in organizations. Surveys and scales are widely used to identify psychosocial risks in organizations. These evaluation methods enable researchers and healthcare professionals to evaluate a large number of participants and analyze the data with relatively high efficiency. Measures enabling a more objective evaluation are based on observational approaches, archive data (e.g., publicity policies, working hours of employees, complaints) or qualitative data. When identifying psychosocial risks, it is necessary to use several methods together in order to obtain the most accurate and reliable results. It is important to ensure the surveillance of psychosocial risks to support programs and policies for the prevention of cases such as stress, psychological violence and harassment at the national and international level.

The increase in psychological violence and harassment cases and not taking precautions causes damage to the cognitive and emotional abilities of employees in organizations in time. These problems may cause a decline in productivity and performance in organizations and an increase in absenteeism, employee turnover rates and occupational accidents that can be appreciated within the scope of occupational health and safety. This leads to many permanent psychological damages in employees who are vulnerable to psychological violence and pressure.

The psychosocial risks that increase even more in the digital transformation of organizations and the problems they will create for employees are discussed in this part. Psychosocial risks cause problems such as work-based stress, mobbing, psychological violence and online harassment in organizations. Measures to be taken to prevent psychosocial risks in organizations that are developing and changing day by day are extremely precious. Taking concrete measures to increase the quality of communication between employees and reduce stress, mobbing and psychological pressures will improve the physical and mental health of employees and contribute to an increase in productivity in organizations, the development of the organizational culture and the dynamic and agile structure of organizations.

Keywords: *Digital transformation, organizational behavior, psychosocial risk, violence, psychology*

References

Berman, S. J. (2012). Digital Transformation: Opportunities to Create New Business Models. *Strategy & Leadership*, Vol. 40 No. 2, pp. 16-24. https://doi.org/10.1108/10878571211209314.

Black, I. S., & Fennelly, L. J. (2020). *Investigations and the Art of the Interview*. Butterworth-Heinemann, 203-215.

Çögenli M. Z. (2019). *Psychosocial Approaches in Occupational Health and Safety*. Konya: Eğitim Publishing.

Davenport, N. Schwartz, RD, and Elliott, GP (1999). *Mobbing: Emotional Harassment In The American Workplace*. Civil Society Pub.

Eryılmaz, M. (2020). A Discussion on Digitalization and its Successors in Organizations. S.109-133.

Gerek, N. (2004). *'Worker's health and work safety*. Open Education Faculty Publications, Eskişehir.

Gökgöz, M. (2017), "Evaluation of Psychosocial Risk Factors in Hazardous Jobs", Master Thesis, Üsküdar University, Institute of Health Sciences, Department of Occupational Health and Safety, Istanbul.

Guinan, P. J., Parise, S., & Langowitz, N. (2019). Creating an Innovative Digital Project Team: Levers to Enable Digital Transformation. *Business Horizons*, 62(6), 717-727.

Jackson, C. A. (2017). Haters: Harassment, Abuse and Violence Online. Bailey Poland. *Computers and Composition* (46), 1-3.

Kompier, M. (2002). The Psychosocial Work Environment and Health—What Do We Know and Where Should We Got. *Scandinavian Journal of Work, Environment & Health*, 1-4.

Leka, S. ve Cox, T. (2008), PRIMA-EF Guidance on the European Framework for Psychosocial Risk Management: A Resource for Employers and Worker Representatives.WHO Protecting Workers' Health Series.

Lévi, L. (2000). Stressors at the Workplace: Theoretical Models. *Occup Med*, 15, 69-106.

Loonam, J, Eaves, S., Kumar, V., & Parry, G. (2018). Towards Digital Transformation: Lessons Learned From Traditional Organizations. *Strategic Change*, 27(2), 101-109.

Meijer, A, & Bekkers, V. (2015). A Metatheory of E-Government: Creating Some Order in a Fragmented Research Field. *Government Information Quarterly*, 32(3), 237-245.

Mergel, I., Edelmann, N., & Haug, N. (2019). Defining Digital Transformation: Results From Expert Interviews. *Government Information Quarterly*, 36(4), 101385.

Morakanyane, R., Grace, A. A., & O'Reilly, P. (2017, June). Conceptualizing Digital Transformation in Business Organizations: A Systematic Review of Literature. In Bled eConference (p. 21).

Portoghese, I, Galletta, M., Leiter, M. P., Cocco, P., D'Aloja, E., & Campagna, M. (2017). Fear of Future Violence at Work And Job Burnout: A Diary Study on the Role of Psychological Violence and Job Control. *Burnout Research*, 7, 36-46.

Söyler, A. (2019), "Psychosocial Risk Factors in Academic Personnel and the Importance of Occupational Health and Safety Education", Master Thesis, Tarsus University, Graduate Education Institute, Department of Occupational Health and Safety, Tarsus, Mersin.

Vatansever, Ç. (2014). A New Dimension in Risk Assessment: Psychosocial Hazards and Risks. *Work and Society*, 40 (1).

Węziak-Białowolska, D., Białowolski, P., & McNeely, E. (2020). The Impact of Workplace Harassment and Domestic Violence on Work Outcomes in the Developing World. *World Development*, 126, 104732.

Yates, J. E. (1989). *The Manager Under Tension*. (Translated by: Fatoş Dilber), Ilgi Publishing, Istanbul.